JOHNNY *Loved* MARY

A WORLD WAR II LOVE STORY

MARY JANE JUZWIN

Copyright © 2019 by Mary Jane Juzwin.

ISBN   Softcover   978-1-950580-82-8

All rights reserved. No part of this book may be reproduced or transmitted in any form or by any means, electronic or mechanical, including photocopying, recording, or by any information storage and retrieval system without express written permission from the author, except in the case of brief quotations embodied in critical reviews and certain other non-commercial uses permitted by copyright law.

Printed in the United States of America.

To order additional copies of this book, contact:
Bookwhip
1-855-339-3589
https://www.bookwhip.com

CONTENTS

About the Editor 1

Foreword 3

Introduction 5

Chapter 1. 1942 – The Beginning of Romance 17

Chapter 2. 1943 – The War Escalates 118

Chapter 3. 1944 – The War Continues at a Great Pace 253

Chapter 4. 1945 – The War Winds Down and Finally Ends 378

Acknowledgements 483

Description of Locations for 1024 Signal Company 485

Bibliography for Locations of the 1024 Signal Company 487

Bibliography 489

ABOUT THE EDITOR

Mary Jane Juzwin previously worked in the Franklin Township Public Library in Somerset, New Jersey. I spent twenty four years there as a Senior Library Assistant. I was able to identify and appreciate many fine stories by various authors.

Since I was privy to all the best titles and authors, I became a veracious reader. Mysteries and romance were my favorites as well as the occasional nonfiction title. Upon leaving the work environment at the end of 2013, I found myself with an abundance of free time.

I started to think about working on a new project to help fill my extra time. Since my brother John and I had inherited our parents' love letters to each other from World War II, we decided to write their unusual love story. We began to separate the letters into categories first by year and then by date. While accomplishing this preliminary task, we began to realize how large this research project had become. After reading a few of Mom and Dad's letters, we became even more determined to write this story honoring them and sharing their unusual love story with other readers. I found it much better to open each letter, read it and write the highlights described by each individual letter. My brother John knows a lot of historical information regarding World War II so he worked with me to clear up any confusion I encountered.

I worked tirelessly day and night on this project. Of course I still had to complete my household duties as best as I could day after day. Both my husband Steve and I took turns babysitting for our grandchildren when necessary.

I began writing my notes in January, 2014 and completed this part of the project in April, 2017. The next step was to type my notes and transform them into a manuscript. In December, 2017 I felt ready to explore publishing options for our manuscript. I signed a contract with iUniverse and began to work with their professional staff to fine tune our manuscript and make it more appealing to other readers.

I received a lot of encouragement and great publishing tips from the iUniverse staff. Finally, my brother John and I were completing our dream of writing our parents' love story. We have dedicated this special story to our children to enjoy and pass on as a family heirloom to our future generation.

FOREWORD

This book is John R. Poslusny and Mary Jane Juzwin's condensed version of the sweet love letters our Mom, Mary and our Dad, John wrote to each other during World War II. Such letters became the primary means of communication for sweethearts to share with each other.

The story of their love and devotion to each other will not only focus on their romance, but will also include some references to historic events that took place during the Southwest Pacific during World War II.

My brother and I feel so fortunate and blessed to have had this wonderful inheritance of love letters from our mom and dad. While sorting through and categorizing these letters first by year, and then by date, we realized it had become a huge undertaking. We counted a total of 620 letters. However, we felt stronger than ever about writing this love story for them and our family.

It took four years to read all the letters, condense them and transfer them into a typed manuscript. My brother helped me to determine which historical information to include as well as verifying the spelling of some of the places dad visited or was stationed in the Army. Dad found 1,001 ways to say "I love you" to mom in his letters. His letters contained so many details about Army life as well as in depth descriptions of the various places he was stationed.

I also highlighted some of mom's family life and the experiences she encountered during the time period when she was writing and reading dad's letters. These handwritten letters are an endearing inspiration to us and to John and Mary's grandchildren. We have dedicated this book to these grandchildren, Jocelyn, Steven, Kristen, Lauren and Nathan.

We consider this to be a tribute to our mom and dad. Our hope is that it will become a family heirloom to be shared with the next generation of our family. This would include John R. Poslusny's future grandchildren and Mary Jane Juzwin's future grandchildren.

We wish to thank our Aunt Doris Kraemer (our Mom's youngest sister) for her keen wit and great memory. We appreciate her sharing the recollections of her family during that time period. She helped us by filling in some important details about our Mom's life as well as our Grandma and Grandpa's experiences. She really helped us create this wonderful *love story*.

INTRODUCTION

Our story begins in the early 1900's when our Grandpa John Regiec (our Ja Ja) met our Grandma Rose while working together on a farm in Pennsylvania.

John Regiec originally started working as a young man in the coal mines of Pennsylvania. He was later able to find work on a local farm. John continued working on this farm while he watched Rose grow from a beautiful child into a lovely young girl.

When Rose turned fifteen years old, John asked the farmer if he could have Rose's hand in marriage. Even though John was thirty five and Rose only fifteen, the age difference did not matter to them. Both the farmer and his daughter agreed to this arrangement.

Since our grandmother was only fifteen and possessed a limited amount of education, she knew very little about becoming a wife. She wasn't familiar with any information about love making between a husband and wife. After they married, our Grandma was told by her new husband that a man would get sick if his wife didn't allow him to satisfy his sexual desires. Rose Regiec believed her husband so the two of them were blessed with many children.

John and Rose travelled across the country to Bisbee, Arizona. There was a copper mine located there and it held a promise of finding a full time job and making some money. This was where they shared their first home together. Shortly after their arrival to Arizona, our mom, Mary Catherine Regiec was born. She entered the world on November 14, 1918. She became the first of ten children joining their little family. John and

Rose welcomed nine more children into their family. Sadly, three of those children died as infants.

Mary showing her birth place in Bisbee, Arizona

Some time later they moved to Manville, New Jersey where John found a job with the help of the WPA (Work Projects Administration). These were hard times for many families struggling to feed and clothe their children. Many people were poor and jobs were scarce. John was willing to do whatever it took to support his family even if he could only find part time work.

Rose became a devoted wife and mother. She worked tirelessly to keep the house clean and prepare meals for her family. Mary was expected to shoulder her share of housekeeping and preparing the families meals.

My mom told me she always saw my Grandma Rose as a pregnant mom. As the family grew, Mary became a *second mom* to her sisters and brothers. She never had a doll to call her own and the family could not afford to buy a bicycle for her to ride. My Mom also told me that one year her only Christmas present was a wooden stool given to her so she could stand and reach the kitchen faucets to wash the dishes and pots.

Our Grandma Rose cooked and cleaned along with teaching her children many life lessons. She had never learned to read, write or tell time, so she made sure her children learned these things. Most of all, Rose and John taught their children to always love and help each other. What the family lacked in finances, they truly made up for in sharing their love. The family included John as the father, Rose as the Mother, and their children, Mary, Margie, Betty, Jeannie, Leon, Doris and Charlie.

Mary (front center) with her siblings

Early Regeic family, Mary is pictured in the back row third person from left.

Our Ja Ja held many jobs over the years. He worked as a maintenance man for Raritan Valley Farms. He could not afford to buy a car for transportation so he walked from his street in Manville, New Jersey five miles through a tunnel until he came to Raritan, New Jersey. After a while, he was laid off from this job so the family had to rely on financial relief from the government.

Finally, he was fortunate enough to acquire a job at a large company called Diehl's Manufacturing Company. He worked hard digging ditches and performing maintenance duties both inside and outside the building. On occasion, he also filled in as a security guard. John was lucky enough to have a kind boss named Tom Thomas. This boss owned a big truck so he'd come to pick John up for work and even take Doris and Charlie to school. At the end of each workday, Tom and John would climb into the truck, drive to school to gather the two little ones, Doris and Charlie, and bring everyone home.

When Mary was not in school learning spelling and arithmetic, she washed dishes and floors in the house. She also helped to prepare meals, take care of her sisters and brothers and even change diapers. Mary had to leave school at the end of sixth grade because her family needed her to go to work and help support them financially. Times were that tough. They also raised rabbits for the experimental pharmaceutical industry. All the children helped to pick grass to feed the rabbits. They had a lot of fun while they worked long and hard.

Even though Mary wasn't able to finish her schooling, she was very smart and wise beyond her years. The family lived through hard times and depended on each other to get through life day to day. Every meal they shared was precious. If they wanted or needed something, they had to work long and hard to earn it. They did not take anything for granted.

As a young girl, I was my *mother's helper* as far as keeping the house clean, cooking and helping with the laundry along with drying the dishes as my mom hand washed them in our kitchen sink. We lived in Somerville, New Jersey in a house that was built completely out of stone by my dad, John and my mom, Mary. It is at this point in the story, where I, Mary Jane nee Poslusny Juzwin first became aware of the existence of these special love letters. Mom and I were sorting through some gift items upstairs in the attic. Mom opened her cedar chest where she came upon the love letters she and dad wrote to each other during World War II.

I was about twelve years old at this time. She allowed me to read some of the letters. I found, to my astonishment, that my dad was not only articulate, but he was also capable of expressing his feelings in a very romantic manner. Some time passed and dad was wondering where we had gone. He came upstairs to see us and ask what we were doing. When I saw my dad I said "Oh daddy, I didn't know you were so romantic". My dad was so embarrassed I had discovered his feelings about mom that he gruffly said "Why did you show her those letters?" This was one of many special times I remember about my interactions with my parents.

After reading only a few letters, my mind was filled with questions about their romance by letter. Mom and I had many bonding discussions while she washed the dishes and my job was to dry and put away all the dishes and silverware. My brother is six years older than me so he always had to do his homework after dinner which freed him from helping with the dishes.

While our mom was very attracted to my dad, writing faithfully every day and sending him letters, she also had some *hot dates* on the home front. I asked her about her *other boyfriends* besides my dad. She was a beautiful young woman so naturally she attracted other young men. At one point, mom was busy dating Tom, Dick, Harry and some guy she nicknamed *Pickles*.

She also told me a funny story about her dating days. She had one boyfriend visiting her at home and they were playfully wrestling on the floor in my grandparent's living room. She happened to look up and notice the time on the clock. She realized she had another date to catch. Without a word, she got up and left the guy on the floor and slipped out the back door to greet her *other date*!

She told me many of her boyfriends begged to *have sex* with her. They even went so far as to drop their pants and plead with her to do the same. However, she told them emphatically she wanted to wait until she married and would then have sexual relations with her husband.

Mom also advised me as a teenage girl to follow the same rule about having sex after marriage. She stuck to this principle so who was I to question her?

If this had worked for my parents, the same would work for me and my future husband. We shared many happy, *bonding moments* in that kitchen together. This was possible because at that time many people did not have dishwashers in their kitchen. I wonder if we would have shared these *special moments* together any other way.

Our story also centers on our Dad, John Poslusny. He was born on March 23, 1919 in Miners Mills, Pennsylvania. He was the second son born to Anthony and Caroline Poslusny. The family consisted of Anthony and Caroline, Stanley, John, Joseph and Walter. Sadly, Joseph was killed in a car accident at a young age. Anthony and Caroline later moved to Belford, New Jersey.

They were proud of all their sons, however, Johnny turned out to be the most handy and helpful with repairs and household chores. As our dad was growing up, he liked to *tinker* with cars, radios and televisions. While attending school, he acquired a passion for playing tennis. He truly enjoyed this sport during his young life. I have a lot of memories seeing my dad fix things around the house and become a *Jack of all trades*. He taught my brother John R. and my husband Steve his handyman skills as well.

When he became old enough to acquire a job, he worked as a *floral designer* for A. Kalma Florist in Matawan, New Jersey. He also enjoyed the polish dance known as the *polka*. It was at this time that *polka bands* became very popular. Dances were held at various Veteran halls and at the Polish American Home in Manville, New Jersey. Mary and her sisters loved to go these dances if they could find a ride. In 1942 most people did not own a car nor did they make enough money to buy a car. Johnny also liked to go to these dances and have fun dancing with pretty girls. He and his friend, Joseph Tye went to a dance at the Polish Hall in Helmetta, New Jersey. It was May, 1942 and Johnny was twenty three years old. The smell of spring was in the air and thoughts of romance were brewing.

Mary had come to the dance with a friend named Stanley Rogozinski. He admired Mary quite a bit, however, she only wished to be a friend to him.

Mary was twenty three years old and met Johnny at this particular polka dance in May of 1942. Johnny only had to take one look at Mary and have one dance with her and he was *in love*. Mary was attracted to this tall, dark and handsome man as well. At this meeting, when Johnny first danced with Mary he told her "I'm going to marry you someday". Mary thought he must be a little crazy to say such a thing to her.

Mary was a beautiful young lady and just wanted to have fun with her sisters and some dancing partners. She was not at all ready to think about marriage. She liked the fact that she attracted many more young men to dance and date as she pleased.

Mary and Johnny shared only three dates. Johnny then wrote a letter to Mary in early June, 1942. World War II had escalated so many young men were being inducted into the service. He said "I will know if I have to go into the Army by the end of this month". "That will give me time to think everything over, but I'm sure I will still feel the same about you". "Of course, there is always a chance I might not pass the physical exam for I have *heart trouble*." "However, my type of *trouble* has never gotten anyone a deferment." "I think you know what I mean".

Johnny was already so in love with Mary that his heart was breaking at the thought of leaving her. Nevertheless, Johnny entered the Army Air Corp. and was sworn into active duty on July 6, 1942. He began to write love letters to Mary immediately as he was feeling desperate and determined not to lose her as his sweetheart.

At this time, war brides and sweethearts often selected a special time every day to write replies to their husbands or boyfriends. Mary looked forward to the mail delivery every day. Her sweetheart wrote to her faithfully at least one letter and often two or three. Our Aunt Doris Kraemer, Mary's younger sister, told us that Mary "grabbed her letters from John with gusto". As she was the oldest of seven children, the family home was very active and noisy.

Aunt Doris also told us "Mary would take her letters, a pad of paper and a pen and find a nice, shady spot under a tree where she could read Johnny's letters quietly". In this way, she could also concentrate on her own replies. She would start a letter one day and continue to write every day of the week before sending it to her honey.

Mary with stationary suitcase sitting on the lawn

Aunt Doris also told us our mom worked in Diehl's Manufacturing Company in Manville, New Jersey later on when she became a young lady. It turns out mom was assembling household fans when she first began working. Later when the war broke out, she made ammunition for the soldiers and parts for the B-29 bombers. As time progressed, many love letters passed back and forth between Johnny and Mary despite the constant post office delays which occurred both in the Pacific as well as the United States during the entire four years of World War II.

Our dad acquired all serious intentions of marrying our mom as soon as he returned home from the Army. Mom also began to realize that dad was the *love of her life* and she began to write her thoughts on marriage. Their letters reflected how close they became and how their love grew stronger with every letter.

Dad was stationed at many Army camps and in each one he described many aspects of his life in the Army Air Corp. He thought of his service to our country as a *great adventure*. He started at Fort Dix, New Jersey then travelled by train to Jefferson Barracks, Missouri. He was then sent on another train to San Francisco, California. Later on he was transferred by boat to the Fiji Islands, New Guinea, Australia, the Philippines, the Netherlands East Indies, Okinawa, Japan and finally to Korea as part of the Occupation Force.

From California he began his *great* adventure on a boat in the Pacific Ocean. He and his company travelled for many days before landing initially in the Fiji Islands. He basically told mom a lot of details about all the places he was stationed from 1942 through 1945. He continued to write to mom daily and went into lengthy details about his surroundings. He also wrote about some of his interactions with his fellow officers and superiors.

After serving four years in the Army, dad accumulated enough points of service in order to secure his release from the Army. He was able to take the first boat heading for the state of Washington. He told Mary about his release but he made sure to warn her that it would be several weeks before he was actually released from the Army Air Corp. This boat trip, however, would take several days. Following that, it would take him six days by train to arrive in Fort Dix, New Jersey. Airline tickets and flying by airplane was only for rich people so most people relied on the train for transportation.

Dad arrived in Fort Dix, New Jersey on November 24, 1945. Ten minutes later he found his bunk in the barracks. However, Johnny was so anxious and determined to get home to collect his car that he jumped over a fence. He noticed he was dressed in his worst clothes but it did not matter to him. He had no patience to wait around for his actual discharge papers to free him from his obligation. He passed the main gate using a fake pass and caught a bus to Bordentown, New Jersey. He hopped on another bus and rode to the other end of town. Then he was able to hitch a ride with a lady who happened to be from his hometown of Belford, New Jersey.

He rushed home, greeted his mom and dad and flew out the door to get into his car and drive back to Fort Dix. He managed to sneak back into his barracks and continued to wait for the Army to issue his discharge papers. He had only one desire at this time and that was to be reunited with his sweetheart, Mary. He called her and told her when to expect him to visit her at the family home in Manville, New Jersey. To his astonishment and pleasure, he arrived and saw Mary's house lit up and decorated for his glorious return. Mary looked more beautiful than ever and they cried with joy and embraced each other.

While Johnny was absolutely certain he was destined to marry Mary as soon as possible, Mary wasn't quite sure she was ready for such a *strong and lasting commitment.* It was one thing to write about marriage and quite another to actually get married in person. Johnny proposed to her as soon as he could scrape up enough money for a diamond ring.

Since they had only shared three dates together, Mary wasn't completely sure of her feelings. She asked her sisters for advice. They emphatically said "Are you crazy?" "That man has been writing love letters to you for four years!" "Besides, he will be a good father to your children." Mary agreed with her sisters and knew in her heart that this man was *the love of her life.* Mary and Johnny were married on June 8, 1946. Money was not plentiful at the time so Mary lent her wedding gown to her sister, Jeannie so she too could marry her fiancé, Frank a short time later.

John and Mary built their *dream home* together in Somerville, New Jersey and it is made out of stone from the Watchung Mountains, in New Jersey. Our home still stands strong in the suburbs of Somerville after all these years. This is where my brother and I lived and grew up to be great adults!

CHAPTER ONE

1942 –
THE BEGINNING OF ROMANCE

On the Home Front in Belford, New Jersey
Mom and dad have met recently and have had two dates.

04/03/42

Dear Mary,

I'll bet you are a little surprised to hear from me. You are *much too nice* a young lady to be strung along so I kept my promise to write to you. I hope everything is okay in your town. My town is forty one miles away from your area. I checked the distance when I was driving home.

On Sunday, I went to a dance in Highland Park, New Jersey using the bus. I danced with a girl from your area who says she knows you *by looks only*. I forgot her name but she did say you are a very nice girl. I agreed with her one hundred percent.

I expect to come over to see you on Sunday if that is okay with you. I have met many other girls, but in my book you are *tops*. We seem to have a lot in common. We both like dancing, we're both twenty three years old and we are both Polish. I like you and I think you feel the same.

Enclosed is a picture of me and I would like to have a picture of you. I want to show some of my friends what a *charming* person you are. I listen to the radio and when I hear the song, ***The Three Little Sisters,*** I always think of you and your sisters. This isn't the only time I picture you in my mind.

I have a personal mailbox so I will be the only one receiving any letters you might like to write to me. I hope you will be home Sunday for it might be my last chance to see you before the *ration board* cuts my *gas allotment.* I have a feeling Uncle Sam might be calling on me this month.

I will close my note now with a hope you can find the time to write to me, even if it is a card. My box is No. 2, Belford, New Jersey. I think you are a very nice girl and I hope we will have some time to get to know each other.

Love, Johnny

On the Home Front in Manville, New Jersey
Mom and Dad are already attracted to each other.

06/03/42

Hello Johnny,

I came home from work and before I could even walk in the door I heard my sister Jeannie yelling. She was leaning out of the window and saying "Hurry up I have something for you". I was so surprised to receive two letters. I also got two letters yesterday so I guess I am becoming very popular.

I was sorry to hear the news about your town becoming too *lonely.* I can say the same about this town of ours. The only thing that keeps this town *rolling* is the Polish American Home. We do have a roller skating rink and a few sociable drinking places but the Polish American Home is the most popular. Maybe Sunday when you come to my house, we'll take a ride and I can show you some of these places.

Say big boy, you better stop praising me so much. I might take your comments seriously. Oh Johnny, the beautiful flowers you brought me are decorating our dining room table.

I could get a nervous breakdown screaming at everyone to stop touching them when they walk in the room. Mother made me laugh by saying "Gosh Mary, I think I'll have to get a new dining room set to match these lovely flowers".

Love, Mary

On the Home Front in Belford, New Jersey
Dad has enjoyed three dates with mom and is already *in love*.
However, he tells her he still expects to be called by Uncle Sam very soon.

06/10/42

Dear Mary,

I don't need anyone to remind me of you. Please believe me when I tell you my feelings toward you do it for me. I've shown your picture to my mom and she thinks you are *just grand*. I certainly enjoyed myself on our two dates. I never had a better time in my life. I only *existed* for twenty two years but after meeting you, I really *lived*.

After seeing you on our third date, I'm even more assured than ever that you are my type. By the way, I will know if I have to go into the Army this month. I will hear about it in the next few days for the next bunch of guys are due to go on the twentieth of this month. This will give me plenty of time to think everything over but I'm sure I will still feel the same about you. You and I are meant for each other.

There is always a chance I may not pass the physical exam for I have *heart trouble*. However, my type of *trouble* has never gotten anyone a deferment. I think you know what I mean. I hope you don't think I have been *too serious* about my feelings for you but my time is getting short. It is very hard not to let your feelings show without sounding too serious especially if they are strong.

I think you know how strong my feelings are for you. You certainly had a *hard* time getting rid of me the last time we were together. I would like to take you to a dance before I go into the Army. I enjoy dancing with you very much. I want to be able to have this *important* memory in my mind while I am away. I would like to come over to see you Wednesday night. We could go to the movies. Don't worry about gas for my car. I can get any amount if I have a good reason. I know you're the best reason I could have. It only takes three and 1/2 gallons round trip.

You know dear when I start writing, I get to a point where my feelings for you take over me. Sure there are a lot of nice girls around, but none like you. You have everything a fellow like me hopes and dreams he could find in a girl. There isn't anything in the world I wouldn't do for you. As I might have said before, you can only come to one conclusion. I am either the *biggest liar* in this world handing you a line of *bull*, or I really feel this way about you from the bottom of my heart. I can assure you my feelings are genuine. I know it's the real thing for I feel it in my mind and heart.

I heard a large group of boys from the Army Air Corp. were sent to Camp Kilmer in Edison, New Jersey. It's a possibility I may be sent there too. It is a *staging* area and processing center for troops who will be sent to various training camps around the United States. I know for sure that in the near future, I will be heading for overseas service where we will be experiencing summer weather.

A bunch of us turned in all our heavy clothing for we won't be seeing much of winter for a while. I don't know when I will hear about this but I will let you know when I am certain. I wonder what my mother is thinking about me now. I'm hoping she has gotten over me being away from home. She took my absence so hard, but I will try to write to her and pop as much as I can.

Love, Johnny

On the Home Front in Manville, New Jersey
Mom tries to depend on her brother to pick up the mail and finds out dad wrote to her but her brother forgot to give her the letter until late in the evening.

06/14/42

Dear Johnny,

You may have more or less thought I forgot about you. Well, I haven't. Friday night after school my brother went to the post office and received your letter. He put it in one of his homework books and forgot about it. When he started his homework late that night, he saw the letter and finally handed it to me. I wasn't able to do any writing at the time for I had a few guests at my house. Finally, I am answering your letter tonight and it will be mailed tomorrow. Therefore, we better put our Wednesday evening date aside because you may not receive this letter until Wednesday or maybe Thursday.

If you still want to go out dancing at the Polish American Home on Sunday, I would be happy to go with you. The dance doesn't start until 8:30 p.m. If you can come earlier, we'll go for a walk, not a ride. That will save you a little gas. I was sorry to hear about that bunch of fellows you know leaving their homes to go into the Army so soon. You might be included as well. Please Johnny, don't leave without coming to see me.

Love, Mary

On the Southwest Pacific War Front in Miami Beach, Florida
Dad has been inducted into the Army and is now stationed in Miami Beach, Florida.

06/16/42

Dear Mary,

Enclosed you will find a picture of a person that looks like someone who could be used to *scare* the neighbor's kids. It works, for I have tried it myself. Also, I don't want you to forget me so I thought having a picture would help.

The Army has taken over all the hotels in Miami Beach, Florida. We must stay in a *total blackout* at night so no enemies can figure out where we are located. I am trying to write this letter partly by flashlight. The nights are *swell* here so we all go to the top of the building. This is where we tell bedtime stories and jokes. We sing songs and most of the boys wear bathing suits. It's a famous hotel but I am not permitted to tell you the name. There are about ninety men to each girl here. I often sit and watch them go by arm in arm. I think to myself *boy, would I like to have Mary here beside me*. I try to prevent myself from feeling too low by taking a walk but it's tough.

I live in a nice room with a fellow who has been married for two years. He is giving me the *low down* on married life. It sounds very nice if the two people involved understand each other's feelings. This little note could come in handy someday. I have a little poem for you:

> It's night now, what a beautiful moon,
> It is a shame darn it anyhow.
> Don't think I'm complaining, I'm just explaining.
> Just keep smiling and always be gay,
> for I am not going away to stay.
>
> Each morning I get up with a smile, and say
> Good morning to your profile.
> I can't be dreaming for my eyes are open and gleaming.
> Here I sit alone memories pass through my dome.
> Clouds may gather in the sky, but there is a sunny day to follow,
> for every sadness there are hearts of gladness.

At night when we get hungry, we climb a coconut tree and have a great meal of coconuts. They sure taste good. This place is full of palm trees and the water is so clear you can see down to the bottom.

Love, Johnny

On the Southwest Pacific War Front in Miami Beach, Florida
Dad thought something was wrong or he might have said something to hurt mom's feelings. Was this the reason he wasn't receiving any mail for the past two weeks? He got a letter and was assured everything was fine. He tells mom about the hot weather and the training the Army is giving their troops to get in shape.

06/20/42

Dear Mary,

You will never know how I felt when I received your very interesting letter. After waiting in line three times a day for the past two weeks, it was great to hear from you. I was feeling *very blue* but your letter sure fixed that. For a while I thought something was wrong or I said something to hurt your feelings. When I found out it was quite the opposite, I was so relieved.

It's so hot here all day long. We drill four hours a day and it's about 98 degrees in the shade. There were four hundred boys taken off the field in the afternoon because of the heat. Almost every day, a couple hundred boys *pass out* and this includes the *big shots*. Everyone gets so hot and weak, they *simply* faint from exhaustion. Most of the time, we *stand* at attention. This means both feet together and no moving even if a bug bites you.

The Army isn't as easy as most civilians think of it. Most people think it's only walking up and down in a uniform. All branches of the Army give military training like I am currently receiving. I must say the *sensation* a soldier gets while marching to the music in front of some *big shot* sure is something. It makes you proud and gives you a lump in your throat. You feel really happy to be an American. In other words, one could be marching in about one hundred different ways to suit many different situations. For instance, there could be a parade or a training exercise. While we were parading in front of the general, his boss and the entire United States Army Air Corp., we had to take our shirts off for about three hours. Most of the boys got sunburned badly.

Boy, do some of the guys drink here until they are broke. Today a fellow fell out of a fourth story window at about 4:00 a.m. He died about two hours later. None of that for me! I intend to stay sober and alert.

Love, Johnny

On the Southwest Pacific War Front in Miami Beach, Florida
Dad explains the rigorous routine the Army expects the guys to follow.

06/22/42

Dear Mary,

The only complaint I have about the Army Air Corp. is it's too far from Manville, New Jersey. Also, they get us up at 4:00 a.m. to eat and exercise. This is how the Army gets us in shape. We rush out at 4:00 a.m. wearing only our *skivvies* for inspection. We get eight minutes to shave, put on a dress outfit, shine your shoes and take a shower. The next thing is walking up five stories to *stand for inspection* by some general. After all this, they inform you that you are to guard the hotel from 4:00 a.m. until daybreak. Luckily, we're able to sleep again. When one can finally go to sleep, they usually call a fire drill about a half hour after you start dreaming about your favorite girl.

After we awaken, we march twenty eight blocks back to the hotel. All the boys put on their bathing suits and march once again for about ten blocks. This is when we get our *warm up* exercises *as if we aren't warm yet* which takes about an hour. Most of us are boiling by this time and *good and tired*. They let us take a free swim and what a *struggle* it is to keep afloat because of our fatigue.

We march out to a drill field twenty eight blocks away. Then we drill for about three hours. Then we march back twenty eight blocks to get our mail and eat. Oh boy, a letter from Mary! We rest for fifteen minutes and continue to march twenty eight blocks to drill some more. Usually, this takes two hours. We then stop and listen to a lecture by some *stiff shirt*. By this time most of us are put to sleep by it all. At about 6:00 a.m. they inform you that due to your *high skill level*, you were selected after much deliberation by all parties concerned to be on K. P. for today.

The theme song we sing now is *the pots and pans will fly over Tokyo when the 354 gets there*. We work seventeen hours straight on K. P. so when we are finished, we return to the hotel. Upon arriving, we are kindly told that our room, or even worse our hotel, has been changed. At this point, we must move out of a clean room into a dirty one mostly located on the fifth floor. There are no elevators so we must climb the stairs. I wanted to show you how the Army works. There's a right way to do something and then there is the *Army way*. Even though there is a distance of 1,653 miles and 42 feet between me from sweet you, I cannot forget you. The miles were measured by one of my friends who was a map maker before the war. I can't wait until we can be together again.

Love, Johnny

On the Southwest Pacific War Front in Miami Beach, Florida
Dad was very happy to hear from Mom. He's not impressed with Florida as it is too hot. He has been classified as a radio man due to his mark on the skills test in Fort Dix, NJ.

Mary Jane Juzwin

06/24/42

Dear Mary,

I received your letter and was glad to hear from civilization again. Florida is alright but as far as I'm concerned, they can give it back to the Indians. It's too hot for one thing and they sure are getting tough with us. I never knew the Army was so strict, they even tell you how to tie your shoes! I have been classified as a radio man because of my mark on the test I took at Fort Dix, New Jersey. I will get basic training and then get sent to an airfield.

I'm feeling very good and my health has improved. My disposition would be greatly improved by a young girl I know back home. She is very good medicine for the body as well as the heart. I now have a fellow with me who has the same *heart trouble* as me *in love, but far away*. We've had a great time thinking about ways to *heal* ourselves. We came to a conclusion that if the cause of our *heart trouble* lived closer to our camp, we might be cured. You can stop worrying about the heat for my training days are over, *thank goodness*. I have spent twenty two days on drilling so for the duration of the war, I will stick to airplanes, radios and jeeps instead.

If you wanted you could hitch hike down here to see me, but I realize that would not happen. I know for a fact you would not enjoy standing around on some road waiting for a ride. If you took an airplane to get here, it would cost $130.00 round trip so that leaves that option out as well. I could call you up on the telephone if you had one for only $2.30 for three minutes of conversation. Oh, to be able to say *good night* to you again in that good ol' three hour way. I sure do miss that.

Give my regards to your family. I will try my best to get this war over quickly. I decided to write a letter without giving you a chance to reply as if I am shipped somewhere else, it would be delayed. I'm not taking any chances on running short of time to write to you.

Love, Johnny

On the Southwest Pacific War Front in Miami Beach, Florida
Dad finds out the custom of playing taps in memory of the soldiers from the last war who died. It is a sign of respect.

06/26/42

Dear Mary,

There is a custom of playing taps in every camp. A bugler blows taps at five minutes to 11:00 p.m. and then another set at five minutes after 11:00 p.m. This is done in memory of the soldiers of the last war who didn't survive.

The other day we all went to a boxing match where only soldiers were fighting. They would start out like champions and after the second round, they would get so tired.

It looked like boxing in *slow motion* after a while.

Yesterday, Al Jolson, the famous screen and radio star gave us a performance. We all enjoyed it. After the show, he walked around and asked the boys where they had lived in the States. I was standing near the exit, however, to my surprise he asked me too.

He didn't know where Belford, New Jersey was until I said "near Red Bank".

Today the Army did something that made me cry very much. I never thought I would carry on like I did. However, you know peeling onions isn't fun! Yes, they finally assigned me to K. P. or *Kitchen Patrol*.

The boys here are *oozing* with knowledge. We are asked to set aside money for *war bonds*. I'm setting aside $18.75 out of my $50.00 monthly payment for future use after the war. If I get a few stripes, I will double that amount. There is a good possibility I will never be sent to the front line. I will always be located about three hundred miles away. I have enclosed a few airmail stamps for you to use so I can get your letters a little bit sooner.

I bought myself an iron to take care of my clothing so I feel like I'm *playing house*. Would you care to join me in *playing house?* Maybe it wouldn't work for I would want to play for keeps. Take care of yourself and write as often as you possibly can. I will be looking forward to hearing from you soon.

Love, Johnny

On the Southwest Pacific War Front in Jefferson Barracks, Missouri Dad's group is small but is considered special. He describes the scenery to mom as he travels through Alabama, Georgia, Missouri and Tennessee.

06/28/42

Dear Mary,

We left Miami Beach, Florida and arrived at Jefferson Barracks, Missouri. The scenery was beautiful and I enjoyed it. We travelled by *passenger* train instead of a *troop* train.

I never knew the Army moved so fast. This train was air conditioned. We went through Alabama, Georgia, Missouri and Tennessee before crossing the Mississippi River.

Our group is small and our squadron is considered special. Something is in store for us. I hope it's for the best. Things move fast in the Army Air Corp. so anything is possible. Our group is the Yhndio Squadron because no one knows where we will be sent. This camp has a two hundred piece band. We also have theaters here so I go to a show once in a while. The seats are like the park benches in Central Park, not too comfortable.

We often have a debate about whose girl is the prettiest. This discussion usually keeps us up until midnight. Now I am listening to the radio and the song that is playing is **I threw a kiss in the ocean**. I happen to remember that it was one of your favorites. You see, I don't forget what you like.

Since I met you my luck has always been the best. You will remain an inspiration to me no matter where I am and I see no reason why it shouldn't continue. If the going gets tough, I'm sure I won't let you down. I am doing this for my country with you first in line. Take of yourself for me and keep smiling. I will try to do the same especially after I read the sweet letters you send to me.

Love, Johnny

On the Southwest Pacific War Front in Jefferson Barracks, Missouri Dad will be in the Army Air Corp. keeping radio equipment in working order and *A1* shape. He assures mom he will be located about two hundred from the front lines.

07/03/42

My Dear Mary,

I don't know what to say first, Mary. Everything seems to be in a general *mix up* right now. I want you to know what I am about to say I mean sincerely. If you should meet someone you like more than me, I guess I will try to get you to like me a little more than him.

If I can't do this, then I don't deserve you so there wouldn't be any hard feelings. I always thought you were much too sweet for just plain old me. The feelings I have for you aren't just a passing fancy or something brought on by the war. I have been around and met many types of girls. None of them have ever taken me over like you have. You're the first girl I can say I really trust.

My position with the Army Air Corp. will always be about two hundred miles from the front lines. My job will be to help keep the radio equipment in *A1* shape. I will be called on to fly occasionally which I think I will like very much. However, most of the time, I will be working with the ground crew. I have received some pistol and machine gun practice. This is in case our airport is ever attacked.

We have some funny boys with us. One fellow was a sky writer. He would write ads in the sky with smoke. One day he got mad and took a plane for himself. He wrote *The boss is a son of a b_ tch*! This did not go over well with his boss so now he has lost his license for flying indefinitely.

Love, Johnny

On the Southwest Pacific War Front travelling from Oklahoma to Texas Dad describes his journey to mom in full detail. He is taking in all the scenery and explaining everything leading up to their destination of San Francisco, CA.

07/05/42

Dear Mary,

I have finally left Jefferson Barracks in Missouri. I am writing this letter on the train and it is pretty hard to write for the train rocks a lot. I can remember the day I called you for the first time. Using a frightened voice, I asked if Mary Regiec was at home and does she live here? I admit I was scared to death because I never called a girl on the phone before. Luckily, you were home and it sure was grand to talk to you.

Sweetheart, it seems like years since we last saw each other but I haven't forgotten you.

We are crossing into Oklahoma and it is filled with woods. I believe we are traveling the southern route to California. The mountains are filled with beautiful colors. There aren't many trees on them so they look like pyramids or volcanoes.

We are now leaving Oklahoma and heading for Texas. We are passing the high oil wells and the air smells like gasoline. We are in Amarillo, Texas which is the third largest city in the state. Everybody waves to us as we travel along the highways. We find ourselves in Gallup, New Mexico. It is a very picturesque city. We have entered Arizona and it is another state that I can say I have been there. Rock piles line each side of the tracks all done by Mother Nature.

We are passing through an Indian village that looks like Chief Wa Hoo is up very early this morning. We just saw a cattle train filled with cattle and that ain't *no bull*.

I believe every train we pass is a troop train. No wonder the railroads are so busy. I don't know if you have ever travelled by train for any distance. You sure get dusty.

There are no showers on the train, only wash basins. We must be in the desert for I haven't seen a ditch, pond or lake. The fields are full of sagebrush and tumbleweeds. The scenery has become tall evergreen trees. Out here there are millions of them growing. I think I just found out where Santa Claus gets his Christmas trees.

We are travelling over the Colorado River and soon we will reach California. Everything is so peaceful out here, one wonders how a war could ever start. We're moving so fast. I see the Sierra Nevada Mountains and the scenery is beautiful beyond explanation. Finally, we arrived at our destination, San Francisco, California.

Love, Johnny

On the Southwest Pacific War Front in San Francisco, California
Dad talks to mom about making a record for her and his *Mama* and *Ta Ta*. He tells mom that this might be his last letter she might receive because

his clothing and gear is being packed. He expects to be on his way to a boat ride in the Pacific Ocean.

07/07/42

Dear Mary,

It sure made me happy to get your letter. If you did let anyone read my letters, I wouldn't care. I want everyone to know I love you. I think you're the *sweetest* thing this side of heaven. Your mother's fear of having an *old maid* around is not true. Anyone who lets a girl like you go should have his head examined.

I'm glad you received the record I sent to you. I was so afraid it would break before it reached you. I hope you like my voice on it. I said *oh* so often because I didn't want to sound like I was nervous. I should have used my southern drawl but with all the excitement I forgot about it. I made a second record in Polish and sent it to *Mama and Ta Ta*. It was a little harder to speak in Polish, but I managed to do a good job.

Now that I am living in San Francisco, California I might be heading across the ocean at any time. I'll let you know if and when this happens. This ought to hold you until then. In the meantime, I am sending 1000,000,000,000,000 kisses to you. This is probably the last letter I will be able to send you because our clothing is being packed and supervised by an officer. This makes me certain that I am on the way to a boat ride. I might be sent east for a number of the boys have been sent there.

My bag contains about 85 different articles weighing at a total of 300 lbs. It sure is a lot of heavy junk to be carrying around. I have been in the Army for thirty days and it seems like ten years. Do you realize I haven't seen you for 720 hours?

Love, Johnny

On the Southwest Pacific War Front travelling to perhaps Fiji or Australia Dad has so much time on his hands so he writes a 32 page letter to mom while he is travelling by boat across the Pacific Ocean.

07/09/42

My Dearest Mary,

Here I am out in the ocean miles from *nowhere*. I never saw so much water in my life. You will probably receive this letter a month and a half from now for it has to travel to many places before it is delivered to Manville, New Jersey. I want to write to you as often as I can. I hope my letters get to you. The trip has been calm so far. Only a few fellows got seasick, but I feel fine. Under the circumstances, I can't help feeling a little homesick. I miss you, darling. I guess I will not be able to see you for quite sometime but I hope and pray you don't forget me.

After we got on this boat, I went to my quarters which are located one deck below. I can get on deck quickly in case of an emergency. We sleep four guys high on hammocks. Lucky for me, I have the bottom one so I don't feel the rocking of the boat as much. Besides if one falls out of the bottom hammock, there isn't a lot of space left until you reach the floor. One fellow fell from the top hammock and got hurt. He was very lucky he landed on his face instead of his head.

The food is surprisingly good. We eat the same as we did on land but twice a day. We thought this was awful at first, but after travelling on the boat we realized we couldn't eat more if we tried. We aren't doing a lot of labor so we tend not to work up our appetites.

There is a store on the boat so I decided to visit it one day. I got in line and stood there for three and one half hours. By that time, I was only the fourth man away from gaining entry. My luck ran out when they decided to close the store. Boy, was I burning mad and fed up as well. The next day I finally got into the store and enjoyed a few bars of candy, a couple bottles of Pepsi and a box of cheese crackers. The only thing I didn't see at all was ice cream, darn it anyway! We are not allowed to take food down below deck because we would be giving the rats a chance to eat. They are carriers of many diseases. If anyone tries to be sneaky and gets caught, they will be heavily punished.

What do you suppose happened to me next while on this boat? No, I didn't fall overboard! A fellow rushed over and grabbed me by the arm. He said "What the hell are you doing here"? This guy is from my home town and lived only a one half mile away from me. He is a naval gunner. What are the chances I would be lucky enough to meet someone from my hometown? He took my breath away!

The boat is heavily armed and convoyed so there is very little danger. I find the boat swell because it is only three years old. It once belonged to a country just over the English Channel. It sure is modern and travelling thirty miles per hour. On the top deck there is plenty of gambling going on among these guys. That's not for me.

The ship is dark at night so no one can see us travel. We go below and sleep away our time. I'm not quite sure if this letter will be censored so I must keep my trap shut on some things. We have many drills such as *man the guns, abandon the ship* or *clear the deck for action*. These drills are very important to prepare us for any situation that happens.

The Air Corp. doesn't have to go on K. P. on this trip so other outfits are responsible for it. The rest of us perform odd jobs that only take a few hours. All I seem to do is walk from one part of the ship to another just passing time. This trip would cost a person $500.00 and I get it free of charge. It's okay, but I do miss you terribly. I have to stay content with looking at your picture.

Love, Johnny

On the Southwest Pacific War Front travelling on a boat in the Pacific Ocean

Dad and the boys are getting sick of the scenery of blue water. He is worried about how his mom is taking the news of her sons entering the service.

07/11/42

Dear Mary,

When we look out into the ocean after five days, it sure makes one a little sick of the scenery of blue water. I did, however, spy a sixty foot whale that looked like a submarine. Our drinking water is rationed and we get two quarts a day. The shower water is salty so it makes getting yourself clean rather hard. Quite a few of the boys are looking forward to growing mustaches.

Australia is probably where we are headed as far as I can tell. Gosh, mail will be slow but I hope I can keep sending you interesting letters. It will be hard for I am not allowed to talk about everything. I don't know how my mother took the news of her sons entering the service. I did not tell her when I left. She might be broken hearted but I hope to cheer her up by writing to her.

The boat has a radio system so every day we hear announcements along with music. Even if it is old music, we ain't very fussy. We do exercises on deck to keep us fit. For the last five nights, I have been dreaming about home and my school days. I am positive I will also dream about you, dear.

With Love, Johnny

On the Southwest Pacific War Front travelling by boat in the Pacific Ocean The crew is informed by the medical officer on how to be careful when they meet bad girls. Dad is reading books, going to mass and watching boxing matches to pass the time.

Mary Jane Juzwin

07/13/42

Dear Mary,

Today we got a lecture from the medical officer on how to behave like good boys when we meet bad girls. Hopefully this information will help keep us out of trouble. The crew is native so we get a kick out of hearing them speak while they work. They wear funny hats and clothing.

Ever since I was inducted into the Army, they keep taking me further away from you and my home. My calculations show I will be traveling over half way around this world. I estimate it to be about 11,000 miles away. I keep thinking of new things to do while I'm on this boat. There is a library full of books to read and we have daily mass in church. Later boxing and some other form of entertainment will be presented.

Columbus was brave to cross this ocean. All we will see for the next twenty days and nights is water, water and still more water. I've seen enough of the sea our first five days to last me a lifetime. On the seventh day of our journey, one of our ships broke down. We waited two hours to get it fixed. Did you ever hear of flying fish? I always knew there was such a thing now I know for sure. We saw hundreds of them fly like sparrows.

We all received a letter from the president on the seventh day of our trip. It was telling us the startling news that *we're now members of an overseas expeditionary force*. My, my as if I didn't know that by now! War sure is expensive. Uncle Sammy has spent over $2,000.00 on me so far and in only a couple of months. It is confinement like this that makes us concentrate on ourselves. This makes us mad and ready to fight! *Grr!* Even though the ship is modern, the air below deck has a *funny smell*. It's the smell of oil filters that help to circulate the air on all decks. It's hardships like these that will make a better man of me by the time this war is over. I know I will be ready to settle down and share happiness with those I love each and every day.

I now eat because it has become a habit. There seems to be no taste to anything. At least, nothing appeals to me. This is the state of yours truly, however, it hasn't got me down. The weather is getting warmer each day for we are heading toward the equator.

I'm writing this letter in the hole of the ship using very dim light. We're all required to wear life preservers everywhere while we are on board. We use them for pillows at night even though they're as hard as a brick. Tonight the air is cooler so I will try sleeping on deck where I can enjoy fresh air. As each day passes, I'll add to this letter. Sometimes I lay in bed wondering what you're doing and wishing I could see you in person. The only way I see you is in my dreams. I can visualize myself coming home, walking down the street and stopping to talk to many people. I also see myself getting into my car and rushing down the road to see someone who is very dear to me. I guess by now, you know it's you. Everything that is happening is because a couple of bums tried to rule the world?

Love, Johnny

On the Southwest Pacific War Front travelling to somewhere in the Pacific Ocean
Dad is worried mom might forget him if she isn't able to hear from him for long periods of time. He is far away from mom but determined to hold onto her.

07/16/42

Dear Mary,

Our ship prints a newspaper. It's two pages long but not much news. I don't know how long this letter will be by the time I reach my final destination. What I do know is your answer to any of my letters will take at least one month to come to me. It sure will be tough waiting for your letters, sweetheart. I'm worried you might forget me if you aren't able to hear from me for long periods of time. We share a large space between us but that's not going to stop us by a long shot.

Please don't ever think anything I said in my letters was brought on by the war. My feelings about you did not spring up overnight. I have felt this way for a while, but one doesn't usually speak about their feelings during normal times. I hope you don't think I'm too serious, for this is how I stand. There I go again getting sentimental, but I can't help it.

One fellow brought his fishing pole and line. He's been fishing during our trip. Some of the boys were hoping he would catch a mermaid. None of us have seen a gal for a long time. There is an old saying I'm sure you've heard, you can't get along with them and you can't get along without them. Looking at the ocean, I can see one hundred miles in each direction. In our position, one would never doubt the world is round. The boats signal each other by lights and code. I pity any submarine that tries to attack us for our gunners have not seen action for so long their patience is almost gone. Their guns can shoot through metal four inches thick and about 600 bullets a minute. Some boys say "If a submarine sends a torpedo shell through our boat, they'll use the same hole to get out".

I wish the boat would turn around and go back. All the boys are sick and tired of this journey. My thought about the situation is *life is so beautiful and I feel it is important to fight for it.*

Love, Johnny

On the Home Front in Manville, New Jersey
Dad sends mom a crate of oranges as well as letters and pictures of himself.

07/19/42

Dear Johnny,

What else are you going to send me? The postman was *kidding* my dad by saying he should get a wagon to hold your crate of oranges.

He was turning away from the window when he got a big surprise. The postman handed him the crate. Of course, you really surprised my sister Jeannie when she picked up your letter with two kisses on the back of the envelope. She said "He is *so darn charming* sending a letter with a kiss for me and one for you, Mary. Now my other sister, Margie wants to go and pick up your next letter so perhaps she too might get a kiss.

Oh Johnny, thank you for the pictures. I like the *natural* looking one best of all. I framed all of them and even took some to the plant. It was fun showing off with your pictures. I am glad you met someone you know so both of you can recall your school days. I'm also hoping your luck stays with you. Johnny, I'm so glad you took me to meet your folks and I'm happy to hear how much your mother likes me. Say big boy, you don't have to hint around for married life to me. Isn't that what we both want? We'll get it when our time comes. You be a *good* soldier boy and do your duty.

They still have those dances here on Sundays at the Polish American Home hall but I seldom go. Honestly Johnny, I work nine hours a day every day and when Sunday comes, I have six to eight letters from you to answer. Then I also have to help mom with the children and the housework so you see what this *little* Mary does in her spare time.

With Love, Mary

On the Southwest Pacific War Front travelling to somewhere in the Pacific Ocean
Dad is filling mom in with all the details of his daily experiences on the boat. He describes the food, drinks and the different living quarters the officers enjoy.

07/20/42

Dear Mary,

Washing our clothes is unique. We tie our clothes to a strong rope and let them tow behind the boat. The clothes wash well but we hope big fish won't eat them for bait.

When I was being sent from Missouri to California, I wrote you an eighteen page letter. While I was still in California, I sent another letter of twelve pages. Please let me know if you've received them. Today I worked in the ship's store. It felt good to do some work for a change. The rest of the day I read books. Finally, I saw a group of boys carrying boxes into the hole of the ship so I decided to grab a box. I knew if I could get past the guards, I would get oranges, bananas and a few bottles of soda. Now I know where they store this stuff. Everything sure hit the spot!

The officers' quarters are like the front rooms back home. They're very different than our quarters. They even have a cocktail bar! My quarters are in the center of the ship. This is the best part because the center of the ship never rocks as much as the front or back. This was a good break for me.

Love, Johnny

On the Southwest Pacific War Front still aboard ship on the Pacific Ocean There are some soldiers playing bingo. They know a lot about Australia and inform dad about the money situation. Dad finds out they will be crossing the equator.

07/22/42

Dear Mary,

It is getting harder for me to write because I'm confined to a space of three feet by one hundred feet. However, don't worry I'll keep writing. They're some soldiers on board with our destination. They speak *jolly old* English. Their game is bingo and they're always looking for players.

We found out a lot of information about their country. By the time you get this letter, we'll be playing with the kangaroos. I am told our money lasts longer in Australia. One can get a six course meal for $.25. This is because the standard of living is low. Each day we set our clocks back a half hour. Pretty soon we'll lose a whole day when we cross the equator. We've travelled 1,900 miles without any land in sight. When I finally set foot on land, I will slug any guy who asks me to go fishing. You have no idea how much cargo and people this ship can carry. We certainly have loads of food.

Good old New Jersey is only 11,000 miles away and about half way around the world. When you stand up in New Jersey, I am just under you, *way down under* as the saying goes. I seem to be feeling better every day. I must be getting used to it all. The other day we enjoyed community singing. We have an organ so we can entertain ourselves and help to pass the time away. I've just read your last long letter again. I think I've read it ten times now. Every time I read it, I feel so much happier. Please don't ever stop writing letters for they mean so much to me, honey. I'd like it very much if you could send me more pictures of yourself.

Love, Johnny

On the Southwest Pacific War Front aboard ship travelling the Pacific Ocean Dad keeps writing faithfully to mom and does a really good job of describing his day to day activities. He is having the *adventure of a lifetime*.

07/24/42

Dear Mary,

The Aussies don't think highly of the British but they sure do like us Americans. We're looking forward to a *royal welcome* as we land. They're so good natured that we were told not to take advantage of them. It rained very hard today so a lot of us boys are on deck taking a bath in the rain water. At least we're having some fun. They're playing songs typical of the South Sea Islands. I guess they are trying to get us in a *good mood.*

Our boat is leading the convoy with a lot of boats behind us. They might be able to catch up to us and I'm hoping this would speed up our journey. I think there are fifteen days to go before we see land. It will feel funny to be standing still for a change. The boat has many horns and whistles that mean something different. We get a good laugh when one horn whistles like a Model T Ford. It's so unusual because we're so far from nowhere.

When I started this letter, I didn't I think I could say a lot. Once I get started, I just keep writing. Honey, I don't know what power you have over me. You inspire me.

Love, Johnny

On the Southwest Pacific War Front still aboard ship in the Pacific Ocean Dad confesses to mom that he met a girl in California, however, he says she was such a *kid.* He tells mom he knew she was a pretty lady and he experienced *love at first sight.*

07/26/42

Dear Mary,

Here I'm still on this excursion which I call it. I have a confession to make. I don't think it's fair of me to keep any secrets from you, dear. The thing is although my time was short in California, I did manage to meet a girl. I've enclosed her picture because I thought you might be interested to see my taste in women. Isn't my taste good? We didn't spend much time together but I hope you understand. She was such a *kid.* In your case, I knew you were a pretty lady and it was *love at first sight.*

I'm just lying on deck with my eyes closed thinking of you. Popular dance and love songs are playing on the radio. I'm thinking to myself *how I used to dance so well with you in my arms.* Mary, I can't tell you enough how much it meant to me. If I think about us being together, it becomes so hard to bear. It is things like this I miss so much.

Love, Johnny

On the Southwest Pacific War Front travelling by boat in the Pacific Ocean
Dad explains two things in this world that would make him the happiest person alive. One would be to win the war and two is to return home to his folks and mom.

07/29/42

Dearest Mary,

I can hardly wait to see you again. There are two things in this world that would make me the happiest person alive. One is to win this war and return to my folks and you.

The other thing would be to hold you tight in my arms. I tell myself I am going to have adventures that I wouldn't miss for the world, even if they are risky at times.

Love, Johnny

On the Southwest Pacific War Front aboard ship travelling in the Pacific Ocean
Dad wonders if mom will be privy to more war news than him. He says the boys on board will be told only what the *big shots* want them to know.

08/02/42

Dear Mary,

I have a feeling you will probably hear more news about the war than I will even though I will be closer to the war zone. They only let us know what the *big shots* want us to know. Only the good news will reach us so that we keep our spirits high. Even though things are a little uncertain, my spirits have not been broken. I sure meet lots of interesting people. Some are *newlyweds*, some are *young* squirts, some old fogies and some are daydreamers. There are a lot of *slap happy punch drunk guys* as well.

Mary, I hope by my letters, I've shown you how I really am as a person. I didn't meet you soon enough before the Army claimed me. I hardly had time to see you and tell you all I wanted to say. I hope what you've learned hasn't disappointed you. It seemed very hard to say what was on my mind because I just couldn't find the right words. I hope I haven't spoiled this letter by trying to explain myself too much.

Love, Johnny

On the Home Front in Manville, New Jersey
Mom has received some very troubling news about her aunts and cousins.

08/02/42

My Dear Johnny,

I received your most *welcomed* letter about a week ago. I'm so ashamed of myself for not answering it sooner. However, I had received some bad news about my two aunts and a cousin. They had all been taken to the hospital for operations. We are very fond of each other and the news broke my heart. I was so upset, Johnny, I could not write to you for fear I might burst into tears and pour out all my troubles. Please forgive me as it is the honest truth.

How are you? I'm hoping you are well as I am *fine and dandy like chocolate candy*. Wanna *nestle* in each other's arms? Oh shucks, how can we do that when you are so far away from me and yet I feel so close to you? Oh, how I miss those nestles, cuddles and the curve of your arms around me. Gosh Johnny, I'm worried about the heat out there.

It seems that not only the war itself is dangerous but everything around it as well. Oh Johnny, do be careful. You say my letters are interesting. Gosh, your letters are full of news, perfect and oh so sweet!

My cousin had two visitors from Camp Kilmer. They enjoyed themselves so much. After dinner, my cousin drove them back to Camp Kilmer and I went along for the ride. I always wanted to visit a *soldier's* camp, however, I didn't know anyone there. I would have liked to see you there and say "hello".

When you last wrote, you said you were going to take a ride in a glass bottom boat. I wish I could join you but enjoy it and pretend I'm there as well. I'm reading your letter and honestly you couldn't possibly tell me more. I love to read your mail and hear about your adventures. Oh, you rascal, I laughed *out loud* about the Army onions!

Johnny, don't fight so hard about getting stripes. You didn't march into the Army with any so just take it easy. You are in the Army, not in prison, so you don't have to wear stripes. As I told you once before, *stripes or no stripes you are my Johnny to me.*

With Love, Mary

On the Southwest Pacific War Front still aboard ship in the Pacific Ocean Dad realizes he's having an easy time now and expects to be quite busy working on airplanes when his group finally lands. He will be checking equipment and fixing planes.

08/04/42

Dear Mary,

My easy days will be over when we land. During the day, I will be assigned to get airplanes ready for nightly attacks on enemy bases. When the planes return, I'll be in charge of checking them over and fixing them, if necessary. I have an opportunity to volunteer as a gunner aboard a fighter plane if I want to learn about it. It will be quite risky, but one has to take a chance once in a while. Don't ever tell my mother about this because she is afraid of flying. As for me, I love flying.

This is only what I have written for my first ten days. My, my who said women do all the *gabbing*. I guess I'm worse than an *old maid*. It has been raining for two days straight. Yes, it is the soaking kind of rain like when we walked to the movies that day. They say *variety is the spice of life*, however, in this place it does not exist. I did discover our boat has a small swimming pool on it but it's being used for cleaning our clothes, darn it anyway! I never knew how good water could taste until the weather turned much warmer. Thirst seems to be hard to please and quench.

Labor Day passed and Christmas is coming soon. How time flies! I must be lucky to get into the Army Air Corp. for I do answer lots of questions about it. There are soldiers who tried to get into it, but couldn't because they didn't possess any working skills. *Join the Army and see the world*. They should say "Join the Army and see the ocean."

On the subject of being spoiled by me, Mary, you spoil me just as much with your sweet letters so we are even. I should have taken up dancing sooner.

Maybe I would have met you sooner. They say, "Life is too short" and I say, *never again will I put off anything*! Why don't you come and see me sometime when you have a couple months to spare? Well, I can dream about it can't I?

While we were stationed at Jefferson Barracks in Missouri, we had to sing the Army Air Corp. song. Now we kid each other saying we should sing this song when we spot some Japs. If we did that, we would surely scare them to death! It is the power of imagination!

Love, Johnny

On the Southwest Pacific War Front aboard ship in the Pacific Ocean
The waves are starting to rise and fall and dad thinks King Neptune is *raising hell* below the ocean. Some of the boys are gambling but dad wants to save his money.

08/06/42

Dear Mary,

The waves are thirty feet high today. It feels just like a roller coaster ride. King Neptune must be *raising hell* below the ocean! I hear such fairy tales from the boys. There seems to be no end to them. Yes, they are quite different than those I heard in grade school.

I'm writing a letter to my mom. I told my brother Walter not to say anything about me for a while. Probably by now, she knows all about my situation. She must be worried to death. I hope to calm her down and soothe her with some choice words in my letter. I hope I haven't broken the censor's rules by telling you too much. I have described a lot about my Army life so far. Perhaps they will get mad enough to send me back home!

Oh yeah, like that would happen, I wish! I must sound as screwy as a 100 year old man!

Our lunch room is always stuffy and steamy. It's so hot that it spoils all of our hopes for relaxation and the consumption of good food. I suppose it will get worse as we get closer to the equator. I must say, however, the coffee is better than any I have tasted since I've been in the Army. The best way to enjoy it is to drink it up on deck where the air is cooler. Today is *pay day* but it is only a partial payment of $5.00. The dice games are increasing by the hour. This guy wants to save his money not gamble it away foolishly.

Remember if you want to send me any mail, try to send it airmail to the San Francisco address, then it will reach me quicker. I look forward to your sweet letters. They keep me going and count a lot in my heart. I hope you have received the locket, pen and the Army Air Corp. emblem I sent to you. I will try to get you something really nice if it's permissible. Don't forget to check in at the Post Office once a week. Your sweet medicine is lasting pretty long. I hope I don't run short of it!

Love, Johnny

On the Southwest Pacific War Front crossing the equator in the Pacific Ocean Dad describes the custom regarding people who cross the equator. All the boys as well as the *big shots* must participate. They had a grand time!

08/08/42

Dear Mary,

There is a custom I found out about when one crosses the equator. Any person who has not crossed it before must be ducked in water or have his head scalped. The crew is getting the large canvas tub ready. I would like to be dunked, besides I need a bath anyway. Quick, somebody throw me a towel and a cake of soap!

Oh yes, I must tell you more about the ceremony we had when we crossed the equator. Everyone had to appear before the King, *dressed* in a costume made of ropes, which put together made a *grass skirt* and the Queen *she wore her curves*. The children were present as well. One had to kiss the royal baby in the most embarrassing place! Each person was tried for some silly reason, and the King would give him his sentence. Then one is *very gently* placed in a chair and thrown into the pool where five men are waiting to dunk me. Following this, one is given shampoo and a shave consisting of ground up carrots, coffee grounds, sand, soap, jelly, potato peels and dish water. All this was smeared over the person's body! After that, one had to bend over and get a *paddling* of about ten hard whacks. *Ouch*! I feel like I've been riding a horse for a couple of hours.

This process changed for each victim and even the *big shots* had to participate. All the boys saw this as a chance to get even so the *big shots* received even rougher treatment. The ship then stopped for a few minutes as part of this custom. During peace time, it calls for a big party with wine, women and song. Everyone was in splits, laughing, hollering and shouting wise sayings. Everybody had a grand time! Beer is usually served but we understood it is not allowed.

Love, Johnny

On the Southwest Pacific War Front landing somewhere in the Pacific Ocean Dad has been spending time studying. He wants to learn all he can before he starts his work. He has been instructed on how to shoot a gun.

08/10/42

Dear Mary,

You should be aware by now that I landed safely. I told my brother Walter to write to you and tell you any news about me. I've been spending lots of my spare time studying. I'm not sure how much knowledge they will expect me to have learned. I'm finding it rather hard because it's been a long time since I've *hit the books*. After all this, I'll be very disappointed if I don't earn myself a rating.

At times it's who you know that counts instead of what you know. It's surprising how many boys have taken up reading for a change. Nevertheless, I don't want anyone pushing me around. While I was a civilian, I thought it was *fun* to shoot a gun. This is only for a few shots because the gun kicks back so much your shoulder aches. When shooting machine guns or large guns, the noise hurts your eardrums. It's not as much fun as people think it would be if they tried it.

I've learned a few words of a new language. *Chop chop*! This means get out of my way you bum! This is what the crew says if they are in a hurry. Remember that time you said I was too nervous? Well, now I'm living life at a slower pace so I've gotten over all that apprehension. My life seems to be running like a storybook with quite a few more chapters to go before it's complete. I'm also hoping I will be permitted to take pictures when I get to my final destination. I will try to send some home to you.

All my friends wrote to me while I was in the states. It was very nice of them, but the letters I really look forward to receiving are yours, dear. Please keep them coming!

Love, Johnny

On the Southwest Pacific War Front on board the ship in the Pacific Ocean Dad is placing himself in God's hands. He believes with his guidance there is no way to go down the wrong path. He also tells mom not to spend all her spare time writing letters. He wants her to go out and enjoy herself.

08/12/42

Dear Mary,

I feel like I'm the luckiest guy in the world. I really mean it. You have no idea how much enjoyment I get from writing these letters to you. I will look forward to your replies. Now, don't try to spend all your spare time answering my letters. I'm sure you can find some other way to spend your time and make it more enjoyable.

Mary dear, the censors may not let me talk much about myself. If I spend lots of time talking about you, I hope you will understand. I have figured out that when I was a civilian, I seemed to be six months behind on my sleeping. I can say I have now caught up on my rest. Such is life, one surprise after another. Anything that happens to me now is being guided by God himself. With his guidance, how can I go wrong?

I hope this letter gets to you quickly and safely. When you go to church, remember to say a little prayer for me. When I go to mass, I will do the same for you. Dearest, I can only hope the day will come when I can say things to you no matter where or when and you'll be there in person to hear them. Mary, I want you to always feel free to say anything to me. If I say anything out of place, please tell me about it. Don't ever feel sorry for me and withhold anything from me. I think it is much more practical this way.

I hope your sisters are well and having fun with their boyfriends. It's too bad we didn't get a chance to go out all together and have a swell time. I can only hope the day will come when I can stop writing about all this and actually start doing it.

Love, Johnny

On the Southwest Pacific War Front in the Pacific Ocean
Dad is dreaming about mom because his mind is filled with memories of her. He tells mom he feels like he is talking to her whenever he writes his letters.

08/14/42

Dear Mary,

Well, it finally happened! After dreaming about everything in general, I had a special one about you. It was one of those dreams where I appear in a lot of places. This is how it went. I was walking down the street and all of a sudden you came along. You put your arms around me and gave me a big kiss. I said, "What was that for"? You said "do I have to give you a reason why I kissed you"? There were a lot more details to it, but it became rather silly. You know, honey, if I close my eyes I can still feel that kiss as if it really happened. I hope to have more of these dreams to tell you about soon.

Summer is almost over in New Jersey. However, where I'm going, spring is just beginning. I'm looking forward to possibly enjoying two summers this year. You ought to see my swell tan right now. Mary, I've been doing a lot of thinking about everything. I wonder if you'll appear differently to me when I finally see you again. I am absolutely sure you will still be my *beautiful armful of love*. Don't forget to tell your Mother and Dad I was asking about them. Oh yes, include your sisters and brothers as well.

All the boys see me writing to you for long periods of time. They like to tease me about it by saying I should forget about you. They think some *draft dodger* has claimed you by now. My answer to them is *forget about kidding me for I know how well we get along*.

Never before in my life have I been so certain that my feelings for you are the real thing. You see kid, a few words from you make me feel so much better. Every time I run short of something, I start writing about you. I wonder why this happens. It couldn't be true, oh yes it could, it is love. When I write letters to you, I feel as if I am speaking to you directly. I hope I haven't said too much to lose the mystery. Do you know what the boys said when I showed them a picture of us together? They said "Woo Hoo, what a babe"! Then they said "Mama buy me one of those" and "Does she have a sister or two"?

I can still picture you all dressed up in a new outfit. You would be giving the boys a chance to cast their eyes on you. I only know they have no idea how lucky they would be to see such scenery like you. I hope they appreciate this opportunity. I still remember the day we went to my hometown and I kept telling and showing you everything at the same time. Time was so short that day. I guess I made you more confused than ever.

That is what I got for waiting so long to bring you to meet my parents and see my hometown. It's a funny thing that everyone thinks his hometown is the best. We just keep saying *Just get me back to the States!*

Honey, I can still remember how I pinned my corsage on your yellow blouse. Gosh, I can remember every day I spent with you just like it happened yesterday. Honey, it sure is sweet of you to spend so much time writing letters to me. I will cherish all of them. I look forward to thanking you when I get back home. Then I can do it in a much better and proper manner.

Love, Johnny

On the Southwest Pacific War Front still travelling in the Pacific Ocean Dad informs mom about the food he expects to have if he ends up being stationed in Australia. He wonders if he will get a chance to see General MacArthur.

08/16/42

Dear Mary,

Every day is the same for we dress as usual. You know we wear the suit with all the trimmings. One gets to know the other boys pretty fast when we are so closely packed. I've made a lot of new friends and when I land I will get to know plenty more at my new location. I just came back from church and went to lunch and I was so surprised to see fried chicken. It was totally unexpected and delicious.

I am told Australia has so many sheep that our meals may always be some lamb dish. Good bye chicken and eggs! I hope my letters don't sound I'm really complaining. This is war so things can't be like *home sweet home*. I am hoping that if I get to go to Australia, they have lots of movies for us. I never thought English could be spoken in so many different ways. One can tell where a soldier comes from by listening to him talk. After hearing all these combinations, don't be too surprised if my voice changes as well. I wonder if I will get a chance to see General MacArthur.

Today I'm going to see some boxing bouts. I hope to see some good fights because there are a few professional boxers on board as well as wrestlers. Oh how I wish I could go to a dance. Personally, I think you are my *best* dancing partner so I guess I must wait on this thought. Most likely I will learn a few new steps when I dodge some Japs.

I hope, by Christmas time, I will hear from you. I know I must make it tough on you to answer my letters for I don't ask many questions. Okay, here I go with some questions. *How does a girl become like you? Did you figure it out by yourself, or did your parents teach you to be a certain type of person? How did you get so sweet and different than other girls I've met?* Now don't hold out on me, tell me all the information. I promise not to tell a soul. We'll keep it a secret between us. My address is: Private John Poslusny (32385094) APO 3028 San Francisco, California.

Unfortunately, I don't know my zip code, but they should know where to ship my mail. The trip this letter takes is more risky than the military adventure I am currently taking.

I feel like I'm getting older every day. It seems like only yesterday that I was nineteen and had never kissed a girl. Mary, you were the last girl I kissed before I left. You will be the first girl I want to kiss when I get back home. Oh, what a great day that will be! Don't forget we have a date for the first Sunday after I invade the United States. I'll plan to come to Manville, New Jersey early and stay as late as you will allow me.

Love, Johnny

On the Southwest Pacific War front still on the boat in the Pacific Ocean The boys had to unpack their bags for inspection. Rumors are circulating about the reason this must be done. Dad is guessing the *big shots* just wanted to keep them off guard and on their toes. He says "that's the Army for you".

08/18/42

Dear Mary,

Today, we had to unpack our bags for inspection. A rumor circulated that someone stowed away a blonde in their bag. Another was either someone stole the anchor or pilfered a rowboat. My guess is the *big shots* saw we're having things too easy so they found a way to make us miserable. They figured making us unpack bags would do the trick. That's the Army for you, always willing to keep you off guard and on your toes!

The reason I didn't mail this letter sooner was because of the censors. I have a swell friend who is married and he tells me how happy they were when he was back in the States. I get mad hearing good things are forced to stop or are prevented because of the war. There're plenty of young people who must wait to be together and suffer this way.

My friend is from Boston, Massachusetts where Boston baked beans are so famous. The secret is to add a half cup of black coffee to them. I would never think of this. He says one will never taste good beans unless you make them this way. It gives them a brown color and flavor. This fellow has a nice wife. He keeps telling me how happy they were.

The first thing I plan to do in Australia is go and order a big juicy steak. I'm just thinking about it and I'm hungry! Quick dear, can you bake me a cake? That ought to satisfy me enough to wait for my steak dinner. The boys are singing **Oh I wish I had someone to hug me, someone to love me**. The words change and we give it the Army touch.

I am getting used to taking orders from the officers now. I don't think I'll get out of the habit. It was easy for the *hen pecked husbands* to get used to but us single guys found it harder.

Here is the latest communiqué issued by the Japs. *On the Australian front, a large force of Japanese soldiers attacked an enemy cyclist making him dismount.*

It was probably an American. After some heavy and prolonged fighting, we were able to puncture his tire and destroy the front wheel. While the loss of the rear wheel must be obvious, the handle bars are in our possession. The frame of the bicycle is still being bitterly contested.

Do you know what the soldier said to the babe at a USO dance? "I don't know how to dance, but I'd love to hold you while you dance". She was *pretty as a picture* with a nice frame too! I really would be happy if I could say *you are my own, my very own*. Gosh, I just can't help saying these things to you. Honey, this is how I feel about you. When I write to you, my heart holds the pen. Dearest, I know I've sort of put you in a spot, but please forgive me because I can't help it.

Love, Johnny

On the Southwest Pacific War Front passing *ghost islands* in the Pacific Ocean The crew lost an entire day by crossing the international dateline. Dad talks about his Navy friend who has a large collection of souvenirs. He is impressed with the large amount he has been able to acquire.

08/20/42

Dear Mary,

We just passed a few small islands with no people living on them. I think we call this a *ghost island*. It's just rocks and water. This is no place for me! I am stuck so please get me out of here! We lost a whole day because we crossed the international dateline.

I was able to visit my Navy friend's room. It sure is better than ours. It looked like the nearest thing to home that I've seen on this boat. He even had curtains on the windows. He showed me his collection of souvenirs. What a large collection! Finally, we had a chat about old times for we know each others family back home. I'll bet you never received a long letter like this one before. There is so much I want to say to you. This is the only way I can keep in touch with you, the time I spend or the amount of pages don't make any difference to me.

One can never tell where they will send me when I do finally get selected for a unit. During the night, everything is in a *blackout*. When we go out, we wear our life belts. They have ropes to keep them attached to our bodies. Sometimes when we are in a dark hall, we fool around by tying ourselves to someone else's ropes. Some boys even tie their ropes to some part of the boat. One time we tied ten men together without being caught! What a mess that was when everyone's lines started to move!

I have a one hour detail every three days so I volunteer for the storage room. This is where all our food is stored. All the fruits are on ice so I don't dare to touch them.

At least I don't taste too many of them. When one is out in the ocean, things like fresh fruit taste very good.

Love, Johnny

On the Southwest Pacific War Front anchored in the bay near the island of Fiji
Dad describes all the scenery in full detail. He also tells mom everything that goes on with his daily life in the Army.

08/22/42

Dear Mary,

Presently, we are anchored in the bay. We will dock tomorrow if we can find a place. The island of Fiji is very picturesque with beautiful trees, hills and mountains. The houses are surprisingly modern. I can see cars and trucks moving along. Most of the vehicles are Army units. In the bay there're some pleasure boats roaming around.

Finally, I got some new paper and it's the airmail kind. I plan to buy a souvenir at each port. Some day I will show them all to you. Mary, it is hard for me to describe all the things I have seen. They are beyond exciting and beautiful. I've seen pictures of islands in books, however, I would never guess I would be able to see them in person. I would trade all these sights in if I could be in my car sitting in front of your house right now. That would mean more to me than anything in this world. I'm writing to you in my hammock while we are passing through the most dangerous waters on this trip. I went to the deck below because it's much better and safer.

Love, Johnny

On the Southwest Pacific War Front landing in Fiji in the Pacific Ocean Dad and the boys are looking forward to going ashore especially after spending so much time on the boat. He realizes they are getting closer to the *danger zone*.

08/24/42

Dear Mary,

Today we landed on an island called Fiji. We're hoping to be able to go ashore if we behave ourselves. Everyone is being an angel. We're doing everything for the *big shots* with a smile on our faces. We go out of our way to please them. We look like very good boys, but wait until we go ashore. On this island, the policemen salute everyone from a *Good Humor* man to a general. Therefore, we salute them in a snappy manner. They are very modern as their hair is worn in a *sweep* style straight up about twelve inches high.

We're getting closer to the *danger zone*. During this trip, we haven't encountered a submarine. We feel very thankful. A boat filled with girls just went past us.

You ought to see how all the boys ran to one side of the boat to see them. This caused the boat to lean over on that side. One would think we never saw a girl before. They were having a party so they waved at us with a glass of beer in their hands.

The dinner room crew and our officers thought we would all get to shore. Some boys weren't allowed to go ashore so this created a shortage of food. We thought there was going to be a *food riot* but we ended up having sandwiches at 8:00 p.m. This wasn't too bad because some natives in row boats sold us some bananas and coconuts.

Love, Johnny

On the Southwest Pacific War Front on the island of Fiji
Dad is entertaining mom by telling her about boys who went ashore and got *tipsy*. He makes her laugh when he describes how they look when wearing shorts.

08/26/42

Dear Mary,

This morning I went to breakfast and saw a lot of boys on K.P. which is kitchen patrol. They were the ones who came back *tipsy* from their shore leave. This is their punishment for drinking too much. I figured that I have been in the water for twenty four days. I think I will probably be here for another eight days or possibly more than that.

Most of the boys bought shorts to wear on board for they are easy to wash. I never knew there were so many knock kneed and bow legged soldiers in the Army until they put their shorts on. I get tired quickly when I'm walking on land. I guess it's too much space after being on board the ship for so long. The officers had a good time as there were many women officers of the U. S. Medical Corp. on leave as well. Though men are married, it didn't make much difference to them.

What I really need right now is a nice big hug and a kiss from you, dear. I would feel better for sure. Woo Hoo! You have me under your spell, kid. Whenever I talk about you, I get all excited. The powers that you possess are strong. I've only been away from you for three months and even with 12,000 miles between us I cannot break that hold on me. No, I'm not complaining, I love it all!

Love, Johnny

On the Southwest Pacific War Front on the island of Fiji

Dad hopes mom has not forgotten him. He says he met girls from many lands but none that possess her charm and beauty. He is enjoying some of the music on board.

08/28/42

Dear Mary,

I hope you haven't forgotten me? This letter should remind you I'm still here. I didn't read this letter over before I sent it because when I tried it put me to sleep! If you find any mistakes, please excuse them. I wish I could send more letters, however, there are no Post Offices or mail boxes in the ocean. I have seen girls from many lands. I talked to them and sometimes they were quite nice. However, I would give up all of them for you, darling. When it comes to thinking about you, I am powerless to do anything else.

There goes the ship's loud speaker playing music. They're playing a song called **Miss You** by Bing Crosby. They sure are rubbing in our loneliness. Now they are playing the Helena Polka. Quick, hold me back from jumping overboard to swim back home to my favorite dancing partner! Don't forget to send me a little picture of you as you appear now. It would certainly do a lot to cheer me up!

I always heard the equator was the hottest place on earth. However, I thought the desert in California was hotter. Your mail should be reaching me more often. However, unfortunately, my letters to you will take longer. This is because the ships go to my location I'm living in and then they go to some other place to be sorted before they deliver the mail to the States. I sent you and my dear mom some pictures. I bet she will be glad to hear from me. I know I was her favorite boy when I lived at home.

Love, Johnny

On the Southwest Pacific War Front moving away from the island of Fiji Dad describes the beautiful full moon but says it's no good without mom. The crew is moving and the sea takes a terrible turn. It's so rough a lot of the boys are sick.

08/31/42

Dear Mary,

Today was my wash day. My clothes do get dirty on board ship. At night we were treated to a full moon. What good was the nice full moon to me way out here without you? The water is so calm today, just like a lake. This kind of night is dangerous for us. Submarines can spot us easier under these conditions.

Now we moved on and we're setting our watches ahead. The sea took a turn and now it is very rough. About eighty percent of the boys got seasick. It was the first time I also felt a little sick. I think it was because I had to take someone's place in the rear of the boat. The poor guy was so sick, he couldn't stand up. The boat was like a see saw. The back would rise up fifty feet and then down again. Oooh, my stomach felt like it was up there while my body stayed down below. This was, by far, the worse day and night on board. Even a few of the sailors got sick!

Dearest Mary, I don't know how to end this letter but I think I should before I write a book! I hope you like it as much as I enjoyed writing it. I might not be able to tell you as much detail after this time because it will be considered military secrets. I think I will always manage to have something to say. Mary, please don't forget I am one soldier boy who really cares for you and loves you. Tell everyone I'm over here putting in my $.25 worth. Be a good little girl and don't worry about little me.

With All my Love, Johnny

On the Southwest Pacific War Front moving on in the Pacific Ocean Dad is feeling *fit as a fiddle* and has arrived *safe and sound* in the *war zone*. He has finally finished his 32 page letter on the Pacific Ocean. He says the Army Air Corp. does not let anyone know exactly where their men are stationed.

09/10/42

My Dear Mary,

I'm still around feeling *fit as a fiddle*. First, I get a needle stuck in me, then they throw more equipment at me. I'll have enough equipment to start my own Army Navy store soon. We've gotten our weapons but I'm not allowed to mention what kind but I think they're the best. This is to protect the air base in case of attack. They're very strict out here so I don't know if and when they censor the letters.

I just filled out a card notifying my folks that I have arrived safely in the *war zone*. They just told me that the only information I can tell anyone is that I'm *safe and sound*. You might never know exactly where I'm stationed. That would be considered *classified* military information. The Army Air Corp. never lets anyone know where men are sent.

I think it will be either Australia or some island in the Pacific. Maybe you will be able to get a general idea where I am by the letters I'll surely write to you.

I might try to keep a diary of all my experiences if I can keep it under cover. I should be able to tell all the little boys and girls how life in the Army was fifty years from now. Here I am going into the prime of my life. I'm just getting to know what life is all about. I'm spending part of it for Uncle Sammy and I'm sure it will make a better man of me. I've heard a saying that goes like this *you can never be a good soldier unless you complain about everything*. I guess it's only natural when it comes to being in the Army but I'm not sure how things are in the Navy.

They say *absence makes the heart grow fonder*. It sure has caught up with me. I could never imagine myself thinking this way. However, as the days come and go, my love for you grows stronger. That's how I know it's the real thing, baby!

Love, Johnny

On the Southwest Pacific War Front relaying details about Fiji
Dad finds this place to be very similar to Florida. He observes many different people and takes notice of their unique clothing.

09/12/42

My Dear Mary,

I thought I would tell you more details about the island where we stayed for a couple of days. There are about one thousand islands in this group. It was a Fiji island. This place was visited by the Japs a couple of times so all the people were prepared. I have enclosed a sample of their money for you to see how it looks. These islands get lots of rain, sometimes three or four times a day. It was raining very hard, but a bunch of us went downtown anyway. A little rain just wouldn't stop us. This place was quite modern and had many cars. This area was similar to Florida with palm trees and lots of different flowers in many colors. Two movies were playing, **Jesse James** and **Skyhawk** with Earl Flynn. It was Sunday so no beer was sold.

This was a good thing for lots of boys would have gotten drunk and lost their shore leave.

The people are Black, Hindu, Indian and Chinese. Both men and women wore dresses with the bottom hem cut in a jagged pattern. They were strong and muscular, but bare footed. Every time we saw a native, they would say "Bola Bola". We saw them smiling so we could tell this meant hello. This wording can mean many things such as *So long, Go jump in the river* and of course, *You know where you can go.* The men style their hair about twelve inches high and six inches wide from front to back. I only saw a few white people besides the soldiers. Some of the *black* native girls are not bad looking for they wear nice clothing to accent their *curves* and have *fancy* hairdos. It's hard to tell whether you're looking at a *babe* or a man because their hair and clothing looks the same. A well dressed person here wears a white dress, a colorful necktie, a yellow skirt and no shoes. This is what the *wolves* wear in this area.

If a boy wants to be fresh to a girl, all he has to do is say "Jig jig", then duck his head or start running. I don't think this meant *Hi Toots*. The cops wear *fancy* uniforms with only a night stick. They are all six feet tall or taller and look powerfully built, however, they don't carry guns. The Indian women wear wedding rings in their noses. They also wear a veil every day. The colors they choose are very bright and the combinations are mixed together. These women are able to carry baskets on their heads without dropping them.

They told us Americans that we wouldn't like it here, because most of these people thought we wanted to stay here. I met a little boy who spoke very good English. He invited me to come to his village six miles away in the jungle. He said I would have a good time for a dance and celebration was to be held. I couldn't go because I had to be back on board ship at 6:00 p.m.

I enjoyed eating bananas. I bought twenty five of them and only paid a total of $.15 for them. I was able to get a large bottle of soda for only $.13.

The merchants soon learned the value of American money. They think we are millionaires because we appear to have so much money. Their wages are very low, about $.40 a day. They work when they feel like they need money. The merchants were friendly and our boys *cleaned out* the store shelves. They bought candy, cakes, ice cream, homemade bread and many kinds of fruit. I went to a New Zealand club and bought eight sandwiches, a cup of tea and a large plate of fruit salad. All of this only cost $.25 so I was quite surprised to find out I could buy so much but pay so little money. Prior to this time, a soldier could buy a house for $4.00. Now they cost $50.00.

One could also buy a very beautiful Indian girl for $6.00. She would live with you, perform maid's duties and offer other services. Woo! Hoo! This practice is illegal now. These Indians are like those who live in India. Some of the girls don't wear much more than a very short skirt and no top. There were soldiers from many lands here, and we all got along well together. We stayed four days and were able to go on shore leave every day for about six hours. Most of the fun started when drunken soldiers came back to the boat. One of them put his arms around the ship's Captain and kissed him. Some boys wanted to beat everybody up and still others were just *slap happy* as they talked and staggered. I stuck to my *malted* milkshakes that I usually enjoy.

All my Love, Johnnie

On the Southwest Pacific War Front leaving Fiji for New Guinea
The boys are treated to a visit from some little native girls who are selling beads. Dad finds out all the native people are under the impression that the Americans are rich.

09/14/42

Dearest Mary,

Some little native girls were selling beads. I guess they were about four years old. We would try to give them a nickel for each string. However, they would say "No, Americans have plenty of money, twenty cents for each, please".

Lots of homes here have beautiful woven carpets. They're made of very strong material. The designs are of their government buildings or something like our Washington, D.C. office building. They look like granite or marble. They can weave many nice baskets and shopping bags. These are all done by hand.

Love always, Johnny

On the Southwest Pacific War Front in New Guinea
Dad is getting to know the people, food and customs in New Guinea. He tells mom there are no parties after 6:00 p.m. It is *blackout* time so the Japs can't see them.

09/16/42

My Dear Mary,

The natives like our names very much so there are many Johnnies' here. We found the British white girls and women very *stuck* on themselves. They wouldn't even say *hello* or bother to look at us. The natives have a very good sense of rhythm. They really sing well. They are able to not only sing their native songs but American songs as well. They were singing **You are my sunshine**. They earn money for food by singing. A penny gets them a loaf of bread and a smoked fish. This is considered one meal for them.

All of the stores close at 6:00 p.m. by law and then there is *total blackout*. That means no parties being held in the hills or villages beyond the city. When there is a party, soldiers from New Zealand, Fiji Islands, Australia and America come together for one party of many nations. Sometimes there are a few civilians. Their drinks are quite strong and one can count on seeing at least one fight at each party. Some boys were so drunk and half crazy. One of them actually started to chew on his canvas hammock!

Love, Johnny

On the Southwest Pacific War Front in New Guinea

Dad does a fantastic job of describing the people he has met. He tells mom about the clothing, the cars and the style of living he has observed.

09/18/42

Dear Mary,

The policemen are the most colorful people on this island. They all have the same haircuts and their uniforms consist of *fancy* buttons and hats. I know you have seen some women wear fancy hats in the States. Well, you ought to see the hats over here! I saw an Indian carrying a small package. Beside him was his son carrying a big package that probably weighed one hundred pounds. It was twice as big as the boy himself. Most of the Indians look like they are wearing a table cloth for a skirt with very bright colors. Women were walking around with very little clothing on them. This wasn't due to the hot weather but it seems to be the style.

If you can get a world map, you can see just about where I have been and where we are travelling now. I still don't know for sure where my boat trip will take me. I can safely say it would be *censored*. In the rivers on the island, men use spears to catch fish. The shoemakers in town sit on the floor with their feet crossed and work on shoes from this position. Only one native in twenty of them wear shoes. The others would scrape their feet on the sidewalk and it sounds just like you and I dancing. What tough feet they must have! They kick footballs barefooted and seem to be as accurate as our players who wear football cleats in the States. The nice grass tennis courts are well kept on the island. I'm told there are some good players here.

Men and women smoke cigarettes made out of tobacco that smells like a $.05 politician's cigar. It was wrapped in old newspaper. In the rivers on the island, men use spears to catch fish. I see many different styles of cars. If you think my *rattle trap* is small, you ought to see some cars here. They are half the size of mine and look like something Abe Lincoln traded in for a newer model. The merchants here want American money.

Love, Johnny

On the Southwest Pacific War Front anchored in New Guinea
The Japs make many claims to victory using false information. Dad finds a way to address his letters to mom to hopefully avoid the censors.

09/20/42

Dear Mary,

The place where we finally laid anchor was reported by the Japs to be completely destroyed two weeks ago. What can one believe these days? The only thing I believe at this time is that we are at war with the Japs. In fact, they claimed *all valuable installations on 2,000 islands have been destroyed.* My My, what startling news! I expect to hear in the near future that I'm a ghost on this ship which was sunk twenty days ago. If I sound a little spooky, check the postmark on the envelope. Who knows maybe it will be from the *other world.*

I purposely used my home address for this letter so that it would look like civilian communication. This way I might avoid any *big shots* from reading it. If they decide to check, I wrote one short letter and then I started another letter. If by chance, my luck runs out and I'm caught, they will lower my status two grades lower than a private.

I expect to be busy as a bee when we settle on land. I could go for a nice *fresh water* shower. I feel so salty that I could never spoil even in the heat. If and when I see Australia, I'll be able to have a big smile. Right now I only have a little grin.

Love, Johnny

On the Southwest Pacific War Front in New Guinea

Dad is getting a kick out of hearing the Australians say "bloody this or "bloody that". He makes sure to tell mom not to write Fiji or Australia or even *blue ocean* in her letters.

09/22/42

Dear Mary,

It sure will feel funny having summer instead of winter at this time. You will be freezing over there while I'll be roasting over here. I have heard the Australians claim we don't know how to speak English.

They think they are the experts when they use the words *bloody this or bloody that*. They use this kind of slang a lot. Don't mention the word Fiji or Australia in your letters. You can say *place*. I might get in big trouble if the *big shots* or censors see it. They're not aware how I was able to get any information to you. A friend is going to mail my letters to you from the U. S. They don't let us say *blue ocean* as the Japs might figure out it means the Pacific Ocean.

Love, Johnny

On the Southwest Pacific War Front in New Guinea
Apparently, the men are not allowed to draw any state maps to pass the time. Dad says this is silly. He feels the Army is foolish to be checking the guys instead of learning all they can about where the Japs are located.

09/24/42

Dear Mary,

I want to tell you a good story. One guy decided to draw a map of Illinois just to pass the time. A corporal saw it and alerted the *big shots*. I'm guessing he thought he would gain the title of Sergeant by this patriotic deed. However, this soldier had to appear before the Commander of our boat and explain himself. They don't want any of us to draw maps because the Japs could see them. Of course, the Japs are free to go to any library and get books or maps. They told him not to make a map ever again and then they said a lot of other *baloney*. I think it's this kind of foolishness that made Pearl Harbor possible. Instead of educating themselves about where the Japs are located, they spend time patrolling us to stop us from making any more maps. If the censor saw this letter, he would never let it go through the mail to you.

We just passed a large school of fish jumping out of the water. They measured about eight feet long and I think there were 98 of them. Oh well, I might have missed a few, dear. We're getting closer to our part of Australia. I will have to close this tiny little letter. So long until ??? XXX kisses all for you!

Love, Johnny Doughboy

On the Southwest Pacific War Front arriving in Australia at last
Dad is happy they have landed in Australia. He worries about how long his letters might take to arrive in the States. He also tries to describe the Aussie money system.

09/26/42

My Dearest Mary,

I arrived in this country at last. This was my first chance to write to you. All of us were very hungry when we landed. I guess it will take me a month to catch up on my eating. After a lot of explanations, we finally figured out a little information about their money. Here is how simple their money is: 1 shilling = $.16 American money, 1 shilling = 12 pence Australian money, 1 pence = 1 Australian penny, ½ pound = 10 shillings or $1.64 American money, an Aussie penny is like our $.50 piece and it is made of copper. If you are a *brain storming* genius with a college degree, you can master the money. It's as clear as mud! It really is swell here!

The cars here are different and old fashioned. The trains are small and look like our 1909 model train. They travel forward and backward. The reason is there isn't any place to turn around. At times they go straight to one town and then backward to another town. At first our truck drivers startled people by going around corners at thirty miles per hour. The people here consider six miles per hour as fast moving. Now everyone has to run across the street in fear of being hit by a car or a truck. They would think N. 13th Street in Manville, New Jersey is a *super* highway. If you stood on a corner and counted the trucks passing by, you would find fifteen out of twenty are American owned and driven.

When I go to a movie, I hear them laughing at silly things. This ends up making me laugh at them instead of laughing with them. I've been here for one month and I can see why Australia hasn't moved forward in the manufacturing field. The transportation and roads are really neglected. However, the cities are surprisingly modern and remind me of some of the medium size cities we have in New Jersey.

Love, Johnny

On the Southwest Pacific War Front in Australia
Dad is impressed with everyone as they are doing some kind of war work. He regales mom with a fancy description of his new home which he calls a *swanky joint*.

09/28/42

Dear Mary,

Cigarettes are a luxury item to civilians because they cost a lot. Our soldiers, however, pay only $.08 each with no tax at all. You can tell this country is involved in a war. Everyone is doing some kind of war work. We got busy making writing tables and chairs. We must work with very simple materials for Australia is in the *war zone.*

It's so nice to have fresh water again without a ration. My new home is a very *swanky joint*. It's basically a tent and my bed is a cot filled with straw. All my gear is piled neatly on the floor. I tell you people who live back home have it easy. If they heard and saw what I have witnessed so far, they would realize war is not easy. The people here have to give up a lot more luxuries to win this war. It's summer now so any kind of clothing one wears is okay. Some soldiers complain no matter how their camp is set up. I guess it's natural for them to voice their opinion.

Love, Johnny

On the Southwest Pacific War Front getting acclimated in Australia
The Australian people are very thankful and appreciate the Americans because they have saved them from the Japs. He tells Mom about the mail status and he misses her a lot.

09/30/42

Dear Mary,

I have to write small and only on one side of the paper. These are the rules. Airmail stamps are hard to find around here but I was lucky enough to get some. Sending letters by airmail is supposed to be faster than regular mail. Honey, I sure do miss you a lot and look forward to getting a letter from you soon.

Rumors fly the minute you hit any camp. I've heard over one hundred that are probably not true. Everything is so different here. This country seems forty years behind the U. S.

The Australian people are grateful to us for we've saved them from the Japs. Women do all the men's work. They only get paid $6.00 a week. The latest time one can leave to go to stores is 5:00 p.m. Almost every store closes for the day promptly at 6:00 p.m.

Love, Johnny

On the Southwest Pacific War Front leading life in Australia
Dad still works on his dance skills, however, the Aussie style is quite different and he finds it confusing. It is also very hard to get around when the town is in a *blackout*.

10/01/42

Dear Mary,

I stopped at a dance in town but I couldn't dance because I had my Army twelve pound shoes on at the time. Their dances are so different. Most of the songs played are ten years old. Their style of dancing is the old fashioned waltz with a little Aussie added. A typical dance consists of three steps sideways, then slide, jitterbug a little and you end with a quick step including spinning and turning. It's quite confusing to me.

The town is in *blackout* so when it's dark one has to dodge people and cars to get around. When crossing streets, it's quite confusing. The reason is traffic comes from the opposite side of the road. There are many small cars, *pocket size* models. In Australia when you say you're going *up north*, you find it warmer. The equator is north from this country. My guess is everything in Manville, New Jersey must be very quiet. Most of the young wolves are in the Army or Navy. I am very lucky to be in the Army Air Corp. and I feel it's the best place to serve your country.

Love, Johnny

On the Southwest Pacific War Front learning more about Australia
Dad knows mom would be curious and want to know about the food being served. He goes into a lengthy description about food and how cheap it is to buy a typical meal.

10/02/42

Dear Mary,

One of my meals was steak, potatoes and vegetables along with a pint of milk. I was able to get it for $.18! What a bargain it was at the American Red Cross. The bread is just as good as our old fashioned Polish homemade bread and milk is even better. The beer is *two times stronger* than our beer back home and it's also rationed. I got a big surprise when I weighed myself as I gained some weight. Scales cost one penny and weight is shown in *stomes*. A *stome* is fourteen pounds. How complicated it is using this system.

I have not seen a kangaroo yet, but I'm sure there will come a day when I'll be able to spot one. Australia does not make too many manufactured goods so most of them are imported from England and the United States. This country isn't as populated as the United States but it's very big. Palm trees grow here like in Florida.

Love, Johnny

On the Southwest Pacific War Front discovering Aussie people and customs Dad is learning about people in Australia, he also gets a chance to talk to soldiers who have been involved in the war in Libya and Egypt.

10/04/42

Dear Mary,

I've heard from many soldiers who've been involved in the war in Libya and Egypt for three years. They tell me we are giving them hell in *censor cutting*. I don't know exactly what I can tell you because a censor is always ready to cut out any type of information they consider classified. I will have to save stories for you and tell them to you after the war is over. I've made some friends so we do have some fun together.

All we do is eat, rest and exercise. Sometimes you see a car with an attachment fly by the camp. It looks like an ice box, a furnace, a gas range or a whisky still. Apparently, it uses charcoal to fuel the engine.

The children here quit school when they're fourteen years old. They are allowed to go to college if they wish. There are many deferred men *mostly old guys* who work on a farm or have government jobs. They trade wool for our goods.

Love, Johnny

On the Southwest Pacific War Front in Australia
The mail is currently *out of sync* so v-letters are rationed to one a week. Dad also informs mom about the store windows which are taped to protect them from bombs that might strike their buildings. He says this also prevents the glass from shattering.

10/06/42

Dear Mary,

I'm still trying to get settled so things are a little out of sync. The *v-letters* or *victory letters* are rationed to one per week. I get a pass every other day to go to the city so I'll be able to see more of it the next time I'm there. Most of the store windows are taped so they are protected from any bombs that might strike them. The tape acts as protection from broken glass. Honey, I'm only 12,000 miles away from home. It's a mere two months of travel. This letter contained a lot of information so I know it will take you a while to reply. So Hon, keep your chin up. So long for now, I'll be dreaming about you.

Love, Johnny Air Corp.

On the Southwest Pacific War Front visiting the local city in Australia

Dad is able to go into the city using a trolley. He enjoys shows which cost only $.18. He notices how delayed the Aussies are when showing their pictures from the past.

10/07/42

My Dear Mary,

I went to the city today and found all the stores closed. I did manage to sightsee a little bit before darkness came. I took the trolley which only costs $.02 to ride to anywhere. It reminds me of a trolley we had in my home town when I was four years old.

Then I went to a show costing only $.18 called **Tugboat Annie**. I was very surprised when they showed us training on the beach back in early July. The parade shown was us marching for General Weaver. I saw our flag indicating what group was marching but it was hard to recognize any of the faces as the scene moved by so fast. Since this activity dated back to July, it shows you how delayed the Aussies are in showing their pictures.

I went to a dance for the second time in the city. The *barn dance* is not like ours at home. Both partners walk together as if they're strolling. The rest of the dance looked screwy! The music is old fashioned and the orchestra cannot start without stopping for a rest.

Love, Johnny

On the Southwest Pacific War Front exploring in Australia
Dad feels the Aussie *babes* are not very pretty compared to Mom's beauty. He tells Mom she is still his *favorite dance partner*. He follows this up with a funny story about arriving back to his tent after a night *on the town*. What a scream!

10/10/42

Dear Mary,

There are many *babes* but their makeup is the work of an *amateur*. It's plastered all over their faces! They're nothing to admire, at least not as pretty as you. I had not danced for so long it felt funny. I saw girls wearing bracelets above their elbows. Every time one dances the *jitterbug*, the dance floor shakes. I still think our American girls are the best. You're still *my favorite dance partner*. My feet got tired quickly. No, I didn't drink too much beer to make me feel this way. The dames are quite sociable. They're curious and want to know everything about the U. S. so they ask a lot of questions.

One night, I got back from town at midnight. I walked to my tent and it's so dark I have to feel around for my bed. My hand feels my bed but also some animal! I must have jumped about three feet. I was *scared out of my wits*! Then I remembered I am a U. S. soldier so I must be brave. I struck a match to get light and there laying sound asleep in my bed were two dogs. They were very nice dogs with curly hair so I pet their heads and they jumped down and took off running. They keep coming back to pay us a visit.

Love, Johnny

On the Home Front in Manville, New Jersey
Mom talks about her thoughts and her dad's comments regarding the war.

10/11/42

My Dear Johnny,

It is a Sunday afternoon and I'm sitting on the front lawn and taking great pleasure in answering your most recent letter. Even though it was a short one, the great comfort I felt was a *cure* for my *sore* eyes and heart.

Daddy is fixing the cellar of our home making it rainproof. What a mess it is! However, I'm glad he is doing it now before the winter weather comes. I'm glad there are no fellows calling upon us three girls at the present time. Sometimes Daddy makes us laugh when we talk about the war. He says "My dear daughters, I'm so happy I have you three and no sons at this time". They would be ready to go far away and Mother and I would be worried. However, when we talk about fixing our home, he says "Why couldn't one of you be a son to help me a little around the house"? He is a *scream* at times!

My sisters want me to go with them to the dance at the Polish American Home because it is being held for the employees of the Diehl's Manufacturing Company where I work. I wish you were here to take me to the dance. If I stay home, I might feel worse. I give up so I'll go and make believe you are next to me. Boy is that tough! The dance was okay. Did you get my letter written in a round circle? Now I'll answer your questions.

1. Yes dear, I'm feeling fine and my family is as well.
2. The weather is lovely and couldn't be nicer.
3. I have written two letters to your brothers and I plan to write to your folks.
4. You bet the single fellows have all gone into the service!
5. Your letters were *censored* and a few words were missing but I could read them.
6. Yes Johnny, I miss you, miss you, MISS YOU! I wish you were here.

I'm still an inspector, however, now I was chosen to be a *Floor Lady* of our department. Maybe you can picture little me overseeing some of those big women and girls. I should feel bigger and yet I don't feel any different.

Love, Mary

On the Southwest Pacific War Front getting used to Army life in Australia

Dad is hoping he will be lucky enough to see a kangaroo. He also tells mom about some of the prices of food. Some of the boys go *AWOL* and he describes what it means.

10/12/42

Dear Mary,

I still haven't seen a kangaroo. The Aussies seem to think us *bloody Yankees* scared them away from our camp. However, the Aussies are swell and ready to help us in any way they can. The only time we stop to *salute* the officers is when we see them with bundles in both hands. Saluting is not as strictly enforced as it was at home. One $.10 fountain pen is worth $1.50 over here. Every day I buy a bottle of milk from the PX store and it costs me only $.06 a pint. We can get lots of beef, milk and butter. *Bikon* is bacon in Aussie. I've also acquired an Australian accent of sort.

There is no electricity in our area. In order to press our clothes, we put them down flat under our mattress and sleep on them. Sometimes we use candles or flashlights. Most of the boys are trying to find an Aussie soldier who lives close to our camp. They are hoping one of them will have a bunch of pretty sisters. If they find this guy, he will quickly become the most popular one in camp. A few boys went *AWOL* for a couple of hours. This term has two means, namely, *a wolf is on the loose* or *absent without leave*.

Love, Johnny

On the Southwest Pacific War Front in Australia
A sergeant assigns Dad to K. P. known as kitchen patrol where he peels a lot of potatoes and is rewarded with cocoa. He sees how some of the guys are wasting their money on gambling. He is always hoping to get letter from Mom.

10/14/42

Dear Mary,

On my fifth day here a sergeant said to me "Johnny some soldiers have it and some soldiers don't, but you have it". When I asked *what do I have*? He said, "You have an opportunity to serve K. P. otherwise known as kitchen patrol." This was my chance to peel a lot of potatoes and drink all the milk with cocoa that I wanted.

Some of the guys are playing *craps* or *dice* in my tent. I have watched them play but I have no desire to waste my money in a game. There is mail call every other day so I hope to be getting more letters from you, my sweetie. It may take a long time for me to receive your letters, but I sure will appreciate getting them.

Love, Johnny

On the Southwest Pacific War Front in Australia
Dad is disappointed with the slow process of mail coming from the United States.

10/16/42

My Dearest Mary,

I haven't received any mail from you lately, however, I'll continue to write to you anyway. I have enclosed a picture of a fellow you know quite well. I sure am glad that I'm stationed in a country where our language is spoken. There are many worse areas I could have been sent to serve.

Love, Johnny

On the Southwest Pacific War Front enjoying outdoor movies in Australia

Dad is very fortunate to be able to see free outdoor movies. Of course the seating is good old *Mother Earth*, however, it is great entertainment for the troops.

10/19/42

Dear Mary,

I just got back from the free outdoor movie in our camp. The picture was **A Yank in Libya**. I had a seat in the lounge. Oh yes, right. A screen is strung between two trees and we sit on good old *Mother Earth*.

There's one movie camera and about the time the *wolf* is ready to plant a solid kiss on the babe, the picture stops. An announcer says Part I is finished and Part II will start in a few minutes. The pictures are very up-to-date. In one part, this *wolf* was trying to get his *eyeful* to marry him. He says "we can go on an ocean trip". All of us hollered "join the Army, we had our ocean trip"! Our whole gang had the same idea and said it at the same time. Every time a kissing scene is shown, all the boys moan. It's so tough to see a scene like that because we are so far away from our sweethearts. Yes, I moan the loudest!

I got quite a kick out of the city in the day time. Almost everybody carries a bag. Even the kids carry one on their backs. When I go back to my camp, I travel by tram. This is a trolley in Aussie language. The trams carry 112 people. The late one can fit about 200 soldiers. We hang all over the tram. It looks like a sardine can. Most of the time, we travel free because the conductor is afraid to climb out to collect money from us.

Love, Johnny

On the Southwest Pacific War Front looking for kangaroos in Australia Dad is told the kangaroos hide in the woods. There are also some things that are rationed even in the Pacific Ocean in Australia.

Mary Jane Juzwin

10/21/42

Dear Mary,

I understand the reason we haven't seen a kangaroo is because they hide in the woods.

I bought a pair of Aussie shorts for five shillings which is about $.80. A malted milk costs only $.05 and you are treated to three full glasses. Everyone is trying to sell something. I tried to sell my tent but the guy wasn't drunk enough to take the bait.

Matches are just as scarce as tires are back in the States. All shoes and clothing are rationed and one must present a coupon to get them. I'm getting used to all the styles. Most of them are about thirty years behind the times. Some of the boys live in the city and get $3.50 a day for living expenses plus the $60.00 a month the rest of us receive.

A meal costs $.18 and a room only costs $2.00 per week. I hope we are assigned to a place like this. It would be quite a financial success. Everything is run by the government. Pay day just passed so we got paid with Australian currency.

Love, Johnny

On the Southwest Pacific War Front in Australia
Dad and his group are given the privilege of seeing a *repairing center* where they fix airplanes, jeeps, cars and radios. He is also assigned other Army duties.

10/23/42

Dear Mary,

We went to another *repairing center* to check it out. This is where they fix airplanes, jeeps, cars and radios. I know how to fix them all but I haven't been assigned to one place yet. Today I was assigned *guard duty*. This duty was for twenty four hours total.

I stood *guard* four hours, then I was off for eight hours and then I completed four more hours. My post was the *main gate* and my duty was to check people's passes to town.

Some of the boys tried to get by me by showing me a copy of the Air Corp. song. Others showed me a picture of their girlfriend. You know me well enough to figure out none of these shortcuts worked. If a soldier falls asleep on *guard duty* he could be fined a large sum of money, shot or put in jail. I did manage to stay awake but I was so sleepy!

Our food is almost as good as home, however, we have no ice cream. Although, we can buy some at our PX store for only $.18 a quart. People wear so many different uniforms over here. Speaking of *v-mail*, the word is that it's not very fast but I will try it out anyway. The writing will be very small so I'm not sure it will be easy to read.

Love, Johnny

On the Southwest Pacific War Front in Australia
Australia's climate is very similar to *good old New Jersey* in the summer. There are some funny stories dad tells mom about the rain and what happens to the tents.

10/25/42

Dear Mary,

The climate is very similar to *good old New Jersey* in the summertime. The only action I've experienced is when one of the tents blew down. It fell on top of some boys during a *rain storm*. The reason this occurred is because they forgot to loosen the ropes on the outside of their tent. The rain causes the ropes to shrink and the tent goes down. We brave boys rushed to the rescue and put the tent back on its track. You should have heard the laughter! Luckily, no one got hurt and we had a good time except our feet got wet!

We have a few mosquitoes at night but we can fix them. The government issues each of us a net for this purpose. The mosquitoes would wait until we lay down and then *dive bomb* us from above. Despite everything I have told you, I'm doing fine.

I'll never forget you, Hon. Anything I do is because I love you and want you to do the same. I seem to be full of energy but no way to use it. If I heard a *Polish hop* and a lady from Manville would dance with me, I could use up this extra energy. I guess I should end this letter so you can eat your *Wheaties*. Save all that extra energy for me.

Love, Johnny

On the Southwest Pacific War Front experiencing a dance in Australia Dad seeks out dances so he can keep his skills sharp. He provides a full description of the dance hall. He also talks about wildlife and a bird who is called a *kookaburra bird*.

11/01/42

Dear Mary,

I just returned from a dance in the city. The hall where it was held was very large but it had an old method of air circulation. Big wings or flaps were hanging across the ceiling and they would swing back and forth. It was motor driven and seemed to work very efficiently keeping the hall cool. When one walks into the hall, a doorman searches each person for bottles. It's quiet and peaceful and they want to keep it that way. Almost all the homes have the same kind of roof. They're made of a sort of corrugated metal or tin so when there is a rain storm, it sounds like Niagara Falls inside the home.

While I was there, I enjoyed a steak dinner. The steak was so tender I could have cut it with a fork but I had to use a knife on the gravy. I also had vegetables, ice cream and a pint of milk for about $.25. The reason the food tastes so good is because it's seasoned. The Army doesn't bother to season food. A typical Aussie week day meal is fish heads and rice. As an added appetizer fish tails accompany the meal on Sunday.

I've gotten a chance to talk to guys who live *deep in the heart of Texas*. Apparently, it is still a very rough place. A shooting is an ordinary occurrence and in some parts of Texas there is no penalty given for it.

We have a bird called a *kookaburra bird*. He's a cross in appearance to a pigeon, a canary and a parrot. His voice sounds like a naughty hyena. One of them made power dives at me the other day. I guess I came too close to his apartment and his family. He had such a temper! One guy woke up and found a large bird in his mosquito net.

These mosquito nets are really life savers. They are truly worth their weight in gold. They help to control our mosquito population. Our camp is overrun with dogs. Every time one of the boys spies a nice dog in the city, he just tucks him under his arm and brings him back to our camp.

Love, Johnny

On the Home Front in Manville, New Jersey
Mom sends dad a big package of goodies for Christmas. She also tells him his letters are *censored* but she can still understand and read them with no problems.

11/01/42

Dear Johnny,

I want to thank you for those *darling* sea shell beads you sent me. Your letters reach me in nine days. I don't think it's bad timing for the *war mail* at the post office. Johnny, are my letters *censored* before you receive them? Your letters are *censored* with only a few words or a sentence cut out, but I can still read them. I sent you a box and I'm hoping you receive it by Christmas. Please let me know when you receive it and what condition the package arrives. The package should contain the following items:

1. One pound box of Shrafts candy
2. One dozen six cent airmail stamps
3. A maroon portfolio with 24 envelopes holder and some writing paper
4. An Eversharp pen & pencil set
5. Two funny books
6. One half ink & pencil eraser
7. One bottle of Watermans ink
8. A large tube of Mennon shaving cream
9. A large can of Mennon talcum powder
10. A toothbrush with floss
11. A large tube of Ipana toothpaste
12. A can of brown shoe polish
13. Two packages of chewing gum (the kind we have now since rationing)
14. Two large white handkerchiefs

I hope you find these items useful and please let me know if you need anything else. The weather is getting so cold. I get up in the dark morning, work all day until 6:00 p.m. and it is getting dark again when I come home. It's quiet in the house for a change so I can concentrate on writing to you. I feel fine but I am getting sleepy. I better go and visit dreamland where I hope I see you again.

Love, Mary

On the Southwest Pacific War Front experiencing amusing events in Australia Many of the boys snore when they sleep. Dad jokes when he tells mom what it sounds like in his tent. Rumors still float around the camp and become unbelievable.

11/02/42

Dear Mary,

You ought to hear some of the boys snoring when we return to camp late at night. It sounds like many prehistoric monsters or all the animals at the Bronx Zoo are camping out in our tent. One of the boys takes our Air Corp. spirit with him when he sleeps. He sounds like a P-47 bomber performing a power dive. Oh, how I hate to get up in the morning! Revile is usually 5:00 a.m. so before I open my eyes, I dress on the run. I stand at attention and wait for my name to be called. I then scurry back to my tent to catch a few more winks until it's time for breakfast.

One fellow told us he's going to tell the government that he didn't pay his income tax. He hopes this story will send him back to the States. We shall see how this tale will end. What a surprise I had when a guy walked up to me. He was my roommate in Fort Dix, New Jersey. His hometown is Red Bank which is very close to my home town.

You ought to hear some of the rumors that float around the camp. One said "The war is being fought all over the world". Then we heard one that said "Hitler has dyed his mustache". Finally, the last one said "Adolph was dead". These are known as *bedside rumors*. The ant hills around here are about ten feet high and they are everywhere.

Love, Johnny

On the Southwest Pacific War Front in Australia
Dad hears many stories about the Aussies, Italians and the Germans regarding how they feel about the war. He recants an amusing story about an experience some guys shared.

11/04/42

Dear Mary,

I was talking to an Aussie soldier who has fought in many battles. He told me that when they capture an Italian soldier, he is always happy to get out of the war. He will even pose for pictures! A German soldier is just the opposite. He would not only be unhappy, he would not be willing to pose for any pictures. The Italian and German prisoners have to be isolated from each other. They are such bitter enemies. If one finds them together in an area, a big fight is guaranteed to follow.

There is some talk about making a formal protest to the Australian government because of the money situation. It seems that their paper money can't stand up under the strain of our dice games. The money wears out too quickly. By the way, I finally found a place where they play modern music. I try to go there just to keep my dancing skills sharp. I am able to go every day.

I must tell you of an experience a few of the boys had to endure. They were put on *shipping duty*. This meant they were packing bundles into a truck. They all thought the actual *front fighting zone* was where they would be heading next. While they boarded the truck it was thought *Oh no, this is it*! It turned out the truck stopped two blocks passed the barracks area and this was to be the final destination!

Love, Johnny

On the Southwest Pacific War Front describing the mail situation in Australia Dad is concerned because his letters must be transported by boat. This will slow down the whole process, however, he will remain diligent in writing love letters to mom.

11/06/42

Dear Mary,

Honey, I know any mail sent to me will be slow in arriving. However, this is due to the fact that it is transported by boat. This will not make me stop writing to you and I hope you continue to write to me, even if it is a short letter.

My last good bye to you leaves me dreaming of the day I will be able to say *hello* again in person to you. I know if I could steal a kiss or two and whisper something sweet in your ear, all my dreams would come true. Well, I guess this is enough of a *note* I have written to you. Give everyone my regards and take care of yourself.

Love, Johnny

On the Southwest Pacific War Front in Australia
Dad is looking forward to taking some pictures of the scenery wherever he is stationed. He wants mom to make sure she sends him more pictures of herself.

11/08/42

Dearest Mary,

Hello honey. I'm camped out so far away from any big town that it isn't even funny. However, with your help, I manage to stay in a happy frame of mind. I bought a camera and expect to have the time to take some pictures of the wonderful scenery out here. I'm hoping you'll be willing to hold on to them if I send them to you.

If you haven't already sent me a picture of yourself, could you ask someone to take one of you just as you are? Maybe I'll have to come back and take it myself! On second thought, I might just capture you instead as that would be much better. Yeah babe!

Love, Johnny

On the Southwest Pacific War Front experiencing the climate in Australia Dad describes a startling weather experience to mom. He talks about the creatures he has encountered around the barracks.

11/10/42

Dear Mary,

I just have to tell you about my startling experience over here! The weather was warm and sunny, about 89 degrees. All of a sudden, it turned cloudy and windy. The wind blew furiously and it started to rain. The next thing was it started to pour hail stones on me. At first glance, the hail appeared to be very small, about the size of marbles. Afterward, the hail stones grew to be the size of baseballs! Some of these came down so fast, they punctured the roof of the barracks. The barracks are typically made with very strong materials. Somehow these hail balls easily made holes in the ceiling. Even the ground was covered. We washed some of the hail stones and made ice water out of them. Finally, the hail ceased and the sun began to shine again. This caused the hail to melt. It seemed to get real warm afterwards, about 85 degrees. What screwy weather!

All around the barracks we catch many strange creatures. One lizard we caught changes its color every time we move it to a new location. This is a gift from *Mother Nature* so the lizard can hide from his enemies. I 've seen him turn green, blue and yellow. He blushes red too! We have lots of dogs. One dog has strong teeth, he'll grab hold of a stick and we can lift him off the ground! He's able to hold his grip for ten minutes. I wish I had teeth like his so I could chew some of the tough beef we get served over here.

Love, Johnny

On the Southwest Pacific War Front watching gambling in Australia Money is disappearing quickly as the boys are getting into gambling. Dad tells mom some facts about the money situation and how confusing it can be to locate an Army unit.

11/12/42

Dear Mary,

One of the boys was a *bill collector*. He says he would knock at the front door, and then run to the back door to catch people as they ran out. When a fellow pays us any money he owes using American money, we say "Stop trying to pass that foreign money around". You see, American money is a thing of the past around here.

Lots of boys are suffering the disease called *broken pocketbook*. Luckily for all of us, a full up-to-date payment is becoming a fact. I'm able to go to town most days for I don't gamble my money. What tales I hear in the Army, there're enough to write a big book.

A half pound note or paper money worth $1.63 seems to last about as long as our $1.00 bill back home. When we go to town, we take money for transportation and dinner. Our money is worth more here than in the States. The modern things one can buy for cheaper prices. Only the old fashioned things are priced higher. The match shortage is pretty well cleared up now. A candle match is now being made. It's covered with wax and smells like a candle when lit.

There are so many different units in the Army. Even the average person gets confused when they try to locate one. Some day, maybe, they will combine some of the units into one which would surely be more simplified. Every time we receive a shipment, we tell the Aussies we will meet them at the *American Legion Convention*. Chances are we will never see them any more for the duration of the war.

Love, Johnny

On the Southwest Pacific War Front describing flies and people in Australia Mom finds out how the flies identify their victims. Dad is enjoying hearing some of the guys singing when they are coming back drunk. The word *bloody* is taboo.

11/14/42

My Dearest Mary,

You ought to see how well trained the flies are around here. First, they peek at our dog tags. *These show our name, hometown and blood type.* They see our blood type and then they *dive bomb* us. This just goes to show you how particular they are about us humans.

It sounds very funny to hear a couple of Australian soldiers singing **Deep in the heart of Texas** as they go walking or rather staggering down the street. A Yank soldier can say almost anything to an Australian girl. When anybody says the word *bloody*, they get so burning mad and ready to fight. The meaning of the word is a mystery and I can't seem to find out what it means. I even tried putting it in a sentence. I said "I cut my finger and it was so bloody". This statement even made them mad, so I give up! What a strange custom. I guess heaven will be full of *Australian angels* for they never say a bad word.

Some of the *hard drinks* are as strong as *paint remover*. The boys never learn their lesson and sure get tipsy! I would rather eat my quart of ice cream and drink my quart of milk every day. By the way, I want to wish you a *Happy Birthday*. I hope to be home on your next one if it becomes possible?

With All my Love I remain, Your Johnny for the next 100 years

On the Southwest Pacific War Front in Australia
Dad realizes how far away he is from mom in the States. He explains the many APO numbers used to identify one's location. He is not happy unless he hears from mom.

11/16/42

My Dearest Mary,

I just can't stop writing to you. All day long I keep hoping I will be able to get back to my camp and spend an enjoyable evening writing to you, dear. The space between here and the United States separate us but I'm still happy to sit down all by my lonesome and have a chat with you using the mail. The mail situation is frustrating because there are too many APO numbers to identify one's location. It seems everybody else is getting mail but not little Johnny! Woe is me!

When the company clerk sorts the mail and I don't get any letters I get mad. I say to him "Are you holding out on me you so and so?" He says "I ain't holding out for anybody Johnny but you just didn't get anything". I walk away complaining to myself, thinking how sad I am because I haven't heard from my sweet gal, Mary.

This is something that depresses me more than Hitler's face. When I lie down at night, I think out loud. One of the boys says, "Why Johnny she's out walking with a 4F *draft dodger* in the park". My heart goes *topsy turvy*. I get hot and cold chills on my face. Then my blood curdles and races with my corpuscles. I eventually gather myself together and pull the covers over my head. I am hoping I can see you in my dreams at the very least.

Here I sit in the shade of my tent stranded only 12,000 miles from Manville, New Jersey. I do have a great tan and sixty five *smackaroos* in my hip pocket. I'm just jabbering to a couple of jeeps but thinking about you keeps me happy.

There is some talk that Turkey will have to be evacuated. This news item is because the Italian and German Armies are running backwards? It could cause a riot and might hurt someone if they pass through Turkey on their way to get to the hiding place somewhere near Berlin. The latest report says the general started running backwards three days ago and only has a lead amounting to three blocks in Manville, New Jersey.

Love, Johnny

On the Southwest Pacific War Front in Australia
Dad is full of stories about Japs. Some are amusing and some are not. He also describes Thanksgiving dinner to mom but he would still like to enjoy a meal with her *in person*.

11/17/42

Dear Mary,

Here's a little dope on the Jap Army. The second class private gained his status because he lisps when he says *Hirohito*. The first class private can actually see when he takes off his glasses. He won a prize for stealing pocketbooks from eighty five year old widows. The fellow who is the private excellence can say "Hirohito" without a lisp and he likes to show off his buck teeth. He likes to chew the bar room rail with his teeth. The major of the cavalry is raging mad because his house was eaten by a bunch of infantry men who got tired of eating rice. Finally, there's a general hanging by his mitts up a tree. He's looking through a pair of binoculars and it seems he's *scared as hell* at what he can see through them.

Well, I better shut my trap before I say something wrong. This letter was written by the same *1A* who has a huge crush on you and he doesn't care who in the world knows this information. Say *hello* to everybody and keep the light in the window burning for me.

Love, Your Johnny

On the Southwest Pacific War front having Thanksgiving in Australia
Dad can't believe his eyes when he saw his Thanksgiving *feast*. All the boys miss their sweethearts and take comfort in the misery of each other

as they discuss their girlfriends far into the night and often until the wee hours of the early morning.

11/19/42

My Dearest Darling,

Gosh honey, today turned out to be a wonderful day for me. It's Thanksgiving and we had a swell dinner. We were able to eat all we wanted and it was quite a feast. We had turkey, potatoes, beets, cabbage, peas, bread with jam, peaches, candy, ice cream and pie. There was also beer, lemonade and coffee. The only trouble was the fact that I couldn't have my favorite desert. *You know the kind I used to moan at when I got it in the moonlight.* Don't tell me you have forgotten about that?

All the boys including me carry on a verbal discussion of each other's girlfriend far into the night and sometimes until 3:00 a.m. If you feel your ears burning at times, it's me talking about you. Here's what happened to me when I received your last letter. While I was reading, I kept walking. My journey continued right past my tent and into the woods. The boys were watching me the whole time. Pretty soon I realized I was in the woods. All the boys laughed and said "You sure got it bad and she has you under her spell". Of course I was guilty but I just smiled and kept my trap shut.

Mary, darling, I miss you so much! Whenever I think of you, it makes me feel happy and yet blue because I can't see you in person. It seems like yesterday since I said good bye. What a time I'd had that night, now I wish I'd stayed longer. Maybe it was a good thing I left when I did because you needed some sleep before your next day of work.

I hope you all enjoyed your turkey dinner as well as I did. We have a lot to be thankful for right now. Well I better close this little note until I find something else interesting to talk about. So long for now and take good care of yourself, darling.

Love, Johnny

On Southwest Pacific War Front hearing good Army news in Australia
The fellows hear some good news about the war with American success on the African front. Dad indulges himself with his favorite dessert which is ice cream.

11/20/42

Dear Mary,

I'm sitting in my camp thinking of you and writing this letter. The Army short wave receiver is broadcasting from a California station. The good news of the second front says American soldiers have had success on the African front.

We have also heard about more success on various other fronts. It's this kind of news we like to hear. The boys all have a big grin from ear to ear on their faces.

There are many orchestras and other radio programs sent across to us over here. It sure makes us happy beyond words but at the same time a little *homesick*. I have indulged myself with a pint of Peter's ice cream. It is the only company that makes ice cream in Aussie land.

Love, Johnny

On the Southwest Pacific War Front observing storks in Australia
Dad is amazed when he sees approximately 1,000 storks resting in one of the fields. He learns some Aussie phrases and his gang adopt a baby kangaroo.

11/21/42

Dearest Mary,

Most of these people have never seen snow in their lifetime. I miss it too! One of the fields has about 1,000 storks just like the same models that deliver cute babies back in the States. I guess the storks decided to travel here for a rest. One thing I know for sure and that is there is bound to be plenty of weddings when this war is over.

When an Aussie asks if you have had your tea, he means *have you had your lunch?*

I went to a lunch room in town and it was pretty late in the afternoon. As I was leaving, I heard the women say "tut, tut." I looked at her in amazement wandering what she meant. Finally, I figured it must mean *so long big boy*.

Here's the latest *underground* rumor circulating now. The American airplane factories will not let anyone pass through as it distracts the attention of the workers. It costs the factory about $800.00 a person with time lost while they're not working steadily.

It sure is swell to be able to listen to a radio any time we want to have a break. We are able to hear the *hit parade* as well as China, Russia, Italy, Hawaii and Japan. We are closer to all these countries than the United States.

You ought to see the baby kangaroo we have for a pet in our tent. He's only seven inches tall. The mother kangaroo had been shot so we took her baby out of her pouch. We feed our baby with an eye dropper and he likes milk. He is very tame. Some day he might grow to be three feet tall. A mother kangaroo gives birth to four or five babies but kills all but one of them. The pouch can only accommodate one passenger by regulation of kangaroo law. It's funny to see him try to walk. He puts his front legs down first and then the back legs pass the front ones. It looks like a *hop* but not a *Polish hop*.

When I get more organized, I will send you a picture of him so you can see what he looks like. He sleeps in a little bag which we hang up for him. He always sleeps on his back all curled up like a rose.

Love, Your Johnny

On the Southwest Pacific War Front hearing lizard stories in Australia Dad checks out some girls at a dance in the city. Australian soldiers who fought in the deserts of Libya tell the boys about their conversations with the lizards.

11/23/42

Dearest Mary,

While I was near a city, I went to a dance where I heard some of the unusual names the girls have here. One girl's name was *Charm* and her sister's name was *Melody*.

I've talked to a few Australian soldiers who have fought in the deserts of Libya. They say the first week you start talking to yourself. Then you start talking to the lizards. When two weeks have passed, the lizards start talking to you and you find yourself listening to them. Another story I heard was in Africa there is a tribe of natives who believe in *a life for a life* and *a tooth for a tooth*. If a native kills a man, his son must live with his mother until a child is born. Then he is punished by death or hard labor. If the man happens to be an orphan, I guess complications arise.

I often wander if I will run short of interesting subjects to write about, however, I think I have enough to last a long time. So dear Mary, remember that I love you dearly and continue to dream about you.

Love, Johnny

On the Southwest Pacific War Front talking with the Australian people Dad's feeling good and notices civilians admiring the American soldiers' dress uniforms. The Australian people are curious and want to know everything about the States.

11/25/42

My Dearest Mary,

I'm feeling *fine and dandy* and I hope my gal and her family are the same. I haven't had my chat with General MacArthur yet. Most of the civilians think we are *big shots* when they see us dressed in our complete uniform. Our outfits are very colorful in comparison to the Aussie uniforms. When the Aussies find out you are from New York, they ask about gangsters.

If they find out you're from California, they ask if you know any movie stars. Almost all of the Australian people want to visit America. Towns here are connected by trains made of wood instead of steel.

Every chance I get, I'm practicing my dancing style. It's quite hard to get used to the Aussie style of dancing, but I manage to hold on to a *babe* and look a little like I'm dancing. All the gals are quite sociable, but one has to *be careful* when talking to them because there are some *gold diggers*. An Aussie soldier might spend $.90 on a girl, a Yank spends three times that amount. The gals also think Yanks are more of a *playboy*.

The style here for a dancing couple is an evening dress for the gal and the man wears a pair of shorts. If the man is smoking a cigarette, he is allowed to continue smoking while dancing. If he doesn't have two pence in his pocket to check his hat, he can wear it on the dance floor.

We're now living in barracks so we have electricity. When we lived in tents, we had to use candles for lights. I never thought I would ever get excited about a lamp, however, we are all anxiously waiting for darkness so we can use it.

Love, Johnny

On the Southwest Pacific War Front investigating beer in Australia
It seems the beer in Australia is much stronger than in the States. Dad is happy getting some mail from mom. He hears some airplanes overhead and can't wait to fix them.

11/26/42

Dearest Mary,

The beer is very strong here so it's nothing to see a drunken bum being slugged and dragged away. As for the U. S. soldiers, there is a strict rule that says "no hard drinks including beer after 6:00 p.m." I've discovered the fact that about ninety percent of the Australian people have bad teeth. Apparently, the drinking water does not contain an important mineral. The dentist must be pretty busy pulling one tooth after another.

We have mail call every day so we get a few letters every time a boat or plane arrives. Pardon me while I slug a *heckler* with a *big mouth* in my barracks. He insists on saying "Why does she still love you"? or "Does she have a sister and what is her address"? or "What kind of girl can she be and will she cook and perform s_ _ acts as well"? I don't like anyone who talks foolishly about my gal or any other gal.

It feels good to hear a few airplanes overhead once in a while. I can't wait until I get to work on them. I was able to go horseback riding today. It costs two shillings an hour which is about $.33. The horse was not as fast as the one the Lone Ranger rides but he wasn't too slow either. I'm a bit sore so today I will only stand and try not to sit down.

I guess I will have to sleep on my stomach.

My bed is my office, table, dining room, kitchen, etc. I can always depend on it to be there for me. What a pal! Each morning I take a cold shower which helps me to open my eyes and wake up. The American Red Cross is swell to us. They allow us to take a hot shower and they provide free towels.

Love, Johnny

On the Southwest Pacific War Front hearing about transfers in Australia Dad says a few of his friends are transferred to a squadron every day. Again, he tells mom about the food. He adds some Australian tales from the past.

11/30/42

Dearest Mary,

Every day a few more of my friends are transferred to a squadron. As of today, I'm a *filler* or a *reserve* and I haven't been assigned to a squadron. When I do get assigned, I hope to travel in a transport plane. If one has to rely on a train, it becomes quite an ordeal. The trains only travel about thirty five miles per hour so it's a long trip.

This country is strictly a *tea country*. This soldier would love a good cup of coffee, some *flapjacks* or some french toast with syrup or honey. We eat some meat but everything seems to taste differently over here. We go on ten mile hikes almost every day to keep *in shape*. You see wheaties are not sold in the stores and spinach has not been invented yet.

I usually get a pass to visit the big city every other day. We don't care if it's dark for we take along some necessary supplies with us. These would be a bullet proof vest, Tommy gun, compass and a book on *how to win friends and influence people*. The PX store downtown is my favorite spot to hang around and see what goods are being sold. I also check to see anyone I might have known from back home.

I heard when the first group of Negroes arrived in Australia, they told the girls they were American Indians. This tale was easy to believe but only for the light skinned boys.

I sure do miss hearing a radio for there isn't any around here except at the American Red Cross building. The wave length is different for Australia so an American radio would have to be *coil rewound* in order to tune into American stations. We have a possibility of a chance to acquire a radio set-up soon which would be a great cure for our loneliness.

Love, Your Johnny

On the Home Front in Manville, New Jersey

Mom tells dad her town is becoming *a ladies town* because so many men have been drafted and sent overseas.

12/05/42

Dear Johnny,

You should see this little town of Manville. It's getting to be a *regular* ladies town because many men have been drafted and sent overseas. When I do go dancing at the Polish American Home, there seems to be enough *young sprouts* to dance. They are between the ages of 18 to 20 years old. My sister, Jeannie and I have fun with them.
Here is a poem for you:

> Soldier boy, I love you so and I want the world to know,
> though you're in the Army now, I make this vow,
>
> I'll wait for you though it may be long you know,
> still you are my only beau and you're the one worth waiting for,
> cause you're the boy that I adore.
>
> and when you're far across the sea, soldier boy please think of me.
> and the lovely hours we spent. The love we shared was ours alone.
>
> I don't know if you'll return dear, makes no difference how or when dear,
> just as long as you return to a heart that's yours alone.

Love, Mary

On the Southwest Pacific War Front hearing news from the States in Australia The poor Army boys in the States are complaining about passes. Dad is not sympathetic for the guys overseas have it rougher. Dad tells another funny story about the guys in his tent. He's bragging to mom about how the guys harmonize when they sing.

12/12/42

Dearest Mary,

I've just heard from a reliable source that there was quite a commotion back home. The news is the *poor* Army boys get to attend only two U.S.O. dances a week and get only fourteen day furloughs instead of fifteen days. The weekend passes were cut to twenty three hours versus twenty four hours. My, aren't things getting tough for the Army boys back in the U. S. Wait until they're sent here where there are no weekend passes. The U.S.O. dances aren't free and we're lucky if we get a clean sheet once a month. We are also missing ice cream and cake but we get plenty of beef and mutton.

Once in a while we must be present for *bed check*. One of the leaders comes into the barracks to make sure we're all here. One of the boys waited until the leader was leaving us and said "Good night Mother". Boy did we have a good laugh! There are lots of orders given out that seem useless but still must be obeyed without question.

That's the Army way. What a swell bunch of fellows we are privileged to have in our barracks. They are full of fun and we get along better than any place I have been stationed in the past. You ought to hear how well we *harmonize* when we sing songs. It reminds me of a *barber shop quartet*. We have a bunch of *bathtub tenors* and *bass frogs* combined into one symphonic splendor. Singing together boosts our morale.

Of course, I would still love to be at a dance with you, sweetheart, hearing an orchestra playing music and dancing cheek to cheek. I guess I can only visualize this in my dreams for the time being. I better close for now. Give my best wishes to everyone back home and keep a smile on your face for me.

Your soldier boy, Johnny

On the Southwest Pacific War Front mastering Army life in Australia

The mail is so far behind that dad has not heard from mom since September 2, 1942. He is adjusting to his work duties and impressed with the skills he's learned.

12/14/42

My Dear Sweet Mary,

I haven't heard from you since September 2, 1942. I miss you very much. My health is okay but I don't feel *chipper* because I need a dose of sweet letters. This would greatly cheer me up . Worse than that is most of my friends are getting mail. Darn it! I know you're writing to me but my mail must be held up at all the APO numbers I've had since I entered the Army. As if this isn't enough to be depressing, the other day our little kangaroo died for no apparent reason. We will miss our sweet little pet.

Another pay day has passed but it doesn't make any difference to me. This shows you that money doesn't *heal the heart's desires*. I sure miss you, honey, and *good ol' New Jersey*. I must have seven wedding invitations waiting for me when this war is finally over. Presently, I have no place to go so I must be content to stay in camp. My work day starts at 8:00 a.m. and continues until 5:30 p.m. I usually work six and a half days a week. After showering and eating dinner, it's almost 8:00 p.m. I can still remember coming to your house and starting my evening at 8:00 p.m. Also, those long three hour good byes we had together were the best!

Here are a few startling things I've learned during the past five months. I have mastered the proper way to tie my apron. I found out I could be more patient while waiting for my meals if I sing the Army Air Corp. song. I also discovered I'm capable of washing and pressing my clothes all by myself. I use the *ultra modern method* of placing them under my mattress and sleeping on them. Finally, I learned how to peel onions, potatoes, pumpkin and squash without cutting off my fingers.

Have you changed your looks or hairdo? How are things in general with you and your family? I still think *absence makes the heart grow fonder*.

Darling, I miss you so much and I'll never stop writing to you until I can see you in person. Our meeting was just like a *fairy tale*. Boy meets girl, boy dates girl and finds out he's *deeply in love*.

Two things I'll have to share with you when I return home. I want to take you swimming *and check out your curves in a bathing suit* either in summer or winter. Asbury Park, New Jersey has a nice indoor swimming pool. The second thing is I would like to take you to Meadowbrook Hall in Cedar Grove, New Jersey and dance the night away to a big orchestra. Finally, I would take you take you on a ride and spend at least two or three hours kissing and hugging you before I would have to say "good night".

Love, Private Johnny

On the Southwest Pacific War Front in Australia
Dad's feeling lonely and truly misses his sweetheart. He hates to get up so early, however, that is the Army way. He is losing patience waiting for the mail from mom.

12/15/42

Hello My Dear,

Here I sit all alone for all the boys went to a movie. I start thinking about you know who *you, of course* so I grab a pen and start scratching. You can tell it's me if you take a close gander at my attempted bit of pen pushing. I hope you miss me as much as I do you.

It is 1900 p.m. which is Army time for 7:00 p.m. You see, sweetheart, there are 24 hours in an Army day but time seems to drag. Waiting for the mail makes me feel like an expectant father. I'm speaking from *hearsay* not experience. Sometimes I just can't see why mail takes so long? On the other hand, I realize I'm not the only soldier boy in the Army writing to his honey and waiting for a reply.

I often wonder how I will feel in a pair of civilian clothes. It will probably make me feel the way I did when I got my first *big boy* pair of long pants and a suit jacket. I find the worse time in the Army is the first ten minutes of each morning. *Oh how I hate to get up*! The best time is when we have mail call and I'm lucky enough to get some fan mail. I live through my letters just as if you were beside me.

Love, Your Johnny

On the Southwest Pacific War Front customizing his tent in Australia Dad is proud of the tent he's sharing with three other guys because it is the only one in camp with a wooden floor built by the guys. He tells mom about telegrams and his latest dream.

12/16/42

My Dearest Mary,

We consider our tent to be of *modern design*. Yes, I say this because it is the only one in camp with a floor made out of wood. The top Sergeant lives in it, the second sergeant, a corporal and that *great lover* with the big last name. *Me, of course*. I hope *Uncle Sammy* didn't wait too long to tell you and my mom where I have been sent.

We are now able to send a telegram for $.40 with three lines. These lines are already written and numbered so I can select the proper ones. I believe the civilians back home can also use this kind of telegram. I received a letter dated December 12 telling me my brother, Walter, had joined the Navy. Boy was I surprised! My mother is probably upset because she isn't used to having all of us boys away from her at the same time. I sent her and Pop a telegram plus a little financial assistance so I hope this cheered her up. I also sent you a telegram, dear, and I hope you receive it. I plan to write to you at least twice a week. My folks will also hear from me just as often. I can send telegrams every fifteen days so no one will worry about me.

I'm *safe and sound*. I don't drink *Australian Mountain Dew* so I always have control of my senses. The place where I'm living now is very safe and we're kept aware of the *war news* at all times.

I know you think I have forgotten you, dear, but as you can plainly see, I haven't. There will always be a hollow feeling inside me and you're the only person in this world that can fill it and make me feel *whole* again. It's definitely you, hon. As I have said before, *You were always good medicine for me.* In my latest dream, I had a date planned with you and on my way to your house my car broke down. I knew I'd be late, get my hands and clothes dirty and feel blue as well. However, when I drove up in front of your house and saw you, I became a different person. You changed my mood from dull blue to bright yellow sunshine. It was that Sunday that I realized my love for you was not my imagination. It was the real thing!

I must end this letter. Say *hello* to everybody and keep your chin up. You are *1A* in my *A1* heart so keep smiling. I will do my best to picture you that way in my mind.

Love, Your Johnny

On the Southwest Pacific War Front working in Australia
Dad has become an expert at washing and peeling potatoes. He also washes pots and pans at K. P. Mom wrote dad a circular letter which was quite unique.

12/18/42

My Dearest Mary,

I'm sitting here resting after having my turn on K.P. otherwise known as kitchen patrol.

I decided to cheer myself up so I started writing to you. My *dish pan hands* are clutching this fountain pen like a mom holds her baby, so gentle and yet firm. My contribution to the *war effort* was washing and peeling a big pot of potatoes including washing a lot of pots and pans that were used to cook them. I did such a good job the *mess sergeant* asked me if I wanted to be a K.P. pusher. In the States, they give you stripes for this job. However, none of that for me!

As of the above date, I have only received your letter written in a circle but no others.

As you can see, this hasn't stopped me from scribbling. I spent half of last night tossing and turning. I just couldn't fall asleep because I had so many thoughts of you racing through my mind. I could remember our dates as if they happened last week. I was visualizing myself sitting in a movie with you holding your hand. I saw tears in your eyes when the story got tense or a little sad. It was then I knew you had feelings and a kind heart. No, don't misunderstand me, I always knew you had a kind heart. Anyone can see this the moment you appear. It's in your smile as well as the way you look at me.

Love, Your Johnny

On the Southwest Pacific War Front in Australia

The mail situation continues to be impossible and all the guys are sick of waiting for their mail from the States. Dad is thinking about the adventures he has had so far.

12/21/42

Dearest Mary,

I always hear a lot of rumors around the camp. Most of them turn out to be false. If I find out any true information, I'll be sure to let you know The sky is beautiful here at night and I wish you could be here to share it with me. Now I know how Robinson Crusoe felt when he had his adventures. This world can be wonderful. I never took the time to sit down and think about it. It took a girl like you to wake me up from my blindness. You showed me what true happiness is without even trying. I do realize that life has its ups and downs so I'm prepared for both of them.

In a few days, I hope to be able to send you some pictures of myself. If you can just keep checking your mail, you should receive them. I'm hoping they don't scare you or your friends. I think I have spent a lot of time repeating some things I have said to you before but maybe using different words. I'll stop now and try not to talk so serious.

If my APO number changes, I will let you know the change of address by telegram.

This might help the mail to find my location quicker. At the present time, my mail has to travel through four APO locations which results in a lot of confusion and delays. During the day, I'm kept pretty busy. However, I spend most of my evenings writing to mom and pop as well as Mary Regiec, my sweetheart. .I never knew I would ever want to do so much writing. Honestly, I enjoy it because it makes me feel more connected to my family and to you of course. I know I wrote a lot in this letter, however, there are plenty of things I still want to say to you. I will save some news for my next letter. I'm hoping and praying I will get a letter from you before the week is over.

Keep up your spirit and may God watch over you and your family. Consider yourself kissed one hundred times by me.

With oceans of love, Johnny

On the Southwest Pacific War Front wishing for winter in Australia
Dad's getting stronger all the time thanks to the Army Air Corp.'s regiment of food, rest and plenty of exercise. He must be content hearing sweet love songs on an old phonograph, however, this makes him miss mom even more.

Mary Jane Juzwin

12/23/42

Dearest Mary,

I am in the nice heat of the day in camp while you are probably freezing back home. I wish I was there to warm you up! Woo Hoo! Snow must be wonderful and I miss it. Darn it, I won't be able to have a snowball fight with you or wash your face in the snow. My health is great thanks to the Army's regiment of food, rest and plenty of exercise. I feel better and stronger than I ever have in the past.

I'm keeping steady company with the lizards, kangaroos and wide open spaces. Tell me honey, are you as pretty as ever? My guess is *Wow and how*. I can hear the boys playing our old phonograph. They're playing sweet love songs while *love starved wolves* sit and stare into space day dreaming. I'm somewhere in Australia where the nights are made for love, however, my sweet Mary is nowhere in sight. She is 13,000 miles away! Boo Hoo!

Letters have come but no letter from my Mary. I've made so many trips to the Post Office that I've just about carved a path from my apartment to it! Sometimes I go four times a day just to make sure. You probably think I'm not able to write anything because of the censor. Actually, I can tell you anything except where I am located in Australia and the work I'm doing for the *war effort*.

We're all wishing for a fresh pack of good chewing gum, however, there is none in sight. Yesterday, we had free beer to cheer us up. We're allowed to drink two glasses per person. I feel very lucky to be alive considering the state of happenings at the present time. I could very well have been one of those unfortunate boys who have died fighting for their country.

Tojo is busy searching for a *glass bottom boat* so he can give his fleet an inspection, we continue to make him regret the attack on Pearl Harbor. I'm hoping to get a chance to see the Hawaiian Islands and try to find his address there.

With Love, Johnny

On the Southwest Pacific War Front observing the wildlife in Australia The boys have adopted a baby panda bear. They are enjoying taking care of him. Dad also describes all the other wild creatures he has seen to mom.

12/24/42

Dearest Mary,

One of the boys here has a baby Panda bear with nice fur on him. He acts just like a human so **Darwin's *Theory of Evolution*** might be correct after all. This bear is small and the only thing he eats is bark from a tree that is very common around these parts. He sleeps in the daytime and goes courting and wooing at night. In fact, he leads a very lively *night life*. I sure miss my *night life* with you, honey.

We have quite a few downpours of rain here. It seems to come only at night. The only casualties I've seen so far has been these big ants which are so plentiful around the camp. They are afraid of the little ants so they scurry quickly away. A few of them get caught running the wrong way up a one way street! After they are caught, they become dinner for the little ants. Ants are supposed to be considered the second smartest insect in the world. Bees are the smartest. I spied a pineapple tree and decided to go and pick some pineapples. I walked a little close to a tree and guess what was staring me in the face? Bees! I ran like hell in the other direction.

We found out there are many strange animals out in the woods. One is a flying fox or large bat that looks like a fox with wings. We came across a *twig hopper* that looks like a piece of wood with legs on it. The birds are quite fascinating to watch and we take pleasure in all their colors and appreciate all the species.

I do miss a lot of things from back in the *good ol' U. S.*, especially you, dear. Christmas is just around the corner and how I hoped I'd be home to spend it with you and my folks. I would make sure Santa Claus was able to take care of you in the proper manner. In Australia, it's very hard to find something *special* or *nice* for one's *favorite armful* as everything is imported. There really isn't anything that is suitable. In closing, I hope you and your family have a nice **White Christmas**. My hope is that everything is *honky dory* at home and everyone is in good health. I hope I hear from you soon.

With lots of Love and Kisses, "Lonesome" Johnnie XXXX

On the Home Front in Manville, New Jersey
Mom and her family are celebrating Christmas but it is not the same because she is missing Dad. However, she continues to write to him and loves to read his replies.

12/25/42

Dear Johnny,

Today is Christmas Day. It used to mean so much to me, however, since the war took you and all my cousins away, it seems like just another day. Of course, we do have a Christmas tree, nuts and candy but it just feels like I am in a *daze*.

I'm so disappointed to hear you have not received any letters since September 1. Believe me when I say I sent you a letter every week and I always put a six cent airmail stamp on it. I think I will try to send this letter as registered mail. I sure hope you get it quicker. I also enclosed a card as well and it is straight from my heart to yours with my *deepest feelings*. I mean it when I say I MISS YOU DEAR SO VERY MUCH! I am sending you a large photo of myself and some wallet size snapshots. I want you to know I will keep on writing and praying my letters reach you in a better order.

Thank you for the beautiful handkerchiefs you sent to me. I'm keeping all my gifts, letters and poems. Johnny, please take care of yourself as best as you can manage. By the way, everyone in my family is fine. They always want me to tell them how you are and believe me when I say you are truly loved.

Your *little* Mary

On the Southwest Pacific War Front celebrating Christmas in Australia
Dad says the only good thing about Christmas Day is the fact that he did not have to get up early in the morning. While he found it hard to get into the Christmas spirit, he tried to make the best of it. Then he tells mom about driving in Australia.

12/25/42

My Dearest Mary,

Today is Christmas Day and for the first time in my Army career, I didn't have to get up at the *crack of dawn*. I took advantage of this privilege and slept all morning. I was able to attend *midnight mass* in a Catholic church a few miles away from camp. It sure feels strange having Christmas so far away from home. The Red Cross did their best to treat us giving each one of us a package containing candy, cake, cigarettes, a sewing kit, etc. I still found it hard to get into the Christmas spirit. If you had only sent me a pine tree and a snowball, it would have helped a lot. I thought of hanging up a stocking but it would have been filled with a few frogs, a lizard or a baby kangaroo in it.

Christmas will not be enjoyable until I am able to come home and spend it with you, my sweet one. Take care and please wish your mom and pop a happy holiday as well as the rest of your family.

Your Loving Johnny

On the Home Front in Manville, New Jersey
Mom receives a bouquet of red roses from Dad for her birthday.

12/27/42

Dear Johnny,

I received your telegram yesterday stating you received my first letter in three months. Oh Johnny dear, I'm so glad you are beginning to receive my letters. I can't imagine where all my other letters were sent. I don't want you to think I am not going to write to you anymore. Rest assured that will never happen. You never know, when my letters start arriving, you might get one every day.

Dear, I have received your *darling* roses. I am thanking you for them with tears in my eyes. I couldn't have been more surprised. Thinking about you so many miles away and yet you remembered me and my birthday. I wish you were here so I could kiss you.

Your *little* Mary

On the Southwest Pacific War Front indulging himself in Australia
Dad is in *ice cream heaven* and decides to eat three quarts of ice cream. Dad is happy to hear mom say she got a dozen red roses from him for her birthday.

12/27/42

Dearest Mary,

I had K.P. the day before Christmas and I enjoyed eating my *favorite snack* which was three quarts of ice cream! While was on duty, I came to a startling conclusion. It turned out to be why we had to get our milk from a long distance away. They can't seem to catch the cows around here to milk them. The horses are so wild, they need their front feet tied together on a short rope. This enables people to catch them and use them when they want to perform some duty.

My boss wrote to me saying he did take care of sending you a dozen red roses from me for your birthday. I wanted you to think I had forgotten your birthday then it would be a *nice surprise*. I bet you thought to yourself *What kind of guy is this Johnny, anyway? He sure is handing me a snow job this means a big line or some baloney. He didn't even remember my birthday! He must not love me as much as he says he does.*

How could you think anything different? Hon, if the roses got to you later, I hope you realize I was thinking of you and couldn't have forgotten your *special day*.

Love, Johnny

On the Southwest Pacific War Front in Australia
A lot of the boys in camp are waiting for Christmas packages from home. At the rate the mail is delivered, it might be February before they receive any of them. Dad continues to send mom pictures of the scenery. He wants to make an album to show his friends and future children what war conditions existed during World War II.

12/29/42

My Dearest Mary,

Quite a few of the boys are waiting for packages from home. The only thing some of them got was a bunch of old hometown newspapers. Most of them would rather not receive or read a newspaper. The reason is because of what you see on the front page. It's usually someone you know who entered the Army about five months after you joined. Now he's a Corporal, Sergeant or Staff Sergeant having a fourteen day furlough. It seems almost everyone who is in the Army in the States gets some kind of rank.

Enclosed are a few pictures of some of the scenery around here. They say *it grows on you* after you live here for a while. Speaking of pictures, I have in front of me your lovely face staring at me. I tried hiding your picture thinking it might be easier on me that way. However, it didn't work so I hung it by my bed so I can gaze at it all the time.

I took a few other pictures which are being developed. They take so long for they don't seem to believe in speeding them along. I don't remember if I wrote a date on my other letter but it was a few days before Christmas.

I just stopped writing so I could eat my Christmas dinner. What a meal! We enjoyed a twelve course meal. The main dish was turkey, peas and carrots, beans, sweet potatoes, pumpkin, fruit salad, mashed potatoes, sardines, squash, catsup, grape juice, beer, hard candy and bread with butter and jam.

Some of the boys tried to get me *tipsy* but it didn't work. I can't see myself getting drunk on the three beers I usually consume. I always said I would need a good reason to get drunk. I have not seen nor found any so I'll stay sober for now.

With Love, Johnny

On the Southwest Pacific War Front in Australia
Dad has finally received some pictures from home which had been mailed on September 17, 1942. He has been showing off with pictures of mom by letting some of his friends see them.

12/30/42

My Dearest Mary,

I received some pictures from home which had been mailed on September 17. They finally reached me now. I can only imagine what other mail is hiding away in some Post Office and has not been delivered to me yet. Now I have quite a few pictures of everybody back home. My dear Mother looks pretty happy under the circumstances. When I look at the pictures of myself as I am now, I think I have changed in appearance quite a lot. Whether or not it's for the better or the worse will be for you to decide, hon.

While I'm writing this letter, you must be enjoying your Christmas dinner at home. Mary, do you remember those pictures we took together? I sent all of them to you. Naturally, I showed them to the boys. There were some that showed you holding your nephew, baby Eddie, so the boys were a little confused. They looked at me funny and said *You always told us you're single and have no children. Here we see your girlfriend holding a baby.* The matter was cleared up after I answered all their questions.

I had been worried about these pictures because I thought they got lost in transit when I was moving around a lot. I can see why I just can't resist you. I remember letting out a big sigh of happiness after I kissed you. Remember that? I better stop this talk before I get too sentimental and spoil this letter. Every time I look at one of those pictures, I think of something else to say to you. One of my friends just received a box of *real, honest to goodness American chewing gum* so I'm chewing my head off! *Yum, Yum!*

Due to the fact that Australia has no snow, Santa Claus had to resort to using a kangaroo instead of **Rudolph the Red Nosed Reindeer** and his friends. He wanted to make sure all the children were not forgotten in *Aussie Land*. His pouch was used to hold the gifts! Yes, I still believe in Santa Claus!

Your Loving Johnny

CHAPTER 2

1943 – THE WAR ESCALATES

On the Southwest Pacific War Front in Australia
Dad has received a letter containing a song. He wants to get more letters from mom.

01/03/43

My Dearest Mary,

I received your letter of December 8, 1942 with the song in it. It sure made me happy. However, the sad part was you talked about your birthday but I could not be there to help you celebrate in style.

Since September 29, 1942 I have written thirty five letters to you. I did receive the letter you wrote in a circular pattern and only one after that. That is two letters in three months. Did you write more letters? Perhaps the mail is moving slower than I thought possible.

I received a letter from my brother, Walter, telling me that you are well. He also said you are now Head Inspector in your department. I am so proud of you.

All my Love, Johnny

On the Southwest Pacific War Front stationed in Australia

Dad is told how Manville and other towns in New Jersey are filled with women. Since most of the boys are in the Armed Services, women are successfully performing in men's jobs. Mom admits she has seen some boyfriends.

01/04/43

Dearest Mary,

Manville, New Jersey is now a *girls' town* is what you said. I know most of the boys are in the Armed Services. However, it sure was sweet of you to tell me about your boyfriends. The only sensible thing to do is to have fun and enjoy yourself. I am glad you are frank and tell me everything. I have always been the same way with you so we understand each other on that score.

That song you wrote is wonderful. It's so well written it's no wonder your friends at work liked it. I know this letter is boring you because I haven't said much about new things. Excuse me, I get so excited whenever I receive a letter from you. I hurry to reply and sometimes my words get mixed up for I have trouble expressing myself at times.

In closing, please extend all my best wishes to your family especially your mother and father. I love you more than ever. So long for now.

With all my love, Johnny

On the Southwest Pacific War Front sending Mom pictures from Australia Dad kids mom telling her there are three guys who love her. He is not quite acclimated to the Army but the Army is to him. He sends her pictures of himself and others.

Mary Jane Juzwin

01/04/43

Hello Dear,

Here is a little secret I'm going to tell you. There are three guys in our squadron who know you very well and think you are a *swell kid*. The first guy is *Me*. That's the fellow who is just crazy about you. The other fellow's name is *Myself*. That's the guy who is always talking about you. Finally, there's the other fellow who is always fighting with *me*. His name is *I* and he insists on daydreaming about you. You see I've got a lot of local competition so I better be careful! Don't you think?

I asked *Me* the other night why I love you. After *Myself* heard of this *Me* got into an argument with *I* so I'm back to where I started. If this keeps up all the time, you might consider it the fifth front of the *battle of love*. This dilemma has been going on over six months with no signs of weakness noticeable except around the heart. The *front* is expected to move closer to Manville eventually. This matter has excited all three fellows. I haven't become used to the Army, but Army life sure has become used to me. I'm happy but I remain always ready to go home at any time quickly. All I would need is five minutes notice. This would be sufficient time for me to get ready to exit from the Army.

Enclosed is a picture of that man again. Later on a few more pictures will follow. The immediate future might be scary so *beware of the WOLF!* Don't ever say I didn't warn you. Mary, I'm afraid sometimes I shouldn't let my mood get involved in my letters. However, then they wouldn't sound natural, would they? Talk louder, I can hardly hear your answer! That's better.

I've started a photo album so when I get back home I will show you a thing or two about Australia. This place has everything except my mom and pop and my sweet Mary. There are also a few thousand other things so I wouldn't make this my future address. There is no place like *home sweet home*. I hope when I get back, the Army will turn me *loose* immediately so

I can see you right away. Baby, look out when I do! I'll spend three hours saying *hello*, about five hours telling you how much I love you and about two hours saying *good bye*.

We both will be excited and real sleepy so I guess we'll need to rest. If only I could get my hands on you now, I'd hug and kiss you until I wake from this dream. Then I would feel like shooting the bugler for waking me! Please keep a little spot for me in the corner of your heart.

With love and all that other stuff, Your Johnny

On the Southwest Pacific War Front in Australia feeling *bush happy*

Mom and dad have exchanged many letters, some of which have been *censored*. Dad battles the *friendly* flies and mosquitoes. Kangaroos and canines continue to hang around the camp. He is happy for the Australian people are very pleasant and respect the Americans.

01/13/43

My Dearest Mary,

I bet while I'm writing this letter you are in bed just dreaming away. The time over here is ahead of you about sixteen hours. Today comes for me and tomorrow for you. I have all the holidays before you.

However, due to my circumstances, every day is the same to me. I don't look forward to any special day except the day when I'm able to start coming home. How is my little gal these days? I hope all is well with you and your family. The soldiers back home must be having the *pick* of the girls. They don't know how lucky they are to be in their native land. I know things are tough back home but there's nothing like being in your own country.

The kangaroos are still hanging around and the canines are as well. One of the dogs has a dog tag on him just like the kind we wear. He is sporting Sergeant's stripes down his side for one of the boys did a painting job on him.

None of us has received much mail lately so we are long overdue. The rain here sure has us fooled. We get set for a big downpour and next thing you know the sun comes out. Then we must open our tent again so we don't roast ourselves. The flies and mosquitoes are just as *friendly* as ever and follow us around for miles. Their friendliness is only surpassed by the Australian people.

I'm sitting on my chair while my blonde secretary is sitting on my *lap* chair taking down what I'm trying to say to you. Pardon me while I pause to straighten my tie. You know one must look neat especially when the opposite sex is within sight. The government has supplied us with anything we ask or desire. As a result, we've been supplied with some of those *Brooklyn gals*. They were sent by one of those flying contraptions so everybody is excited about Army life and stuff. Woo! Hoo! Well, we all can dream, can't we?

Due to the movement on the part of Uncle Sam, a lot of fellows have given up the hope of ever getting back to the United States. This mood I'm in right now is called *me bush happy* by the Australian natives. The sky is full of stars and a big round moon outside. It's just the right kind of night for getting out of gas in my *rattle trap* with some gal, preferably my sweet Mary. We could find a nice, quiet place where we could talk about the weather or who will be the next president. We could also discuss who will break down and give **Little Orphan Annie** a home. Wouldn't that be ducky?

Be sure to keep in touch with me as to the appearance of your house so I will be able to recognize it when I get back. You are the one person I will never forget. I'm pretty sure you wouldn't forget me either because I have a face that haunts anybody who ever dares to look at me. Well, this is enough of this bunch of the latest new from *down under*.

Keep a spot in your heart for me.

As always with lots of love and kisses, Johnny

On the Southwest Pacific War Front getting an official title in Australia Dad writes to mom using some *cool* Army stationary. He is proud to say he is now a P. F. C. which is a *Private First Class*.

01/18/43

Dearest Mary,

In your letter of November 4, 1942, you asked me to let you know if there was anything you could send me. Well honey, yes there is one thing. If you could wrap yourself snugly and jump into the first plane heading for Australia, that would be wonderful!

I was officially made a P. F. C. This is a Private First Class so I now have the distinct privilege of wearing one stripe. I sure was glad to achieve this. I've been in the Army for seven months. It's been an awfully long time to be away from you. Oh, how I wish I could have my own way with life right now. I'd be right in your front room this minute just making a general nuisance of myself. Oh baby, what I would do to you! Woo! Hoo!

Army life puts hair on your chest. It must be that cereal and *cat beer* I've been drinking. *Cat beer* is Army slang for G. I. milk. I know they are sure making a new man of me.

Every letter you write is read by me several times. This is the nearest thing I can do toward talking and being with you. Distance is supposed to make one forget people and things. In your case, however, I feel like thirty elephants and just can't forget you.

Mary, I remember everything that ever happened while I was with my favorite gal, you hon. It was some of the happiest days of my twenty three years of life. I can recall everything as if it was yesterday.

With kisses and an armful of Love, Your Johnny

On the Southwest Pacific War Front *hanging with* the guys in Australia

Dad and his friend Dominic know how to repair radios. He also had an opportunity to play some tennis. He had not played in a long time so it felt good. He explains what the term AWOL means and he loves to tell mom funny animal stories.

01/19/43

My Dearest Mary,

Remember the letter you wrote to me before I left the United States? I have read it so many times that I've just about worn out the paper by handling it so many times. It was a good thing I got some other letters from you just in the *nick of time.*

My friend, Dominic and I are still together. He went to school to learn Radio Repair. We have that experience in common. In our tent, we have two *Pollacks*, one *Swede* and one *Dutch* fellow. Of course we are all Americans but we are called the *Foreign Legion* section of this company.

The other day it rained a lot. After the rain stopped, there were so many bull frogs jumping around in our tent. One of them accidentally jumped into one fellow's bag.

It was quite a sight! One of the guys caught a large bull frog and put a cigarette in its mouth, Freddy frog smoked until he got sick. What a mess he made!

I had an opportunity to play tennis the other day. Although we only had one good ball to play with, it felt really good to swing a racket once again. I played for seven years in school and I still managed to remember how to score points. My mind was willing, however, it was very hot so I had to quit after two hours. My feet got tired as well. I guess *old age* is starting to catch up with me.

I don't believe I ever told you about what happened when I was at Jefferson Barracks in Missouri. There were eight fellows or rather soldiers in one tent. One fine day these guys decided to take a vacation from Army life. They call this going *AWOL* otherwise known as *away without official leave.* The whole bunch left that night. The next morning an inspection was made by an officer. He found three signs on their tent. One said *For sale cheap – inquire at tent across the street.* The other one said *Out for lunch* and the third *Will return later.* The boys got caught a few days later and that was the last time I saw them. As I was leaving camp the other day, I got a glimpse of them splitting rocks and I found out they've been assigned a lot of detail work.

When it rains, it doesn't soak into the ground because the soil is too hard. The water just rolls away and makes large ditches. One day after the rain quits, the ditches are *bone dry*.

Oh to be home again where things are under your own control. Here they tell you when to wake up, when to eat and what work you will be doing for the day. Enclosed is a picture of my *swanky apartment*. Although the picture didn't come out very well, it gives you a general idea of my swell living quarters. Well, I will say *so long mate* as they say in *down under* Australia.

As always, Johnnie

On the Southwest Pacific War Front learning how Aussie's speak in Australia Dad is hearing different words and phrases the Australian people speak along with their accent. He sees more night insects. He tells mom how the natives *fashion* their hair and an interesting story about nursing mothers.

01/21/43

Dearest Mary,

When I got here *somewhere in* Australia, I thought I could spell and talk in English. However, after being here a short time, I found out the Aussies think I cannot. They heard me talk and they said *Oh, a Foreigner.* I said "No I'm from New Jersey." They replied "Well, that accounts for your accent". If you want to hear something funny, just ask an Aussie to pronounce aluminum. You would never know what he was trying to say. Sargent is spelled Sergeant. When an Aussie says "Put one gallon of petrol spirits in my Louie", he means *fill my car up with one gallon of gas.* Center is spelled centre. Even though we're English, we speak differently.

I spent half the night wrestling with mosquitoes who managed to get under my netting. It was dark outside, so there I was using a flashlight to try and capture them. I finally got them. If you think you have seen lots of funny night insects, you ought to come over here. All one has to do is put a light on outside and watch them creep in. They're all sizes, shapes and colors. Some of them are *funny looking* but they are harmless.

I had a wonderful experience the other day. I got the chance to drive a truck on the wrong side of the street. It was the first time I was able to drive since I've been in the Army Air Corp. It sure brought back memories from the past. I can picture myself in my old *rattle trap* that we used to take for rides and then share those sweet kisses.

Enclosed are a few Australian coins. The shilling is worth about $.17 of American money. The sixpence is worth $8.50 in American money. The three pence is worth about $.05 of American money. I will make sure I bring home a lot of shillings. The music boxes at home take a quarter and a shilling is the same size.

I've talked to some boys who were in New Guinea. Oh, the tales they told me. It seems the natives like our old razor blades. They usually shave by pulling all their hair out. They roll their hair into two strings with coconut shells and give them a sharp yank. I don't know if I should tell you about this but I will. It's not unusual to see a native woman nursing a baby on one side and an animal *usually a piglet* on the other side.

All the boys felt bad for the native women because they walk around with no top on and don't seem to care. Well, some of the boys thought they would do something kind for these women so they gave them their white short sleeve undershirts to wear. The women proceeded to cut two holes in each shirt and flip their breasts out. A man has four wives and he lets the women do all the work. He strolls around trying to see how many marks he can make on his face. You are considered *a good looking man* if you have plenty of marks on your *kisser*.

Today is January 21, 1943 and your Christmas gift package for me hasn't arrived. There is still hope I might get it soon. I will send you a telegram the moment I get it. I hope everything is just fine in your *neck of the woods* and I hope to hear from you soon.

Love and kisses, Johnny

On the Southwest Pacific War Front talking about pictures in Australia Dad is missing mom terribly. He also misses dancing with her at the Polish American Home in Manville, New Jersey. He describes how he feels about her picture. His letter has been marked *censored*.

01/24/43

Dear Sweetheart,

How I miss you! Words cannot describe how I feel. I finally received your letter of October 11, 1942 in which you say you were sitting on the front lawn of your house writing to me. You mentioned the Polish American Home dances. Oh, how that *hit my spot* and I missed you even more. I'm glad you went to the dance and gave all those young squirts a break. You know dear, you look so young in this picture. Everybody who sees it says "Johnny, are you robbing the cradle?" They think you look like you're eighteen years old. When I tell them you are almost twenty four years old, they can't believe it. I also tell them they should see your mom as she looks very young as well.

When you last replied to my letter, you answered all my questions. Here's what I have to say. "I wish you were here so that *vicious man* as you call me could tell you a few things. *I want to know if sugar is so sweet, how come you haven't been rationed yet?* You told me that your new title at the plant is *Head Floor Lady*. You get to boss all the other babes around the place. It must be fun and very good experience for you.

I think it's very sweet of you to write to my folks to give them some news. Thanks a lot. They always said you were a *very nice* girl and liked your ways.

Love and kisses, Johnny

On the Southwest Pacific War Front in Australia
Dad finds it fun to share some funny stories about *Tojo*. He wishes mom could be next to him enjoying the scenery.

01/26/43

My Dearest Mary,

I haven't much to say that's new but here is a little *dope* on the war. It's about this fellow called *Tojo* from Tokyo, Japan. We're making plans for his funeral. We figured out it'll take forty men to carry the beer and pretzels we plan to serve at his repass. We will also need three *ice men* who need to be *fully equipped*. Ten bartenders will take care of us and everything will be *on the house*. It will be a grand and glorious party!

I have just about made up my mind where I might be able to get a job when I get back. It will probably be where my two brothers worked as well. I should be able to make a recent income for us to live on and we will be quite comfortable. Honey, you know what would be paradise for me right now? If I had you here by my side so we could sit on a blanket together on the grass. It'd be fine with me if we sat close together and looked at the moon and stars. I better stop talking for it's impossible!

My mom finally sent me twelve rolls of Kodak film. Boy was I happy! This should be enough film to take ninety six pictures! Don't be too surprised if you find some in my letters. Some of the poses might be rather silly, but it's fun to be that way sometimes. The development of the film is done for free by the government and it will take about three weeks.

I am not permitted to use the background for my pictures but I can still enjoy shooting some of me and my fellow soldiers. Please understand that it is a strict regulation concerning any of the photos taken over here.

I saw a very good show the other day. It was called **The Yank in the RAAF** *Royal Australian Air Force*. The stars were Tyrone Power and Betty Grable. I tried to imagine that you were here with me and I was whispering in your ear. However, my imagination wasn't a strong enough substitute for sweet you.

Love, Johnny

On the Southwest Pacific War Front going to a local dance in Australia The boys go to a *moonlight* dance, but for dad it is not the same without mom. He sends remarks to her about how Aussie *babes* talk.

01/28/43

My Dear Mary,

Well, I was able to get a short furlough so I did some sight seeing. Leaving the Army routine even for a short time period does make one feel so different. I can safely say I feel three percent more like a civilian. Honey, I went to a *moonlight* dance. It was held outdoors at a skating rink. It was *very cool* but I certainly missed *my little Mary*.

The remarks made by some of these Aussie babes sure are something. For example, one gal was wearing wings. When she was asked who the wings belonged to, she said "He's a tart gunner on a P-38". I have news for her, a P-38 is a single man fighter and is not big enough to carry a lot of ammunition. Some of the cooks in the kitchen tell these girls they are *chefs on a B-24 heavy bomber*. The bomber doesn't even have a toaster on it!

I hope you are alright yourself. As for me, well, I'm still living. One of the songs played on the nickel machine was **Me and my gal**. Of course I was thinking of you and really missing having my arms around you. I just know there are many letters from you waiting for me at my unit. I can't get back soon enough so I will have the pleasure of reading letters from my sweetheart.

My Section Chief went to Officers Training School. It was hard for him to decide whether to attend Officers Training School or just go home. He said the training was excellent. Afterwards he finally did go home. He sure was a *swell egg*.

Did you ever get the picture I sent you of the New Guinea native girl? They are considered natives like those in Africa. Here's a little info on the Aussies. They have *legal lotteries* called *caskets*. What a term they use for this activity. Recently I saw an odd sign that said *no naked lights within forty feet*. This was near a gasoline plant. I see and hear so many strange expressions. For instance, if you dance with a gal, when the dance is over she says "Please escort me across the snow". I think they say this because some Yanks give the girls a *snow job*. Their sense of humor is very different.

Love, Your Johnny

On the Southwest Pacific War Front receiving Christmas packages in Australia Dad is elated when he gets mom's thoughtful package for Christmas. She packed a lot of tasty and useful items for dad which made him feel joyous for a change.

01/30/43

Dearest Mary,

Today I received your Christmas package. It came to me in *A-1* shape. Everything was carefully packed its no wonder it travelled through the mail so well. The items you sent are tasty and your selections were thoughtful. I figured out the reason your Christmas package took so long to reach me. Santa Claus had to use kangaroos instead of reindeer.

Here are a few questions and answers for you. No, I didn't eat all the candy at one time and get sick. You also sent me a rubber eraser. Is that a hint that I should stop drawing pictures for you? Thanks for all that material used for writing letters. Looking at all the supplies you sent, you made sure I will not run short and stop writing to you. I'm using the portfolio, pens, the special ink and paper. It was very sweet of you to send me these useful items. Every time I eat a piece of that real *honest to goodness* chocolate candy, I'll remember who sent it to me. We all like the books and candy. By *we* this means the fellows in my tent. We are *all for one and one for all* just like a happy little family.

Now I'll try to let you in on the latest *gossip*. I heard this while I was standing on the corner of 13th Avenue and *Mary* Street in Manville, New Jersey. The rumor is that a fellow in the 11 Sig. Company in Australia is crazy about a certain gal from New Jersey.

Here is a story that a Sergeant told some rookies. *Frequent water drinking prevents becoming stiff in the joints. Yeah* replied one rookie, *but some joints don't serve water.* We have soldiers here from all parts of the country. Each one has their own story to tell. I was just interrupted by one of the boys who spotted a kangaroo. Luckily, I had my trusty camera nearby so I grabbed it and got some shots of him. Of course, I had to bribe him with one of your candies so I could get him to pose for me. I'll make sure I send you a picture of the handsome kangaroo as soon as I get some developed.

Hon, maybe some of your *ex-wolf* boyfriends are living here in my camp. Meeting you took the wolf out of me so now I'm as gentle as a lamb? You don't know what taming powers you possess dear. It's quite amazing! You got what it takes with plenty to spare.

Lots of love and kisses, Johnny

On the Southwest Pacific War Front waiting for mail delivery in Australia As usual the mail is *held up* at various locations so dad hasn't heard from mom for early a month. He expresses his love by identifying his feelings. He goes horseback riding and ends up very sore. He complains about the hot weather.

02/06/43

My Dear Mary,

Although I haven't heard from you for nearly a month, it doesn't stop me from writing to you, sweetheart. I'm warning you that this is going to be a rather sentimental letter for a change. I feel that way so much today. I just can't keep my feelings for you to myself. You have touched me in a way that no other girl has in the past. I will always tell you how my heart feels and when I write to you, my heart holds the pen.

I love you because of how sweet and thoughtful a person you are to me. Also, your sense of humor and personality make a hit with everybody. Your taste and neatness combined with your *full of life pep* is so rare a possession. You make me feel so wonderful anytime you are near me. Sensations happen inside of me that I never knew existed.

Your love for children is deeply shown by your excitement when you see a youngster. Your way of cuddling so close to me is so sweet anyone with a heart can feel your warmth. You are sweet without trying and just naturally being yourself. Every time I saw you, I liked you more and more. There seemed to be no end to it. After being away from you for seven months, it still leaves me loving you more than ever. I feel like you are a part of me. I know all the happiness I feel is a small amount of joy that is in store for us if we continue our courtship. I hope and pray we do just that.

I realize I'm taking a chance by telling you all this. You might answer me by saying "Johnny you are too serious for me". Well Hon, I am to you what you want to believe. Remember, no matter how you feel, I want you to know I'm a *sport* and can take anything with my chin up.

Now I will change the subject. The other day I went horseback riding. Boy was I sore! Never again I say until the next time. I had a rather hard time getting along with this horse. It seemed every time he went up, I'd be coming down so we sort of connected. I have to say it was a lot of fun.

When I said "Giddy up", he just stood there. I guess he couldn't understand my foreign accent. I decided to try out an Australian accent and to my surprise it worked.

The rest of the day I suffered through the heat. It gets so *damn* hot around here during the day. I have acquired an *awful vise* while I've been living here. The climate is so hot I eat about a quart of ice cream every day.

The portfolio, writing paper and pen works swell for me. I'm writing to you while I lay in my bed dressed only in my shorts. It's much cooler this way. I heard from my Mom and Pop and they are well and getting used to us being away from home.

Love always, Johnny

On the Home Front in Manville, New Jersey
Mom is told dad's Army fellows think she is a *babe*. Mom's little brother and sister write letters to him. The whole family asks about him and misses him.

02/07/43

Dear Johnny,

Today is Sunday and the sun is shining but it sure is cold. The wind is *howling* outside like a mad dog on a lonely night. I forgot to tell you that I wrote a beautiful letter to your old boss. That owner of the florist did a *wonderful* favor for you by making sure I received those flowers.

You said your Army fellows think I'm a *babe*, eh! They tease you saying you *robbed the cradle*, but when you show them a large photo, I wonder what they will think of me. My sisters and I had fun playing *blind man's bluff* and threw snowballs at each other.

Oh Johnny, my little sister and brother came running into the room and showed me some letters they wrote to you. I must carry out their wishes and send them to you. Honestly, I was surprised myself when they showed me what they wrote to you.

With Love, Mary

On the Southwest Pacific War Front with an explanation of the mail in Australia

Dad tries to give mom the details about how the mail is stored as well as what the reasons are for the delays in mail from the States to Australia.

Mary Jane Juzwin

02/11/43

My Dearest Mary,

Today I received your beautiful Christmas card and that ever so sweet letter as well.

Gee honey, you sure are something getting the letter registered and telling me you will send all my letters that way. It's very nice of you but it's not necessary for it doesn't speed up the mail any quicker. Honey, you are too sweet for words. The mail is slow because the *boot where mail is stored* fills up quickly on board the boat. Some mail is very slow because the boats cannot steer a straight course. This is due to the direction of the submarines. I try to write twice a week to you and I will always do this no matter where I am stationed.

Let me explain why I said I received only a few letters since September 1, 1942. I was still cruising along on a boat to my first destination so that had to be the reason I didn't receive your mail. I probably confused you a little but I hope by now you are all clear. I'm glad you received all my little gifts. I tried so hard to find something nice for you, but I had so little success. If by chance I come across something appropriate, I'll grab it.

Hon, I haven't gotten your pictures yet. You really couldn't send me anything better than that. As soon as I get your pictures, I'll be sure to write back to say thank you. I'm in a safe area so there is no need to fret over me. I did get all the gifts you sent me in the Christmas package in perfect condition and try to thank you for them as best I can.

I heard from my boss. He followed through ordering red roses for your birthday. It was a mix-up for the letters came at different times. Some day, I'll be able to write to you without any explanations. Don't worry, I have everything a soldier needs except you.

Love always, Johnny

On the Southwest Pacific War Front describing the wonderful events in Australia
Dad has cheered up immensely because of his promotion to P. F. C. and he is now able to *sport* some stripes on his uniform.

02/12/43

Dearest Mary,

Many wonderful things have happened to me recently. On January 1, 1943 I was elevated to a P. F. C. which is Private First Class. This cheered me up an awful lot.

Then I received all the great things you and my mom and pop sent me. Now I'm told I am a non-commissioned officer or in other words a Technician Fifth Class. Yes, I'm a Corporal with two stripes and I feel like the happiest soldier in the world. It feels rather strange to have the boys call me *Corporal*. Before my promotion, they called me all sorts of names. This Army will *kill me with kindness* instead of the Japs. When I first heard the news of my promotion, I thought I was dreaming. I actually had to sit down for ten minutes to recover my senses.

My mom and pop will be proud of me when they hear this news. My salary will now be $79.00 a month so when I get released I'll have plenty of money for anything. I'll be able to save $70.00 a month, still have spending money and help out my mom and pop too. I think I have said a lot in this letter so I'll save some things for the next one. Please give my heartfelt wishes to your family and tell them what a nice daughter they have.

With happiness and so much love, I remain, Your Johnnie

On the Southwest Pacific War Front in Australia
Dad knew mom would be overcome with emotion when she received his roses for her birthday. The *ultimate* mystery is not knowing what location

he will be sent to in the Army. Of course, if he had a choice, he would choose Manville, New Jersey.

02/14/43

Dearest Mary,

I had an idea you would have tears in your eyes when you got my roses for your birthday. You, *softy* you! Please don't try to thank me for them, rather save it for my return to home. It was very cute of you to send me those lips on your letter. They sure made me feel *homesick*. You say you read my letters more than once. You would be surprised how many times I read yours as well. Remember, I play for keeps. Honey, I always try to answer all your questions. All the things you mentioned about yourself are clearly stated in your very sentimental letter.

Now, I will get down to this *angel business*. I'd like to be your *angel* if it is possible for you to be mine. If you think I'm close enough to an *angel*, you certainly are enough of an *angel* to me with plenty to spare. How about we play as *angels* in dreamland?

One never knows where he will end up in the Army. If I had any choice, I would pick Manville, New Jersey. That would be ideal. I could continue my service to the country while spending more time with you. Until I see you in my dreams, I'll say *good night*.

All my love, Your Johnnie

On the Southwest Pacific War Front talking about the Aussie people Dad still doesn't understand Australian money but he manages to buy things. He is questioning why young girls are wearing such heavy clothing in this heat. He wants to stroll down the road letting mom wear his hat when he gets back to the States.

02/17/43

Dearest Mary,

I will start this letter by telling you a little about Australia and its ways. A girl here who drives a 1927 *Model T Ford* or *reasonable facsimile* is considered *glamour girl #1* in her town. I have a lot of fun with the store owners. They say an item costs "a shilling and a tupence". I ask, "How much is that?" Finally, they say it is *a shilling and two pennies*.

I was walking around town and it was time to dismiss students from school. I saw this group of girls about fourteen years of age coming down the street. You ought to see what clothes they were wearing. They wore thick stockings, heavy sweater dresses and a pair of gloves. I couldn't believe my eyes when I saw them as the temperature here is one hundred degrees and very humid. The outfits they wear are standard when attending Catholic school.

The news from home is always good to know even though it is old news. Mostly, one hears about all those convoys of ships getting ready to leave port for the war zone. It is almost a complete change from civilian life.

My only wish was to be granted a long enough furlough to be able to come home in a uniform. We could go for a stroll down the street and I would let you wear my hat. I remembered you once told me you would like to wear a soldier's hat. However, one cannot always catch a break.

Now I want to talk about my favorite subject. You are my favorite for anything, anytime and any hour of the day. Remember how we used to dance together? When we danced around those corners, I liked to steal a kiss from you. You seemed to cuddle so close to me and I loved it so much. I realize everything I'm missing.

Love and kisses, Your Johnny

On the Southwest Pacific War Front in Australia

Dad can now describe how he has been feeling in the Army Air Corp. He is glad he has been assigned to one camp so he can get more acclimated.

02/18/43

Dearest Mary,

The first three months in the Army, I was a *wandering* soldier boy travelling from one camp to another. I felt like a ball player without a team to call my own. Finally, I was assigned to one camp and everything improved approximately eighty five percent. I found myself actually starting to enjoy this strange new life. I guess I felt this would be a new adventure for me. Of course, everyone has a bad day once in a while. There're days you feel so lonely and blue. The next day the sun is shining and a little letter from home comes to the rescue. Hearing from you makes all the difference. I'm very happy my classification with you is just like the *Army 1A*. I do a lot of daydreaming and I imagine so many wonderful things happening to me.

I can't keep myself from thinking a lot of them will come true. My only wish is to be granted a long enough furlough to be able to come home in a uniform. We would stroll down the street and I would let you wear my hat. I remembered you once told me you would like to wear a soldier's hat.

You know hon, I would never do anything to offend you. However, I can picture the expression on your face when you touched my hair and found a lot of *grease* on it. I only put *grease* on so I can look neat.

I have seen such nice scenery such as Miami Beach, Florida and the trip on the very blue Pacific Ocean to get here. There are a few places I am not permitted to mention. Yet after seeing all these places, I'd be more excited to see my hometown or your home town again. I don't have much more to tell you in this letter. I must go to work very soon. Rest assured I will have more to say in my next letter.

Love and kisses, Your Johnnie

On the Southwest Pacific War Front in Australia
Dad is finally receiving some mail from mom. He's looking forward to having dinner with her and her family.

02/20/43

My Dearest Mary,

Here it is approximately 205 days since I last saw you. It seems like an awfully long time. Please remember to thank your mom for inviting me to dinner at your house. I'm sorry I'll be a little late, perhaps twelve months at the very least. Tell her I appreciate her kind invitation and I'll be looking forward to dinner and a visit with you and your family.

When I received your letter with the initials M. P. on it, I thought the military police were looking for me. I completely forgot your name is Mary Regiec *someday to be Mrs. Mary Poslusny*. Yesterday I was sewing my corporal stripes on my jacket. I kept thinking about the time you were hemming your yellow dress. I was watching you and I noticed how carefully you moved along to fix the dress just right. I always say *a girl is dressed just right when her dress is a little tight in all the right places.*

I don't know if you remember my car, but it certainly is a *rattle trap*. If I were at home, I'd probably be walking instead of driving. If this war keeps going, people will have to put a sign on their car saying "Don't take this car to the scrap pile, I'm still using it".

The boys here are always kidding each other when they see you get a letter. They say "I didn't know anyone in your family knew how to write". Usually I say "I'll have you know I came from the part of New Jersey where people know how to write".

In our camp, we're always hearing rumors. One time one of the boys said, "We've got moving orders"! All at once the boys got excited and thought we're either going to another camp or back to the states. The real news was we had to move a tent.

I'm closing this letter and saying "I miss you so much sweetheart."

Love, Johnny

On the Southwest Pacific War Front in Australia
The guys are enjoying radio programs from San Francisco, England, India and a few French programs. The war news from Tokyo is not accurate and they dish out a lot of propaganda. Dad is very satisfied with his status in the Army Air Corp. and says he would not trade it for any civilian job.

02/22/43

Dear Mary,

Here at camp we're able to hear radio programs from San Francisco, England, India and a few French programs. Of course we hear some from Tokyo as well. We don't bother to listen to the programs from Tokyo for it is made up information and is not accurate. No kidding, I heard our Captain say that the Japs claimed our boat was *sunk*. One of these days, they will learn the truth. About one hour ago, I heard a radio program from the States. It was all requested dance numbers. They played one of my favorite songs called **I don't want to set your house on fire, I just want to light the flame in your heart.** No other words have had the same impact. I wouldn't trade my place in the Army Air Corp. for any civilian job. One has no idea what an experience this Army life will have in store for you. After the war is over, no one can say I was a *draft dodger*. I'll have plenty of overseas service to my name.

You must have had a swell time at your birthday party. Wow, you have reached the old age of twenty four. It won't be very long before I turn twenty four years of age too. I shall say "hello and so long to everybody". Take care of yourself, honey.

With Oceans of Love and a Kiss on each Wave, Johnnie

On the Southwest Pacific War Front writing on *cool* Army stationary in Australia
Dad wants to take mom ice skating and swimming. He can hardly wait to get back to the States to do this. Now he is telling her about ice cream and beer.

02/24/43

Dearest Mary,

Here I am out in the sun and you are probably freezing yourself to death. I'd gladly give you some sun if you could spare me a big hunk of snow. I hope you haven't gotten into too many snowball fights. Have you ever been ice skating? If you don't already know how, I'd like to teach you how to do it. Of course, I will have to hold onto you or you'll be learning it *the hard way*. What I mean by *the hard way* is trying to skate alone and falling on the ice. Besides, I have never seen you in a winter outfit. I'm sure you would be as sweet and curvy as you have appeared in the summer.

I can hardly wait for the time when we can go swimming. I would dunk you for sure, then I would rescue you. We could go to the ocean and swim in the big waves. I'm thinking of all the activities we will enjoy together when I get home. All this *paper talk I've* been writing is only a substitute for when I will be able to see you in person. That will be a day I know I will never forget.

I'm hoping our unit comes home early. I only say this because we have been overseas for a long period of time. However, one never knows what will happen in the Army.

My brother, Walter sent me a few good pipes and some tobacco. I never cared much for smoking but I do appreciate him thinking about me.

I just came back from the American PX where I ate a quart of *homemade ice cream*. Boy, was it a treat! Australian ice cream tastes about as good as our $.18 a quart kind back home. If one needs something to cool off, I certainly won't be a *fussy eater*.

Our mess hall has a radio. When we eat supper, I turn on a program from the States. They play the *hit parade* and a lot of songs I heard at dances. Some of the titles are **Scatter Brain, I don't want to walk, I want to ride in the willy with you, My last good bye to you, Oh how I miss you tonight** and **When you wish upon a star**.

The other day I heard a good story. It seems when an airplane flies up in the very hot section of the *Far East*, the soldiers put beer in it. It is very cold when a plane flies at a higher altitude so in this way the beer gets nicely chilled. It sure makes a lot of soldiers happy. It takes a *Yank* to think of these things. Now *little rascal* of mine, you, of course, if you're a good girl, I'll try to bring back a kangaroo. You can practice being a mom before you become one. Would you like that?

With love, Johnny

On the Southwest Pacific War Front performing K. P. in Australia
The Army has many ways to get the men to do what they want. Dad is peeling potatoes in the K. P. kitchen. He learns about how the unit is motivated to perform K. P. and feel good about it.

02/25/43

Dearest Mary,

Here's the way the Army gets you to like K. P. They hand you a bag of potatoes and a peeler and tell you every time you peel a potato, you're helping to beat one more Jap. With our thoughts focused on this, we peel like *hell*. Before we realize it the pot is full of potatoes. Our unit is pretty lucky because we only get K. P. duty once every eighteen days. I don't mind it for the cooks treat us very nice and everything is done quickly.

Now it's time to tell you how the frogs, lizards, kangaroos, wild horses and those friendly mosquitoes are doing. They are all alive and well. I haven't seen Adolph, the kangaroo lately. I'm guessing he's out *wolfing around*. The mosquitoes are the only thing that reminds me of New Jersey.

You know, Mary, I feel so much at home when I visit you. Everyone who lives in your house, especially your mom and pop are so swell. Keep smiling and I'll keep writing.

Love, Your Johnnie

On the Southwest Pacific War Front discovering mysteries in Australia Dad is discovering mysteries all the time and wonders why some girls back home are *suddenly* interested in writing to him. He is pondering many other amusing mysteries.

02/25/43

Dearest Mary,

I've been in the Army for about seven months now. There is a mystery I discovered since I turned in my civilian status. It seems all of a sudden the girls back home have begun writing to me and say I'm a pretty nice guy. When I was at home, I didn't have enough money, didn't wear the right clothes and didn't own a 1942 sports car. I also didn't look enough like Clark Gable to rate getting a date with a girl.

Another mystery I have pondered is why does a fly pick my nose to execute a fast landing while I'm standing at attention and can't use my hand to bat him away? Why does it have to rain on my off duty time instead of my working hours? The biggest mystery is why did I wait twenty three years to meet the *girl of my dreams*?

Perhaps God had a *plan* for us as to when and where we would meet. At any rate, here I am half way across the world from you and yet I feel closer to you every day. I would never have met you if I chose not to go to that dance in Helmetta, New Jersey. It took a lot of effort to boost my confidence and ask you for a date.

All the boys over here want to express their deepest sorrow for all the *hardships* our soldiers back home have to *endure*. Oh yeah, it must be awful! The other day I read an article about Jimmy Jones. This *poor soldier* had only two furloughs in 1942. He is a *stay in the barracks hero*. He also had to be brave and face all those *horrible enemies* walking down Broadway in New York. In his home town, he would only have a weekend pass every week and a copy of the Army Air Corp. song. Gee, that's really tough! I could tell you more about the soldiers in the States complaining about their situation but I won't do it. This is because I would probably blow a fuse in my brain.

Please Mary, don't you think the boys overseas are trying to make people back home feel sorry for them. Sure, if these boys wanted to lie, they could say they kill one Jap every day before breakfast and two Japs on Sunday. I am only telling you this because only a *bragging soldier* would make up such a lie to make himself feel important. Most of us will never come close to fighting the Japs. I've heard more *complaining* and *squawking* while I was still in the states, than I could ever hear overseas even if I was here for the next five years!

I went on a motorcycle ride with an Aussie I met in town. We took a ten mile ride and it sure felt good to travel without walking or marching for a change. I haven't heard from my Mom lately. However, I always remember how she would fix my clothes for me so I could shower, eat and get dressed all in about forty minutes.

This way I could travel to see my sweetheart in record time! Gee honey we're both so lucky to have such sweet mothers and good fathers. Don't you think so as well?

At my first date and dance with you I said something special to you. I wonder if you remember what I said. "Someday I want to marry you". You are the first and only girl that I feel so strongly about above all the other girls I have met. I actually get tears in my eyes when I write to you. I have seen many girls and after only one date, I can tell what type of girl they will be. You are different. I was always a gentleman with you for I knew you were a lady.

Are there many dances going on in Manville? I hope you take the time to go to them and have some fun. After all, you must keep up your dancing skills for me. I think this is enough idle chatter for one letter. I love you and think of you constantly. I look forward to seeing you again and I know it'll be one of the happiest days of my life.

Love, Johnny

On the Southwest Pacific War Front with more stories in Australia
Dad has discovered more amusing stories about the Aussie people. He tells mom he is looking for something special to send to her brothers. He is thinking how Americans could make good money selling goods in Australia.

02/28/43

Dearest Mary,

Yes, it's that man again who is crazy about you and keeps writing to you from overseas. I hope my letters are reaching you. If you don't hear from me, rest assured I am still thinking of you. I would have to be a victim of *amnesia* for me to forget you. I'm going to try to find something special for your brothers. I know if I were a kid again, I would be *tickled to death* to receive something in the mail from a soldier in Australia.

One funny thing about the Aussie soldiers is that about eighty five percent of them are left handed. Most of them have false teeth and their style of clothing is old fashioned. They like to grow mustaches so I tried to grow one too. It came in pretty good, however, one day I was trying to get fancy and trim it so I accidentally shaved it off.

Our soldiers like eggs for breakfast at least two times a week, while the Aussies only prefer to have them once every other week. Most Australian people don't travel a lot or go on very long trips. A ten mile ride to them is like a hundred mile ride we take. There are so many ways a person could make some money here if one had some cash to get started. Someone could get a large batch of handkerchiefs, embroider them with the saying "Hello from Australia" and sell a lot of them in this town where I'm stationed.

The steaks they serve at the American Red Cross are a tender delight to eat. They treat us well so we appreciate them. I just hope we'll be together to share the future. I can picture you saying "Boy, that Johnny is a *jibber jabber* always talking and talking".

I heard almost everybody in the States is being called to serve their country. Even *draft dodgers* and guys who think they're something big will have to serve in the Armed Services. I imagine owners of Model T 1942 classic cars will also be included.

At the rate the Russians are pushing the Germans, I don't think that part of the war will last too long. After that all the planes being used there, they will come here and get into this fight over Tokyo. I predict Tokyo will probably *burn down to the ground*. Of course your little Johnny will have to patch them up and get them in working order.

Now sweetheart, I want you to take good care of yourself for me. Countries separate us, but you're a part of me as my right arm is to my body. Maybe you think I don't have the right to feel this way, but it's beyond my control. My only desire now is to get home so I can whisper sweet nothings in your ear.

Love and kisses, Your Johnny

Johnny Loved Mary

On the Southwest Pacific War Front taking pictures in Australia
Dad's been taking pictures of the boys he shares his work duties. He sends them home to save. He took pictures of his friend *Pokey* and tells mom about their friendship. There is another amusing story about guys in his tent and a description of a day in the Army.

03/04/43

Dearest Mary,

I'm writing this letter to you while I'm on C. Q. *captain's quarters*. I have to answer the phone and direct the calls to the right person. It's not usually busy in here so I have some extra time.

Today we had an inspection of our outfit and a G. I. camera man took a lot of pictures of our personnel. It's too bad I can't get a copy of the picture, however, I was able to take a few pictures of the boys with whom I share my work duties. In the middle of the night, I heard my tent mate call out a loud noise. I jumped out of bed so I could help him. I suddenly thought we might have a runaway kangaroo attacking us. It turned out he was being attacked by our ever present *friends*, the mosquitoes.

Here is a typical Army day for you. We are noisily awakened at 5:45 a.m. for role call. Once that is done, we have some exercise to keep in shape. The Sergeant will say "Now we will execute some arm exercises". Then he gives us a demonstration. However, we're half asleep and it's totally dark outside. This makes us blind to his movements so we just wave our arms around hoping we got it right. My friend *Pokey* and I are always having fun joking around with each other.

I would help him with anything and he would do the same for me. I'm hoping the pictures I took of him come back soon so I can show you what he looks like. He wears glasses and tries to flash a big smile with a lot of teeth.

The more news I hear about foreign countries, the better I like my *good ol' USA*. I am happy and proud to be an American citizen. I must say our way of life is so much better than some other countries. How are your movies back home? Here they are mostly old films of romance or some other old tales of soldiers. I always get a peculiar feeling when the show begins because they play the **British National Anthem** first and then our **American Anthem**. We all stand motionless until both of these are finished. I don't care much for British pictures for their sense of humor seems so silly. Watching a show alone is no *great thrill*. Remember how we would cuddle close together as we watched a movie? I miss all those special times we shared.

Here is a poem I read in an Army book written by U. S. Army Private Gerber:

> I've got a gal so far away and she is fair and pale,
> but how can I send my love to her when the censor reads my mail?
>
> This gal is, oh so very sweet. I love her *willy nilly*.
> but how can I tell her of my love, when in print it looks so silly?
>
> So read my letters gently, sir, even though they're not meant for you,
> but for a girl so far away, I scrawl this silly goo.
>
> And when you read each letter, sir, and laugh with profound delight,
> Remember sir, another censor reads every letter you write.

Pretty cute lines don't you think? I don't care what I say or write to you or who reads it. I want everybody to know how I think of you and what a sweet gal you are to me. Honey, I feel like the luckiest guy in the world because of you. Some people go through their lives and never find a girl to share their love or life at all. Mary, I must say good night to you. I'll say a little prayer for us and make a wish for us to be together.

Love, Johnny

On the Southwest Pacific War Front in Australia
Dad enjoys listening to the radio and it goes a long way to keeping up the boy's morale. He gets treated to a taste of being the *man in charge* of a platoon. He enjoys drilling the guys up and down the field.

03/06/43

Dear Mary,

The other day I bought a small portable radio from one of the boys for $20.00. Now I have about ten percent more of the comforts of home. It's small and can run on a battery or with electricity. It sure gives us many hours of enjoyment. When I get back home, we can use it at the beach or wherever we go to just listen to the music.

Last Friday, I had a most enjoyable experience. There are platoons in our company. Whenever the first and second leaders of our platoon are absent I being a *Corporal* have to be the *man in charge*. I took the whole platoon and drilled them up and down the field. They also have to drill to the right flank, then to the left and finally to the rear. After this, they have to go *left oblique* and then *right oblique*. Following this, they must form a column left and right and about twenty more different movements. It felt so good to be the *officer in charge* of giving out the orders. I'll never forget this experience for it only comes around once in a life time. Even though we are overseas, we still have to drill in order to keep in *tip top shape*.

I'm listening to my new radio so now I have about everything I need except a car, a few thousand letters from you and at least 999,000 kisses from my gal back home. In other words, I'm trying to make the best of my Army life. I'm always very happy to read any letters from you. They are so typical of your warm personality and they help me see an imaginary picture of how you are at any given time. Honey, you are to me as bees are to honey. Oh, so sweet! How I wish I could show you my appreciation in person. This would be the only manner in which I could do justice.

Love, Johnny

On the Home Front in Manville, New Jersey and the United States
Mom tells dad all food items including butter are *rationed*. Tires and shoes are also being *rationed* because the Army needs rubber to make tires for the fighter planes. Everything must go to the war effort. Mom strained her eyes working on war materials.

03/07/43

Dear Johnny,

I don't know where or how to start. I don't know how to come out with it. Oh heck, I better start to ask you this question. You'll be shocked at my *forwardness*, but I have tried time after time to lead you up to the matter but somehow never succeeded. Since it has been on my mind for several weeks now, I have decided to ask you. Ever since I met you I counted on you as a friend, but as weeks and months have passed us by that friendship started to grow into something so beautiful and *sincere* that it had become indescribable.

I never thought, my darling, that such a problem could enter my mind. You know you are the only person I would dare ask such a question. Johnny dear, do you think the Lone Ranger should sell his horse if he gets drafted? Ha! Ha! I didn't play a fast one on you for a long time so you can't blame me for trying can you? It was fun writing to you and *teasing* you a bit to keep up your morale, don't you think?

Oh yes Johnny, did you hear of all the stuff that's *rationed* now? All food including butter and shoes have been *rationed*. Only three pairs of shoes per person per year. Boy am I glad I don't go out much anymore as clothes are going to start to be rationed soon too. I understand you men are all *rationed* too and that is not fair.

I can't write much now. You see Hon, I told you I work in a different plant now and I'm the Head Inspector there. I work with such fine materials as a *micrometer, blue prints,* and all kinds of *gauges* and *bearings.* This might be *Greek* to you but they are all fine and very delicate with very fine letters and numbers on them which have to be read quickly and correctly. I've been doing all this for eleven months now.

I think my eyes became strained. I awoke one morning with large *puffy* eyes and they were bloodshot. I got frightened so instead of going to work I visited the doctor. He examined my eyes and first he thought I had *pink eye*. It turned out it was *eye strain*. He gave me Aregrole salve in a small tube and it's black. I laid down and Mom put that salve in my eyes. Oh Johnny, it looked so awful that Mom cried and got so scared. I tried to calm her down but after awhile I fell asleep. She ran to the doctor to check up on me as she thought I was going blind! The doctor laughed and said "just continue to put the salve in her eyes and everything will be alright". I went to work each day and then put the salve on at night.

Isn't that a good excuse for not writing to you? Now I'm better and back to reading your letters and writing to you. It was nice that you called me an *angel* so you think I could call you an *angel*? You have sent me everything any soldier can possibly send his sweetheart and I feel truly like your sweetheart.

Mom and dad dressed up as they wanted me to go with them to pay for our home tax and fire insurance. All those things are in my head and I have to attend to all our main bills. I guess I am the oldest and *most capable* so they always turn to me. They keep my head and hands full but I don't mind as I know they love me and I'll never have another mom or dad to take care of again. We girls have to laugh at them at times.

Oh Johnny I feel so bad as my foreman and I are good friends at work and he got a call to go home because his 27 year old son has *heart trouble*. I know that he is in danger so all I can say is "while there is life there is hope". We'll see what tomorrow brings. The foreman trusted me with all the keys to our department, all our toolboxes and compartments. Well you should see me with all those keys, I look like I own a jail.

Love, Your *little* Mary

On the Southwest Pacific War Front talking about conditions in Australia Time is passing by for dad and he feels like Army life is *perpetual motion*. He dreams about mom, repeats his dream to her and he's happy.

03/07/43

Dear Mary,

Here I am somewhere in Australia where a letter means more to a *Yank* than any amount of money. Here where the young boys go to school barefooted, and the men hang around in their shorts. The theaters sometimes have no roofs and where every day is the same except when mail is received. Army life is like *perpetual motion*. It just keeps going on and hours, days and weeks pass before your eyes.

The other night I had a rather funny dream. I had gotten to your house a little early to take you out. Since you're the oldest child in the house, it was always your job to do housework before you're allowed to go out at night. I was so anxious to go out with you that I grabbed a broom and started sweeping. Soon your Mom came along and caught me. Then you came down from upstairs and caught me as well. We all burst out laughing with each other. We did go out and I remember getting rewarded with a sweet good night kiss from you.

Mary, I'm listening to the radio and wishing I could be dancing the Helena Polka with my favorite gal. I used to steal a kiss or two while we made our turns. I guess I was a *bad boy* after all. Perhaps this Army life has *tamed* me down. Honey, the sky is so beautiful here. I wish we could share this scenery together. All I do is sit, look at the sky and get all wrapped up in my thoughts. Everybody always sees me writing to you and they remark

"How do you do it all the time"? I tell them if they met you, they would know the answer. I won't tell them because it is a *military secret*.

Today I saw a large group picture the camera man made of us. I look pretty good for a change. I think we might each get a copy but I don't think we'll be able to send them home until after the war is over. It would be great to be able to show our kids some day. *Here is a picture of your old man in his Army outfit with all his Army buddies.* Well dear, I must close this letter. I'll be thinking or dreaming about you.

Love, Your Johnny

On the Southwest Pacific War Front listening to war news in Australia Dad hears good news about the air and sea battle near New Guinea. His letter is clearly stamped *censored*. Now that he owns a portable radio, he feels more informed. He thinks the Aussies are catching on to American music. He is also observing more boys gambling.

03/08/43

My Dearest Mary,

I'm writing and listening to the news about the big air and sea battle near New Guinea.

I guess the Japs got a taste of the *Yanks* that time. Don't feel you have to write and tell me war news now that I have my portable radio. I'm mailing an ashtray I made and two pocket knives for your brothers. The reason I have sent you so many things at this time is because there may come a time when I won't be permitted to send anything home.

I went to a Red Cross dance and had a pretty fair time. It would have been one hundred percent better if you were there. The Aussies are catching on to our music. However, the dance floor is too small and crowded to do any *real good* dancing. I just keep *ducking elbows*. I'm also watching my *dogs or feet* for they do get stepped on quite a bit.

When Americans first arrived here, we played with dice. The Aussies wondered what a large crowd of boys were doing. It's nothing for a fellow to either win or lose $200.00 in one night. As I said before, I'm saving my money for our future. I'll be glad to get back home so I'll have a reason to get all dressed up for you. I have now designed a system hereby I'm guaranteed to have a dream. I sleep three nights without a pillow. On the fourth night, I lay my head on my pillow and sure enough I enjoy a dream. Maybe I should get a patent on this system. What do you think?

Since I've entered the Army, you have learned more about me than when I was a civilian. I just hope and pray you are not disappointed with me. I assure you I'm trying to be *just plain Johnny*, a young fellow in love with a girl who is also being herself. Well honey, I must end this letter for now. May God bless you and your family.

With all the love in the world, Your Johnny

On the Southwest Pacific War Front still stationed in Australia
He is trying to keep up with the latest *war news*. He tells mom about *propaganda* the Japanese are reporting. He also says *war news* is getting better every day. Dad is full of details about the dances he's attended. He tells mom how much he loves and misses her.

03/10/43

Dearest Mary,

Last night after my work was done, I turned on the short wave radio. I tried to get some music on but the atmospheric conditions here in the tropics make radio reception difficult at times. I finally tuned in to a very loud station playing popular songs from the United States. The announcer was very well spoken and made remarks such as *Don't worry boys, everything is fine at home.* He said this in between each number. He also played a song in honor of that *good old American beer* Budweiser and Hoffman.

When the program was over, the announcer said "This is the zero hour". Then he paused and said "This has been radio Tokyo" so it was a Japanese station after all. Then he started to give some news about all the *success* the Japs were having. He did not say anything about the *air and sea battle*. We get a big kick out of all the *baloney* they dish out on their programs.

Last Friday, the Red Cross dance was different. The *master of ceremonies* announced *this will be the Cinderella dance.* All the girls each took off one shoe and put it in a basket. The basket was dumped into the center of the dance floor. It was a scramble of boys rushing out to claim a shoe. I got one and the girl wasn't too bad looking. All the girls got their shoes back so everybody got a kick out of it. The boys wanted to take off one shoe and do the same, but that would not work for most of our shoes look the same.

The camp shows are having double features so we get to see plenty of movies without ever leaving the camp. I read in the newspaper that the soldiers back home are only allowed one cup of coffee a day. Here we can have all we want to drink. The men who go to a technical school earn a P. F. C. rating when they graduate. My friend, *Pokey*, went to school for five months while I earned my P. F. C. rating on my merit alone.

Every day the war news gets better and it looks like it's our turn to be on the offensive.

I hope it will all be over soon before you have a chance to forget about me. Mary, you make it so easy to love you. You're always so sweet to me. After our third date, I knew in my mind and heart you were the answer to all my hopes and desires. I saw a movie where soldiers came home and how happy their girls were after that long period of time. I tried to picture you and I seeing each other after a long time and I think it will be exciting beyond all imagination.

Love, Your Johnny

On the Southwest Pacific War Front in Australia
All the boys are grinning because finally a large bundle of mail was received. He checked with the fellow at the Post Office and was told he would be receiving a *registered* package after lunch.

03/12/43

Dearest Mary,

Today there are many boys walking around with big grins on their faces. No, it's not another rumor about going home. It's because after a month of very little mail, a rather large bundle finally reached us *down under*. I did receive two letters but none from you so you can imagine how I felt. Finally, I came across a guy who works in the Post Office so I asked if all the mail had been distributed. He said "Yes, but I have a registered package for you". The Post Office was closed for lunch. I couldn't wait for it to open.

Yes honey, I FINALLY RECEIVED YOUR LARGE PICTURE! Yahoo! The feeling I experienced is one I will never forget. Sweetheart, you are more beautiful than ever. You looked so sweet and real. There isn't a more excited soldier in camp when mail arrives. I can't concentrate on my work if I'm wondering about my letters from you.

I showed your picture to all the boys and you ought to have seen the looks on their faces. You made a hit with them all. Our company is small so we always feel more like a family. We share each other's enthusiasm for family pictures of any kind.

You're quite an actress posing in so many different ways. I sure got a warm heart looking at them all. Mary, I like the way you styled your hair in the big picture. You should always wear it that way. In one of your pictures, you're waving. How I wish I was there to receive and return that wave. It looks so natural and the *tomboy* outfit is very becoming on you. You should have worn that outfit during the summer we were dating. You must've spent the day changing from one outfit to another. I hope my large picture comes out half as good. Honey, I must tell you I'm a *softy* for while I'm writing you this letter, I have tears of joy in my eyes.

Love, Your Johnny

On the Southwest Pacific War Front hearing from his parents still in Australia Dad's parents tell him about babies being born, how everybody seems to be engaged or married so he might end up a *bachelor*. Dad is thrilled he has mom's picture.

03/15/43

Dearest Mary,

I received a letter from my mom and pop. It is the first in over two months. It seems everything is fine there. Mom keeps telling me about all the babies being born in my town. She says everybody I knew back home is engaged or married. I guess I'm the *only* single guy and I may end up being a bachelor! Maybe I'll be able to do something about this situation when I get back. At least no one will accuse me of not trying to rescue myself from a life as a *hermit*.

I keep looking over at your picture after I write every few lines. Honey, this picture will be treated as one of my most cherished possessions and will stay with me no matter where I go. I often wonder how you stayed single for this long of a time. I guess some guys' eyesight must be bad in Manville. How they ignored noticing you is beyond my comprehension. All the things you do to me and say to me are so wonderful. I have to pinch myself to make sure I'm not just having a *beautiful dream*.

I'm just letting you know I'm writing this letter under the mosquito netting because they would *eat me alive* if I was anywhere out in the open. At the present time, I feel I have everything in the world, but I'm missing one important thing.

Of course, it's you Mary and I do miss you so much. I know I've said an awful lot in this letter, however, I don't believe in holding back my feelings.

Your Soldier Man from far away, Johnny

On the Southwest Pacific War Front in Australia.
Dad wishes mom a happy *St. Patrick's Day*. He wonders if he will have to teach his mom how to wake him up in *Army style*.

03/20/43

Dear Mary,

I hope by now you received my letter telling you I got your beautiful picture *safe and sound*. You also told me how you feel about cats since one bit you in the past. I was bitten by a rooster once when he thought I was cutting in on his territory. That is how I got the little indentation of a dimple on my left cheek.

In your last letter, you mentioned that because so many people are getting married, you feel like an *old maid*. Now that is not a good feeling. I know a fellow who would like to do something about this matter. I never thought I would meet a girl who is so sweet and considerate. Honey, you told me that the picture you sent was *second best*. I can't see how that could be possible for it was such a beautiful picture.

It sounds like it's really cold in your part of the world. Now if I were only at home, we could help each other keep warm and keep our minds off the cold! I am wishing you a happy *St. Patrick's Day* to you. Today is the day the great Irish warrior made it impossible to pass up such an occasion. I always put on my green socks to celebrate.

I will have to teach my Mom how to wake me up when I get back. I'm thinking I'll have to buy her a whistle or teach her how to play a bugle.

That way when I get back home, she can wake me up in the morning in *Army style*.

Do they still hold dances at the Polish American Home? Why does my radio have to play all those love songs that remind me of the joyous times we shared at dances? You know my dear one, one of these days I'm going to write a letter without becoming sentimental, but I doubt it very much. Let me know when you receive the ring I made for you out of a *coin*. I hope you'll like it. I'll close for now by saying "Thanks a million for everything, especially your love". May God protect you for me until I return.

Until I can hold you in my arms again I remain, Your Johnny

On the Southwest Pacific War Front in Australia
Dad was very pleased to get mom's Valentine's card. It's getting cold at night and he has to use two blankets, a coat and his work clothes to keep warm. He describes the many different birds he has encountered.

03/16/43

Dear Mary,

I received your Valentine's card and it was a pleasure. Thank you for the red lips on the paper. The line about a guy in a uniform who weakens your resistance made me laugh. Look what you've done to me. Don't ever stop! I eat the attention you give me. The nights here are getting awfully cold. I have to use two blankets and a coat with my work clothes on to sleep at night. Brrr! We have a parrot in our camp who talks. He says "Censor the Japs" and many other things that are only appropriate to be heard by us. His vocabulary includes a few naughty words and we have a lot of fun listening to him. There are many different colored wild parrots that fly around like crows.

In the next few days I expect to be *shot!* It will only be a *shot* in my arm to help make me immune to diseases. Of course the doctor looks down your throat *clear down to the soles of your shoes* to judge how thick they are on your feet. I'm glad the Army is smart enough to take such precautions. Take good care of yourself for me.

Love and kisses, Your Johnnie

On the Southwest Pacific War Front writing from Australia on *cool* Army stationary
Dad sends mom a picture of himself but he says it was not his best picture because the sun was strong and he was caught *off guard*. He continues to enjoy listening to his radio.

03/22/43

Dearest Mary,

Yesterday, I sent you a large picture of myself plus a few things all in the same package. I'm sure you'll be surprised how this large picture turned out. It's not the best picture of me because the sun was rather strong that day and I was caught *off guard*. Your picture is right in front of me. It inspires me every time I glance at it. You are a darling.

I'm listening to a program from Atlantic City, New Jersey and it is being played for all the Army Air Corp. boys *down under*. We like all the programs from the States. All the modern songs are played and we sure enjoy hearing them. There is a custom in Australia called *dance tea*. Instead of playing *dinner music* for tea which is considered a meal over here, an Aussie says "Have you had your tea?" He means did you eat your supper yet?

Honey, I just came back from a camp show. It was a pretty good *gangster* picture. Yes, the hero got his girl and they lived *happily ever after*. There is no future in being sad all the time. It gives one wrinkles and a bald head. This is not for me! I'm in a very happy mood tonight. There is no particular reason except the fact that I'm *head over heels in love*. I heard from home that a lot of my friends have been shipped overseas since I left. A few of them are in Africa so I'm really lucky to be in a *civilized country.*

My dear Mother always walks two and one half miles round trip to the Post Office just to get a letter from one of her sons. I try to write as often as I can so I don't disappoint her or worry her. I wish I had a sister who would keep my mother company around the house while her boys are gone. I'm old enough to realize this matter now. I am thinking of you all the time.

With love, Your *little* Johnnie

On the Southwest Pacific War Front writing to people in Australia
Dad has written to one of his high school teachers and hopes she is surprised to hear from him. Dad says there are a lot of characters with many stories to tell in the Army.

03/27/43

Dear Mary,

I hope you're happy and everything is okay with your family. I have written so many letters to all my friends but only a few have answered. I am hoping you are getting my mail quickly enough. I even wrote to one of my high school teachers. Yes, she was *an old maid.* I told her a few things about Australia. I started her letter by saying "It has been over five years since you had the misfortune to have me as one of your pupils".

I bet she was surprised to hear from me.

The boys wonder how things are going to be back home. It will be strange to live as a civilian and be in charge of our own lives again. The Army is full of characters. Each fellow is different and has a personal story to share. This experience has shown me a lot of things to make me understand life and has opened my eyes to things I took for granted.

I'm going to ask for a furlough soon. I'm pretty sure I'll be able to get it. I should get about ten days so I can visit a large city here in Australia. Having a little freedom will be very nice. We're supposed to e thirty days a year. In *wartime* it's up to the commanding officer. He has to approve our time as much as he can spare us.

Here is a good story: A corporal went to see his commanding officer and said "Sir, I wish to request a weekend pass as my wife is expecting." The commanding officer *being a family man* understood so he said "Sure, I understand, I hope things work out okay". The next weekend the corporal repeated the same scenario and got his weekend pass. Finally, when he asked his commanding officer for a pass a third time, the Captain said "What in the world is your wife expecting?" "Me" cried the corporal. He was made a P. F. D., which is a private for the duration.

Tonight I expect to go to a Red Cross dance to keep my dancing skills sharp. Hearing music and having a decent meal will feel good. I wish I could meet you again on the dance floor. You can count on me to think of you and miss you terribly.

Yours forever and a day, Johnny

On the Southwest Pacific War Front in Australia
Dad is not allowed to tell mom any war news now because all information is being *censored*. The Japs are interested in any news they become privy to at this time.

03/28/43

Dear Mary,

I finally received a letter from my big brother, Stanley. Everything is fine with him and his family. He told me that my younger brother, Walter sent some gifts from Cuba. Now I know I was right when I said he was there. Have you received the Australian coins I sent to you?

I think of you and you can bet how often during my day. Presently, you must be sure that I mean every word I ever said to you. You must have realized I wasn't trying to win your confidence so I could take advantage of you when we were alone. Don't ever think I'm losing interest in you if you think my letters sound a little dry. It's awfully hard at times to say something new if there is very little going on. On the information side, there is not much I can tell you for the Japs might be glad to hear anything I would say or write.

I had three full days off this week because I worked nights and I finished all my work in two hours. This allowed me to get extra rest, however, I'm not always this lucky. I know there might be times when you have forgotten about me. This is to be expected as it's been a long time since you last saw me. Of course, the sad thing is we were just getting to know each other. I hope you only forget me for a few minutes. I'll never forget you, dear. I expect to take a few different pictures so be prepared to get anything. I've taken pictures of kangaroos but I haven't figured out how to make more copies of them.

Honey, you have probably noticed that I numbered all the pages of this letter. Those pages that have no words or numbers on them represent that empty feeling. I hope I'm still *1-A* in your Army. You sure are with me and always be my *one and only*. My feelings for you are guided by my heart and are one hundred percent true. I must close now and here is my hope you are okay and say "hello" to the rest of your family for me. I love you so much.

All my love, Johnny

On the Home Front in Manville, New Jersey
Mom is reminiscing how and when she and dad met and what was said on their first date.

03/29/43

Dear Johnny,

Do you still remember how we met? Honestly, I thought you forgot, but now that I know you still remember, I guess you always will. I will never forget.

Guess what Johnny, remember I was at that dance in Helmetta, New Jersey with the fellow named Stanley Rogozinski? I met him at my sister Betty's wedding day four years ago. He was a nice fellow but I only cared for him as a friend. Although he begged me to marry him a few times, he said, "I'll always regret the day I took you to that dance in Helmetta, New Jersey".

I can't get over it, Johnny. After all we only knew each other two months before you left for the Army and look at the way we feel toward each other.

Love, Mary

On the Southwest Pacific War Front receiving letters in Australia
Dad gets eighteen letters from home, but none from mom. He worries something could happen to mom and he would not know about it for months. He sends her a letter clearly marked *censored* by the person listed on the envelope.

03/31/43

Dearest Mary,

Today I received eighteen letters from all my friends back home. I looked through them quickly but I didn't find a letter from you. Woe is me! You can bet my excitement died down and came to a *screeching halt*. Yes Honey, one letter from you would have made me happier than all those letters together. I always make it a practice to reread your letters carefully and make sure I answer all your questions. I'm lying in bed thinking about the things I want to say to you. I took a casual look into the beautiful sky tonight which is very full of stars. Gee, it's tough to be alone on a night like this one. I guess I will feel this way until I am able to come back to my *little Mary*.

Time is supposed to move fast but it isn't moving fast enough for me. Sometimes I think this war will last fifty years. Other times it looks like it could be over in a few months. If you could see my face now, you wouldn't have to take a second look to see how lonely I feel tonight. Hearing from you with letters dated two months behind makes me worry that many things could happen to you during that period of time. For this reason alone, I'm not worth much as a worker until mail arrives and I'm able to read your letters. If you ever told me we were through, I'd feel like the saddest person in the world. It scares me to think I could lose you over this period of time. However, one has never lived if one has never experienced love. I have never been as happy as I was when I met you.

Now I would like to change the subject for a few minutes and show you how an Aussie talks. This is a *made-up* story: I came home from work and had tea *supper*. Then I dressed up and decided to go to a dance so I could jazz *dance* a little. I jumped into my *lorie* or *car* and started her up. Bang, the front tyre or *tire* had a puncture so I got out and fixed the *bloody* thing. I finally got it fixed so I started her up again to make sure the *bloody* thing was in working order. I pulled into a depot or *gas station* and had the man put one gallon of petrol spirits or *gasoline* into my *lorie* or *car*.

I arrived at the dance and was ready to do some jazzing or *dancing*. I spotted a babe and asked her for a jazz *dance*. She said, I'm sorry I'm engaged. I politely congratulated her and she gave me an odd look. What she meant was someone else had asked her to dance. I saw a babe dressed up in all the latest colors. Her face was all made up. Soon it got very late and all the babes had to go home. I left and went to a store next door to listen to the *wireless* radio. It proved to be a big disappointment because it only had two volumes and *tubes*. I called it a day and went back to my hide away or *house* with the mosquitoes, kangaroos, spiders and lizards.

I thought I better be a good boy for a policeman might put me in a box or *cell*. Oh yes, if I ever said *bloody* to an Australian babe, she would be highly insulted. It would sound to her as if I called her the worse thing one could possibly say in the *English language*. This is how the *Aussie* language sounds to an American Yank like me!

Love and kisses, Johnnie

On the Southwest Pacific War Front talking in Australia
Dad continues his story telling mom about trains in Australia. He is still missing his *favorite dance partner*. He's lucky to have a guy in his tent who gets the New York Daily News as it does contain some local news from the U. S. He also sends letters that are clearly marked *censored*. It is *April Fools Day* and the guys are full of ideas for fun.

04/05/43

Dear Sweetheart,

The other day I saw a train coming down the track at about fifteen miles per hour. It was the *latest* style. It seemed to be about the same thing Abraham Lincoln used for transportation. The train slowed down before a small hill because a truck was on the track. The train had to back up two miles so it could make enough speed to climb the little hill.

It's only 1:00 a.m. and I just got back from a Red Cross dance. I don't feel sleepy so I'm writing to you by the light of the moon. Oh Baby! Actually, I did have to use a flashlight as well. Yes honey, you are still my favorite person. No other person could ever take your place. I really mean that!

I consider myself pretty lucky to have a fellow in my tent who gets the New York Daily News. Now I can read all about my section of the woods. Thank goodness. *April Fools Day* passed with only a few boys getting caught causing tomfoolery. Yes, some of the stories heard were the following: We're leaving soon for the States. We're getting paid with different money than the last time. Also 100,000 Japs and 31 Yanks got killed when a Jap tried to take away a pack of Lucky Strike cigarettes from a Yank. Well, that will give you an idea of the variety of tales we heard. It's nothing for us to hear Christmas carols on an Aussie radio station. You see we couldn't seem to tune in to any carols when it was that holiday time. Now it's almost Easter and we can hear plenty of Christmas carols. Who knew? I tried to find some Easter cards to send home but there wasn't a single one in any of the stores.

The other day, I talked to a teacher. He told me he gets eight pounds a month teaching fifth grade English and arithmetic. That's only about $25.00 a month. An Aussie soldier gets $25.00 a month, while we get $50.00 a month in the States and $60.00 a month when we're overseas. This just goes to show you the people over here don't get much *dough*.

Honey, I would appreciate it if you could wrap a few *good old United States pennies* in one of your letters. I haven't seen American money for a long time. I do have a twenty dollar bill but no coins. Thanks a million. Did you ever get that Australian money I sent to you? It should have reached you by now. Let me know what you think of them.

Here's a poem for you:

> I held her tightly in my arms, obsessed by all her lovely charms.
> She's the kind of glamour girl, who puts your head in a whirl.
> I speak words so tender, she whispers "I surrender"!
> As my heart beats heavily I wake and hear it – Reveille.

I am extending each and every one of you a *Happy Easter*. I hope by next *Easter* I will be living in your part of the world.

With an armful of kisses and a heart full of love, Johnny

On the Southwest Pacific War Front reading the headlines in Australia

Dad is sending mom a recent picture of himself. He's still amused by some headlines in the Aussie newspapers. He finds out butter is now being *rationed* in the United States.

04/07/43

Dear Mary,

Today, I'm sending you a large picture of myself. It's a recent one so I hope you like it. Please let me know if I have changed for the better or worse. Yes dear, I'm making sure you don't forget me. That's why I haunt you with all these letters and pictures. I understand butter is now being *rationed* in the States. Too bad!

I continue to be amused by some of the Aussie newspaper headlines. I read one that stated "Three thousand Germans killed on the Russian Front". "In New Guinea, three Japs were killed in a patrol clash". These rumors go from one extreme to another. The war news has been very positive lately which means a lot to us. We hope this war is moving to the end. You know Mary, I wish I was able to get a twenty five day furlough and come home to see you. Unfortunately, this is not an option.

I do hope you're not working too hard. You need some time for fun and a little pleasure. All work and no play make life awfully boring. Have you looked at one of my pictures lately? You have! How can you stand it? Did it frighten you into forty one nightmares?

Hon, I'm in a very happy frame of mind. I'm a little *screwy* but it's fun to be that way once in a while. Don't you agree? I have a feeling I will get a letter from that *little Mary* of mine very soon. It's been almost twenty five days now since I received your last letter. Now, I better quit all this chatter before I drive you *buggy* or something.

With an armful of love, Johnny

On the Southwest Pacific War Front discouraged about the mail in Australia Dad has seen three large mail deliveries, however, he has not received a letter from mom. He is starting to worry something could be wrong.

04/09/43

Dearest Mary,

There has been three large mail deliveries lately but I didn't get a letter from you yet. Is there anything wrong? Maybe you're sick and can't write to me because you don't want me to know or worry about you. Maybe you don't want to write for you're discouraged about this *long distance* romance. Maybe I might have said something to make you mad at me. I hope there's really no problem and it's just the mail coming slow. There is no way of knowing being I am so far away from you. I want you to be frank and honest with me. Come straight to the point if there is anything wrong. Maybe in a few days, perhaps I'll get some letters from you and that will change everything. Then I will laugh at myself for ever thinking there was anything wrong between *your Johnny* and my *little Mary*.

Gosh, my heart sunk when I got eight letters and found none from *my favorite gal*. My Mom and Pop tell me they receive my letters in about eighteen days or less. It is my hope that you must be getting my mail. This situation would not alarm me so much if I were not already *so in love* with you. I'll never be my *happy go lucky* self until I hear from you. I have never felt quite like this for any girl. Don't feel sorry for me as I don't want anyone to pity me.

Sweetheart, one letter from you is enough for me anytime. I had hoped I would hear from you before I left on my seven day furlough. Had I known about the present situation, I wouldn't have requested it at this time. It's going to be hard to enjoy myself as things seem to be in the dark and my hopes and dreams are at stake. However, I haven't given up hope. My Mary has not let me down yet. Consequently, before I leave on April 22, 1943, I'm sure I'll get something from you to put me straight.

If you have met someone else, let me know. It would be better to find out now, rather than later. If this is the case, it's your life and I have no business trying to change it for you. Honey, you are your own judge and know best what you need, desire and deserve.

Everybody should have the freedom to make their own choices.

Six fellows in our small company have received rather unhappy news from home. They were always so sure of themselves and their girlfriends at home. They would say "I don't have a worry in the world" or "It can't happen to me". Then the bad news came by mail. They have lost their girlfriends to some other guys. Now they have nothing to look forward to when they get back home. Everything is shattered now. There is no one else in my life and no one could ever take your place in my heart. I say this with all sincerity. I had indications that my chances were not hopeless and I might have a chance to have you for my own. I still believe I have. When I left you that night, I knew I had met my *girl of the future*. Even though nothing was discussed about our futures, we both agreed we wouldn't consider any commitment until the war is over.

I feel as though I'm talking to you directly when I write. I have your picture in front of me and you look so sweet. It looks so real, I feel like I can reach out and touch you. Ever since I met you, everything seems to go in my favor just like a dream. I still have all the faith in the world about you and believe you're my one and only choice. You have a very kind heart that you've shown me so many times during our short friendship.

Now I will change the subject. At the last Red Cross dance, I started to talk to a fellow who I presumed to be an Aussie. He spoke with a strange accent very much like a fellow from Brooklyn, New York. He was also dressed in an Aussie outfit. I finally asked him what city he had lived in originally. To my surprise, he said he was from New York. He's helping Aussies learn American customs and language. One never knows who one will meet the next time.

It looks like everything at home is being *rationed*. How many coupons does a fellow need for a date with a babe? I guess dating will never be *rationed*, not yet anyway. My ex-boss wrote and told me that I was written up in the overseas section of his local newspaper.

Every time I go somewhere, I come across many interesting people. Most of them are coming from New Guinea for a furlough. One of these guys tried to give me a five cent cigar. No, he didn't just become a *Papa*. He was able to get a box of American cigars from home. Now he'll smoke at least seven cigars a day until he finishes the whole box of fifty. Of course, he chews half and smokes the other half. I'm in a swell tent and I enjoy being together with such nice, *down to earth* guys like these. No matter what happens while I'm overseas, I will still look forward to my homecoming to you and my folks. You are a part of me and mean so much to me always.

Love, Your Johnny

On the Southwest Pacific War Front with *censored* letters from Australia The Army seems to be concerned enough with our boys so they show them a movie about *how to be a good boy when bad girls are around and what happens if you choose to be bad*. Dad is also enjoying playing volleyball with his friends.

04/13/43

Dearest Mary,

I just came back from the camp outdoor movie and guess what picture I saw? Give up? It was **When Johnny comes marching home**. It was a very good picture and it had an added attraction. This was *how to be a good boy when bad girls are around and what happens if you choose to be bad*. It was enough to make even the dumbest person open his eyes. This picture is about war and it makes one hope this war ends soon. I think every school should show it to the appropriate class so they could be more aware of these consequences. They would realize they could ruin their lives forever just by being ignorant of the facts. These outdoor movies do plenty to keep our boys from getting a *Section 8* classification. This is when a person is missing *a few screws* and ready for the *nut factory*.

The volleyball team of our company played against the headquarter officers. It was a *bloody battle* but we finally achieved a victory. One of the officers always *sticks up* for us. There he was all alone on the other side of the net just *razzing* all the captains and the majors. Boy, were they burning mad!

Now I must have you mumbling under your breath saying "That Johnny must be overcome by the heat". It won't be long before you will able to go swimming. We never had a chance to go during the short time we were together. We have a lot of *making up* to do when I come marching home again. I'm behind on a lot of things especially that *medicine* you so capably dish out! Ooh! How I will I stand all this waiting? According to the Army Air Corp. doctors, I'll pull through with *flying colors*. I'm sure you have plenty of it left.

I took a few more pictures with some of the fellows just to add some more glamour to the poses. I hope my Mom will be sending me more film. Think about it honey, I'll be able to show our kids how the *old man* looked in his *hay day*. It's a nice thought, don't you think? I try to number my letters but I may have mixed up some of the numbers. You see how my mind is working. I jump from one subject to the next. I always come back to writing about you. I wonder why? I'll give you one guess, I'm truly in love. Do you think I could be cured? I'll give you 99 years of my time if you care to try and cure me. In closing, I'll say "May God look after you all like he has with me."

With all my love, Your Johnny

On the Southwest Pacific War Front discussing the orchestra in Australia
The mail continues to drag between the States and Australia. Dad was surprised to see more players in the orchestra at the dance he visited recently.

04/17/43

Dearest Mary,

Hello Hon, it's that fellow again. You know he is the guy who is sort of *crazy* about you. Your last letter I received was dated February 7, 1943. That's over two months ago and seems like a lifetime to me. When I don't hear from you during that length of time, it makes things worse. Take it from me, you'll never know how much. My furlough was approved for fourteen days. However after two days, something came up and I was forced to cancel it. I can't tell you the reason it happened but suffice to say it was a very good one. I may be able to take one again in a month or two.

I went to a dance last Wednesday and was surprised to see more players in the orchestra. They played some real *modern songs* we used to dance to when I was a civilian. It looks like I won't forget how to dance after all. When I heard a lot of foreign music, I thought I had forgotten some steps but don't worry this is not the case. It should be easy and enjoyable but I was really missing my *favorite dance partner*. Never fear, my sweet, just give me three Polish hops and I'd be back in shape again. I miss that *hold me ever so close* way of dancing we enjoyed so much.

I haven't seen rain for a while. It's the *dry season* in Australia. In order to get wet, I have to swim in warm water. Nothing could replace the Atlantic Ocean, it's always cool.

Honey, do you realize you are twenty four years old plus 155 days? Why it seems like yesterday that your birthday was upon you. How time flies! I realize now that maybe I was a bit hasty in asking you if anything was wrong between us. I think I figured out the reason the mail has been so slow lately. I've been reading all the letters you have sent me again. You have no idea what they do to me. They were all so sweet!

I hope I'll still be able to *weaken* your resistance when I finally get home. Resistance is a *thing of the past* as far as I'm concerned. Whenever I get to see you, nothing will hold me back. Resistance is a thing of the past. One letter from you makes me feel you don't care for me then the next letter sounds the opposite. Maybe that's the way life should be all mixed up. I always have faith in you and I know you will do the right thing when the time comes. Honey, you see how frank I am to you. Honestly, I can't hold back my feelings any more.

I am splitting up a group of pictures and wrapping them up in four or five pieces of cardboard. You should expect to receive them in the near future. Hopefully you have received a recent picture of me. I think it's done more justice to me than all those small pictures I sent you previously. This should give you an idea how your man looks right now. I hope you notice a difference in me. One is not considered a man until one serves in the Army or a while. Let me know if you think my change has been for the best.

With Love and Kisses, Corporal Johnny

On the Southwest Pacific War Front at *Easter* time in Australia
Dad wonders if mom bought herself a new hat or suit for Easter. Dad continues to listen to music to pass the time. Sometimes he thinks this war will never end.

04/18/43

Dear Mary,

I am hoping you all have a nice *Easter* this year. I plan to attend *Easter* services over here as well. What is *Easter* without a new hat or a new suit? Did you buy one of these this year? If you did, I would greatly appreciate seeing you in a picture.

It seems the gas and tire ban is steadily improving so things should be a little more lively for a change. One day, I'll catch up on the news but it's quite a long way behind me.

I'm on C. Q. *command headquarters* duty and listening to a performance by Bing Crosby with a lot of other good singers. One feels like sitting and day dreaming. I'll bet dances are going on at home. Nothing should stop you from going for I know you enjoy them. I'm afraid you'll have to teach me the *hop* all over again. My feet and yours will have to get acquainted all over again. Don't you think so? Sometimes I'm afraid this war will never end. One day we hear good news then bad news in papers and on the radio. All we can do is hope and pray for a positive outcome.

Apparently, Japan planned to seize European colonies in Asia to create a large defensive perimeter stretching into the Central Pacific. The Japanese would be free to exploit the resources of Southeast Asia while exhausting the over-stretched Allies by fighting a defensive war. In order to prevent American intervention while securing the perimeter, it was also planned to neutralize the United States Pacific Fleet and the American military presence in the Philippines from the outset. On December 7, 1941, Japan attacked British and American holdings with near simultaneous offensives against Southeast Asia and the Central Pacific. These included an attack on the American fleet at Pearl Harbor, the Philippines, landings in Thailand and Malaysia as well as the Battle of Hong Kong.

These attacks led the United States, Britain, China, Australia and several other countries to formally declare war on Japan. The Soviet Union was heavily involved in large scale hostilities with European Axis countries and maintained its neutrality agreement with Japan. Germany, followed by the other Axis countries Italy and Japan declared war on the United States in solidarity with Japan citing as justification, the American attacks on German war vessels that had been ordered by President Roosevelt.

I keep telling you about myself. You should be sick and tired of it all. Yes, I'll continue to write but I think I talk about other subjects. I'll never stop loving you forever and a day. You'll always be close to my heart.

Love, Your Johnny

On the Southwest Pacific War Front located in Australia
Dad is thinking so much about mom. He tells her this letter will be about their relationship. Mom's letters really cheer him up. The boys have a lot of dogs in camp who have proven to be good pets.

04/20/43

Dear Mary,

In my last letter, I said I would try to write about something different. I tried but I found it impossible. This letter will be about us, Johnny and Mary. Please understand it's so hard for me to do otherwise. Now is the time to face everything. I didn't consider myself to be weak, however, since I met you I found my weakness, and it's you. I just can't picture myself alone without you. You are a big part of my happiness and nothing could take your place. Saying *I love you* in a thousand ways in letters, wouldn't do as much as ten minutes alone with you. If you care for me, you'll know these are not just *choice words*. Whenever I have a *dark day*, I just pull out my letter box and read a bunch of your letters. They affect me and actually help to *cure* the blues. I feel like you are so close to me and yet so far away. All I see is a *beautiful dream*. I can hardly wait for the day to come when I can see you and hold you in my arms.

I started this letter early this morning and now I'm on the midnight shift so I have a few hours to myself. I started at midnight and continue on this shift until 8:00 a.m. By the way, the radio music is swell from 4:00 a.m. to 6:00 a.m. I get tomorrow off. The next day I'm not on duty until 4:00 p.m. so at least I'll be able to get plenty of sleep.

I think I've answered your questions and I try to make sure of that all the time. There are three dogs keeping me company in camp. It makes it seem more like home to have them around. We always have lots of food so they don't want to leave us. There was talk of getting rid of them, but it never happened because they've proven to us they are nice pets.

This is all for the time being so I will close with a hope you all share a nice *Easter*.

Love, Your Johnny

On the Southwest Pacific War Front finally receiving some mail in Australia Dad finally receives mail postmarked March 31, 1943 and tells mom it is the first letter he has gotten since February 8, 1943. He had been worried about her but is now content with her *Easter* present of a letter. He is concerned about her eye strain.

04/25/43

Dear Mary,

I finally received your letter postmarked March 31, 1943. This is the first letter I got since February 8. That's about forty days. At first, I dreaded the idea of opening it for fear of what I would find inside. Soon afterward when I saw how thick the letter was, I realized everything was okay.

What a swell *Easter* present, I couldn't have asked for more. Gee, when you are happy, everything seems right. I hadn't heard from you for so long, I was thinking of so many awful things that might have happened. Now I've learned how foolish my anxiety was and all is clear.

You should have heard my sigh of relief. Please do understand and forgive me for ever thinking anything was wrong. I couldn't picture you abruptly stopping to write to me without first giving me a reason. I'm awfully sorry to hear about the trouble you are having with your eyes. I can see how your eyes must have gotten strained. I do hope and pray you get well soon. It's terrible having anything like that happening to you. I wish you didn't have to work so hard, but I know you accept it. Don't give me that innocent look, you are as guilty as you can be.

The *rationing* of food, tires, cigarettes and other essentials back home must be tough. However, that's better than taking orders from a Jap or a German. When this war is over, we will be much more thankful for all the good things we have in our lives. Hopefully, we'll appreciate and protect this wonderful world for us and for the future.

I sent my mom one of your snapshots. She was very pleased. You have no idea how glad I was that you remembered my birthday. I was waiting to see if you were going to say something about it. As far as sending me any presents, a letter from you is the best kind. Close your eyes, picture me but not for too long. It's not good to torture yourself.

I keep thinking about your sore eyes and I'm hoping the salve helps them a lot. I know it takes more than a pretty face to do the work you're doing. You're not only pretty, but you have brains as well. This is a rare combination for anyone to have. All this time you were suffering with your eyes, and yet you kept reading and writing to me. How could you be so cruel to yourself? However, you know I appreciate it.

Yes, I realize 99 years isn't long enough to prove that I love you, so I'll have to give you 100 years. I'm hoping to get back home before all the other admirers take over. You say you have a lot of keys. You had better lock all the doors and windows if you expect to keep me away. Even a *sawed off* shotgun your Pop might use couldn't do the trick. On the silly side of things, I know you just love the thought of going to the dentist again. My teeth are okay now so I won't be giving the dentist any more pleasure to explore my mouth. I still have plenty of molars left to chew that *tender* meat they serve over here.

If you find you're not able to write me a long letter, just drop me a short one. Anything

I hear from you is great. Thanks a million, Darling.

Love, Johnny

On the Southwest Pacific War Front still in Australia
Dad is hopeful mom's eyes have healed from the strain of *war work* she is involved with at her job. He continues to regale her with more Australian stories.

05/01/43

Dearest Mary,

I hope your beautiful eyes are all healed and back to normal. I'm sure you have taken care of yourself so your troubles should be over.

I'll attempt to tell you some things about Australia and its people. Most people have never gone on a long car ride or gone swimming. It seems they've never rode on an elevator, subway or train. Most have never owned a refrigerator or a small freezer. A two story building is the tallest they have ever seen. One never sees more than one car for each family and it is usually at least eight years or older. Most of their houses are one story. Milk doesn't come in bottles but is sold from door to door like oil at home for the stove. The roads are rather poor, the buses are very old and small and they don't even leave from the main street.

In Australia children go to school up to the seventh grade. One is allowed to quit school at age fourteen or go barefooted if you wish. If one wants more education it is college.

When you're in a restaurant you're not given napkins, toothpicks or water. I have travelled a lot and I haven't seen road signs and service stations are almost nonexistent.

Most of the people are very religious and around *Easter* all the stores were closed for four days. If you see anyone outside after midnight it is considered very late. You and I would be deemed *bad people* for staying out so late. There are no afternoon shows because the theaters have no roofs to protect one from the hot sun.

All laundry seems to be hand washed as there are no laundry mats or dry cleaning stores.

The standard of living is very low. A *poor* person in the States would be considered average here. Yes Hon, they say "This is the land of opportunity" but I wouldn't stay here if they paid me. It's the *good old United States* for me. You couldn't find a better place to live. This ends my commercial on Australia.

Hon, I live through every letter I receive from you. Now take that grin off your face, you know darn well you have me under your *spell*. However, I don't know if you feel the same way about me. There is no hurry for my heart waits patiently for your answer. When you feel your answer is ready, it will be fine with me. Now for the latest *sugar report,* I still love you madly but my disposition would be much improved if I had your presence. It's never too soon for me to hear from you.

With plenty of hugs and kisses, Your Johnny

On the Southwest Pacific War Front discussing soldiers' *behavior* in Australia Dad expresses concern that his camp is getting very strict. However, he is elated to hear the war in Africa turning into a victory for our troops. He is enjoying some very good shows. They are shown outdoors and projected on a white sheet attached to two trees. His letter is written on *cool* Army stationary.

05/06/43

Dearest Mary,

This camp is getting very strict. If one doesn't behave, the guard house is where one is sent thereby giving up freedom. A soldier has to be a gentleman at least among his men. As for the Japs, I am told *anything goes* and usually ends up with crazy results.

I saw some very good shows recently. Did the **Star Spangled Rhythm** play in the States yet? I saw it about six weeks ago. One of the fellows in our company runs the shows so sometimes we have an afternoon show as well as an evening one. Admission is free if you're accompanied by a blonde or a kangaroo. Unfortunately, both are very scarce. I saw another very good movie. It was Abbott and Costello in **Buck Privates**. It was very funny and seemed to be another soldier picture with a lot of things only a soldier would understand.

The war in Africa has turned into a victory for us. I get the impression that the war there will reach its peak soon and be over before this one. This is good news to all of us boys.

Keep smiling and I will try to picture your face in my mind. Who knows, maybe this will make me smile as well.

Love, Johnny

On the Southwest Pacific War Front playing tennis in Australia
Dad has an opportunity to play tennis with a very good female player. He is proud to say that he won the match and earned another stripe on his uniform.

05/08/43

Dear Mary,

The other day I played tennis with a very good female player. She works at the telephone exchange and has played with a lot of the boys in our company. The word is she has beaten most of them. I decided to try my winning chances with her. She was very good but I had a little too much speed on the ball so I beat her rather easily. It felt really good to play with such a good player for a change. Tennis balls are scarce over here so we have to use old ones to play. If a player hasn't learned good strokes, both backhand and forehand, it becomes hard to put a decent tap on the ball.

All of this activity results in a *fly away ball* that sails all over the place with no control at all. There is a way of hitting the ball hard and yet it will drop fast and stay in the court. I'll have to teach you the game some day.

Honey, it was very sweet of you to tell me that I'd be *your Johnnie* and it doesn't matter to you how many stripes I have on my uniform. The same day you wrote to me wishing me luck, I got my second stripe. I'm also very happy to hear you enjoy wearing my locket around your neck. It's very nice of you to think enough of me to do this.

Today, I also got a letter from my old friend in my little town of Belford. He told me he saw my mom and took the time to talk to her and cheer her up. Then he proceeded to tell me all the other local news. Boy, did I hear plenty. It seems a few wives are having a *fling* with other men and they're not concerned about cheating their husbands. You know honey, my love for you is true and I would never try to hurt you in any way.

All my love, Johnny

On the Southwest Pacific War Front in Australia
It is very hot in Australia and dad and his gang are doing whatever they can to stay cool. All information continues to be *censored*, even pictures of the Australian scenery. He is happy to report the *war news* is positive.

05/12/43

Dear Mary,

The latest news from the States is that this is *fall in love* week sponsored by some company who has just the thing to help people. What in the world will they think of next? Enclosed is a picture of the gang enjoying a bottle of beer one hot day when the temperature was 100 degrees in the shade. I'm sorry I couldn't be in it for someone had to hold the camera.

John (front center) having a beer with his Aussie buddies

I heard a good one the other day. A fellow took some pictures in the States and had to board a boat before he could have them developed. He then took them to the developer and the pictures were refused because the censor said the pictures *gave away too much Australian scenery*. It turns out these pictures were taken in Texas! Yes, it could only happen in the Army.

The *war news* has been very good during the last few weeks. It looks like it's our turn to do something and I hope we respond soon so we can proceed to clear up this war. Our men are hoping we catch a break and they give us our own shower. In the past, we had to walk about four blocks just to take a shower.

I can't wait to be with you again so I am able to show you how much I love you. It would fulfill all my desires. Thinking of you and hoping I will be back soon to continue our romance right where we left it in the past.

All my love, Your Johnny

On the Southwest Pacific War Front serving in Australia
Dad does not need anything to remind him of memories with mom. He warns her he will still have some *jungle* in him so she better watch out.

05/14/43

Dearest Mary,

Here I am half way around the world away from home and I don't need anything to remind me of you. I think about you during my day and night. I couldn't forget you if I tried. Yes, I did test myself to see is there was any doubt in my mind. I'm happy to report that my love for you will surely pass all future tests. I realize that my chances of you feeling the same way are slim but there is hope yet.

As for attention honey, what little I gave you was only a sample of great things to come in the future. You understand I will still have some *jungle* in me so I might be more vicious than ever. Look out, I'm warning you be prepared for a lot of great love.

Love and kisses, Your Johnnie

On the Southwest Pacific War Front providing the *inside dope* in Australia Dad is describing his activities that he is currently involved in for the Army. He is still *in love* with mom. He talks about another orchestra he has heard.

05/17/43

Dear Mary,

You are probably wondering what I'm doing in this man's Army. Well, here is the *inside dope*. I get up in the morning, still sleeping with my eyes open and then I eat breakfast. Afterward, I go back to bed to catch a few winks until I hear a very annoying whistle. This whistle is to let us know when it's time to go to work. I stand outside my tent, now only half asleep with my eyes open and answer *here* when my name is called. Then I either have a day off or I go off to work. Lucky for me, this is my day off so I go back to my tent and take out all my medals. I've got over two hundred medals so I like to shine them once in a while. I earned them but I can't tell you the reason for them for it is a *military secret*.

Then General MacArthur and I have our *daily chat* about a few points on the war. It's getting late, almost 3:00 p.m. I'm starting to feel like I haven't accomplished a thing all day so I get out my Hollywood gun. I shoot a few hundred Japs just to be mean. When I hear the 5:00 p.m. whistle, I quit for the day. I only work forty hours a week. What I do after that is a *military secret*. Wouldn't you like to know?

Honey, you are always on my mind and I can't possibly ever forget you. I hope you feel at least ½ as much toward me. Keep your heart open for me.

Love and kisses, Johnny

On the Southwest Pacific War Front operating in Australia
Dad and the gang are enjoying all the benefits that the Red Cross provides for them. He tells Mom about the music he has heard and what show he has been able to see.

05/21/43

Dear Mary,

I just got back from a Red Cross benefit program. The new orchestra is a fourteen piece affair and makes me feel *right at home* especially when they play the songs in the American style. On the program is *Miss America* of this *one horse* town. She grants us her presence. She's not a bad looking babe, but her outfit was awful. It was as loud as a fire engine and it hid all her *curves* and that sort of stuff. She was a blonde and with that outfit she looked like a *big Mama*! No doubt you know her type. The announcer was quite an actor and put on a good show. He can mimic many of the screen and radio stars. His impersonation of President Roosevelt was the best I've ever heard.

Very soon the American Red Cross will open its new lunchroom and dance floor. I'm told it will be done up in a completely new fashion. With the new dance floor and all this good music, all I need now is you honey. Then I would be so content. I guess I'll never achieve that feeling until I'm back with you. Things look so different when we are together. What strange power love holds! There will never be a good substitute for love.

Love, Johnny

On the Southwest Pacific War Front serving in Australia
Dad is working in C. Q. which is *Commander's quarters*. He has to answer the phone, direct calls and fill out any reports assigned to him. He tells mom about the *v-letters* or *victory letters*. He wants mom to send him some as they are received very quickly. He has not heard from her in over thirty five days. Gas *rationing* has begun so all the fuel will be used for the planes and jeeps that the military operates.

05/26/43

Dearest Mary,

Today is my turn in C. Q. *Commander's quarters* so I'm sitting here listening to my radio. I heard that gas *rationing* will be strictly enforced again so no one can enjoy any more *pleasure riding*. Honey, *v-letters or victory letters* are being received every day with good speed so don't forget to use a few once in a while.

However, they do not seem to return to the States too quickly. This is the reason I don't write more of them. I'm sorry I couldn't write more often this week. It's been awfully hard to write especially when I haven't heard from you in over thirty five days. *V-letters* have been coming through in ten to eighteen days. This is much faster than other mail and remains steady.

I should be getting used to not hearing from you often, but I'm having trouble accepting this situation. I guess you know that by now. I must be quite a pest!

Of course, you are my special gal and you try to write to me as often as you can. I do appreciate it. In the past year, I've written over five hundred letters and only received about one hundred twenty in return. Now I can see who my *true friends* are by how they write.

The States must be rough on you girls. Maybe it's because there is a shortage of boys to take care of you. This is a questionable subject for there are eight million boys in the Army at home and only one million overseas. I hope this experience doesn't change me too much. You too no doubt will be changed and I'm pretty sure I'll be more or less a stranger to you. Won't it be fun to get acquainted all over again? All I can hope for is that you are willing to give me a chance. It's all up to you, dear.

The ban on packages being sent overseas has been lifted. All we need now is to place a request so when the letter and envelope is shown, permission is granted by the Post Office. Anyone can send any things to us that we might need. I don't need a thing, all

I want is you honey, so don't worry about me. Well, honey I have just about *run short* of writing for the time being. Shut your eyes, try to picture me in your mind and I just threw you a bunch of kisses. I hope you got them.

Until my next letter, I remain Your Johnny

On the Home Front in Manville, New Jersey
Mom is reminiscing about her and dad's first meeting date.

05/31/43

Dear Johnny,

I listened to the radio and heard the Joe Lys orchestra. Boy, what good *old* memories entered my mind. I could see a girl in a teal green suit, sitting down watching the dancing feet that were gliding past her. All of a sudden she saw in front of her a slender dark haired young gentleman bend down politely and ask "May I have this dance"? Then she heard herself say "I believe so". From then on, oh you know the rest of that *sweet*, short but never *forgotten* story. That was the beginning of the love story about the couple that met in Helmetta, New Jersey on May 18, 1942.

Love, Mary

On the Home Front in Manville, New Jersey
Mom informs dad how hard it is for a single girl not to get serious with any guy until the war is over. She is, however, willing to wait for him and continue to write to him.

06/01/43

Dear Johnny,

This darn war! I'm glad I don't have a *steady* boyfriend much less a husband at this time. I just want to be *unattached* and that's how I want to stay until the war is over. I'll have my chance then to prove to some man that marriage was worth the wait.

I just thought that I would say "Come home Johnny". You are included in this *grab bag* of men. I don't mean it that way Johnny. What I mean is that after this war when and if I get married I want my husband to be with me every moment. That's what married life is for, to share and share alike and to have and to hold. I'm trying very hard not to choose a husband before this war is over. Please try to understand how hard it is for a girl. All I can do is sit, listen to the news on the radio, read the newspaper, think, hope, dream and pray that the war will end soon. Then we can be sure of our promises that we are always writing in our letters. Please Johnny, don't get tired of writing to me. I'd be sick if you stopped writing to me. I get twelve to fourteen letters from you in two weeks. I don't know which one is the nicest. You did propose to me in that letter and that does mean the world to me. Jeannie and I go to the Polish American Home dances and I pretend I'm dancing with you. That way I don't miss you so much.

I would like you to try to listen to a song by Ella Fitzgerald. It is called **There will never be another you**. This song reminds me of how I feel about you and I'm hoping you will feel the same way once you listen to the words.

Love, Mary

On the Southwest Pacific War Front in Australia
Once again, he is writing using some *cool* Army stationary. Dad is treated to a furlough and he is wishing mom was with him. He talks about the WACS who serve in the Army but mom is his *favorite gal*.

06/03/43

Dearest Mary,

This letter might be the only one you receive until June 17, 1943 for that is when I'll return from my furlough. While I'm on vacation, I'll be thinking how much nicer it could be if I were spending it with you. That would definitely be *heaven*! I went to town and saw another movie about the Germans. At this rate, the movies are winning this war. I hope it will not continue for a long time period.

On my way back to camp, I almost ran over a kangaroo. There are many of them around here especially since winter has arrived. They are the funniest things when they try to run. They jump up and down on one foot.

My friends wrote and told me that those WACS *Women's Air Corp.* are not bad on the eyes. Women weren't inducted into the Army when I lived at home so I never had the pleasure of meeting them. You'll always be my *favorite gal*.

Your loving soldier, Johnnie

On the Southwest Pacific War Front in Australia

While perusing the Red Cross building, dad is surprised to find another soldier from Leonardo, New Jersey where his high school is located. He's still enjoying various music programs on the radio. He sends mom an Air Corp. ring hoping it will serve as a constant reminder of his love. He tells her about his *night watchdog, Musso* and how he acts.

06/06/43

Dear Mary,

In our Red Cross building there is a large map painted on the wall. It has little flags placed in the location of each boy's hometown. I went to check if anyone I knew was shown and much to my surprise, there was a fellow from Leonardo, New Jersey. That's where my high school is located and is about one and one half miles from home. He is a Second Lieutenant flyer and he graduated with my big brother, Stanley. This was only one year before my graduation. You can imagine how I felt when I saw his name and town, it sure was swell! I spoke to him and he told me a lot about my town, the fellows he knew and just things in general. He's married to a girl from my graduating class. It was one of those furlough affairs, only ten days and then good bye.

Now I'm listening to a command performance. It's a program from the States to troops in the South Pacific. These programs are in a much higher class than those of the Aussies because we have the money to back them. Today it's Van Monroe and his orchestra, Kenny Baker and Judy Garland plus a bunch of other good singers.

Enclosed is my Air Corp. ring. It can serve as a little reminder of me so you don't forget my face. I hope you like it. I think you can figure out how to place it on a chain and wear it around your neck.

I don't know if the fellows in my tent are kidding me, but they say I was chanting *Mary* in my sleep last night. I really don't remember anything about last night except our dog barking at 3:00 a.m. He's my *night watchdog*. I have taught him *Yankee ways and manners* so he understands us completely. Confidentially, he's almost smart enough to seek shelter from the rain. His name is *Musso* and he is named after *Mussolini* himself. There is a great resemblance between dog and man.

Tojo, Hitler and Mussolini

No doubt, I've changed in appearance, but that old feeling I have toward you lives on and shows no sign of ever weakening. You will always be my dream come true.

With All the Love I have for a girl who is *tops* I remain, Your Johnny

On the Home Front in Manville, New Jersey
Mom's worried about battles and tells dad not to be too brave but take care of himself.

06/07/43

Dear Johnny,

We had a few men return from the battle and visited our plant. We all stopped working one day last week and heard their speeches. Oh Johnny, I couldn't sleep for almost a week thinking of all they told us. That battle you're in is *awful*, I know. Please Johnny, I do hope you take care of yourself and don't be too brave.

I wish I could do something about this war situation if only I could join the Wacs or the Waves. There are a few girls leaving the plant to join but I wonder who would help Mother and Dad. They depend on my help around the house and with the children. I want to do my share helping out so I guess all I can do is work in a defense plant and help make ammunition instead of using it.

Love, Your Mary

On the Home Front in Manville, New Jersey
Mom and dad have sent and received many letters. They're getting to know each other quite well.

06/19/43

Oh Johnny, it was a *lovely* warm day and I had fun at work. I even walked home from work and that's three miles. Mother always keeps your letters and gives them to me after I eat dinner. She knows if I get them before dinner, then I don't pay much attention to my dinner. Your letter was dated May 6, 1943 and you wrote that it was letter 49 but Johnny you're wrong for this letter makes about 149 at least!

Here is another song for you called **I'm Yours** sung to the tune of **Dear Mom**:

> I'm yours, I love you so much I can't sleep a wink.
> When I go to bed, I lie there and think about the day we met,
> It is in my memory yet, and I love you, I'm yours.
>
> When we were in school, I carried your books, and helped you
> to learn of far distant nooks. The time slipped away but you are
> still in my mind, cause I love you, I'm yours.

When we're apart, you're right here in my heart. So please think of me, I want you desperately. Try hard to want me, taunt me, I'm yours.

If you will say "yes" I'll kiss you and then, we'll tie our love knot and be together again not for a day but forever amen. For I love you, I'm yours.

Love, Mary P. S. Now remember, it's only a song!

On the Southwest Pacific War Front in Australia
Dad is getting to know the natives and finds them very interesting. He tells mom he thinks these natives are descendants of others who happily enjoyed chopping off people's heads and eating them. They also eat insects. He says some guys like to drink their sorrows away but that is not for him. He also brags about his reputation as an *expert potato peeler*. He sends her a handmade bracelet.

06/22/43

Dear Mary,

I saw many natives here the other day and you ought to see the colors of their hair. One really strong man with a *Charles Atlas* build had orange hair. They dye their hair just like women do in the States. This fellow's complexion was five shades darker than licorice candy. I had no doubt that he had too much exposure to the sunlight. His orange hair made a sharp contrast to his *fire engine red* draped garment. This only covered a space of about fifteen postage stamps across his body. These natives are of the ancestors who took *great joy* in chopping someone's head off and making a delicious meal of it. These particular natives have more foresight and reason so they stopped this practice. Now they eat ants *sunny side up*. A very noble deed on their part, don't you think?

Some guys here like to drink their sorrows away. One friend of mine decided to try this and now he can swear in seven different languages.

There are no pubs or bars in Australia. It is our *swimming hole* that we use to drown our sorrows. Mother Nature doesn't seem to mind. We get soaking wet and feel refreshed again.

My reputation as an *expert potato peeler* is widely known and I do some other things quite well. I'm very glad the bracelet I sent you fit so well. I have made over fifteen bracelets now and I'm able to get $3.50 for each of them very easily. The movies are now shown in three different places, however, I don't enjoy them as much as I did when

I had a shoulder to lean on and a *darn sweet* gal beside me. I keep thinking about all the swell times we shared before and also the ones we will have in the future. This is all for now.

With all my love, Your Johnny

On the Southwest Pacific War Front finally receiving mail in Australia Dad is so mixed up because he didn't receive mail for a couple of months and *Bang* he got three letters all at one time. He is privy to the knowledge that some of the fellows lost their girls, however, he is elated to hear from his sweetheart. He is also enjoying some of the fine cuisine that Australia offers. He also meets a sailor from Manville, New Jersey who actually knew who Mom was and says *she is a swell kid.*

07/03/43

Dearest Darling,

Gosh, I'm so mixed up now, I don't know where to start. Here is the situation. I got no mail for a couple of months and then *bang* I receive three letters all at one time. They are all so long and very sweet. I feel rather silly when I jumped to a conclusion and assumed the worst. Honey, you didn't forget me after all and boy am I happy. You ought to see me grinning from ear to ear.

You see, twenty fellows in our company lost their girls because they didn't or couldn't write. The girls got married leaving them flat with no explanation. They always said "It couldn't happen to me" but it turns out it did happen. I guess the more I heard of this, I thought it would be my fate too. I just couldn't figure out why you wouldn't have told me about it. Now I know I was wrong. I'm so happy you're still my sweetheart!

I must tell you a bit about my furlough. I figured I should see a little bit of the town so I went to a restaurant and ordered a big steak. I can just picture you with that hungry look on your face. I understand meat is scarce in the States. I enjoyed a big steak, well done with eggs. One gets steak and eggs as a common meal for breakfast, lunch or dinner. The whole meal costs $.40 so you see meals are cheap over here. Afterward, I went for a walk and came across some sailors. I stopped and asked them if anyone was from New Jersey. Surprisingly, one said "Yes I'm from Manville, New Jersey". I almost jumped out of my shoes! Then I asked him if he knew a girl named Mary Regiec. He said he knew you well and that his friend had a date with you a while ago. I asked him what he thought of you and he said "she is a swell kid". Finally, he asked me why I was so interested in this girl named Mary, so I told him all my thoughts. Who knows maybe some day I'll run into one of my rivals!

The people in town were so friendly so I decided to spend my ten days here. I went to some dances but I didn't see any girls like you, of course. I also rented a bicycle for $.40 a day and rode around most of the day. I took my camera but I didn't have enough film so I went to a drug store and talked the man into giving me some film. He did this for he liked Yanks and had already just about sold all of his film to them. I took a lot of pictures which I will forward to you later on.

With all my love, I remain, Your Johnnie

On the Southwest Pacific War Front in Australia
The guys feel the *fourth* of July is just another ordinary day in the Army. A new rule is assigned by Washington, D. C. They have received a lot of

requests from parents who have a son or daughter in the service whom they haven't heard from in a long time. Letters are being *censored* and sometimes there are sections that are cut out because the censor feels it is *classified information*.

07/04/43

Mary Dearest,

Today is the *fourth* of July but it's just another day to me. I try to stay positive by thinking each passing day is bringing me closer to my dreams. Our company has a rule now that everybody has to write to his or her folks once a week. This ruling is because Washington, D.C. has received too many requests from worried parents asking why they haven't heard from their sons or daughters. You see many people just can't think of any thing to write about so they are hesitant. If I didn't think the *world of you,* I wouldn't be able to write as much to you. I always carry a pad of paper during the day, if I think of something I want to say, I write it down so I won't forget.

You mentioned that my letters were *censored*. I am very careful about what I write, but one never knows what you can say or not tell people. Consequently, I try to write whatever I want occasionally just to see what happens. All your letters mention a lot of weddings for the soldiers can marry any time they wish. Over here it's not hard to get an Aussie girl to marry someone because they all want a ride to the States. You see us *Yanks* are more *dashing* than the Aussie men and we treat the women better. Aussie men treat their women quite rough and have a very old fashioned outlook on life. I'm told Australia was first settled by prisoners from England. The major problem here is transportation. The roads are in bad condition and the wage scale is very low.

Well Mary, I will close now and I am wishing you a million hugs and kisses from me to you.

With love and memories, Your Johnnie

On the Southwest Pacific Front serving in Australia
Dad had acquired the impression that mom might be done with their relationship. Then he almost *jumped for joy* as he received a twenty-four page letter from her. He told some of his friends about it and they could hardly believe it. It is not common.

07/08/43

Dear Mary,

You have no idea how surprised I was when I saw your heavy letter you sent. I thought I was *seeing things*. It looked like there was a possibility you had sent my letters back because you were done with me. When I opened the letter and saw twenty four pages, I had tears in my eyes. Honey, you are so sweet to me. I feel like *jumping for joy!* When I told some of the fellows I got a twenty four page letter, they couldn't believe it for it just isn't a common occurrence.

I'm glad you liked the friendship ring I made for you. It might not look like the best I could make, but it is from my heart. Now about the Aussie money I sent you, doesn't it look so different than ours? I heard we now have a *victory penny*. I miss you something awful, Darling, and I want you to know I'm still in love with you as much as ever. You are my *one and only* as far as I am concerned.

Dreams of Love, Johnnie

On the Southwest Pacific War Front reading mom's letters in Australia
They are starting to talk about what mom calls this *marriage business*. They both agree that it will be better to wait until they can be together again before considering marriage.

MARY JANE JUZWIN

07/10/43

My Darling Girl,

Yes, I'm still a soldier and I am sticking around, but I wouldn't want to stay here forever. My homecoming gets closer each day even though it seems so far away. I like the way you express yourself about this *marriage business*. I also agree it is better to wait until we can be together again before we even think about marriage. It's so sensible and it sure shows me what a *sweet lady* you are to me.

No, I'm not tired of writing to you. It makes me so happy to write a letter to you or read one of your letters. It is music to my ears to hear you say my letters are beautiful and this means so much to me. Be good and think of me as I do you.

Armfuls of Love, Johnny

On the Southwest Pacific War Front in Australia
Dad has trouble catching up with mom's letters. He especially liked the song called **There will never be another you** that she told him to find.

07/17/43

Dearest Mary,

I have mailed you a letter every three days since the *fourth* of July and I still find myself so far behind in answering your letters. I'll catch up sometime. You say when you go to a dance, you close your eyes and try to make believe it is me dancing with you. You're taking a chance when you do this, if I was someone else, I'd never let an opportunity like that pass me.

The little song called **There will never be another you** sounds very appropriate for us. The singer, Ella Fitzgerald sure is talented. I am sure it would express all our feelings perfectly. Thanks for telling me about it.

I hope your feelings haven't changed toward me and if they should I would hope you tell me right away. I am closing this little chat with you for now. So long kid.

With love and kisses, I remain Your Johnnie

On the Home Front in Manville, New Jersey
Mom tells dad she went to a dance with her sister but missed him being beside her.

07/20/43

Dear Johnny,

Here I am sitting up in bed with my stationary suitcase near me. No, I am not sick. I thought I would get in bed, get comfortable and write until I fall asleep. This way, I won't have far to go to get to *dreamland*.

My sister, Jeannie begged me to go with her to the dance so I made her happy by going with her. It was the first time I went in almost three months. I had a good time but honestly, Johnny, I was thinking about you and missing you the whole time.

Love, Mary

On the Southwest Pacific War Front sending mom pictures from Australia Japs are always reporting false news about their role in the war. Dad tells mom how Aussie girls dress and act when you talk to them. They all dream of marrying a *Yank* so they can come to the U. S. He learns news about Italy surrendering. He's looking forward to getting newer materials and supplies for the Southwest Pacific War Zone.

Mary Jane Juzwin

07/26/43

Hello Sweetheart,

I can picture you sitting by yourself on the front lawn. That sounds so wonderful and peaceful I wish I was there to join you. I'm happy to hear you received six letters from this soldier in one week.

I want you to be prepared to meet a *ghost* for you have to keep in mind that the Japs sunk my ship seven times while I was sailing across the ocean. At least this is what they claimed that happened. It's magical how they invented a way of sinking ships so many times isn't it? Your collection of pictures from the Armed Forces must be getting large. I hope my pictures are the only ones you cherish. You know what I mean. You say you brought my picture with you when you were sitting on the lawn. I hope the neighbors didn't get to see it. I hate to scare people. I am soft hearted that way.

Our meals are very good. The infantry men have it very tough when it comes to food or other things.

Most camps have very good food under the circumstances for we are the *best fed* Army in the world. Don't ever think you are not doing your share for the war effort. You're doing your job so skillfully it does more to help win this war than joining the WACs. I'd like to tell you more about the WACs, but I'll save it until I can get back to you.

Now a little about the Australian girls, they are just like any other girl back home, however, their environment makes them so different. They don't know how to dress and will believe anything you tell them if you keep a straight face while talking. Their taste in color is awful and their make up is *plastered* all over their faces. Almost anyone would like to see the States and marry a *Yank*. They are old fashioned compared to American girls whose actions give them away. They do not possess much glamour and

I still prefer my *beautiful Mary*. Until I see you in my dreams, I'll say "good night, sleep tight my sweetheart."

Love and kisses, Johnnie

On the Southwest Pacific War Front hearing war news in Australia
Dad is looking forward to hearing about the end of the European war. He explains that once this happens the South Pacific would finally get first choice in military supplies and airplanes. The problem is the Japs are relentless and refuse to give up. He is tired of *patching up* old planes temporarily for our American pilots to use.

07/31/43

Dearest Mary,

Today I heard news that Italy surrendered. The war news is good and I hope it continues to move to an end so this war can be given more attention. This way the South Pacific would finally get first choice for materials and supplies. It would also include more men and better planes. I am tired of *patching up* old planes for our American pilots to use. I guess they had enough in Europe but these Japs are relentless. They're too clueless to figure out their number has come up.

Gosh, nothing has been going right lately. One of the tubes in my radio burned out so I can't play it now. I'm hoping I can get a replacement soon if one of the guys is able to get one for me. Dearest, I hope my mail has been getting through the *maze* of mail coming from here and is being delivered promptly. All we have to do is keep our chins up and just keep writing to each other. I'm sure everything will work out in the end for us. You're the one person I can count on to stay beside me.

With love and kisses, Your Johnny

On the Southwest Pacific War Front serving in the Army in Australia

Dad explains a lot of unpleasant things have happened in the past three weeks. He says his conduct as a soldier has been excellent, however, he was caught without dog tags.

08/01/43

My Sweet Mary,

I know it has been some time since I last wrote to you. A lot has happened to me in the past three weeks. Things have caused me very many unpleasant days. I never was so disappointed in my life. After serving in the Army for about thirteen months with most of it overseas, I find that all I have worked for is over. My conduct as a soldier has been excellent with only one discrepancy. I was caught without my dog tags, which should be worn at all times. I got restricted to camp for four days.

I have written everybody a *v-letter, victory letter* telling them the same story so I hope the news gets through. If I were home, I could show everyone the facts. My conscience is clear. The only rating I really care about is how I rate with you. That's all that is of any importance. I do hope you'll stick with me and have faith in me for I have never let anyone down. My big promotion will come when I get my Army discharge. Then I will be free to do and say whatever I please. I will end this letter now.

With all my heart, I love you truly, Your Johnnie

On the Southwest Pacific War Front in Australia
Dad hears some encouraging news on the radio about the invasion of Sicily by allied forces. He is impressed with the work women are doing back in the States.

08/04/43

Dearest Sweetheart,

Last night on the radio I heard more information about this invasion of Sicily by allied forces. It made us happy to hear we're starting to move faster. It is happening initially in New Guinea and now in Italy. Who knows where the situation will go next? I'll bet you have a map of the South Pacific so you can see what I'm talking about. My mom listens to the Australian news more than ever since I got here. You can continue to send me any poems or songs for these boost my morale. I'll bet you hear a lot of news at the plant where you work, hon. You girls do lots of composing and I guess you run the place. I understand most of the work is done by girls these days due the shortage of men in the States.

Our dog, *Musso*, is something. When one of us plays a harmonica, he joins us and just about *eats his heart out* because he thinks we're crying. You ought to see his hair stand up when he barks at a stranger. We had to register him because it is an order here. My, what noises he makes in his sleep! He's just one of those things around here that help to make us feel more at home. He sure does a good job.

In closing, I want to write a little verse on how I feel about you: My heart may be lonely, while I'm waiting for my one and only.

However, I smile sweetheart for I know, the day will come when we will show each other dancing and romancing like we used to go. Trying to forget things I miss is like asking me to leave with no kiss. I can hardly wait to see my sweet one, and say we don't have to part anymore. I keep wishing my dreams come true. I'll return to you and cherish the memories dearly as these keep me smiling, not weary.

Love always, Your Johnny

On the Southwest Pacific War Front in Australia

Dad has been very busy constructing a wooden floor under his tent. This is a great way to stay dry when the rain comes down and soaks into the soil. Our Dad was a *Jack of all trades* and he figured out how to build many things over the years. mom originally thought she would become a WAC to help out the *war effort*. Dad explains to her that she is a *valuable* defense worker. She realizes how important her work contribution is and that it is directly used by our American soldiers.

Army tents on wood pallets

08/07/43

Dearest Mary,

The war situation gets better by the hours although my radio is on the blink so I'm not exactly sure of anything right now. I sure miss my friend, the radio. I've been very busy the last two days putting in a wooden floor in our tent. It was a hard job because the only wood I could find was all different lengths as well as different thicknesses. After it was all done, everyone appreciated it. It is so much better than a dirt floor and we stay dry as well as dust free. We also made a frame for our tent. A tent with a frame is much better because it raises the tent higher which really gives us more room. The tent is big enough for five men without crowding.

Do you feel as though you know me better now since I left for the Army? My friend *Pokey* is now married. His wife wanted to join the WACs but she couldn't do it as she got sick. She knows now it's better to stay home and be a defense worker like you are instead. A defense worker helps make things us soldiers use directly in the war effort. Besides, if you join the WACs, you'd have to wait for discharge papers to be set free.

Mary, if you have any control over your pictures, I wish you would stop them from staring at me. Only kidding, don't stop for I love them. Your pictures are always at the side of my bed. I like to be able to lie down and gaze at them every so often. I hope you don't object! Hon, you're the sweetest girl I could ever hope to meet. I am a lucky guy.

Love and kisses, Johnnie

On the Home Front in Manville, New Jersey
Mom informs Dad about her brother Leo's job and why she convinced him to quit.

08/15/43

Dearest Johnny,

My brother Leo got a *scolding* from me and I made him quit his job. All the boys from ten to sixteen years of age get a job for the summer. Most of them go to the farms to pick vegetables. That's not so bad and they make about five to ten dollars a week. Then there are other farm jobs as well. My brother thought he would be smart and get a different kind of job. He got a job as an ice man's helper.

He worked about two weeks and each evening he would come home late, exhausted and wet as carrying ice blocks is not fun. He got tired and wet and be like that for the rest of the day. It would hurt me to see him like that. However, he would pay no attention to me when I asked him to get another job. This one will ruin his health and then he could not help

Mother and Dad once in a while. He took his time thinking it over. Finally he got frightened and agreed to quit. Thank God for that!

Love, Your *little* Mary

On the Southwest Pacific War Front in Australia
While mom's sweetheart is serving in Australia, both of them know marriage is a big step. However, they can rely on their faith to guide them.

08/16/43

Dearest Mary,

It's a funny thing kid, every time I get a *v-letter*, I write two pages answering it. I now look forward to getting mail from you every four days. It sure is sweet of you to spend so much time on me. After all, you are home and could be doing other things. I feel like getting my hands on you and just keep hugging and kissing you until you holler *murder*!

You're right when you say *Yes, I do* it's a big step. We don't know what married life is like yet. Marriage has hidden benefits and it's up to us as a couple to bring them out. It also can contain some bad times, but when it's true love, all turns out well in the end. Faith will guide us as it did when we met. As long as this war is continuing, we have to hold on to our love and hope and pray. I'll do all I can to make your dreams come true. All my dreams depend only on you. I hope it won't be long before we are throwing pots and silverware at each other and sharing all those happy times married life has in store. I could say I love you *in more than a thousand ways* and yet two words cover it, *true love*.

Every time I look your picture, I think of more to tell you. Everybody who sees it thinks you are a *swell looking gal.* That old saying *love is blind* just doesn't work. The thought of holding you ever so tight in my arms again just fills my heart with joy and warmth.

Love, Your Johnny

On the Southwest Pacific War Front recalling some memories still in Australia Dad is reminiscing his favorite times spent with mom. These memories keep his morale positive. He also tells her about all the items he can buy at the P. X. store.

08/18/43

Dear Mary,

I'm just sitting here taking it easy and listening to my radio. Tomorrow I will be on K. P. which, by the way, will be my first in over six months. Remember when we took a walk in Doris Duke's Park and how dark it was when we left? I keep thinking of all those swell times we had together. It sure keeps my spirit up.

We have coca cola about four times a month at our P.X. *Post Exchange* and it goes very quickly. It only lasts about two hours. Our supplies are limited for most things but we can get plenty of canned goods. These include cheese, hot dogs, beans and spaghetti. We have ice cream every day *which you know I cannot do without* and also a drink that is similar to Pepsi cola.

What are some of the movies showing at home these days? This will give me an idea what to expect eight months from now over here. All my thoughts of you are centered around the happy occasion when we will meet again. I miss you more than anything. You'll always hold the key to my dreams and my heart.

All my love, Your Johnny

On the Southwest Pacific War Front enjoying a steak in Australia
Once again, mom gets a letter from dad clearly written *opened by U. S. censor*. Dad thought he was in *steak heaven* as the guys were treated to plump, juicy steaks. He says it was a *great day* because he also got to eat a pint of ice cream, which is his favorite dessert. He is displaying his talents

by making a gas stove out of a gas barrel. He is also able to make candle holders for the Chaplain.

08/28/43

My Dear Mary,

I'm still trying to recover from staring at your picture. I'm telling you honey, you're something else. My heart is still going *pitter patter*.

We had a big treat the other day, namely, t-bone steaks about the size of a Sears catalog. We thought we were in *steak heaven*. On top of this, each man got a pint of ice cream for dessert. Boy was it a great day!

It's raining now and I just started to boil some of my clothes. As usual, I can see rain if it's wash day. I made myself a gas stove from a gas barrel and it's working like a charm. It is nice and warm in my tent. I'm starting to make a few candle holders for the Chaplain. He needs them for our church. I'm also working on a bunch of ashtrays. I have decided to make a very serious attempt to grow a mustache. So far, it is growing in nicely. I haven't decided whether I should tame it to sweep up or down on the ends. How do you think I would look with *handle bars*?

Recently, I heard good news of my best friend who was captured by the Japs during the Pearl Harbor bombing. He's now a prisoner of war in Japan. At least he's alive for I heard many wild stories about what happened in Pearl Harbor. Just keep an eye on the newspaper, kid. This war is starting to *flicker* and there are plenty of surprises to come.

As always, Your *little* Johnnie

On the Home Front in Manville, New Jersey
Dad kids mom wondering if she knows how to cook. Mom is not shy and tells him how it is and what foods she has cooked.

08/30/43

Dear Johnny,

I want you to know that you are the one person in my life that I am *patiently* waiting to see. I want to take a walk with you and you alone! You wanted to know how well I cook. I can boil water for noodles or rice and I know how to fry an egg, that is cooking isn't it? I'm a *country* gal so I even know how to roast a chicken. I say I am a *country* girl but I do know about the latest fashions and tips about the *city slickers* too. You just try to put one over on me.

Oh, by the way, you asked me to give up the idea of becoming a Wac so I never gave it another thought. I'm so happy when you tell me to smile at things and I hope you are smiling too. Honey, I wore your wings on my jacket yesterday. Boy did they look nice and I'm very proud of them and you, of course.

Love, Mary

On the Home Front in Manville, New Jersey
Mom and dad talk about the latest movies and what's happening in Manville, New Jersey at this time.

09/05/43

My Dear Johnny,

Your postal telegram came yesterday and it made me so happy. I was able to go to the movies for the first time since the end of June. I saw **The Hit Parade of 1943** and it was swell.

I want to tell you that the Government is building homes right across the street from us. They are *temporary* homes for the defense workers. They will only be here for two years after the war and then the homes will be destroyed. We don't know who will be living there and we are a bit concerned. In the meantime, you should see the mess! There are tractors, trucks and steam shovels everywhere. The children get so dirty after playing in that dirt.

It's a *miserable* day and I feel tired. Mother took a look at me and said "I want you to take a nice, *hot* bath and I'll give you a *rub down*". Boy, do I feel swell. I have a wonderful mom and I plan to have the same compliment given to me some day. Wow! What did I say? Oh well, I mean it.

I try so hard to begin a letter and finish a letter without an *interruption* but it just isn't possible. However, I am *so wrapped up* in this letter I couldn't stop to fall asleep even if I tried. Mother and Dad went shopping for shoes for the children. They're also enjoying their twenty sixth wedding anniversary. They are so cute together. Sometimes Dad takes Mom in his arms and says "how about we step out tonight"? I often feel like they are still honeymooners.

I know how much this home means to Mother and Dad. I wanted you to know that we are a happy, *loving* family. We understand we must take the bitter with the sweet. It's the sorrow and hardships we live through that brings our hearts together. Dad and mom have experienced lots of hard times, but they stood together and faced them. I hope you and I will feel this way and also have some good times, joy and happiness. Our little family kept growing. We never seemed to have enough money to pay the mortgage and feed the family. My idea was to quit school and go to work. The only job I saw was domestic help so I took it. I didn't mind and I worked nine years.

We all helped to keep us going. Although I have done more than the others, I know they will never forget it all. I was the only one working for a while but I was lucky enough to find both my sisters a job. My sisters Betty, Margie and I worked very hard and helped our family. Betty got married and it was Margie and I who worked. Dad worked off and on earning barely enough to feed our growing family. We got along fine until dad got laid off from his job. Luckily, we were able to get relief from the government but it didn't seem enough for us.

With Love, Mary

On the Southwest Pacific War Front in Australia
Dad is exploring the town and finding some *culinary delights*. Australia is basically a *tea country*. The uniforms the American soldiers wear attract the gals attention because they look *tailor made*. They want a *Yank* to take them to the States so they can get *bar happy*. Dad remembers to explain to mom why the K. C. is engraved on the ring he made for her. Then he tells her a funny tale about the Commander of another group.

09/05/43

My Sweet Mary,

Every day here I see something funny. I went into a store to get a *malted milk*. Instead of regular *malted milk* containers tin cans were used to mix the contents. Then it was done with an egg beater. The Aussies are strictly tea drinkers and when riding on a train there is a place on the engine boiler where they can get hot water for their tea. The Aussies are strictly *tea drinkers*. When riding on a train, there is a place on the engine boiler where they get hot water for their tea. A little boy who might be three years old is given steak and eggs for breakfast. This entrée is an everyday meal suitable for any time. They go to theaters with no roofs. If it doesn't rain, you can enjoy an entire film.

Our uniforms sure make everyone stand up and take notice for they look so much like *tailor made*. All the gals think they will get a *Yank* to take them to the States.

Here is a funny story for you. Remember when I told you I made a wooden floor and a wooden frame for my tent? Well, the Commander of this new group who is moving to our location, told us "You guys better clean this place and clear out all your stuff before my men get here". He gave us such an attitude so we all decided to chop up the wooden floors and frames so they would be sleeping on dirt again at this location. Upon breaking up all the wooden floors and frames of the tents, the boys and I had to get a big dump truck to haul everything away and drive it to the dump. When we got to the dump, the guy there tells us we cannot dump our stuff because we are not authorized. I tried to tell him there is no other place I can dump this stuff. He still insisted telling us we could not drop our load there. I moved our truck a few feet forward and then dumped our load. Upon seeing this maneuver, the guy took a *pot shot* at me but he hit the truck instead of us. Alls well that ends well!

The ring I sent to you dear is made in Kansas City, Missouri. That is the reason the initials K. C. is engraved on it. This small bit of news is just a little something I recently discovered. Honey, it's almost impossible for me to find anything useful to buy for you. Most of the merchandise is old fashioned and too common. I do hope I can find something special to get before I leave Australia. If I don't find anything, the place where I will be going soon doesn't even have a store.

Always yours, Johnny

On the Southwest Pacific War Front in New Guinea
Dad moved to a new location but does not see much activity. This means he has a new APO address, APO 503, 1024 Sig. Co. (am) Service Group, San Francisco, California. The first thing he hangs is a picture of his *favorite gal*. Dad describes his furlough in Ingham, North Queensland, Australia. He is happy to report his flight to a new company.

09/08/43

Dearest Mary,

There is not much going on in my new location because there are no towns or villages to visit. When I arrived here, some commotion was taking place.

Upon asking, I was told that a blonde woman was seen seventy miles away. I guess this was really an *event* so it's no wonder everyone got excited. I have all my stuff straightened out now in my new location. I hung up your big picture and I also have a little picture of you in my mirror. I enjoy checking out my favorite gal whenever I need to cheer up a little. I get tired of looking at myself when I'm shaving.

I spent a very enjoyable furlough in Ingham, North Queensland, Australia. I also had two days of it in Townsville, Australia. The P.X. here carries lots of things that surprised me. I bought a big bar of chocolate and some chocolate milk that is mixed with hot water to make a cocoa drink. Yum! We seem to see many canned fruits so I think I will have as good a selection to purchase as I did in my previous location.

Oh yes, I travelled by plane most of the way to my new company. I heard everyone who ranks up to a Sergeant is getting K. P. duty, so chances are I won't get it too often. The trees are very tall around here and the vines hang down from the top of them. We can see a movie almost every day. It's a quiet place where nothing much ever happens.

Here I am hoping your mail catches up to me soon in this location. I will miss it more than you'll ever know possible. So, until the next time, I'll say "So long".

Love and kisses, Your Johnny

On the Southwest Pacific War Front hearing encouraging war news in New Guinea
The boys hear more news about Italy giving up and surrendering. Dad enjoyed an eight day furlough and thought it was certainly nice to be a civilian even for a little while.

09/11/43

Dear Mary,

I just heard more news about Italy giving up and surrendering. Gosh, things look good for us, don't they? As I mentioned in my previous letter, I had an eight day furlough. It was a nice change to be a civilian even for a short while. Now I can safely say I have fully recovered from that experience.

I hope and pray my next furlough will place me in Manville, New Jersey right in front of your house. No Hon, I haven't forgotten the way to your house for the love in my heart will be my guide.

I'm hoping you are not working too hard, dear. I know you hold an important job in the plant. Probably they call on you to help out. Tell me more about the shortages or the *rationing* there.

> Eve said to Adam "I've not a thing to wear, all in despair,
> when Adam wanted a walk for fresh air.
> But it is strange to relate that an hour Adam did wait
> Then Eve inquired "Is my fig leaf on straight"?

Well kid, I might sound a little screwy in this letter but I'm always happy when I write. Keep a spot for me in your heart. I love you so and I'll never stop.

An armful of love, Your Johnnie

On the Southwest Pacific War Front explaining new activity in New Guinea Dad is now located in a new company where he must, once again replace an old floor with a new wooden one in his tent. The natives eat raw birds, lizards and ants.

09/12/43

My Dearest Mary,

Today I got your *v-letter* dated August 20, 1943. This makes the first letter in three weeks. I was overjoyed to hear from you sweetheart, for I miss you so very much. However, with me *jumping* all around the world, it's no wonder I don't receive your letters quickly. I always get a lump in my throat when I read your closing remarks. I love to read *all is fine now and I'm still your Mary*. What else could a fellow like me want to hear?

I spent a rather long and hard day replacing the old floor in our tent. The other boys helped out, however, the boards were all different sizes and that made the project go slow. We had to execute the job as quickly as possible for it rains here without notice.

I saw some natives today and I never knew that men wore *sarongs* but here they do.

They are hard workers and we pay them more money than they ever got before. Their salary is $1.50 a month and they are happy to get it. Of course, we also offer them a hat, a pair of shoes, some beads and some American cigarettes. They like all these things so they don't mind working for us.

They carry their bow and arrows with them and all of a sudden they started looking up through the trees. I wondered why and finally one of them shot at a little bird about the size of a robin. They made such a *fuss* over this action, one might think it was an Army camp getting excited over a girl passing by. The natives eat the birds *raw* and also on their menu are lizards and ants. My, what an appetite! They wear bracelets on their wrists and all the way up their arms. A lot of these are made of snake skin.

Native woman from New Guinea

The days pass by here faster than the other place I lived. It seems like I don't get a chance to get anything done and before I know it, it's time to *hit the hay*. I do mean hay for my mattress is made of it. I keep my big ears *glued* to the radio for the news is getting hotter than a *firecracker* by the minute.

I hope everyone is in the best health. I'll see you in my dreams.

Love always, Your Johnny

On the Southwest Pacific War Front observing natives in New Guinea Dad describes the *zoot suit* riots in Los Angeles, California. He also tells mom how little clothing the native women wear at the beaches.

09/15/43

Dear Mary,

I just came back from a nice, cold shower and I feel like doing something. However, when I look around, it's just trees and more trees so you spend a quiet evening at home just like people back home do after they collect their old age pension.

I saw some native women today. They passed our camp with a bunch of kids. Their clothes were very simple. They wear much less than you see at the beaches back in civilization. Only a few of them wear shoes and the reason isn't because they lost their ration books. They stick to Mother Nature and try to sell you everything for a small sum.

I took some very interesting pictures on my way to this company but I'm afraid I wouldn't be permitted to send any home due to military secrets and all that sort of stuff.

I see Eleanor is over here. No, I don't mean a new gal. I mean Mrs. Roosevelt for she is on a tour of some sort. That gal sure gets around.

I heard about the *zoot suit* riots in Los Angeles, California. I understand they were a series of racist attacks between Mexican American youths and white American servicemen stationed in southern California. White servicemen and civilians attacked and stripped youths who wore *zoot suits* because the outfits were considered unpatriotic and extravagant during wartime especially since rationing of fabric was required for the World War II effort. The *zoot suit* war is all over, things must be rather dull in the States.

I wish my newspapers would catch up to me for I'd like to hear more news about home. Well kid, I have rambled on for three pages now and I think I'm finally talked out.

Loving you so much from the bottom of my heart, Your Johnny

Mary Jane Juzwin

On the Home Front in Manville, New Jersey
Mom tells dad about the war hero, John Bonjovi visiting her town and about the parade that was held for him.

09/19/43

My Dear Johnny,

Today is Sunday and the house is quiet for a change. I wanted to tell you about the war hero who was in town today. His name is John Bonjovi. We had a big parade for him moving through three towns. It started in Manville, then Somerville, through Raritan and ended in Dukes Park. This hero killed 38 Japs. My goodness, he sure is the *talk* of the town. He will return to the Army soon.

I am doing my favorite thing right now and that is writing to you. I really wish you were here next to me and I could tell you lots of things in person. Oh Johnny, I miss you so much. I haven't heard from you for three days now, but I understand the mail situation. You spoiled me, you rascal!

Love, Your Mary

On the Southwest Pacific War Front wearing a *grass skirt* in New Guinea
Dad has such a great sense of humor he decides to dress himself as a *native* with coconut shells on his chest and a *grass skirt* covering his legs. He promises mom he will get someone to snap a few pictures and send them to her.

09/19/43

Dear Mary,

In a few days, I plan to get all dressed up in the most modern clothes around here. It will be a *grass skirt* worn a few inches above the knee cap. I will make use of some shells to form a top and it will be a very *daring* outfit. I promise to get some brave volunteer to snap a few pictures of me. I'm sure when you receive a picture of me in my new outfit, it will reveal the savagery in me. Oh well, you would have found out one of these days anyway. I guess it is okay.

Honey, I miss you an awful lot and could never forget you. I feel very happy and blessed for I have a girl who stood by me through all this war business. Keep a spot for me in your heart always.

Love, Your Johnnie

On the Southwest Pacific War Front keeping busy in New Guinea
Dad's morale is cheerful as he has just read two *sugar reports* from mom. The boys look forward to getting mail from their sweethearts because their romance is long distance.

09/26/43

Dearest Mary,

I just got through reading two very nice *sugar reports* from you. Remember, there are no rations involved. I saw another movie yesterday, and as usual I held hands with a ten foot snake all during the show. I hope you aren't jealous.

This *long distance romance* stuff is okay, but there is nothing like close quarters. Oh, what I could do with a car, a radio and you. I'm going to have a lot of catching up to do with you. You'll have to build up your sleep for I'm afraid I'll want to see you very often. Thinking of you and keeping myself happy for you are so darn sweet.

Your loving soldier, Johnny

On the Southwest Pacific War Front in New Guinea

Dad happily shares the story of one of his friends playing the harmonica. He tried his first taste of *jungle juice* and it took his breath away. He is thrilled to receive eight letters from mom. He's sending her a ring made out of a *Jap zero* and fashioned by himself.

10/12/43

Dearest Darling,

One of the fellows in my tent is playing one of my favorite pieces on the *mouth organ*. **You are my sunshine** and I'm thinking of you, of course, hon. I had my first taste of *jungle juice* and it took my breath away! It's the same as the kind that is made at home by amateur bootleggers. No more for me, I've had enough.

I realize you are a busy girl so if I don't hear from you for a while, I will understand. Honest, I won't get worried this time. You make me feel so good when you close your letters like the one in which you state you have *all the faith in the world in me* and *trust me*. I hope this is true for trusting me with your heart. We both miss each other a lot. However, when people have to be ruled by monsters, we must realize everyone has to do his or share to fight this oppression.

Until the next letter, I close my letter to the *sweetest girl in the world* my *little* Mary.

As always, Love, Johnnie

On the Southwest Pacific War Front in New Guinea
Dad continues to receive more of mom's letters through the mail system. Mom keeps asking him what he would like her to send him for Christmas. However, Dad is stuck in the jungle and will not be able to send a gift to her in return.

10/16/43

Dearest Mary,

The clouds may be out in the sky today, but it is a wonderful day for me. I received eight letters from you. This attention on your part is like a *dream*. I never knew it could happen to me. However, I can read about your love for me in black and white so I don't have to pinch myself to see if it's true.

You keep asking me what I might want for Christmas. I wish you wouldn't make so much *fuss* over it. I understand how you feel for you are thoughtful, so you want to send me something nice. However, I'm helpless over here because the jungle hasn't anything to offer that I could send to you.

If you ever get your hands on some film, any size will do, I would really appreciate it if you sent me some. I will gladly repay you for them. If you should get any, pack them in wax paper for the climate here is very wet and they might get soaked.

Remember, I'm a *one girl man*, and I don't mean *one girl at a time* with a string of them.

At last I know you definitely received my thirty two page letter when I left San Francisco, California and set sail on the ocean. The only clue I had was you said "Boy, you sure write long letters". You have no idea the trouble I had to send that letter to you without it being *censored*.

I'll be looking forward to receiving those letters from the girls at your plant. I guess you all feel like sisters working together and writing to your sweethearts as well. You say your folks are waiting for me too. You also said they wouldn't let us be alone. I'll be around for a while, but baby I'll jump in my car with you so fast that they will think we've eloped or something. There's nothing like being alone with one's sweetheart.

I can just see you staring at me as though you haven't seen me for a long time. However, honey if you close your eyes when I kiss you, I'd hold you so tight you'll be afraid to open them for fear they could pop out.

With love and kisses, Your Johnny

On the Southwest Pacific War Front describing conditions in New Guinea
Surprisingly, Dad has not encountered many hungry mosquitoes in this location and is he relieved. He tells mom he wants to visit one of the largest cities in southern Australia when he gets a chance to have a furlough.

10/17/43

Dear Mary,

I sure can imagine how your little brother, Leo felt when he got his first long pants. I remembered how important I thought the occasion was for me. I guess I felt like a *really big boy*.

This day is very wet because it's been raining on and off all day. This place is surprisingly free of mosquitoes so it's very nice. However, we sleep under nets something like a little baby uses just to be on the safe side. I plan to go to one of the largest cities in southern Australia when I am able to go on a furlough again. I think I should be able to find something nice for you. One of these days, I'll send you a ring made from a *Jap zero* for I already have the material. I think I'll put two little hearts on it and a place for your initials.

Love, Johnny

On the Southwest Pacific War Front noticing some jungle animals in New Guinea
Dad has seen some interesting birds in the *bush* who swing on vines hanging from the tops of trees. He also encountered some lizards. The

crew had fun playing a baseball game between the guys with three grades. They won the game!

10/18/43

Dear Sweet You,

I'm glad you are able to figure out my letters. You can also say anything you want so there is no need to *beat around the bush*. Speaking of bush, you ought to see this jungle. So many vines are hanging from the tops of the trees and these birds are making a lot of funny noises. I bet there are many babies and young mothers.

I am missing you something awful! I don't think I will have to walk into your dining room when I get home. I'll bet you'll be at the front door before I can shut the motor off of my car. I can't tell you enough for words cannot show you how much you mean to my heart and the rest of me. I guess I will have to show you when I get the chance.

I just saw a lizard climb a tree. Such happenings occur in the wild life of Johnny. We did have fun the other day when we played a baseball game between us K. P. guys and the last three grades. We beat them and did they holler! Everyone up to a Sergeant gets K. P. duty. This was my first game in a long time and my arm feels as heavy as lead.

I have your pictures hanging all over the place so any way I turn I can see you. I couldn't ask for better scenery. I feel *sleepy* so I hope we will be together in my dreams tonight.

With loads of Love, Your Johnny

On the Southwest Pacific War Front hearing positive war news in New Guinea It seems our American pilots are frustrated because the Japs are not sending enough planes in the air for them to shoot down. Dad tells mom about natives wearing snake skins around their hands and stomach.

10/20/43

Dearest Mary,

I am a boy who is in love with a very nice girl. However, I find it very hard to show her how much I love her. Please tell me what to do. Shall I marry this girl or is there some other way? I myself cannot think of a better way.

The war news continues to be very positive so I do hope to return to my favorite gal very soon. Our pilots are very frustrated at the Japs for they don't send enough planes in the air for them to fight. Sometimes our pilots get practice by flying around each other to see who gets their target.

We have another dog here who looks about the same as *old Musso* but it is rather hard to keep him around. Someone takes him away but he always manages to return to us.

These natives have snake skins wrapped around their hands and stomach. I guess it's the latest rage. I have a better looking picture of one but I'm afraid to send it to you. This picture would definitely cause some people to go *native*. Don't you dare! I see them with their *upsweep* hairdo. Usually they like to put soap in their hair and let it get hard. When I show you the picture, you'll get a general idea how they look.

That is all for now. I miss you more each day.

Love and kisses, Your Johnnie

On the Home Front in Manville, New Jersey
Mom and dad are teasing each other and being *so romantic* in their letters.

10/23/43

My Dear Johnny,

That was a *swell* description you told me about the men changing on account of this war. If you can't do better than to make love to a ten foot snake, then don't do anything. Darn it, how can I go on thinking you're cheating on me with a snake when all I can think of is your arms wrapped around me.

Oh honey, of course I'll be glad to receive one of those ashtrays you keep talking about made from shells of large guns. They must be quite something and I'm sure Mother and Daddy would like them too. I am certain they would be proud to have them and show them to people when they come visiting our home.

Also Johnny, I would not object if you send some pictures to me of native women. In fact it's about time I received some interesting pictures of or from you anyhow.

With Love, Your Mary

On the Southwest Pacific War Front living in the jungle of New Guinea Dad says the jungle and he get along very well. They have a few air conditioned rooms at this location so the guys relax in them to stay cool. He is reminiscing about the past when he used to rush home from work, eat, shave, shower and dress all in forty minutes so that he could drive to Manville, New Jersey.

10/23/43

My Dearest Girl,

I'm writing a few words to let you know I am still very much alive and all that sort of stuff. The jungle and I get along well. I'm sitting in one of the few air conditioned rooms we have here. It feels like *pure heaven*. It's so cool and I'm looking forward to getting my coca cola very soon. Only a limited bunch of us can get them for the machine can handle only so many bottles. The extract is sent here and then they mix the drink thus saving a lot of space.

I drove a truck the other day about the distance from your house to mine. I kept thinking how I used to rush home from work, eat, shave, shower and dress all in forty minutes to jump into my *rattle trap* and start on my merry way to see you. Those were the days. How could I ever forget them?

Well Dearest, don't celebrate too much on your birthday. Remember I'll be thinking of you that day more than ever if that's possible. I feel so blessed to have a girl who thinks so much of me. Take care of yourself.

Your loving sweetheart, Johnny

On the Southwest Pacific War Front in New Guinea
Dad informs mom the work she performs at the plant is serviced by he and his fellow coworkers at this location. Mom's friends graciously wrote notes to dad to cheer him up.

10/25/43

My Darling Mary,

Today while I was busy fighting the Japs on K.P., I was handed a letter from my gal, Mary. It was the one that contained those nice notes from your girlfriends. I can tell that they think the world of you. Be sure to thank each one for me. I will look forward to meeting all these girls for they mean an awful lot to you.

The work you do at the plant is often serviced by your Johnny. It is important for you and your fellow co-workers to know they are really helping the *war effort*. In fact, we use your materials every day.

Life was very dull until you came along and filled that *lonesome feeling* in my heart. Now when I think of you, I get a certain feeling that's very hard to explain. If my heart could talk, I'm sure it would say "Mary is the dearest girl any fellow could ever hope to meet". I miss you so dog gone much Hon. If you ever gave me the air, I'd be a very sad *dog face soldier*.

I am writing this letter with a flashlight and outside it's raining very hard. The time doesn't matter for I'd rather be doing this than anything else. I still can't get over how I rate such a nice girl like you. When I think of holding you in my arms again, it gives me a lump in my throat. I'm so sorry you are going to spend another birthday without me. I just have to shut my eyes and be content to dream about you. Keep smiling dear and remember somewhere there is a lonesome soldier boy waiting to see you.

With all my heart to you, Love, Johnny

On the Home Front in Manville, New Jersey
Mom praises dad by saying he has grown up a bit and found himself to be a real man.

10/30/43

My Dear Johnny,

Honey, it is a Sunday afternoon and I'm at it again. I am trying to answer these twelve letters I received from you this week. Mom and Dad were so happy that you remembered them as well as me. Johnny, my dear you just can't imagine how my daddy and mother feel toward you. You are their son and no one can tell them any different.

You have grown up a bit in the Army and found out that you are a real man. When I met you, you were still a kid. *What was that I heard you say?* There is one whole pint of ice cream to one man. Oh you hog you, it is kind of hard to get ice cream here, you know.

I know you love ice cream so I am happy you can get it over there. I do manage to get some almost every day as they sell it in the cafeteria at work. *Huh, what's that I heard you say?* I have some nerve calling you a hog. Oh honey, don't feel bad about it if you are my *little hog*, I'll be your *little piggie*, okay?

"Let's not waste a short furlough here — I haven't eaten ice cream or had a beer in months."

You say your friend got captured by the Japs. It's too bad about that. I only hope he can live through it all and come home to tell us all about the Jap prison. Oh how dreadful!

Soon I will try to get some boxes and fill them with goodies for you for Christmas. I am not going to tell you now what I will put in the boxes for I want it to be a surprise and I don't quite know what I will buy or what will fit in them yet.

Love, Your Dear Mary

On the Southwest Pacific War Front watching gambling in New Guinea Dad is always thinking of the future so he saves his money. He has observed many guys gambling and becoming *low on funds*. The Aussies do some work for the Americans, however, they really need their *tea time*.

11/04/43

Dearest Mary,

Gosh honey, it's a lovely night out and the moon is so beautiful. I never looked at the moon so often before because I looked at you instead. You say you wrote twelve letters in one day! You must think of me a great deal for I know it couldn't be so easy for you to spend so much time writing to me. I can see you put your *heart and soul* in them.

I am saving my money like I always have. There are many boys who are *low on funds* because they gambled or drank away their money. I haven't lost the value of money like so many others have.

Eleanor only visited the U.S.O. commando camps here, so I wasn't able to see her after all. There is a good joke about her over here. General MacArthur asked for help. He had many conferences with big shots and still didn't get what he wanted. After all these encounters, they sent Eleanor. Even though she is a woman, she gets things done and is really tops. I meet many boys who have been close to the front lines. They tell me many interesting stories about the Japs. They say it's all in our favor so hopefully we don't have to wait too long before this war is over.

Here is some more interesting stuff about the Aussies. Many of them work for us in our offices. At about 10:00 a.m. they all march out with their cups to have their tea. It is quite a sight. I think a lot of the Aussies will be rich after this war. Any place where our men are located, a lot of money is spent. Most Aussies make more money in two months from us than they did in a year in normal times. Many of them plan to see the States. They never realized *white people* could be so different and have so much. Most people, namely, ninety percent of Australians, lead a very simple life.

Be sure to give my best regards to your Mom and Pop. They sure will make swell in-laws.

Loving you from the bottom of my lonesome heart, Your Johnny

On the Southwest Pacific War Front using his talents in New Guinea Dad is putting parts together to build a short wave radio. The natives are willing to help the guys do some work around the camp. The guys get a *kick* out of the songs they sing while their working.

11/09/43

Dear Mary,

I'm still trying to finish answering your eighteen *v-letters*. My portable radio does not work here. However, I have found enough parts to build one for short wave. The portable radio will be used for the regular broadcast band.

The natives are doing some work around our camp and they sing such *lovely* songs.

They sound like they all have toothaches. I got a few shots in my arms today. It was done to prevent different illnesses. It's quite an experience but it doesn't hurt.

Every word you've written to me deserves a kiss when I get back. I can't even to count them. Sweet, I hope I can see you soon. I'm afraid you will forget me as time goes on.

As always, Your Johnny

On the Southwest Pacific War Front in New Guinea
Dad is enjoying the scenery and sending mom more pictures to save. She has another birthday without Dad but he wishes her a lively celebration with friends and family.

11/12/43

My Darling Mary,

Enclosed you will find a reasonable sample of some scenery around here. Some stuff, eh kid. I realized I keep sending you all my best pictures and I have sent my Mom only a few. I better send more to her. Writing to my Mom and Pop is hard for you are always on my mind. You are much easier to write to by *a long shot*. I got it bad, huh! This morning when I wrote a letter to them, I started to address it and automatically wrote your name and address before I caught myself. You see what you do to me!

You should see some of the pictures the boys painted on the side of trucks. Our favorite is some babe with *lots of those curves* that make you want to whistle. I guess you know what I mean. Our water truck man has a big police dog. He will stick by the man all day and he always rides standing on the roof of his truck. You could almost put a saddle on him and take a pony ride.

Okay dearest, this is enough for now. I sure ramble on, don't I? I think it's so much nicer to share everything so their will be no secrets between us.

With love in my heart, Johnny

On the Home Front in Manville, New Jersey
Mom gets some boxes to send Christmas goodies to dad once again. However, her sister, Jeannie plays a *trick* on her and hides one of the boxes.

11/13/43

My Dear Johnny,

Honey, let me tell you a story about the boxes I got for Christmas and how cute Jeannie stole one of my Christmas boxes from me. You see it was very hard to get these *special* boxes this year to send across the ocean to you. Somehow I managed to get four of them in Plainfield, New Jersey. That is the limit to send to one person across to another in the service. They would only sell me four boxes.

When I came home with them, I found out that my sister Jeannie was looking in every store around here for one of those boxes for your brother Walter but she was unable to buy one. When I bought enough stuff to fill your boxes up, I found out I didn't have enough time to send them all from me for I could only send one each week and I wanted to send them all before October 15, 1943. So I got smart and I addressed one from my sister Betty and before I started packing your boxes I found out one was missing. I looked high and low but I just couldn't find it. I kept asking Mother how come all of the other three boxes are exactly where I put them but one is missing.

Jeannie kept saying, "Mary you don't need four boxes, I'm sure you don't." Then she would change the subject or she would say, "you only have enough stuff for three boxes, Mary do you really need the other one?" Finally, I put two and two together and said "Jeannie where is that other box?" Isn't she a doll to steal that box and hates to admit it. Well she laughed right in my face and so hard tears rolled down her cheeks. Here is a list of stuff I sent you for Christmas. I do hope you receive them and they come in handy. After all you men are far away from your families this holiday and you deserve at least a few things from home.

Box 1
12 assorted meats
6 different charms
1 pkg. cherry sour balls
10 assorted chewing gums
1 bag of sweethearts
1 box of Planters peanuts
1 box Ludens cough drops
1 pkg. charcoal gum

Box 2
3 pkgs. Of razor blades
3 rubber erasers, 1 tube pencil lead
3 neckties & 6 handkerchiefs
3 pairs socks & 1 pkg. playing cards
1 small Dr. Lyons toothpowder
1 small address book
1 half 'n half tobacco
1 bark dog tobacco & 1 square pipe

Box 3
3 song sheets & 1 autograph book
2 funny books
1 pkg. of 16 air mail envelopes
4 small Rite form memo pads
30 v-mail stationery pages
2 skin thin tablets
1 tin of my homemade peanut brittle

I hope you enjoy all the items I picked out for you. I miss you very much.

With lots of Love, Mary

On the Southwest Pacific War Front in New Guinea
Dad is sad because mom is having another birthday without him there to celebrate with her. The bugs are plentiful so he is being attacked on all sides.

11/14/43

My Darling Mary,

Today is the day my *little sweet one* has her birthday and Woe is me! I kept thinking about you all day *more than usual* and all the nice things I could have done for you. I do hope you had a great time even though I couldn't be there.

Oh Baby, am I in the *groove* right now and you're the cause of it all. You vicious woman you, some day I'm going to tell our children what you've done to me. Oh no, just to rub it in the song on the radio is **Home sweet home** of all things. They have very good programs on tonight but listening to the radio alone is no fun compared to the way we cuddled up to hear it.

Pardon me, while I brush off two Japs. Don't get too excited as they are Japanese beetles crawling on my bed. I guess they are seeking company but it won't be me. I'm going to have to cut this letter short. I'm being attacked on all sides by bugs. The light always attracts them. Closing with all my love and hoping to be by your side for your next birthday.

Love and many Kisses, Your Johnnie

On the Southwest Pacific War Front growing a mustache in New Guinea Dad is amazed there was no rain for one whole day. He still suffers *heart trouble* as he misses his sweetheart. He got himself a small tent. He tells mom he is in a safe area so she shouldn't worry about him. The worst thing is ice cream might be scarce at home as well as in New Guinea.

11/15/43

Dear Mary,

I just got through serving my sentence on K. P. After the mess sergeant let me out *on parole*, I made a quick retreat to the showers. That covers my action against the Japs for today. We have had an awful drought. Just think of it, no rain for twelve whole hours. Ain't it awful? This just one of the *horrors* of war in the jungle!

You say ice cream is scarce at home too. Now that is a *tragedy* for you know it is my favorite dessert! I guess we'll be lucky if we get two quarts a year.

I guess my mustache caused quite a *commotion* from the sound of your letters. Well, I'm just trying to see what it'll look like for the heck of it. I'm thinking of using the *handle bar* style. It will make me feel like a grown man riding a bicycle, don't you think?

Dearest, I still have the same *trouble with my heart* since it is back there with you and it gets worse every day. You mean the world to me and don't you forget it! I am closing with lots of love and many kisses. I remain yours forever.

Your *wandering boy,* Johnny

On the Southwest Pacific War Front in New Guinea
Dad has set up camp in New Guinea where he has a tent to himself. He tells mom this area is very safe so if she hears any wild rumors just disregard them.

11/19/43

Dearest Mary,

I'll go right into telling you why your Johnny was so busy this past week. You see dear, I got myself a small tent about 15" by 15" and now I have a tent all to myself. I spent a lot of time getting it set up and I made a wooden floor for it. I am all alone except with the company of your pictures hanging up all over the place. You're *darn swell company* and you tuck me in to sleep every night and reward me with a sweet dream kiss.

In case you are interested, I am somewhere in New Guinea. Don't get excited for I'm okay and in a safe place. Don't listen to any stories you might hear about this place. I heard many of them before I got here. They all turned out to be a big bunch of *baloney*.

I am in the *combat zone* but it has its advantages. It is strictly *all work and no play*. My work consists of the following items. A *Tech Sergeant* in our outfit removes a radio from his plane by cutting a few wires. Then he gives the radio to P.F.C. Johnny and I take it apart to fix it. I do my share to keep them flying. The Fifth Air Force is a place where it means more than other camps in Australia. I also restring antennas on our planes so the pilots are able to talk on the radio for longer distances. Another of my skills was to develop film of the Jap airfields so our guys can locate them easier.

We've been getting eggs every day, two to each man and apple pie two times a week. It is easy on the stomach. I eat my spinach too! I just have to keep in shape for I know I could never keep up with that *full of pep* gal of mine. I hope you've been taking your vitamins for you'll need strength for all my plans. I want your heart to be *strong and wide open* for a *yes*. Be prepared and remember you are reserved to me only.

With all my Love, Johnny

On the Southwest Pacific War Front informing people about Jap losses in New Guinea
Dad is now permitted to reveal Jap plane losses. He also describes a Japanese motor plane and says the Japs don't own too many bombers.

11/21/43

Dearest Mary,

You bet we'll take long rides in the country and even go on hikes. I'll really give you a *workout*. Keep sending me your *sugar reports* for I eat up all the *sugar* you can send.

We are permitted to tell about Jap plane losses now. Some time ago, the Japs tried to *dive bomb* a place in New Guinea during the day. We listened to the *fighters* go after them. Boy, it was something like keeping track of history. Our pilots said "There goes a Jap let me have him". It was a *mad scramble* for there wasn't enough Japs for them. A few of our pilots were disappointed. We heard this on the radio, every time a pilot shoots down a Jap plane, he circles camp and gives a *low flowing roll* with his plane.

A Japanese motor plane is easily detected for its two motors don't run even at the same rate of speed thus producing a funny sound. The Japs have very few bombers. Flying high at night, they have about as much chance to hit anything as a *needle in a haystack*.

The Japs lost all their planes in that dive bombing raid.

I don't mind telling you when I'm writing to you, I find it hard but I try my best to think of something interesting to say to you. You may meet better looking boys than me, but you'll never find anyone who loves you as much as me. When I get back, I'll really show you what I mean.

I just got done repairing the lights on some jeeps from the States. They put a switch across two wires and when you hit the switch it makes a *dead short* blowing the fuse. Rather than fight the war in the dark, I put on my trusty raincoat and located the trouble.

That *Miss* in your name just has to be removed and that is all there is to this fact. I will close now for it's a good night for rest and sleep. See you in my dreams so don't disappoint me.

All My Love, Johnnie

On the Home Front in Manville, New Jersey
Mom and dad miss each other terribly but are happy to keep each other's pictures close by so they can see and think about one another no matter where they sit. Her letter was written on *cool airplane stationary*.

MARY JANE JUZWIN

11/22/43

My Dearest Johnny,

Boy is it good to sit here in this warm kitchen with your picture in front of me and me writing to you. I always have your picture with me no matter where I go to sit and write to you. Sometimes I even sleep with your picture pressed close to my heart. I couldn't ask for a more quiet and enjoyable evening, unless of course you were here next to me.

I thought it would be fun for you to get your friends to sign the autograph book and put down their names and addresses as well as telephone numbers. Who knows? Maybe some day we will be able to visit them after the war when they return to the states.

With Lots of Love, Mary

On the Home Front in Manville, New Jersey
Dad praises mom to other guys but she says he should see how she looks right now.

11/27/43

My Dear Johnny,

You shouldn't praise your girl so much to the other guys. If you only knew how she looks. This summer she rode the horses so much that she became bowlegged. She fell down the cellar stairs and knocked her teeth out! She couldn't get a good dentist to replace them as they have all been drafted. So she had some old fossil set them in for her and are they a beautiful set of *buck* teeth!

Then she got a bright idea that her hair was getting dark so she shampooed it with peroxide and it turned a *bright orange* sort of color! To top it off, she worries something awful about you and has become run down, pale and thin. Now you have a bowlegged, buck toothed, bleached hair, skinny dame and you are showing off with her.

With my Love, Mary

On the Home Front in Manville, New Jersey
Mom and dad tease each other by saying dad is a *wolf* and mom is a *wolfess*.

11/28/43

Dearest Johnny,

The fellows kid you because you write to me so much. Well, if you only knew what I go through here, you would be surprised. I'm telling you dear, everyone who visits us at home finds me writing to you. Honey, do you have all the letters I sent you? Oh, I doubt it. I don't think that you are able to carry all those letters with you, are you Johnny? Don't worry about my letters to you as I have made a copy of each and every one so if you have lost some, you can read them when you come home.

Was I surprised to hear you say *"all the wolf"* is out of you. No wonder all the fellows say, "Mary, you little *"wolfess"*, will you dim those lights in your eyes and show that beautiful smile of yours". That only makes me laugh and light up more. Did you receive my Christmas packages as yet? I wasn't allowed to send any bottles, therefore, I couldn't send you ink. However, I will try to send it again. I also ordered the pen point for your pen. You see it's very hard to get them now. I hope I get them soon.

Dear, you say whiskey is very expensive out there? It is expensive here too. Boy are we trying our hardest to get a quart of whiskey for Dad for Christmas. It is six dollars a quart if you are able to get it in some place that you are very well known.

Love, Your *little* Mary

Mary Jane Juzwin

On the Southwest Pacific War Front enjoying Thanksgiving in New Guinea Dad is still in his *one man tent* but he says some very friendly mice keep him company as well. He reads the local newspaper and says everything one buys helps the *war effort*.

11/29/43

Dear Mary,

Well, I have fully recovered from my Thanksgiving dinner. What a meal! Even if it was Aussie, it was very good. I hope you and your family shared a nice Thanksgiving. What I wouldn't give to spend Thanksgiving with my gal and her wonderful Mom and Pop.

I'm still in my *one man tent*, only now I have someone living with me. No, it's not a native but it's very friendly mice. They are swell company. They tickle my toes and play football in my hair. Mickey Mouse's team won last night.

Look at me, I seem to be writing downhill. I just let myself go and I feel as though I'm talking directly to you. I get a big kick out of the home town newspaper. Everything one buys these days help the *war effort*. Well I have done my bit for this time. Keep smiling dear and I'll always smile just as long as I have you in my life.

Lots of Love and Kisses, Johnny

On the Southwest Pacific War Front now somewhere in the Philippines The boys are grinning whenever they see the mail man and receive letters from home. Dad is looking forward to running his hands in mom's golden hair, pulling her ears, rubbing her nose and showering her with kisses.

12/03/43

My Sweetheart Mary,

I'm now somewhere in the Philippines. I'm just taking a few minutes to tell you a little nonsense and all that sort of stuff. You should see the boys' faces when mail comes. Their grins look just like those dimples on your knees. All of us just drop everything and run to the mail man. We all want him to call our name and give us some communication from home.

Did you hear about the man who:

1. Pulled his teeth out so he could chew his gums?
2. Poked his eyes out when he heard he had a *blind* date?
3. Threw his nose out the window so the wind would blow it?
4. Took a chair to the hospital so little old Granny could set in?
5. Went to a flower shop to see a *defense plant*?
6. Wouldn't pay his bus fare for his name was *crime* and *crime doesn't pay*?
7. Took his whiskey up to the roof because he wanted a *drink on the house*?
8. Swallowed some bullets so he could pass the ammunition?
9. Thought Peter Pan was a toilet?
10. Put two bald headed men together so they would make an *ass of themselves*?

That is all the nonsense I have for the time being. I'm sure I'll think of some more. I can just hear you laughing like you always did, so happy and so naturally sweet. I long for the day when I can run my hands through your golden hair, pull your ears, rub noses and just shower you with kisses. Of course, you will be completely helpless.

Love and Kisses, Johnny

On the Southwest Pacific War Front somewhere in the Philippines

Dad is enticing mom by describing a *highway movie* otherwise known as a *drive-in movie* that he would like to share with her. He asks her to send him a picture of her folks.

12/05/43

My Darling Mary,

Oh, what a night! It's the type of night I would love to be with you. I have my furnace heating, it's my pipe in case you wanted to know. However, I get even warmer when I think of you. Your pictures do so much to me. I think I'll wear them out just looking at them. By the way Hon, don't you think it's about time you sent me a picture of your Mom and Pop? Do you think you could make one and send it to me?

There will be no movie tonight but I often think how nice to would be for us to go to a *highway movie* otherwise known as a *drive-in* movie.

It's the kind where you sit together in the car and watch it from there. Have you ever been to one like this? Make sure you write your list of things we want to do in the future. Of course, I have to come home first in order to get started on that list.

Give my love to everyone. You know you will always have all of my love. It's almost time for *lights out* and I must have my dream of you.

With all my heart, Johnny

On the Southwest Pacific War Front in the Philippines
Dad tells mom it has been two years of war for the Yanks. He's proud of his h*andy man skills* and feels like he is doing his share in the *war effort*.

12/07/43

Dear Sweet Mary,

Today makes two years of war for us Yankees. I'm so thankful I'm in the Fifth Army Air Corp. If I had been in the infantry, I'm sure I would have been shot. I always was a guy who got mad once in a while and when I did *all hell broke loose*. Besides since I am handy at fixing things, I feel like I'm doing my share in the war effort. I am still pining for a dance with my *favorite dance partner*.

We have some fellows from the States who sing. One of them is singing all the latest hits. Gosh, I'd love to try some of them out on the dance floor with my *favorite partner*.

I haven't seen native women lately. I guess it's the same story, *I have nothing to wear*. They don't wear much in the jungle. I'm getting sleepy so I better close. It would be wise of me to close before I say something I shouldn't. How do you like that line?

Lots of love, Johnny

On the Home Front in Manville, New Jersey
Mom enjoys sending a poem to dad.

12/12/43

My Dear Johnny,

I thought you would enjoy this little poem entitled **G.I. Issue**:

> Sitting on my G. I. bed, my G. I. hat upon my head,
> My G. I. pants, my G. I. shoes, everything free so nothing to lose.
> G. I. razor, G. I. comb, G. I wish that I was home.

They issue food that makes you grow, G. I. want a long furlough!

You get a belt, your shoes and your G. I. tie, everything free, nothing to buy.
You eat your food from G. I. plates, buy your needs at G. I. rates,
It's G. I. this and G. I. that, G. I. haircut, G. I. hat.
Everything is government issue, G. I wish that I could kiss you!
Pretty snappy, eh kid? If you want to send me any funny stories or poems, I would love to read them.

Love, Mary

On the Southwest Pacific War Front in the Philippines
Mom sends dad a sweet card and it made him feel warm and loved. He feels like he is the luckiest man alive. He misses seeing snow and wants to take her ice skating.

12/16/43

Dear Mary,

Today I got two very nice cards, one from you and the other from your family. Darling, your card was so sweet it made me feel all warm inside. Baby, if you feel that way about me, I'm a *dead duck*. You sure got me close to your heart and I feel like the luckiest man alive. You are the first girl that ever sent me to bed with tears in my eyes. I'll never stop feeling this way toward you and I hope you stay the way you are right now.

How's the snow these days? I haven't seen any in two years now. My radio and I are keeping steady company. I would feel lost without it. Have you gone ice skating yet or maybe you still have to learn? When I come strolling home, I'll teach you. When I say home, I mean your home for it feels like my home as well. Remember there is a soldier boy who is just eating his heart out for you.

With all my love, Johnny

On the Southwest Pacific War Front enjoying music from the Philippines

Mom sent dad an autograph book and he is enjoying having his friends write in it. He had trouble getting ink in the past but now he has all he needs.

12/18/43

My Darling Mary,

Well Dearest, here it is only seventeen days before Christmas and where am I located? Oh well, I'll have to make the best of it. I received seven *v-letters* today and I feel so much better now. In one of them you told me you wrote fourteen letters in two days. Boy, is my radio playing such sweet songs. I sure am helpless to do anything about it. I'm sitting here barefooted with my big toes *flapping* in the breeze.

I'm enjoying doing the thing I always look forward to and that's writing to my Darling Mary. You sent me the autograph book and I'm having fun letting some boys write in it. As for using ink, I can get all I want now.

There are a lot of *Yanks* around and *Tojo* should be hearing from us in the near future. This jungle is not bad. Of course, there are no bright lights or dance floors. However, I feel like I'm doing something now rather than when I was in a commando camp before.

I understand the boys back home want to be *relieved* from all that *horrible* atmosphere and baby we sure would like to help them. Remember, I could never do my feelings justice in letters alone. I've learned a lot about life in the Army. I'm set to settle down with my sweetheart and enjoy all those good things in store for us from married life.

Only you could show me the way.

With Love and a Big Heart, Johnny

On the Southwest Pacific War Front seeing natives somewhere in the Philippines

Dad's group gets a *kick* out of the natives who love nail polish and *strut around* like kings. One native even tried to drive a truck. He gave his friends quite a scare!

12/21/43

Dearest Mary,

The other day we had some natives in our camp area helping us to do some of the work. When we line up in a straight line to present ourselves, what do you think happened next? The natives jumped in our line and giggled very loudly. I guess they were enjoying themselves. Some of these natives have very big stomachs on them, and we often wonder where they get their beer. They love nail polish so one of the boys gave them some. They got so excited. One even *strutted around* like a king while others made all kinds of designs on their ladies. They can't speak English so this presents a problem when you want to tell them to work longer. However, when it gets closer to quitting time, one of them starts talking with a Bronx accent. They are not so dumb after all.

One of the natives said "Me make machine go". He got into a truck and after giving him some instructions on how to steer, he tried it out. However, he got mixed up and tried to steer from the bottom of the wheel with both hands together. The others on the truck yelled because they were afraid. When he finally caught on, he could steer as straight as an arrow and then they cheered him on. They are very friendly and rather good workers.

I'm glad you got my cards and understand those Aussie Christmas cards. You say I praise you too much to my folks. I could never tell them everything so don't be so modest. You are the best. How is the snow and ice? I've forgotten how it looks and feels. Don't worry, I can still remember what you look like, baby.

With Happy Memories, I remain, Your Johnny

On the Southwest Pacific War Front hearing *war news popping* in the Philippines
Dad gets word that American troops have landed in Rabaul, Australia. He is hopeful thinking this will speed up the war. Dad and his friends are enjoying mom's homemade peanut brittle in his Christmas package. He especially liked getting a picture of mom.

12/23/43

My Dear Sweetheart,

Today I received the package you sent with all those useful things. Thank you so much and you can be sure I will put everything to good use.

I hear our troops are landing near Rabaul, Australia and it looks like things are *popping* now. Our Air Corp. sure gives the Japs gray hair, that's if they have any hair. I met some boys who were over those targets and they can't see how the Japs can stand it. Too many bombs makes a person go *bomb-happy* and they go insane from it all. I'm guessing most of the Japs have a *screw loose* or something.

These attacks led the United States, China, Australia and several other countries to formally declare war on Japan. The Soviet Union was heavily involved in large scale hostilities with Europe. The axis countries maintained their neutrality agreement with Japan. Germany declared war on the United States in solidarity with Japan citing as justification the American attacks on German vessels ordered by Roosevelt.

I'll say "good bye" for now. I am thinking of you so much and missing you a whole lot.

Lots of Love, Johnny

On the Southwest Pacific War Front spending a holiday in the Philippines Dad is truly grateful to have received mom's peanut brittle. He has been able to find some bottles of beer but it is not as strong as *jungle juice*.

12/24/43

Dearest Mary,

Here it is the *night before Christmas not a creature is stirring* but a good deal of mice and I ain't kidding. I'm very busy mending my stockings so I can hang them up. I don't expect to find much in them, just a few snakes and perhaps a little lizard.

I'm on K.P. duty tomorrow but it won't be too bad because there will be three times as many K.P.'s on duty. After the show last time, we had one bottle of beer for each man and it sure *hit the spot*. Of course, it's not as strong as *jungle juice* but it goes down nice and cold anyhow.

Darling, the peanut brittle you sent was very tasty. Just ask the boys if they enjoyed it after I told them you made it yourself. So far everyone is living large. I guess you are a good cook. There wasn't anything I liked better than to receive your package with your picture first. I am a different person without you.

By now you should know I'm in New Guinea but don't you start worrying your pretty head about it. This place is very safe and has been for some time. Well Dear, I do hope Christmas finds you happy as can be. That's all that matters to me.

Love, Your Johnny

On the Southwest Pacific War Front in New Guinea
It's Christmas Day but dad is on K. P. duty. He shows everyone mom's picture. He is lonely but writing to mom makes him feel more connected.

12/25/43

My Darling Mary,

This day is different. Well it is for I'm on K. P. fighting Japs, the pots and the pans. What a battle, but I emerged *without a scratch* and my stomach was full of chicken.

Everyone who comes in my tent sees your picture. They always ask "Is that your wife?" Of course I have to say "no" even if it hurts. Some day I will be able to say "yes" that is after you say "yes" first. How are the States? Did Little Orphan Annie find a home? Did Dick Tracy catch up with *Pistol Packing Mama?* I can imagine how those *boy crazy* girls you speak of carry on. Some day they will regret it. It only takes one mistake to *wake them up.*

Did I ever tell you about my brother's cars? Walter has a 1939 Studebaker sedan. Stanley's car is a 1942 Ford V-8 and my car is a *rattle trap*. Oh well, it sounds like that anyway. You have to admit it *parks* pretty good, eh kid. You can bet I miss it terribly. I do hope you miss it too. These lonely *spells* we get are awful but at least you have your family to cheer you up. It's quite different with me.

If you can handle me in a *delicate* manner it remains to be seen. Pretty sure of yourself, eh kid. I have just about told you everything about myself at this time. I'll close with a heart full of love and a big wish to spend next Christmas together.

With all my love, Your Johnny

On the Southwest Pacific War Front anticipating a rest for New Guinea troops Dad is expecting to be going on a ten day leave where he will go to MacKay, North Queensland, Australia which is reserved for New Guinea troops. He thinks he will have many questions to answer about the war when he gets home.

Mary Jane Juzwin

12/29/43

My Darling Mary,

I expect to be going on a ten day leave soon and it will feel good to get back to Australia again for a visit. I will go to MacKay, North Queensland which is a place reserved for New Guinea troops.

This distance between us sure is something but I feel our hearts are closer than ever. That means a lot to this soldier boy out here in the jungle. Some day I'll show yours truly how much and baby just prepare yourself for all the good things to come.

As I sit here all by my lonesome, I think of all those happy hours we spent together. I'm positive now that I really neglected you. I only saw you three times a week. Ain't that awful? I have opened my eyes now and will do much better when I return home. Of course, should you object, your Pop can get his gun out and fix me. I know it will be rather hard to get you alone. There will be so many questions asked, such as, how many Japs did you kill? I just tell the truth and say "I didn't even see one".

Your Loving Johnny

CHAPTER THREE

1944 – THE WAR CONTINUES AT A GREAT PACE

On the Home Front in Manville, New Jersey
A New Year begins quietly at Mom's home. She still looks forward to dad's letters and has to be content with that form of *keeping in touch*.

01/01/44

My Darling Johnny,

Happy New Year! I have Mother by my side while I'm writing to you. This is how I'm spending my time on New Years Eve *ringing out the old and ringing in the new*. I'm looking at your picture and I have tears in my eyes. I'm wishing we could be together. Some of my tears are happy because we still stay in touch by writing. It is wonderful that we're still sweethearts only with tears of sorrow because we can't be together on account of this war. I want you to remember nothing can take away the happiness we have shared. I keep memories and happy thoughts of more times we shall spend together.

There is a quarter of a moon and the stars are shining brightly. I'm sitting in the living room where I wish you were with me. Mother is calling me to come downstairs for she knows I feel *very blue* and she doesn't want to leave me out of her sight. I join her with a heavy heart. I'll say my evening prayers and go to sleep with your picture beside me.

My love to You, Mary

On the Southwest Pacific War Front still on leave in Australia
Dad is teasing mom by telling her about his very frequent visitor, namely a nice, *big fat* mouse. He says it's the kind that make women scream and jump up on a table but he assures mom her will always remain at her side to protect her.

01/05/44

Dearest Mary,

I'm a bit *screwy* this evening but happy as usual. How are you? Did you see the New Year in or did you sleep through it? I stayed up until 3:00 a.m. Has my mail been coming through? I know I got a few letters numbered wrong, but I think you can figure out which one was written first.

I've been receiving a very frequent visitor who is just passing through my tent. It is a nice, *big, fat* mouse. You know the kind that make women scream and jump up on a table. They don't seem to realize when they do this, their dress flies up above their knees. I bet you are afraid of them, but don't worry because I will always be there to protect you.

The jungle is fine but as usual I say "Jungle, I want to go home Johnny". It's almost time for my coffee which I must have before I go to bed. Some of those sweet kisses took care of me but that was before I heard from Uncle Sammy. Now I have an awful substitute.

Well my sweet, I will say so long for now.

With Lots of that Love Stuff, Johnny

On the Home Front in Manville, New Jersey
It is winter now and very cold. Mom or her sister, Jeannie has to walk over a mile to get to the Post Office to pick up any letters.

01/06/44

Hello Sweets,

How is tricks with you? Are you a good boy and have you been taking care of yourself? I wrote you some letters but I didn't get a chance to mail them but I will soon. I hope to be able to go to the Post Office. The cold weather is the worst part of winter. Writing letters isn't so bad but mailing them is awful because we have to walk over a mile to get to the post office. The Post Office is closed when I get up to go to work and then it is closed before I come home from work. Thank goodness for Jeannie as she goes to pick up the mail for me.

We had rain most of the day and especially around the time I was coming home from work. I got all soaked! After all I do have fifteen blocks to walk home from the bus line. I was so cold that I stripped all my wet clothes off and got into a nice hot tub and took a bath. It felt so good!

All my Love, Mary

On the Southwest Pacific War Front returning to New Guinea
Dad is excited to find a lot of mail for him. His *little shack* is still standing and he assures mom he has plenty of room for her letters so he wants her to keep them coming.

01/06/44

My Dear Mary,

I had a few days furlough but now kid, I'm back in camp. Everything is the same here. There are a few new faces but my *little shack* is still standing. I was delighted to find so much mail waiting for me. Eighty percent of it was from you so now you know why I'm so happy. Darling, how could you ever think I would throw away your letters? I have room for one thousand more so just keep them coming.

This is *leap year*. How about leaping in my direction? It's not too far to go. I certainly would be waiting for you no matter how long it would take to get here. Take good care of your heart for me. Consider yourself kissed *good night* although it would be much sweeter in person.

Lots of Love, Johnny

On the Southwest Pacific War Front still in New Guinea
Dad tells mom should he get home before the war ends, he'll try to be sent to Fort Monmouth radio school. He expresses sympathy as she was *stuck* in bed on Christmas Day.

01/09/44

Dearest Honey,

If I should get home before the war has ended, I will make a *large* attempt to be sent to Fort Monmouth radio school. It's only four miles from my home. I haven't got the lightest idea how the Army will handle my return. I'm just trying to think ahead.

I'm glad to hear the battle of what department you should work in is over. You must be a very valuable, knowledgeable worker on the *A1* list. You're always on my *A1* list, baby. Please go to all the dances for I want you to have a good time. Make sure you remember our dances as well.

Baby, you're *stuck* with me. I'm so sorry to hear you spent Christmas Day in bed with a sore throat. I spent mine fighting the Japs on K.P. that day.

The picture I sent you of myself must be getting a lot of attention. I'm jealous of my picture because I can only imagine it slept under your pillow. Woo Hoo! Oh well, some pictures have all the luck.

A Heart full of Love, Johnnie

On the Southwest Pacific War Front in Australia
Dad is on his leave staying over night with a swell bunch of guys from his old company. He assures mom that he is still many miles away from the Japs. Even on leave, he still continues to keep her in his mind and heart.

01/11/44

Dearest Mary,

I finally got started on my leave. I'm much closer to my destination. I'm staying over night at a detachment of my old company and they are a swell bunch. I am many miles away from the Japs. How these places change from dirt roads to paved roads sure is something. Uncle Sam doesn't waste any time.

We enjoyed some swell ice tea for lunch today and I guess I had about six cups of it. Boy did it taste good! Last night a bunch of us went swimming in the ocean around 9:30 p.m. We had a great time! The water wasn't too warm for a change. Of course, you weren't nearby so I didn't get a chance to dunk anyone. Rest assured, there will come a day for that.

Dad roasting a pig

Even though I'm on leave, I just can't get you off my mind. Why would I want to do that anyway? Darling, things are working out nice for me and my luck continues to be good. Perhaps I will be home by mid-summer so we could have a date to go swimming. I can't wait to see you in a bathing suit with all those *lovely curves*.

Lots of Love and Kisses, Your Johnny

On the Home Front in Manville, New Jersey
Mom writes dad a letter using *funny war stationary*. The whole family suffers as they all get colds and the *grip*.

01/16/44

My Dear Johnny,

I guess I'm punished for showing off by telling the girls in the plant about the letters you send me. Everyone in our family had colds and I had the *grip*. I could feel that tight burning grip around my throat and chest and it sure got me down.

Honey, I am proud of you and what you're doing so of course I tell my friends and family about your letters. Now I have twenty one letters of yours to reread and answer. I just don't know where to start. I'm getting better now so I'll write as many letters as I can. I hope you are feeling well and having some great adventures.

Love, Your Mary

On the Southwest Pacific War Front playing tennis in Australia
Dad has an opportunity to play tennis with two very good players. They gave him quite a workout but he did manage to beat them. He's not accustomed to being free and doesn't know what to do with himself.

01/18/44

My Dear Mary,

Yesterday I played about four hours of tennis with two very good Australian players. They sure gave me a *work out*, however, I beat them anyway. Australia is a *tennis country* and just chock full of good players.

I rode all around town on my bike and checked out everything, except you of course. Darn it anyhow! No matter what I do I can't get you off my mind. Who would want to do this, not me? I know there must be at least six letters waiting for me back in camp. I can't wait to go back and enjoy reading them. Half the time, I don't know what to do with myself. I'm not accustomed to being free this way.

I hope you haven't been worrying your pretty little head about me for I'm very safe. Being in the Fifth Army Air Corp. makes it this way. The Japs haven't got a chance to reach us by air and that's the only way they have.

Darling, waiting for our day together seems so much closer now. I know you'll never disappoint me for being with you is all I ever want. With tears of joy I say this, that's how much I mean it. Remember, I mean every word I say from the bottom of my heart.

I do hope I'm still *A1* with you. I'm going to the theater and I'll try to make believe you are sitting next to me. I'll feel alone but I know you'll be there in spirit.

All my Love to You, Johnny

On the Southwest Pacific War Front in Australia
Dad wants to keep his dancing skills sharp for mom so he attends any dances he can find. He tells her the jungle *makes one quiet* and listen to animal noises. She is happy to find out he's not wasting money on drinks at a bar.

01/20/44

Dearest Mary,

Here I am somewhere in Australia enjoying my leave. I hope it's my last one overseas. In the evening, I went to the dance as usual. I spent my time dancing every dance on the floor. Why would I want to sit them out? I can do all the sitting I want in camp. As I dance, naturally I talk to the victims and some of the answers I hear are very funny. I say to them "My you dance very nicely". They come back with "Now take it easy Bud, I ain't got my snow shoes on". The *snow job* is a common expression around here. I'm guessing it will be listed in the Aussie dictionary. The definition of a *snow job* is more than three words said to an Aussie babe by a Yank.

The first two days I couldn't get used to talking to anyone. I'm telling you the jungle *makes one quiet* so you can listen to the animal noises. So many Yanks spend $100.00 a week for drinks and that adds up to $300.00 after three weeks. Please don't think I throw money away like that. I don't believe in throwing my money away on nothing. I think of you and love you so much.

All my Heart filled Love, Johnny

On the Southwest Pacific War Front hearing war news in Australia Dad hears *through the grapevine* that both the European War as well as the Pacific War is going *great guns*. He enjoyed another movie starring Loretta Young. He says mom should have heard the boys whistle when she came on the screen.

02/01/44

My Darling Mary,

Last night I had a dream about you. I think it was because I had some fruit cake that my sister-in-law Marie sent me. I dreamt I was home for four days and for some unknown reason I couldn't go to see you. Boy, I was really trying, but before I was able to find the problem, I woke up. *Darn it*! I never did figure out what the problem had been. I know this may sound like a *snow job*, but honestly cross my heart it's true.

I have heard that the European and the Pacific wars are going *great guns*. When I was listening to my radio the other day, it was mentioned that Germany is telling its people that Berlin is *in danger*.

I saw a swell picture last night called **Now or Never**. You ought to hear the boys whistle when Loretta Young came on the screen. She has what it takes to make a sweater look good. You sure have it too so there, as if you didn't know it already.

Here is a *corny* joke for you. There was a salesman who worked in a furniture store.

A pair of newlyweds walked in and said they wanted twin beds instead of one bed for she was a *timid soul*. They picked out two twin beds. The salesman then said "You better buy a rug as well". "Why" asked the couple. He said, "You must have a rug between the two beds". He added "Too many couples have told me they wished they had a rug because they wore out the floor walking back and forth between the beds".

You see hon, why I don't want twin beds. If you are as innocent as you claim, you should believe the reason I stated. However, we do know the difference eh, Hon? Now don't blush for I can't see you anyway. I feel like a monkey tonight. I could just climb all over you if only I could get my hands on you.

I got a large amount of Jap *Paso money* so I'm sending some to all my friends. Of course you are definitely one of my friends so you will get some in the mail as well. You are my sweetheart and will always be first with me.

All my Love, Johnny

On the Southwest Pacific War Front catching up on rest in Australia Dad indulges himself with an all day rest. Mom teases him by adding an imprint of lips to her letters. *Tojo's* stations say his location was bombed and completely destroyed.

02/14/44

Today was my day off so I spent all day sleeping, no kidding this climate makes you want to sleep. I received a few letters from you with those luscious lips on them. Baby, don't do this to me, so close yet so far away.

Those lips look so tempting and this Yank can't wait to get down to *real business.*

I'm listening to some very good American music. It's especially for troops in New Guinea, the Aussies and the Yanks. This music is coming from a Tokyo radio station. They think we will fall for their *baloney.* Mary, how would you like to hear one of *Tojo's* stations say that this place was bombed. It was completely destroyed. I guess you can consider me gone with all my pals. Of course, they didn't even send a butterfly over our area during those raids they mentioned.

Oh, the life of a man in the jungle! Pull over and greet a vine or two hanging from a tree, but first make sure it's not a snake in disguise. Keep smiling dearest.

Lots of Love and Kisses, Johnnie

On the Southwest Pacific War Front in Australia
Dad is trying to get caught up with answering mom's letters. He is telling her to be patient while he checks on the rotation of men for the month's quota.

02/15/44

My Little Darling,

I'm still trying to get caught up with answering your letters. You must talk the gals' heads off at the plant. Imagine them telling you they're dreaming about me. I think it's best not to plan too far in advance as far as we are concerned. The past year's rotation has averaged two men a month for its quota. I am about twenty fifth on the list. It seems they don't think of you until you have thirty four months of service. I have about five more months and then maybe something might happen with my rotation.

Now darling, don't get all excited. It's only my impression and nothing is official. Don't get your curves in *a tizzy*, but please do take care of them for me.

All my Love, Johnnie

On the Southwest Pacific War Front still on leave in Australia
Dad's hoping the rats haven't carried his tent away. He misses the winter season and all the *fuss* mom always made every time he visited. He can't wait to say "meet my future wife" to his family and friends and watch their eyes pop!

02/16/44

My Darling Girl,

I'm still on leave and I hope the rats haven't walked away with my little tent. I'll fix them if they try anything. I bought some poison for this purpose.

I hope you haven't been catching many colds this winter. Winter must be something. I've almost forgotten how snow looks. Please be very careful and try to stay healthy for me. I really miss the *fuss* you made every time I came to your house. I do receive letters from home and they always ask about you. They know I'm happy when things are okay with us. I'll be so proud to say "Meet my future wife" and then watch their eyes pop!

Listening to the radio makes me *cry for joy*. Our troops are jumping the islands closer to Tokyo and things are really happening now. I have to say I'm very lucky to be in the Army Air Corp. The boys in our company are handy like me and we've a lot in common.

I was so afraid I would lose you after the last night we spent together. I'm happy it turned out very different. I bet you thought you wouldn't hear from me after a while. Little did you know what went on in my heart.

We started to call each other dear and now it's more serious. Am I glad I learned to dance. I don't believe I told you that story. At first I took six lessons, after that I practiced on my *victims*. You're a *really dangerous girl* and in a way I like so that's why I fell in love with you. Keep up the good lovin'.

Lots of Love and that sort of sweet stuff, Your Johnny

On the Southwest Pacific War Front leaving Australia back to New Guinea Dad will be leaving tomorrow for *wide open* space and the jungle. He enjoys ice cream and malted milk knowing it will be some time before he is able to enjoy another treat like that.

02/17/44

My Darling Mary,

Well, tomorrow morning I leave for the *wide open spaces* and the *jungle*. I feel very satisfied right now. I spent all day drinking. No, not the hard stuff! I only had ice cream and malted milk because I know it will be some time before I see another treat like that.

I went to the dance as usual getting in my last fling. I saw a funny thing this afternoon. A car started off like a *house on fire* in first gear. Then the fellow tried to put it in second gear, he accidentally put it in reverse. The darn car jumped four feet in the air and went backwards. The car was going pretty fast at the time so it was a miracle how it ever got into reverse. I don't think you know how to drive, but baby you sure can park.

Darling, I can't wait for our first date when I get back home. I have so much to tell you. I really want to show you how much I love you. The first date we had before I went into the Army Air Core, I told you "some day I'm going to marry you". Baby I meant it! The sweet memories of you keep me going along happily in my work so I can do my part for this war. If I said "I miss you a lot" it is only putting it mildly.

Lots of Love and Kisses, Johnny

On the Southwest Pacific War Front in New Guinea
Dad is reminiscing about his family who think mom is *tops*. He starts talking and planning all the places he and mom should visit and how he wants to show her off as *his girl* to his relatives in Passaic, New Jersey.

02/18/44

Dear Sweet One,

I was very happy to hear about my brother visiting you. Their letters say they think you are *tops* and that goes for the rest of the family as well. I wish someone would take a picture of you in your bathing suit and send it to me. As you know, I'm anxious to see you and your *curves* in a bathing suit.

While I was in Australia, I did come across a few British sailors. I understand from what they told me that Asbury Park, New Jersey is just full of *babes with curves*. That's one place we must go to see together when I get my release from this Army.

My commando mission to McKay is over now. I'm wishing to be sitting on the sofa with you at night and the rest of that *togetherness* stuff. I'm sitting here *all by my lonesome* listening to the *wireless* radio. In case you are interested, the programs are swell. I'll be glad when I am able to take you to Passaic, New Jersey to meet some of my relatives. They are a swell bunch and I can't wait to show you off as *my girl*. Hoping to see you soon and missing you an awful lot.

Lots of Sweet Stuff, Johnny

On the Southwest Pacific War Front in New Guinea

Dad is working in the jungle and waiting for real *honest to goodness* ice cream. He is enjoying the U. S. O. shows and looking at mom's picture. He says tomorrow is rifle *inspection* so he is polishing his *trusty* rifle.

02/23/44

Dear Lonesome One,

This is Lonesome #2. I'm *sweating out* the ice cream machine because we plan to have *real, honest to goodness* ice cream tomorrow. Hurray! We all enjoyed the U. S. O. show and most of the fun comes from the crowd. Such ideas the jungle puts in your head!

Your picture is looking at me in the usual way and I feel like doing certain things but of course, I cannot at the present time. Once again, it's a beautiful evening outside here. I always write to you at night for we spent many nights together. Somehow I feel right *in the groove* at this time.

Each day brings me closer to when I get to be a U. S. O. Commando. I admit it will be rough fighting all your charms, however, I have a *special* plan to handle the situation. Tomorrow is *rifle inspection* so I polished my trusty rifle. It's just a check to see if we are taking care of our equipment.

This *drafted* heart of mine misses you so much sweetheart. Please keep your pretty face full of smiles for me.

Lots of Love Stuff, Johnny

On the Southwest Pacific War Front still in New Guinea
The news of the war is it is *moving at a great pace* and the Japs are *catching hell* now. Dad is pleased for there's a new First Sergeant and it is one of the *old* boys in our outfit.

Mary Jane Juzwin

02/25/44

Dearest Kid,

I'm just sitting around doing nothing so I made the great decision to write a *sugar report* to you. Enclosed you will find a pen I picked up for you in Australia. You must have quite a collection by now. I'll be glad when I can be added to your collection. The news about the war is that it's *moving at a great pace* and the Japs are *catching hell* now. I have some more *native* pictures to send to you in the near future.

We have a new First Sergeant now and it's one of the *old boys* in our company. He's a swell guy and we are all glad to see him get the break. He will jump from Buck Sergeant to Master Sergeant as far as we can tell at the present moment.

My radio is playing *full blast* with such wonderful programs. I know they would be so much better if you were by my side. We could be enjoying all that *great nonsense*. Have you forgotten what it was like to be together? All I need is a *big hunk* of you and I'd be *perking on all my cylinders* at a great pace. Of course, I'd behave. If you shut your eyes when I kiss you, I'll make sure you get an awful lot of attention. I'll have you *gasping for air*. Ain't I a brute? I frighten myself especially when I look in the mirror.

The boys are giving our departing Lieutenant a party and I assure you there won't be any water. We all hate to see him leave. We could call him by his first name and it was okay with him. The usual way is *Sir this* and *Sir that* but not for him. Well Dearest, without trying I have completed a letter. See what you do to this guy!

Closing with All my Love to you, Johnnie

On the Southwest Pacific War Front in New Guinea
Dad praises mom for her ability to *secure* packages and thanks her for the mushroom soup and salami. There is a young Filipino boy working

with the group. He is only fourteen years old and has *successfully* killed seventeen Japs. He wants to stay with Dad's group wherever they go. He is also enjoying music in the Mess Hall.

02/28/44

My Darling Mary,

I received your fifth package today and it was in very good shape. It is the one with the mushroom soup and salami inside. You see, hon, packages do get here eventually. They usually get wet or some fall apart if they are not secured properly. You sure know how to *secure* a package. It's no wonder they come through intact. You're some package yourself. You're my *sweater* gal. There are two kinds of *sweater* gals, one looks as big as a *sweater* and the other looks swell like you.

Here is a little poem for you:
   Bee as it may, a bee is such a busy soul.
   He has no time for birth control and that is why
   in times like these there are so many sons-of-bees.

We have a young Filipino boy working for us. He's a swell kid. At fourteen, he joined the guerillas and went into the hills to fight the Japs. He fought for three years before we got here. He has seventeen Japs to his credit officially and has an American Army rifle with a permit to carry it. He was a guide for a long time and is an excellent shot with all our guns. He uses slang just like us and he wants to stay with us no matter where we go.

Well my Darling, I wish I could show you in person how much I appreciate all those packages. Take care of yourself, my sweet one.

All my Love and Kisses, Johnny

On the Southwest Pacific War Front serving in New Guinea

Dad complains, once again, about the mail that has been painfully slow. He is listening to a new radio station from Port Moresby, New Guinea. General McArthur spoke as well and dad is hoping to finally get some *real up-to-date* information. He asks mom if she got the *Merino* wool foot rug he sent while he was on leave in McKay.

03/02/44

My Dear Sweet One,

Here is a little note that I have *cooked up* during my lunch hour. I just had a very good meal. We had French fries and a lot of regular things prepared in a way that made one enjoy them. We now have a radio in our Mess Hall so we enjoy music while we *beat our gums* with this horse meat. There is no ice cream but I knew it wouldn't last. Boo Hoo!

Did you get the rug I sent you while I was on leave? It keeps your feet warm when you get out of bed in the morning. Of course, I hope my letters keep your heart warm. The rug is made of the finest wool in the world called *Merino*. I do hope you don't think it is too nice to use. It was the best thing I could find in McKay. Of course, had I gone to Sydney, I could have gotten something else for that is the modern part of Australia.

Some people still don't know there is currently a war. If someone shot his mother-in-law, he would get the complete front page in the newspaper. Yet the large attacks in Rabaul, Indonesia only get a few lines. It sure is a *funny* world.

Darling, we are in love and we both know it. Isn't it wonderful at times but awful at other times? Having you for my sweetheart is like a *beautiful* dream.

I just heard a bell and we stuck our heads out thinking it was a *work call*. However, the first Sergeant said "ice cream".

You could hear mess kits rattling all over camp and it sounded like bells on a truck back home. Everyone made a *split second run* to be the first in line. Yeah, man it sure was good chocolate and vanilla! Well kid, this is all for now.

Lots of Love Always, Johnny

On the Southwest Pacific War Front in New Guinea
Dad sends mom a hilarious picture of himself *sporting a grass skirt* with shells on his chest. He has been rather busy repairing planes, jeeps and radios. Dad is lucky enough to receive a visit from a friend from his old company.

03/04/44

My Darling Mary,

I know I say this a lot but I haven't heard from you in over a week now. It feels like a long time so you see how you have *spoiled* me.

Enclosed is a picture of me going *native*. Some legs, eh kid? I hope the pose isn't too much for you Hon, but that's the way they look over here. Of course, it's become my *best* outfit. Notice the leg work. I'd like to see you in an outfit just like this.

Since fellows have been going home, I've been rather busy repairing planes, jeeps and radios. I am beginning to like this work more each day. When I *fooled around* doing work before, I never had the equipment like I have on hand now. I have learned a lot.

I'm getting used to this jungle gradually, but it is a *dead place*. We have not heard of any *Jap trouble* for a long time. They must be too busy running toward Tokyo. Don't forget to save me a *big hunk* of your love, sweetheart.

Loads of Love, Your Johnny

On the Home Front in Manville, New Jersey
Mom wishes dad a very *Happy Birthday* and sends him her love and a big kiss.

03/05/44

My Darling Johnny,

I just thought I would drop you a few lines as I have very little to tell you. Oh yeah! Did you have a *very Happy Birthday*? I hope so, or am I too early? Anyway, here is a big kiss for you. Johnny, how is my heart behaving? Oh now I remember where it is. You took my heart all the way overseas with you. You better be careful with it. Oh honey, I have so many of your letters to answer. Honestly dear, you are so wonderful to take the time to write to me so often.

I'm writing this letter right in my new bedroom. We had to make an entrance for the people upstairs, so we made a wall along the stairs. Mother and I bought a lovely *studio* couch and a nice little chest of drawers. At night, we open up the studio couch and it serves as a bed for my sister Jeannie and I. It looks lovely, but it is a little chilly as we have no heat in this area yet.

Dear, did I tell you I received your peanut can with the Australian ring and the other ring? When you get back, we'll both wear rings and we can be kind of twins. Okay?

Love, Your Dear Mary

On the Southwest Pacific War Front in New Guinea
Dad enjoyed a visit from a friend who is from his old company. He says this man is on his way home after completing three hundred hours as a radio *gunner* and he was able to come away with *barely a scratch*.

03/06/44

My Darling Mary,

How is your heart? Is it still warm for me or am I in the *dog* house? I was lucky to have a visit from my friend who is from my old company. He is on his way home after completing three hundred hours as a radio *gunner*. He was very lucky to come away with *barely a scratch*. The nearest he came to getting hit was two feet away. He had been in all those major victories you've been hearing about at home.

Life is awful without you and when we *tie that knot* things will be so wonderful. I can hardly wait, but I know I have to be patient. Remember somewhere there is a boy who is *eating his heart out* over you. That's me, of course.

Good night Sweetness, Johnnie

On the Home Front in Manville, New Jersey
Mom thinks about dad so much that she pictures him in her travels to and from work. She actually went to the bakery and got a roll of paper five feet long because she wanted to write a very long letter to him that was the exact height of herself.

03/10/44

Honey,

We have a new bus driver who takes us to and from work every day. Boy, I'm telling you he looks just like you. I couldn't take my eyes off him the first few days. I thought *Oh my, maybe that is Johnny. Maybe he came back and got a bus driver's job and forgot he had a girlfriend here. Maybe he has lost his memory and does not love me anymore.*

The thought almost drove me crazy, but after receiving a few more letters from you, I regained my mind! Then I knew it was another fellow. However, I'm telling you his looks, ways, actions and especially his black hair reminded me of you. Don't start worrying about me now because I realize I was wrong.

A month ago, two girls from Jeannie's department named Tessie and Ida, Genevieve, Jeannie and I went to a *vaudeville* show and movie in Bound Brook, New Jersey. While we were there, we saw another fellow that looked so much like you that he made me cry. I am such a *cry baby*! This fellow played approximately six different harmonicas and he sure was great. It only costs ten cents to go from Manville to Bound Brook. The bunch of us girls had a *grand* time, however, I wouldn't want to do it too often. I might get *spoiled*. However, I do hope to take mom and dad out someday soon to the same places.

The following Thursday some fellows came to visit us. We were folding some of mom's wash so they helped us. Well, everything was going along fine until we came to dad's *long* underwear! After that we came to my brother Leo's underwear and some of mom's personal things as well as our personal items! Oh how *red faced* and embarrassed we were! We burst out laughing and ran into the other room. My mom thought we were going crazy until she found out what all the excitement was that took place.

The other day, we met two other fellows, Murlie from Kentucky and a Polish fellow named Chet. We walked downtown and had some soda. My mom invited them in for dinner. When that Polish fellow saw what we were going to eat for dinner, his eyes nearly *popped* out! Mom had made potato, cabbage and prune dumplings. After dinner, we all went for a walk downtown. When we got back home, I got *devilish* and turned out the lights in the living room. We danced to the music by the light of only the radio. After a while, the fellows left to catch the 10:45 p.m. bus to New Brunswick, New Jersey.

Johnny darling, when are you and I going to dance by only the light of the radio? The music will be playing on the radio and the music from our hearts will also be heard in our living room. I can hardly wait! Honey, I have to go downstairs and give my sister Jeannie a hand cleaning the house. I'll hurry *like the dickens* to get done and return to finish this letter. If I can't make it, you can picture me with a little house dress on and an apron over it. My hair will be tied up in a kerchief and I will be wearing ankle socks with my little house shoes. What a sight!

I don't remember how I ended this long letter although I went to the bakery and bought a long roll of paper. I wanted to write a very long letter. I folded it in half and kept writing. The letter measured five feet long which is my exact height and sixteen inches wide. Sweetheart, let people say anything they want. I only know one thing and that is you are meant for me and I am meant for you. I must owe you a bunch of letters. Somehow, I can't catch up with you. Remember now, I'm not complaining, only explaining. I can write to you all day and night and never run short of words or get too tired.

With Love, Your Sweetheart

On the Home Front in Manville, New Jersey
Mom is truly in love with dad and they are getting very comfortable with each other. She is amazed he picked out a perfect rug for their bedroom.

03/12/44

Dearest Honey,

You mean so much to me. Darling, what a big surprise I got when I received that beautiful fur rug. I love it! It will look beautiful in our bedroom. How do you know what I like? Honey, you're certainly spoiling me. Honestly, I can't get over the fact that you are so different from all the fellows I've been out with on dates. You seem to know everything about me.

I will keep on dreaming until you come home and make my dreams come true. I hope you enjoy reading my long letter as I enjoyed writing it for you.

With Love, Mary

On the Southwest Pacific War Front sending pictures of natives in New Guinea Dad tries to picture mom in a suit and how she might look as a *housewife*. He likes the *innocent, shy* look on her face but he doubts she is completely innocent. He points out the fact that he needs a wife because he has a hole in his pants. Dad's birthday is soon and he is sending *Yank* newspapers for mom to save.

03/14/44

My Dearest Love,

Today I feel happy for many reasons. The main one is I received a letter containing the pictures of the whole family. I enjoy your *cute* figure. Boy you're *some eyeful* dressed in that suit. You're worth at least one half dozen whistles by passing *wolves*.

I see the way you will look as a *housewife*. I'm not a bit disappointed, but I'll have to *slow you down* for you work too hard. I'll be your helper so you can hold me in your arms and tell me I did a *good* job. That *shy* look on your face is cute, however, I doubt you're that innocent. I see what you'll look like after I come home from work. You'll drop everything, grab *no not me* a can opener and say "Honey here's your supper".

Enclosed is an *awful* picture of the natives and myself. Notice the hole in my pants, doesn't that prove I need a wife? I am sending you some *Yank* newspapers to save for me. Now I have a general idea how you look when you are wearing your bathing suit. Boy will I be glad to stroll along the beach and pass all my *wolf* friends. Remember there will come a day when we can plan many more activities to do together. I will make you very happy now by closing my big mouth!

Lots of Love and Kisses, Johnnie

On the Home Front in Manville, New Jersey
Mom and dad have to settle for just hugging and kissing each other's pictures. They have sent each other some poems and songs as well.

03/22/44

Dear Johnny,

It seems so long since we last talked face to face. I don't mind reading your letters and answering them but it is definitely not the same as person to person. Oh Johnny, I can't wait until you come home and take me in your arms and kiss me. As for the present time, I guess I will have to settle for just hugging and kissing your picture.

I have a little poem for you:
>It seems so very strange the way we two met.
>learning to care through letters we sent.
>My heart will remember, my mind can't forget.
>
>I'll cherish the pins you gave me.
>Your wings I'll wear over my heart.
>Your face in my mind grows clearer.
>I pray we shall never part.
>
>Recalling our first meeting the way we smiled as we stared,
>hoping that you felt and I was hoping that you cared.
>before we two had to part I knew deep in my heart,
>no matter what the future holds, we will never grow apart.

Love always, Mary

On the Southwest Pacific War Front in New Guinea

It's Dad's birthday, however, it feels like any ordinary day for there is no celebration when one is in the Army. He tells mom the reason New Guinea is rough on him is because he can't see his *Darling* Mary. He is sending more *Yank* newspapers for her to add to the collection.

03/23/44

My Darling Mary,

I bet you can't guess what day it is today? Yes, it's my birthday and the second one away from home. It's just an ordinary day for me. I didn't even have a *nip* of *jungle juice* all day. The mail delivery has been awful lately. I'm guessing the postman is asleep or something. When I get home, people will ask me if New Guinea was rough on me.

I'll tell them "You bet, because I couldn't see my Mary for what felt like a lifetime." This is why it was so rough for me.

I'm sending some more *Yank* newspapers along to you today. I could make some remarks in them but then I would have to worry about the censor. Please save them for me so I can show them to our kids some day. Some of the articles apply to us and a good part of it is filled by the Fifth Air Force of which I am also a representative.

Well Darling, think of me as I do you and don't ever lose hope.

All my Heart, Johnny

On the Home Front in Manville, New Jersey
Mom and dad's relationship is growing closer with every letter they send and receive.

03/23/44

Hello Darling,

How are you? I am fine but sometimes I feel blue especially when I think of you so far away and in danger with this war. I am thinking of the little song called **You'll never know** by Ella Fitzgerald. The words help me to focus on you and I. It helps me to feel more connected to you. This is how I'm feeling right now. I miss you very much.

With Love, Your Sweetheart Mary

On the Home Front in Manville, New Jersey
Mom is now addressing dad as *Darling* and she is concerned about his health.

03/26/44

My Darling,

You speak of coming home quite often. Then you ruin it by saying it's only a dream and you'll have to pinch yourself a few times to make sure it's true. Don't you believe in miracles? Well I do.

You also tell me of how awful that jungle is and I know how hot and miserable it is. I know how lonely you are in that *hell hole*. Then you try to cover it up by saying it's because you miss me too much. Sweetheart, that's the same with me sometimes but wait until you come home to me. It will be our *heaven* and our life shall begin anew. We shall live again in each other's arms.

Your Honey, Mary

On the Southwest Pacific War Front in New Guinea

Dad is wondering whether he will gain a higher rank because of his overseas service. He says he has gained a lot of knowledge.

03/26/44

My Darling Mary,

Sweetheart, I got your reply from the last letter I wrote. Gosh honey, I didn't mean to make you feel so blue. After receiving your sweet letter, I felt like digging a hole and crawling inside. I don't know what got into me. It must have been things around here that put me in a *bad* mood even before I got your sweet reply.

It looks hopeless for me to get *something to show* for my overseas service. I know you will love me no matter what rank I hold. I have gone through so much in comparison to these who come from the States as Sergeant or a higher rank. As for gaining as much knowledge as I can, I've been made a Corporal twice in two months for two different companies. I would like being a Sergeant. When I get home, I don't want to be pushed around by some *egghead* who acquired a rank of Sergeant in three weeks fighting the *battle* of New York City.

I know what kind of girl you are and boy am I lucky. I found the most wonderful girl who is clean, honest and sweet. You are also thoughtful and baby you *swept me off my feet!* Honey, don't you ever think I'm playing with your heart. Ever since I told you I was going to marry you, I've been preparing for our future. Yes Darling, you mean the world to me. We are sweethearts and we will remain united that way.

With All my Love, Johnny

On the Southwest Pacific War Front in New Guinea
He receives a surprisingly *large* letter from mom. Dad requests some time off from his work schedule. He asks his *Section Chief* for extra time so he can read it. He showed the letter to the *Chief* so he would believe the request.

Mary Jane Juzwin

03/27/44

My Darling Mary,

I was so surprised to get your *large* letter. I want you to know I'll never worry about you again. All day long, my friends kept asking me to let them read your large letter. I think they were jealous. I asked my *Section Chief* if I could have the morning off. He asked me why and I told him I have a long letter to read. I showed him how *big* the letter was so he wouldn't think I was trying to put one over on him.

Darling, I can see you really care for me and even if you had been trying to keep me guessing, that letter gave you away. Yes, your heart spoke to me.

Now I know for sure how you really feel about me. I got your birthday card and I knew you wouldn't forget me. I spent that day just like any ordinary day because nothing is celebrated in the Army when you are overseas. Besides, there wasn't any *jungle juice* in sight.

Having you as my sweetheart even while I am so far away, makes our *love test* a real one. It is wonderful to think in only three months we were able to realize how much we care about each other. I wish I could keep hugging and kissing you until you holler *murder!* I haven't kissed my girl for twenty two months. Do you see what I mean when I say "It's girls like you that make war so rough on us boys".

Have you looked around for a good spot to put our tent? As I explained to you in the past, I can't just forget about living in a tent. I know I wouldn't have to sweat in a *chow line* and just you wait until we get started on creating our *baseball team*.

Your letters sure *snapped* me out of that disappointing mood I had been experiencing for over a week. Your letters are so different from those first short ones. You are more comfortable with what you can say without me getting the wrong idea. You were even afraid to call me *Darling* then.

However, look at you now, so brave and sweet. You're always sticking by me and I appreciate it.

Love Always, Johnnie

On the Southwest Pacific War Front in New Guinea
Dad is answering mom's *large* letter by kissing the lips she stamped on it. He is ready to settle down, get married and tell the stork to bring a black haired baby boy to them.

03/29/44

My Dear One,

I finally get to answer your *large* letter by kissing the lips you sent on it. That's a preview of the treatment I expect to get when I come rolling in.

Here is the latest *corny* joke:

> A New Guinea *old timer* says "As I live and dream in this jungle, I dream of a *white mistress* but it all turns black to me now!

Gosh honey, you seem to have so many feelings and you cry over the silliest things.

I guess I'll have to get used to that. You always take things *to heart*. By the way, be sure to save me some room in your heart. I'm trying to keep *in shape* for you.

Love, Johnny

P. S. I feel so proud and happy to say "I have a wonderful girl waiting for me".

On the Southwest Pacific War Front in New Guinea
The most *dreadful* thing happens to dad. He receives a letter from mom that is all *stuck* together. He makes the best of it by reading only the front

and back pages. He does not want her to spend all her free time writing to him. He thinks he will have questions from his future kids asking if he ever saw Japs during the war.

03/31/44

Hello my Sweet,

The most *dreadful* thing happened. I never knew it could happen to us, but it did. I received a letter from you and all the pages were *stuck together*. I was only able to read the front and back page. Even so, I'm always satisfied with anything I receive from you whether it is long or short.

Don't spend all your time on me. We will have at least seventy five years together and you might get sick of me. Yes, about fifty years from now, I'll be telling our kids how I went overseas to fight the Japs but I never saw one *face to face*. I did see some Jap planes but only from far away.

Yours always, Johnny

On the Southwest Pacific War Front in New Guinea
Dad is excited as he informs mom that his company has their own radio station. A *lonely warrant officer* arranged for this benefit. Dad says he is a *swell egg*. He describes the girls' area which is *fenced in* by wire to keep the *wolves* away.

04/01/44

My Darling *Pin-Up* Girl,

It is April Fools Day so I feel right at home in this great little *shack* in the jungle. My radio is *blaring* like I'm hard of hearing. Our neighbors like to hear our company's own *jam session*. Yes we now have our own radio station. We can talk for about two hours and *kick* the Red Cross out. This makes our hearts *jump with joy* while we hold on to our tent pegs and have a picnic with *bully beef* otherwise known as *horse in disguise*.

The program accepts song requests so we're getting phone calls. We own one hundred and fifty records so we play until we make ourselves homesick. This is due to a *lonely warrant officer* who is a *swell egg*. A Red Cross gal is announcing for us. You ought to see how the girls are *fenced in* by wire as they sleep. It's to keep the *wolves* away!

I'm glad you received the rug for our bedroom. It's meant to keep your feet warm, but don't be afraid to step on it as I removed the *sleeping snake* from it before I sent it to you.

Dancing in the dark sounds like fun. I'll be looking forward to our dances in the dark. I know we'll do lots of things by the light that shines from our hearts. Some boys have one girl to come home to and it is their Mom. I have everything because I have you. You are the only woman I could ever hope to love. Save a spot in your heart for me.

Love always, Johnny

On the Southwest Pacific War Front in New Guinea
Dad wants mom to keep her muscles in shape so they can go places and do things when he gets back to the States. He also wants to dance *in the dark* with her.

04/03/44

Sweetheart of Mine,

Twenty two months is a long time to hold a secret. I can't hold one for more than two days. I'm getting to look and feel like *Sad Sack* each day. No kidding aside, I have *jungle* in my blood stream and you in my heart, of course. I'm letting you know I'll go *Tarzan* the moment we see a tree on one of our little walks in the country.

Hon, my target is your heart, my mission is a little talk and a little walk, with you wearing a little ring. A little of everything and plenty of you! A little of you and lots of Woo! Boy can I really pitch it. You have no idea. Also, it would be great if we created a *little Johnny* as well.

Remember we have a date to go and do things so keep your muscles in shape and don't let them *drape*. Don't worry about your hair for I can't wait to run my fingers through it. I like it better when I push it around like I did in the past. Good night, my sweet. I wish I could reach over and hold you tight and really say good night.

I'm yours, Johnny

On the Southwest Pacific War Front in New Guinea
Dad reiterates that he gets a *big kick* out of the *local* hometown newspaper. He tells mom stories about how the war and its soldiers are portrayed in the paper.

04/05/44

My Darling,

I got a *big kick* out of the *local* hometown newspaper. Three boys were shown who have spent twenty seven months in the Army in the States. It states "Here are a few pictures of men *at war* from our district". While somewhere on the back page, was a story about a fellow who just returned home from the *war zone*. He was only featured in ten lines on the back page saying "Here's one of our men in the service".

This goes to show you people don't know the score about things. In fact, if I said something about the *bloody battles* fought around New Guinea, most people would say they never heard of the place.

While I have been away or at dances, I had girls who literally *threw* themselves at me. It didn't mean a thing to me for I've got my *one and only* back home waiting for me. Hon, I'll always leave the front door of my heart open for you. Keep your *lonesome* self for me and no matter how lonesome you feel, your Johnnie is even worse.

As Always, Your Johnny

On the Southwest Pacific War Front sending magazines from New Guinea Dad is happy sending mom a bracelet he made for her and asks if she has been getting his *Yank* newspapers. He reports the Japs are *on the run* and our soldiers are close behind.

04/07/44

My Darling Mary,

Today I'm sending you a bracelet which I made special for you. I think it might be a little too big for it is one quarter inch larger than the one I sent you before. Let me know how much bigger it is so I can make one that really fits you. Use your *calipers* to measure down to the $1/100^{th}$ of an inch to be sure it's correct. If you wish to polish the bracelet, use tooth powder, you know the kind you use on your *false* teeth. Of course, if it's too big, you could go *native* and wear it around your leg.

As summer is just around the corner, you should be ready to put on your shorts and give the boys a peek. Woo! Hoo! Have you been getting the *Yank* newspapers? I think I sent about thirty five of them to you so far. Be sure to save them so I can tell you and show you some of the scenes in it that happened where I was located at the time.

Mail has been poorly received here and it will get even worse. The Japs are *on the run* and our soldiers are close behind them. Places such as Australia and parts of New Guinea aren't very important any more.

Well kid, I have spoken enough. Be sure to think of me often as I do of you.

Love and Kisses, Johnny

On the Southwest Pacific War Front in New Guinea
Dad is amused by mom's reply regarding the *grass skirt*. Dad is delighted when he receives the *large* picture of her in a bathing suit.

04/13/44

My Little *Hula Hula* Girl,

I'm still laughing about the way you answered my question regarding the *grass skirt*. Let me know if you feel the same about it when you receive it. Oh I torture myself when I think about how wonderful it will feel to hold you in my arms, gaze into those eyes, kiss those warm soft lips, run my hands through your hair and finally hold you close to my heart. I was surprised to get the *large* picture of you in a bathing suit and I loved it! *Va Va Voom!* Your figure is an eyeful. I know you keep my picture under your pillow. It has spent so much time there and I wish it could talk. I bet I'd hear plenty for it goes with you even to the tub. I wonder if that picture *blushed*?

So, my love, I live for the day I can see you running toward me with your arms wide open. I'll give you a long kiss. I'll make you so breathless you couldn't say "Stop Johnnie" even if you wanted to tell me. Would you really want me to stop?

All my Love, Johnny

On the Southwest Pacific War Front in New Guinea
It is very quiet now and dad feels like a *commando* for a grave yard. He is reminiscing about how he and mom would sit in the car and listen to the radio. He also enjoyed having her lean on his shoulder.

04/14/44

Hello Sweet One,

How is my *heartbeat* these days? All is quiet here and I feel like I'm a *commando* for a grave yard. I am still happy to see my *sweater girl* and *pin-up*. I don't go to bed hungry for food, however, I still have that *empty feeling* in my heart. Are you ready to fill up my heart?

I always lay back in bed just thinking of what I would like to do when I arrive in your backyard. Hon, I'm telling you there is so much I want to do with you. We can really *step out* and do things up in *real* style.

The best of all were those sessions we had sitting in my car with the radio playing. I really was *in heaven* with you leaning against me. I would kiss you and say "I just can't go home yet". Then I would imagine a few thousand more kisses just like that one. Make sure you save me a few million for you owe me so many.

Lots of Love, Your Sweetheart Johnny

On the Southwest Pacific War Front in New Guinea
Dad is amazed by the letter he received from mom where she told him a million things using only a few words. He read the prayer she wrote and it answers everything for him. Now he understands her so much better.

04/15/44

Dearest Mary,

Boy, I never knew a girl could write a letter like you did. You told me a *million* things in it using only a few words. That prayer you told me answers everything for me. I understand you so much better now.

Love is so hard spending all this time away from you. I get sick thinking about it for I can't get you off my mind. I would never have been so straight to the point had I not felt you and I are in love and meant to be together. Love is such a *funny* thing. One day you are happy and the next day you are *blue*. I know this will change to permanent happiness when we are back together in each other's arms. Darling, you are *tops* with me. Many of the boys tease me because they lost their girls in less than a year. As long as you are with me, I will be the *happy Johnny* you know and love. I'm just starting to live. It took you to make me realize *love feels like the most wonderful feeling in the world*! Sweetheart, sleep tight and keep your tears of sorrow away. Use only tears of joy.

Love Always, Johnny

On the Southwest Pacific War Front in New Guinea
So many *screwy* things have happened around Dad's camp. He discusses them with mom but cannot figure out what they mean which leaves him scratching his head for answers. The natives like to eat *chicken heads*, old meat and *corn willy*.

04/16/44

My Darling *Pin-Up* Girl,

I'm telling you now, you are the first girl I have ever called *sweetheart* and the last one as well. I am *roped* and if you think I want to get away, just hold on tight for you're going with me.

So many *screwy* things happen around here. A guy fixed a broken watch. When he was done, he still had five parts left over. The watch works better now than it did before. Another fellow has a pipe that looks like a *coil*. It's a long pipe hooked onto his regular pipe and it makes a complete circle around his neck.

The natives who work outside the Mess Hall always have a big feast of *chicken heads*, old meat and *corn willy*. I can't wait to be able to sit across from you and share a good meal. Hon, when I come home, I won't need a moon or stars.

Why should I look at them when I have heaven in my arms and not a care in the world. I know I will have plenty of love and charm all wrapped up in one bundle. What a bundle! Woo! Hoo!

With Lots of Love, Johnny

On the Southwest Pacific War Front in New Guinea
Dad hears and sees so much *monkey business* going on behind husbands and wives backs. He says the boys are cutting down large trees so that if they fall, they won't damage anything, namely, dad's *big, little* tent.

04/20/44

Dear Honey,

I've got my big *flat* feet propped up in bed while writing to you. I'm telling you hon, this war has caused many people to change. There is so much *monkey business* going on behind husbands and wives backs. That is the case over here, just as much as in the states, if not more.

We've been cutting down large trees. One was eighty feet high and a few feet around. This tree looked bad because the termites made a meal out of it so it had to be chopped down. My *big, little* tent was right in line with it. We had cable wires pulling to one side, however, it did land right on my tent. Luckily, I was prepared for I had removed all my important things. When it crashed on my *apartment*, it just crushed the tent. Fortunately, I only had to replace three ten foot boards and I ended up with the same tent without even a hole.

We all shared a big laugh out of the situation. We did have an accident happen when a tree fell, so we didn't want to take any chances. Now I can sleep with both eyes closed.

Keep your spirits up, my *little* one.

Love and Stuff, Johnnie

On the Southwest Pacific War Front gambling in New Guinea
Dad finds out it doesn't pay to *gamble* one's money on horses. He informs mom about the custom of going to horse races on a Sunday afternoon. However, he finds this practice *silly* because parents do not allow their daughters to attend a dance or a movie on Sunday night. It makes no sense to him! He is thrilled to report his food situation has improved and he has eaten rabbit, steak, chicken and mutton all in one week. For dessert they served apple tarts. He tells mom not to worry about her cooking skills as he *ain't fussy* and will eat anything.

04/22/44

Dearest Honey,

I went to a horse race this afternoon and won a *big fortune*! I placed a bet costing $1.53 on a horse and when he won, I collected a grand total of $.42. I did all that *sweating* and *blowing my big mouth off* for that! All I could say was at least my horse won the race. The Aussies really go *crazy* for horse races. They wouldn't think anything of going to a horse race on a Sunday afternoon.

However, should their daughter want to go to a movie or a dance on a Sunday night, it is forbidden. Consequently, we didn't have a dance on Sunday but we had a show for us boys only, no babes allowed.

This doesn't exist in the southern part of Aussie land for the people there are more modern thinking and *really in the groove.*

Our food situation has improved. We had rabbit, steak, chicken and mutton all in one week. We were able to eat all we wanted plus the fancy stuff like apple tarts. Don't believe the Jap radio saying that we are *being starved*. It's a funny thing about food in the Army, some boys say "Boy, that meal was no good" or "What awful food". Yet if they ate the same thing in

Sydney, they would think it was very good. Sydney is a big furlough city. So, you see hon, it's all in the mind.

I guess I can eat anything and be satisfied so don't feel the need to study cooking for I *ain't fussy*. However, by all means don't ever change my favorite dessert which is ice cream for I love it so much the way it is.

Honey, if there is anything you want *real bad*, I wish you would tell me so I can get it for you. Make sure you say "hello" to your Mom and Pop and the rest of the family. I think I have just about talked my ink pen to death. I'll close for now giving you time to recover from this mess.

Love always, Your Johnny

On the Southwest Pacific War Front in New Guinea
Dad thanks mom for the palm cross he received in her letter of April 2, 1944. He tells her that wherever the Army goes, there is always a church service even close to the *front lines*. Dad relays the information that the planes and ships are being utilized for more important things rather than to deliver mail.

04/24/44

My Darling Mary,

I received your letter of April 2, 1944 with the palm cross in it. Thanks hon, it was very nice of you to send it to me. Yes no matter where the Army takes you, there is always mass even very close to the front lines. There are no palm crosses here, but they hold as many masses as you have at home. I admit I haven't been going too often.

Yes my sweet, it will be swell to go to church with you. I will be proud to be seen with you anywhere. I mean that, honey. Okay, you say you didn't get any mail from me for a whole week. Well kid, you listen to the radio and read the newspapers. The planes and ships are being used for more important things.

Remember I write one page a day so just keep that pretty face smiling and don't worry. It's funny the way we carry on telling each other not to worry and yet we both worry anyway. I am happy even though we are so many miles apart. So long, my sweet one.

Love always, Your Johnny

On the Southwest Pacific War Front in New Guinea
Dad assures mom that there isn't a thing in the world more important to him than her. He says he would like to come home to a nice, *fresh* wife dressed in a *cute house dress*.

05/04/44

My Dearest Mary,

Today I got your letter of April 23, 1944. I can't understand it, with so much to do on your day off, you *torture* yourself by writing to me with my picture in front of you. Don't you ever waste your breath asking me if you will be mine always. I do want to be with you and there isn't a thing in the world I need more than just sweet you.

Haven't I proved that to you yet? If you think you're not going to *retire* after we are married, you better start thinking differently.

I want to come home to a nice, *fresh* wife all dressed up in a *cute house dress* and have my meal on the table in a *nice fashion*. I'll feel like *sweet sixteen* just because you look that way. Now isn't that better than getting home the same time as your husband and having a mad rush to cook something for dinner? What an awful sweet mess we have with each other's heart. Well Hon, I'm going off to the Mess Hall. Grr! I could eat anything because I'm as hungry as a *wolf!*

Love, Johnnie

On the Southwest Pacific War Front in New Guinea
Dad makes a hilarious remark to mom regarding their *false* teeth and their *wooden* legs. He wants to know if she threw in any *hops* for him at the last dance she attended.

05/09/44

My *little* Mary,

Yes Hon, our first night together after our *little* trip down the aisle will be one we will never forget. We will be careful to keep our little foot rug clean. I'll even take off my shoes and *park them* under the bed.

I'm still waiting for my *false* teeth to come. Think about it, we can place our teeth side by side on the dresser. Of course, our *wooden legs* would fit under the bed. Then we will be all set for our pillow fight! You frighten me the way you say I will be kissed like I have never been kissed before. Maybe I better stay away. You sound *dangerous* and I'm the guy who knows about it.

Did you throw in a few *hops* for me at the last dance? You didn't throw your leg *out of joint*, did you? I am still the *same old Johnny*. I am happy, healthy and still very much in love. I miss you and love you so much, sweetheart.

Love always, Your Johnny

On the Southwest Pacific War Front in New Guinea
Dad cannot believe how his relationship with mom has grown. He would like to help her more by contributing household items to her *hope chest*. He is getting ready to *welcome* a little boy with his black hair and any other children that may pop out.

05/10/44

My Darling Mary,

Today I received your letter of April 11, 1944 and I sure got a *kick* out of it! You are so sweet to me. What you have done to me in just three months cannot be described in ten books. I want to do so much for you but it is impossible from where I'm located. That's not only giving you attention or love. We could be filling up your *hope chest*. I hope you will be ready for the little boy with my black hair when he arrives in the future. I know I am ready for him and any others that may pop out!

Love and More Love, Johnny

On the Southwest Pacific War Front in New Guinea
Dad missed mom terribly this past week as he went to the movies and saw some *steamy,* love scenes. When he listens to his radio, the Japs put a *scrambler code* on the same station to prevent our boys from hearing the *correct* information.

05/11/44

Dear Sweet Mary,

Oh how I missed you this past week. Sometimes I go to the movies and what happens, I feel worse because I see *steamy love scenes*. Gosh honey, I really have some days when I'm in *bad shape*. Don't you dare stop writing to me. Your letters really keep me going. It could be a *dark and dismal* day in the jungle, and after I read one of your letters the sun *shines* in my heart.

I'm listening to my radio. Every time I hear the news being broadcasted, the Japs put a *scrambler code* right on the same station to try to prevent us from hearing the *real* news.

Remember how I used to tell you to get closer to me while was driving? I doubt if I ever have to ask you that again. I love the way we feel about each other. Well dearest, I have rambled on an awful lot and told you very little news. I had fun talking about things we feel about each other so much. I am closing with all my heart's love to you.

Lots of Love Stuff, Johnnie

On the Southwest Pacific War Front in New Guinea
The radio station the guys are running is getting more popular each day and does contribute a long way to better morale. Dad is trying to make some sense about ranks in the Army but he can't understand it. He says "that's the Army for you".

05/12/44

My Darling Mary,

I am sending along some more *Yank* newspapers. After reading these newspapers, a lot of lonely boys dream about waking up in the morning and finding a WAC in their tent. I can say I'm not one of them for I am yours and that's final. Our radio station is getting more popular each day during our two hour request program.

It looks like most of us will be rewarded for our *faithful* overseas service. Here is what the Army is going to do for us as things look now. We're going to have the *great thrill* of seeing a jeep *straight from the States* come into our company. This jeep will have very high ratings thus preventing any one of us from getting any higher up the ladder. Figuratively speaking, the fellow who would take my place, should they decide to send me home, will have at least *two times* as much rank as me yet no one in our company can do a thing about it. It makes no sense but *that's the Army for you.* Only one high ranking USO Commando coming into a department prevents six boys from getting one rank higher as no spot will be open.

Now Hon, you see what I am up against. I can't return to you with a *high* rank like all those home boys do it. I'm the *forgotten man*.

I know what your answer will be, but I feel differently about the situation. I still have you and as long as I rank *1A* with you that is all that matters. My commanding officer came over on the same boat and he is doing his best for us, but the *higher ups* have blocked him.

Mail is still painfully slow, however, I know you are by me always. Please keep your heart *warm* for me.

Love and Kisses, Your Johnnie

On the Southwest Pacific War Front in New Guinea
Dad excitedly relays all the places he has visited now that he is *permitted* to share this information. He has had and is continuing to have a *great adventure* in his life. He describes *jumping in trenches* when Jap planes are flying overhead.

05/14/44

My Dearest Mary,

I can now tell you some of the places I have visited since I landed here. The regulations are not as strict as they were originally. In Australia I have visited Brisbane, McKay, Townsville, Charter Towers and Ingham all in Queensland. In New Guinea, I visited the battle fields of Brenia and Sananada of Buna. Also included is Oro Bay and Port Moresby. I have flown over the Owen Stanley Range where the Japs were *pushed* when they tried to get into Port Moresby. I also flew over the Coral Sea where a great naval battle occurred. I expect to visit more of these places one of these days.

Enclosed is a picture of a battle area in Buna. It shows how tops of trees were *shot off* by shellfire. At Buna, I went to the famous war cemetery where so many Americans are buried. They have an Aussie cemetery and both cemetaries are maintained. I witnessed a war burial where an Aussie was killed by a *dive bombing* courtesy of the Japs.

I have had to *jump* into a trench a couple of times because Jap planes were flying overhead. It was at night but luckily the Japs didn't see me or cause damage. Queensland isn't the best part of Australia. I understand Melbourne and Sydney, as well as some of the southern cities are the best. However, I have not had an opportunity to visit them. They are the most modern. Brisbane is similar to Newark, New Jersey, however, it seems different because Aussies are there. There is none of that *modern design* stuff.

We seem to be the *forgotten men*. It is very disappointing, but what can we do about it? It's beyond me how men in the Army for thirty years make it their *career*. My only happiness is you. Some day I'll tell you and show you in person what I mean. As long as I have you, I will have happy moments. I am closing for now.

With All my Love and Kisses, Your Johnny

On the Southwest Pacific War Front in New Guinea
Dad asks mom if she is enjoying the *hit* songs. Of course, he likes to listen to them as well, but it is not the same without mom by his side. He jokes with her saying "Do you realize you will have to introduce my feet to yours again so we can dance together?"

05/16/44

My Darling Mary,

I am back again *in a flash with some more trash*. Summer must be knocking on your front gate now instead of me. Make sure you send me a picture of how you look in your bathing suit. Honey, aren't the songs *swell* these jungle days? All I can do is listen to love songs, but I would rather be in the arms of my *sweet* Mary. I know the songs would sound so much sweeter then.

I have a joke for you. Did you hear what Mussolini said to the German people? He told them he was going to be put on public display and admission would be charged to see him. I heard he was to be put in with the monkeys in the Bronx Zoo in New York and shown free. Of course, the monkeys would *object*!

Do you realize that you will have to introduce my feet to yours again? I only know the *jungle hop* and a few *native* dances. Some of these dances occur only in the presence of babes who are dressed in *almost nothing!* That's out for me!

I have been studying on how to make the little boy with black hair and I feel I can arrange it with no problem. Ha! Ha! Well kid, I must be getting to bed for I have a date with a pillow on my bed. I always see you in my dreams and I hope you see me as well.

Lots of Love, Johnnie

On the Southwest Pacific War Front in New Guinea
There is *encouraging war news* being broadcasted about the European War. Dad loves to talk about musical numbers and dancing in his letters. Mail is being received at a *snail's pace*. Dad is trying to figure out the Army's policy for sending guys home.

05/17/44

My Dearest Mary,

How is the world treating you? Are you enjoying my *sugar reports*? I sure would like to put my *big* feet under your kitchen table and let you serve me a nice *big* dinner. Yum! Of course, the usual dessert I get from you will do very nicely.

Isn't the news from Europe *encouraging*? I hope things start *popping* soon. I bet some of the *hit parade* numbers you hear are *swell* for dancing.

I miss my *workouts* on the dance floor with you. I haven't *trampled your feet* for such a long time. You'll have to teach me to dance again and other things. I'm living in a different world over here.

I've been sending you the **Guinea Gold** newspapers when I see something of interest in them. However, I do prefer the **Yank** newspaper more don't you? I hope you also like this *Yank* a little too! Well kid, I must be closing now. I'll always be yours if you want me that way. I sure do want that, too.

Love and Sweet Memories, Your Johnnie

On the Southwest Pacific War Front in New Guinea
Dad helps sort four hundred letters, but doesn't find any for him! He's not sure how the Army handles sending men home. He says he heard some guys went home for sixty days and then got sent back overseas. Dad discusses how to prevent malaria and says he may have to keep taking the *little yellow pills* for quite a while to prevent it. He and the boys observe the natives' custom of *gazing* at themselves in the mirror and *enhancing* the color of their teeth by mixing and eating three kinds of *wild fruit*.

05/20/44

Dearest One,

Well it is pouring *cats and dogs* outside. A bunch of us are watching a big tree. Every time it rains, a few trees fall. Everyone comes running when they hear just one *crack* of a branch. Mail continues to be *awful* as usual.

Long time no hear from my *one and only*. I just finished sorting four hundred letters and not a single one for me. Darn it! You bad girl! I'll forgive you though, honest hon.

Honey, maybe this *sending home business* isn't very good. Some men get *sent home* to the States for only sixty days and then get *sent back* overseas again. That's awful because there are so many men who haven't been overseas even once. We heard of a fellow who was sent home and he developed malaria the second day. If and when I do come home, I'll have to keep taking those *little yellow pills*. I should take them for a while as they are used to prevent malaria from *taking over*. I might have some symptoms of it, however, I'm not concerned because I'm taking the drug. It's harmless because the dye was invented by the Germans. Of course, I might look *a little yellow* in the face. If you can put up with this mug of mine, I'm sure a little *yellow coloring* wouldn't make any difference.

You ought to see the way these natives look at themselves in their mirrors and play around with their hair. No kidding, they do this more often than you would in a day. They eat three kinds of *wild fruit*. When they mix these three fruits together, it makes their teeth *red*. This makes them very happy.

Rumor has it that beer is on its way, but I'll have to see it to believe it. In fact, I'm not going to believe anything in the Army anymore unless I see it. I haven't changed a bit, I'm still your *victim*. Give all my love to the girl you see in the mirror and be sure to give her a nice big *smackeroo*.

All my love, Johnny

On the Southwest Pacific War Front in New Guinea
Dad continues to wait for the mail. He suggests a carrier pigeon might do a better job of delivering mail. Mom has informed him that the meat *ration* has been lifted. Dad thinks everyone will make up for lost time by gorging on meat. He hopes the gas *rationing* situation is fixed before he comes home.

05/22/44

Hello My Sweetheart,

Boy, have I been *sweating out* the mail deliveries this past week, but it didn't do any good. I guess I'll have to send out a *carrier pigeon* and hope he can deliver the *sugar reports* faster.

I see the *meat ration* has been lifted for a while. I bet everyone is making up for lost time. I do hope the *gas business* is fixed before I get home. It will be very hard on me not to come to see you every day. However, even if I have to use a bicycle, I'll get there.

The Japs and the Germans sure are *nervous in the service* these days. I wouldn't be surprised if I get to see the Philippines before I come home. Our troops are about one thousand one hundred miles away as compared to three thousand miles away in the beginning. The *infantry boys* are not having any fun. They are required to be fully dressed, wear leggings and salute everyone all over the place and all the time.

In the Army Air Corp., we walk around with *less* clothing. The sun tanned *native* babes give the infantry boys a *snooty attitude*. They don't deserve this as they really go through a lot. Well Hon, I put you through a lot just reading this letter so I'll close now.

All my love, Johnnie

On the Southwest Pacific War Front in New Guinea
Mom receives a large picture of dad and the boys in his unit. He also sends her some money to celebrate their *two year* anniversary away from each other. He wants her to buy a new dress, hat or use it to get her hair done at the beauty parlor.

05/25/44

My Darling Mary,

Enclosed you will find a money order for $20.00. It is my present to you for our anniversary. I have been away from you for two years now and it feels like much more than that. Now don't try to send it back for I can't cash it anyway. I want you to go out and buy yourself a nice dress, a new hat or get a permanent wave. I hope it is enough to get anything you want. After you do this, please write and tell me how *pretty* you look in what you bought.

I will be very happy to hear from you. It took me three days of my *spare* time to earn it. You will see the ash tray and airplane I made to earn the money. I will be sending you one as soon as I finish making it for you. Honey, I hope you don't think it's not proper for if you do, I'd feel very unhappy. I do make a lot of extra money here for very little labor. Remember there isn't a thing in this world I wouldn't do for you.

I hope the Mother's Day card got through the mail to your Mom. I think my Mom got hers already. I mailed both cards the same day so they should have reached both places at approximately the same time. Honey, you're really lucky because I have saved my money for you. I am filled with love and pep and plenty of things that are a *military secret* to me. Now, wouldn't you like to know?

Keep your chin up and let me know how *beautiful* you look after you spend the money order on something for yourself.

Love and all that Sort of Nice Stuff, Your Guy Johnnie

On the Southwest Pacific War Front in New Guinea
Dad has been camped out in New Guinea or Australia all this year. He analyzes the similar ways both he and mom have been raised. He still sends money to his mom and dad, however, a portion of his salary is being saved for his future with his *sweet* Mary.

Mary Jane Juzwin

05/29/44

My Darling Mary,

In this letter, I'm going to tell you a few things about the man you are going to marry. I come from a *poor* family just like you. We take care of our own property and the taxes are paid. Our cars are fully paid off as well. All this was made possible by my brother, Walter and me. Everything was paid off about three weeks before I left for the Army. When I got my furlough in the States, I worked twelve days out of the fourteen just so I could make a little money to take along with me when I entered the Army.

I had $50.00 to my name. I did, however, own my car. I left some money for my Mom and Dad so they would be on *even terms*.

I decided to help them a little and at the same time save money for myself. One day before I sailed overseas, I wired myself some money. It finally reached me two months later.

During the past twenty months, I've been sending $20.00 a month to my Mom and Dad to help them along. My Army salary is about $80.00 a month. Out of this total, I have $16.60 taken out each month for insurance. Also $18.75 for a bond I never see as it is automatically taken out and then sent home. I have the rest of my savings in *soldier's deposits*. This is a bank in the Army and the only way to get money out is for a reason such as *sickness in the family* or for *marriage*. I have never gambled the whole time I've been in the Army.

Well honey, this will give you a general idea what a *poor man* in love can do if he finds the right girl. I owe all my happiness and success to you, sweetheart.

Love and Kisses, Johnny

On the Southwest Pacific War Front in New Guinea

Dad tells mom he's been *keeping company* with a bunch of infantry men who served in the Battle of Buna Sananda. He enjoys hearing stories of their adventures. They tell him about the hospital the Japs captured and how the nurses surrendered and the Japs were *pushed into the sea*.

06/06/44

My Darling Sweet One,

This week I have been *keeping company* with a bunch of Aussie infantry men. They were in the Battle of Buna Sananda. Here are some stories they told me.

One time the Japs made a *raid* by plane over them. They must have dropped their garbage for down came lots of bottles and tin cans. They were used to make the noise like bombs exploding. Before they hit land they whistle. When the Japs landed, they were half drunk and each one had some kind of brew but no food. There were several bodies found that looked like the Japs *cut out* parts of them and ate them. They told me about the hospital the Japs captured. The place was surrounded, but the nurses and men would not surrender. They were given five chances to give up and then the place was rushed. In a few minutes, the girls came running out and shouted "Me girl, don't shoot". They had their breasts showing out of their dresses so the Jap soldiers would believe them. Finally, the Japs were *pushed into the sea*. A lot of them waded out in the water and pulled the pins out of hand grenades to blow themselves up. The prisoners that were taken didn't have the slightest idea where they were.

Many of them died due to malaria because they wore shorts and didn't take any medicine. The fellows who told me this story were my age.

They had been in the infantry for four years *without a scratch*. They said when one is *in the jungle* some things were hard to find. There was tobacco but no matches, a desire to write a letter but there was no paper.

What makes this interesting is the fact that I had visited these battlefields in the past. These boys turned out to be a *swell bunch* and would do anything for you. Well Sweet, these are only a few of the true stories I heard right from the men who witnessed them.

Love, Johnnie

On the Southwest Pacific War Front hearing *good war news* in New Guinea Dad expresses concern for mom's mother who was sick on Mother's Day. He is encouraged to hear the *good news* of the second front when the U. S. invaded North Africa and Italy. Dad compares the Fifth Air Force building in New Guinea to the Astoria Hotel in New York. He says some people in the States think the guys overseas are living in nice, tall buildings, however, the truth is they live in tents.

06/08/44

My Darling Mary,

Today I received ten *v-letters or victory letters* all dated around May 23, 1944. What a girl! Darling, I feel so happy all over, I don't know where to start. I was sorry to hear that your mom was sick on Mother's Day. I hope she is better now.

Did you hear the good news of the second front when the U.S. invaded North Africa and Italy? I hope everyone who *celebrated* at home realized for every beer they drank, ten American boys lost their lives during the same time. Perhaps when news of some of the boys that were killed reaches their families, maybe people will finally be *convinced* that a war is being fought. Eighty percent of the United States population don't believe it.

I must tell you about a picture I saw. No kidding, the picture was called **Joe Something**. It was about the Fifth Air Force in New Guinea. They showed a big fancy Officers Club 4elike the Astoria Hotel in New York. There were plenty of beautiful girls and all the drinks in the world. The building was painted and the furnishings were very fancy. Boy, if that wasn't the *biggest fraud* I have ever seen.

People back home think it's that way here. All we have here is a lot of tents in the jungle. There are plenty of roads and we count ourselves lucky if we get a little orange juice once in a while. Here is what a pilot told me about shooting Jap zeros down. *It's just like a girdle, one Yank and it's down.*

With All my Heart, Johnny

On the Southwest Pacific War Front in New Guinea
Dad cleans his *house/tent* and finds a picture of himself in the *grass skirt*. He tells mom he wasn't wearing any underwear under the skirt. He was terrified when his knife slipped down inside the skirt narrowly missing his precious *manhood*. Dad sends her a ring and hopes she likes it. He sleeps all morning at times with rats that like his *apartment*. He describes hamburgers made of rabbit and says kangaroo is tasty as well.

06/15/44

My Darling Woman,

I just finished *cleaning house* and I sure had a lot of your letters *scattered* all over the place. After I had a final peek at them, I stored them safely away with the others. I finally found the picture of me in the *grass skirt*. I thought I sent two of them to you. Do you remember? Now about that picture of me, I want you to know that the grass skirt was the *only* thing I had on at the time. If you look closely, you will see a knife handle. The knife was as sharp as a razor and while the *grass skirt* picture was being taken, it slipped down inside the skirt. This really scared me because I almost cut off something *precious* and I don't mean perhaps.

Please don't worry if you aren't getting my mail regularly for there are many reasons it just isn't coming through quickly. At one time our mail stayed at our Post Office and took a *nap* for about ten days due to bad weather or no transportation.

Then it had to travel to another place to be sorted so that takes time. Then it might get on a *slow ship* to the States that also causes delays. Air mail doesn't always travel by air to the States.

Enclosed is the ring I promised to send you. I hope you like it. Tomorrow is my day off so I can stay up late. I can sleep all morning along with a few rats that like my *apartment* as well. One day a rat dragged my Reader's Digest about ten feet away so I decided to set a trap for him. No more problems with him! I might give him to the natives for they say rats taste like hamburger. Speaking of hamburgers, we had some very good ones yesterday made of rabbit. We get rabbits once in a while and kangaroos both of which are tasty.

Well dear one, I must stop for now because I have a *date* with my pillow.

Love and Stuff, Johnny

On the Home Front in Manville, New Jersey
Mom misses dad terribly but says she is willing to wait for him and it will be *heaven* when they get together again.

06/19/44

My Dearest Johnny,

I thought you might like this poem about Hitler and the devil.

> Hitler called up the devil on the telephone one day.
> "Hello" was Hitler speaking, "is old man Satan home"?
> "just tell him it's Der Fuer who wants him on the phone".
>
> The devil said, "Howdy Adolph", Hitler said "How are you"?

"I'm running your show on earth so tell me what to do".
"What can I do" the devil said "dear old pal of mine".
"You don't need any help from me, you're doing mighty fine".

"Yes, I was doing fairly well until some time ago
When a man called Uncle Sam told me to go slow".
He said to me "Herr Hitler, we don't want to be unkind,
but you've raised enough cane so you better change your mind".

I thought democracy was a bluff and he'd never make it so,
He soon had put me on the spot and told me where to go.
"That's why I called you Satan, I need advice from you,
for I know you can tell me exactly what to do.

Satan said "Dear partner, there is not much left to say.
The United Nations will make it hotter than I can any day".
"I'll be ready for your coming and I'll keep the fires all bright.
I'll get your room all ready cause you know you'll lose your fight".
"Yes, I know your days are numbered, you'll soon be all washed up.
So hang up the phone, put on your hat and come on down with me".

I thought you would fine this poem interesting. Take care of yourself for me.

All my Love, Mary

On the Home Front in Manville, New Jersey
Mom receives a special ring and a nice ashtray that dad made for her. Now she can't wait to get a *hope chest* to save some household items for them when they marry.

06/23/44

My Honey,

You surprise me in so many wonderful ways when you send me such lovely gifts like the ring you made me with two hearts on it and also the nice ashtray. Now I can't wait to get myself a *hope chest* for our little home. I'll be so proud to show my friends the gifts from you then.

This was a short busy week. I hardly know where the days have gone. I know that last Sunday I wrote you a long letter and then Monday evening I got so excited about receiving your eight letters all at one time. Then Wednesday I received another one making it nine letters all together this week.

Lovingly, Mary

On the Southwest Pacific War Front in New Guinea
Dad reminds mom that all *v-letters* are photographed so she should be careful what she writes in them. He says only the *v-letters* not written in dark ink cannot be photographed.

06/27/44

My Darling,

If you want to picture me, try turning off lights. I'm sure it would be much easier for you to have me around because my face wouldn't be *scaring* you into doing things. I don't know if you remember but all *v-letters* are photographed so you must be careful what you write on them. The only ones that aren't photographed are those written with light ink.

How is my *better* half? Do you still love me a little? I hope my letters are interesting to you. I try my best to make each one different. I should be more up-to-date on my letter writing to others, but the words don't come out like they do for your letters. I miss that *close quarter love stuff* don't you? I would enjoy plenty of that *love stuff* that I ain't been getting for the past two years. My wish is to hold you in my arms, but right now I can only do this in my dreams.

Love and All my Kisses, Johnny

On the Southwest Pacific War Front in New Guinea
Dad was happy to receive two of mom's *sugar coated* reports. He thinks the bracelet he sent her was stolen for packages are opened to see if any government property is being sent home. He is thankful and optimistic looking forward to acquire such a swell Mother-in-law and Father-in-law. He is amused when mom tells him how much her bus driver looks like him.

07/01/44

My Darling Mary,

Today I received two of those *sugar coated* reports and it's about time. I'm guessing the bracelet I sent you was stolen for they open all packages to see if any government property is being sent home.

Yes, I'm sure I'll have a swell Mother and Father-in-law. Your Mom and Pop were born in the States so I think this makes them more modern thinking. My Mom and Pop were born in Europe so this is why they are old fashioned in their ways.

You thought the bus driver looked just like me. That's pretty interesting. Go easy kid, you never know where I will show up so I might be the bus driver. I must say any girl who can say I'm handsome must really be *in love*. Therefore, you got it good and you have been stung by the *love bug*! Well *little* woman, this *old* man has to close for now.

Love and Kisses, Johnnie

On the Home Front in Manville, New Jersey
Mom has received many *love letters*. He also shows her his *charm* by sending her sister Jeannie a letter. He sent her a *lovely* bracelet and a cigarette case for her father.

07/08/44

Hello Sweet One,

How are you coming along? Darling, it has been such a busy week that I feel very tired but not too tired to write to you. It was so kind of you to send a letter to Jeannie when you sent one to me. Now I have exactly thirteen letters! In one of the letters you explained how to put that ashtray and airplane together. Whenever you tell me you are sending me something, I can hardly wait to receive it.

Honey, you should see the moon tonight. It reminds me of the song, **I'll be looking at the moon, but I'll be seeing you**. That's one song that makes me want to crawl into your arms and stay there.

Today I also received your lovely bracelet. I love it so very much. Daddy can't stop showing off his cigarette case. He keeps telling his friends about *his soldier son* from Australia. He is so proud of you. I like the other bracelet I received from you a long time ago, too. They are both made of silver coins but are so different that I don't know which one I like better. The ring you made matches both bracelets beautifully. Darling, you treat me too good! Even though I have received a package every month from you, the best package I am waiting for is you in person.

All my Love, Mary

On the Southwest Pacific War Front in New Guinea
Dad informs mom about the many couples who have been split up by the war. He tells mom men that are coming home can now wear their overseas

stripes. He says his company has a lot of radios to repair because they are able to get parts easily and quickly.

07/11/44

Hello There *little* Woman of mine,

How's my *little lassie* with the *classy chasse?* I read a story recently about this fellow who got some letters from his girl at home. First her letters said "Dearest Bill", then "My Dearest Bill". After a few months it was "Darling" then "Sweetheart". Another letter said "Dear Bill" and finally "Dear Friend". You would be surprised how many cases are like this.

I bet over seventy five percent of single men in our company have lost their gals. Some guys think they have their sweethearts. Later they receive a letter with P.S. at the bottom saying "I was married last week".

I never knew I could have anything to say to you after two years time, but I see I can hold out for another ten years. The men coming home now can wear overseas stripes. One is for each six months of service so I'll have four of them on September 1, 1944. Boy, do we have a lot of radios in our company. Other people are envious of us because we can get radios and parts easily and quickly. Oh well, I guess this is enough for today, but I'll never have enough of you, my sweet one.

All my Love, Johnny

On the Southwest Pacific War Front in New Guinea
Dad feels like *Sad Sack* and he looks like it. He explains how he thinks most people feel about the war. He tells mom about Japs who don't give up as they feel *honorable to die*.

07/12/44

My Darling Mary,

I am having another one of those exciting evenings. What I mean is I have *nothing* to do. I had no mail today which makes three days with no mail for anyone. I feel like *Sad Sack* and probably look like him.

Most people think this war is a *pushover* here and they don't pay much attention to it. It was announced that we lost about the same amount of men in Sipan which is an island belonging to the Japanese as we lost in the initial landings in France. It's tough to fight someone you can't see even if he is two feet away.

These Japs don't give up even when they're *licked*. They think it is *honorable to die*.

A soldier in New Guinea doesn't have a town to visit after hours like those civilized places where war wages. Out of the eleven months I've spent in New Guinea, one half of the time furloughs were *frozen*. Some of the time *rest leaves* to McKay were not available. This covers all the *dope* for today so I'll close now.

Your Dreamer Boy, Johnny

On the Southwest Pacific War Front in New Guinea
Dad sends mom two *native* combs to help her with her *hair trouble*. He says he feels his handwriting looks a little better because he was finally able to get some American ink. He thinks of her every time he hears music.

07/14/44

My Dearest One,

I have sent you two *native* combs to help you with your *hair trouble*. They were made by a well educated native who is cleaner than a lot of people I know. I hope you will like using them. Did you ever receive the ring I made from a Jap zero? Let me know how it fits with your dress and figure.

Notice my handwriting looks a little better because I finally got some *American* ink. *Aussie* ink is so thin it is like water. Have you been behaving yourself? Out here in the jungle, I don't have much choice so I take life as it comes day by day. Honey, every time I hear music, I think of dancing with you. Boy how I miss that! I haven't had the pleasure of stepping on your feet for such a long time. Well, this is today's chapter of *Jungle Johnny's* life without a wife.

Love and Kisses, Johnnie

On the Home Front in Manville, New Jersey
Mom tells dad her new address. She wants him to stop teasing her about her false teeth.

07/16/44

My Darling Johnny,

Today I decided to write and tell you that we now have a mailbox of our own at the Post Office. Now my address is: Miss Mary C. Regiec, North 13th Ave., P. O. Box No. 255, Manville, New Jersey. You see there are so many people with my same last name that the postmen get the letters all mixed together.

You say you saw the picture called **Sweater Girl**. I'll just have to get a sweater for myself and have someone take a picture of me to send to you.

You asked me about my teeth. I don't know how I ever walked around with my old set.

These new ones are swell. Another thing Johnny, will you please stop teasing me about them, for crying out loud. You just wait until you get home so I can tease you as well. So long, Monkey.

Love, Your future *Sweater Girl* Mary

On the Southwest Pacific War Front in New Guinea
Dad is surprised to get two regular letters and twelve *v-letters* all at one time. He plans to send his mom a *grand* to put in the bank for him. Dad is now the last Corporal in Radio Repair who is an *old timer*. He tells mom to go to dances but if she really wants to stay home and write letters he will not argue with that.

07/16/44

My Darling Mary,

Boy did I receive a surprise today! I got two regular letters and twelve *v-letters*. I was *in heaven*. I found out there's no risk sending any money orders home. I expect to send *a grand* this month to my mom so she can put it in a local bank. I always keep the receipts of all my money orders so I can collect them if any get lost.

Finally, our *big headquarters* permitted our *local headquarters* to give out some ratings. Now I am the *last* Corporal in Radio Repair who is an *old timer*. I have the same amount of time as seventy percent of the men who are waiting to go home.

Darling, you sure are something. You're always wondering if I really mean what I am doing or saying to you. Honey, haven't I told you I *play for keeps?* I'd never tell you one thing and mean another. How could anyone be so cruel as to tell a girl he loves her and yet not mean what he says? You're the first girl I ever fell in love with completely.

I did think I liked some girls before, but never like my love for you.

Honey, I wish you wouldn't stay home from dances just to write to me. However, if it makes you happier to stay home and write, I certainly cannot argue with that decision. Well dearest one, I have many letters to answer and I don't know where to start. I would really rather start my future with you in person. So long, Sweetheart.

Love and many Kisses, Johnny

On the Southwest Pacific War Front in New Guinea
Dad's happy to report he has gotten a new Eversharp fountain pen so mom does not have to get him a new point for his old pen. He was also able to get a *waterproof* watch.

07/17/44

My Dearest Mary,

I didn't mean to get you *excited* when I had that fellow address my letter for me.

When I want to know how you act or feel, I just shut my eyes and say "Now how would I act if I were Mary and loved Johnny the way he loves Mary". It works every time.

I got myself a good fountain pen. It's an Eversharp so don't worry about getting me a point for the old pen. A boy who was going home sold it to met. I also got a *waterproof* watch so I'm fixed up for a while. I remember how we used to walk down the street together. Every one hundred yards I wanted to kiss you but I didn't want to scare you. I also remember how the store manager said "Whose car is that with the far away plates"? Then he said "That guy must really love that girl to be willing to travel so far".

Loving you, Your Sweetheart Johnny

On the Southwest Pacific War Front in New Guinea
Mom asked dad a serious question so he is now repeating why he *fell in love* and what he finds so *attractive* with her. He praises her for being honest and not trying to make him think she is an *angel* like other girls tried to do with him.

07/18/44

My Only one,

You asked me a very serious question so hold on tight while I tell you why I *fell in love* with you. I will tell you how I know I'm still *in love* with you even though I haven't seen you for twenty four months and nine days. You are the first girl that filled that *empty* feeling inside of me with love.

I like the way you *fuss* with your hair and the way you *cling* so close to me. I could spend the whole evening with you, not even talk much and yet feel like I'm *in heaven*.

You are also the first girl that made me *fight* for her love. I had to practically hit you on the head before I could find out how you felt about me. You are the kind of girl who wouldn't hesitate a moment to *slug* me over the head with a rolling pin and then hold me in your arms *crying your heart out* hoping you didn't hurt me so much. When I'm out with you, I don't feel I'm with a girl who's innocent and doesn't know the answers.

You never tried to make me feel like you are an *angel* like so many other girls try to make you believe. Everyone wonders how I can feel happy yet not discouraged about a lot of things. I also like the honest way you talk to me in your letters. You are the first girl that makes me feel like being a *bad boy*, and yet something inside is telling me no, not like that Johnnie. I see a girl who can act *young and carefree* and yet know how to be sensible about things.

Your memory of the little things in life shows me that everything has a meaning to you and affects you. You don't try to *dress up* like a rich girl with a lot of *face paint*. Nothing or no one will ever mean more to me than sweet you.

With All my Love, Your Johnny

On the Southwest Pacific War Front in New Guinea
Dad says he thinks mom waited for him to *pour his heart out* before she would tell him how she feels about their relationship. He says he's *sort of wild* from living in the jungle.

07/22/44

My Dear Woman,

Hon, you must admit you were *beating around the bush* when you told me how much I meant to you in our first few letters. I realize now that you really wanted me to *pour my heart out* and tell you how much I love you and what you mean to me.

Did you hear the one that goes like this? Why does a woman have a waist line? It's so she can hang her figure on it! I realize I'm *sort of wild* from being in this jungle. Do you think you will be able to handle me when I get back home? I expect to go swimming this afternoon. Of course, I'll be a good boy with the mermaids. It doesn't seem right for me to go swimming alone without your *curves* and waves beside me. Oh Darling, I get such a big kick out of handling you this way and teasing you in my letters, but it would be so much better in person. Give my love to your Mom and Pop and the rest of the family. So long, Sweetheart.

Lots of Love, Johnny

On the Southwest Pacific War Front in New Guinea
Dad is so excited because he received a second batch of *pin-up* pictures. He tells mom these pictures are done so men can see the reason they are fighting. He says people in the States are lucky for they never had to experience a bomb alert.

07/23/44

Dearest Mary,

I received your second batch of *pin-up* pictures today. Did you know the reason *pin-up* girls have such *little* outfits on? It is done so the men can see better what they are fighting for in this war. Woo! Hoo!

It looks like the war in Europe will be over before the end of the year. Our whole naval fleet is in this war for Adolph has no fleet left. He isn't interested in *military secrets* anymore. All he cares about now is *where the hell can he live* after this war ends?

People back home in the States are lucky for they never had to run to a bomb shelter or hear a bomb striking a target. If you only knew how much money is used to run and supply a little company like mine. You would be able to see how those *big bosses* of the factories in the States make money. This ends today's issue of my report card. I hope it rates an *A* with you, sweetheart. You will always be *1A* in my life. So long for now, monkey.

Love and lots of Kisses, Johnnie

On the Southwest Pacific War Front in New Guinea
Dad is getting ice cream at the usual *coffee hour*. He says it was his first dessert in five months. He is looking forward to a time when he can take mom out to a *fancy* place and have a nice meal. He also wants to take her to what he calls an *outdoor* movie or *drive-in* movie. He thinks he should

trade in his *rattle trap* of a car and replace it with a baby carriage. He sends his letter using a *cool* Army envelope with a war scene on it.

07/24/44

My Darling Mary,

I got a *big* surprise this evening. I went down for my usual cup of coffee, and much to my delight we had ICE CREAM! It was my first in five months and it sure *hit the spot*! Hon, I haven't had a drink of water that didn't contain chlorine in it for almost two years now. Chlorine makes it safe to drink so I'm used to it now.

Hon, I can hardly wait until we can go to some *fancy* places and have a nice meal with ice cream sodas of course. We just have to go to that *outdoor* movie. Imagine a whole car seat just for the two of us. I could *feel at home* seeing a show with you in my car. I'd probably be looking at you more than the picture, but it would be heaven anyway.

In the old days, I was *breaking my neck* trying to get to your house and hoping my car didn't break down. I sure was conscious of the old *rattle trap*. If you can put up with it, I guess I can as well. My darn *rattle trap* of a car does create problems. I always had trouble with the fuel pump. I think I should *trade it in* for a baby carriage! You used to get nervous and then I'd kiss you and you would relax and forget about it. That medicine is the *cure* for a lot of things. This is all for now, my sweetheart.

Love to You My Sweet One, Johnny

On the Southwest Pacific War Front in New Guinea
Dad is *reminiscing* about the first time he met mom at a *polka* dance in Helmetta, New Jersey and what he said to her. He notices tears in her eyes when he walked toward her after his induction into the Army. He tells her that the U. S. government will be offering loans over a twenty year time period with very low interest.

07/25/44

My Darling Mary,

I'm remembering our conversation the first time we met on the dance floor. I said "Mary, I have just made a startling conclusion!" You said "What is it"? Then I said "Some day I'm going to marry you". Now isn't that a funny thing to say on a first date? I never talked about marriage to anyone but you and I surprised even myself by mentioning it.

I'll never forget those tears in your eyes when I walked toward you after my induction.

It was so *cute* the way you tried to *hide* them. It was then you made my heart beat *so fast* I knew I wouldn't give up loving you. However, I'm afraid you'll have to teach me how to kiss. You realize it's been way too long since I had the pleasure of kissing you.

You know hon, the government is going to give loans to people over a twenty year time period with very low interest. If we're able to get that plus all the savings I will have, we should be able to pay for our *little love nest*. Be sure to save those *lips* and *curves* for me.

All my Love, Johnnie

On the Southwest Pacific War Front in New Guinea
Dad sends mom a package with two *native* combs, a book on Queensland, Australia and a picture book about the Battle of Buna. In addition, there was also a book on the Fiji Islands. He asks her if she has had a chance to go swimming. He explains to her that in the jungle he swims in his *birthday suit*.

07/26/44

Dearest Mary,

I sent you a package with two *native* combs, a book on Queensland, Australia and a picture book of the Battle of Buna. There was also a book on the Fiji Islands. I visited the capital city of Sunia. I'm hoping you received this package in good condition.

Did you go swimming this year? I bet you look *swell* in a bathing suit. Out here in the jungle, I'm a *native at heart* so I swim like Tarzan in my *birthday suit*. I feel funny with a pair of pants, socks and shoes on. Oh well, I'll have to get used to civilization one of these days. I'm sure you can tame me down for you know the secret to my weakness. My weakness is you, Hon, and the cure is to have more of you around. It will be *heaven* when we finally get to spend our lives together.

Lots of Love, Your Johnnie

On the Southwest Pacific War Front in New Guinea
Dad gets the *score* about the WACs from his friends. The men camp out in tents but it's quite an *expensive proposition* to house the WACs in New Guinea. The WACs are housed in *wooden* barracks with *perfect* plumbing. Dad says the Australian Women's Army does not have fancy or expensive items. They are treated like the men and they do a *darn* good job.

07/30/44

Dearest Mary,

Today is the day our beer is here. I'm eating pretzels and drinking my allotted three bottles of Budweiser beer. Of course three bottles is just about enough to *gargle* in most of our throats but it is better than nothing.

Some of the boys who have passed through tell me a lot about the WACs. Yes, it's true what they say in most cases. Of course the WACs in New Guinea have *wooden* barracks and *perfect* plumbing. In fact, their home in the States wasn't as *nice and modern* as the one in New Guinea. A tent is *good enough* for us men, but it's an *expensive proposition* to have the WACs over here. I figure one must pay at least three times above the cost of the *average* man. The average WAC can't do as much work as a man from the States. The Australian Women's Army doesn't enjoy glamour or fancy expensive items. They are treated just like the men and they do a *darn* good job.

Boy, it sure is raining *hard* outside. I can remember the rain we had when we walked home after the show. You ought to have seen the large *handsome* rat that came to visit me yesterday. He was as big as an *average American cat*. I wish you were here to see him so I could hold you close when you jumped and screamed. Well my sweet one, I hope everything is just fine with you on these *lonesome* days and nights. You can do what I do which is keep the picture of you nice and close. So long, sweetie.

Love and Kisses, Johnny

On the Southwest Pacific War Front in New Guinea
Dad is delighted to receive mom's letter with her *kiss* print on it. He sends her a picture of some Jap equipment taken by infantry men. Hon, you don't need to keep an extra copy of your letters for I am saving them all.

07/31/44

My Darling Mary,

Today I received the letter with your *kiss* print on it. You know this will do for now but it would be much sweeter in person.

I have enclosed a picture of some Jap equipment taken from them by infantry men. The flags are supposed to be *good luck charms* and are usually worn in the lining of a helmet. Add this to our collection of pictures. Be sure to save all of them so we can show them to our children some day.

Keeping an extra copy of the letters you write to me is not necessary. I am saving every letter in a safe place. Hon, I'll cut this short now for it's getting quite late. I sure miss those good night kisses from you and I will need a lot more when I get home.

Love and kisses, Your Johnny

On the Southwest Pacific War Front in New Guinea
Dad tells mom about the natives, in particular the women. The native women do all the work and carry *heavy* loads while the men stroll around with nothing in their hands. He says the *Yanks* have *won them over* for it's a common sight to see a native dressed in a *Yank* uniform.

08/01/44

My Darling,

Another month has started and my 26th month for me overseas. I wish some of the rumors would come true. It's a nice, sunny day out here today so that will help dry up some of the mud.

The natives here are *very* clean. The women wear the most clothing while the men only have as much clothing on as a *sheet of paper*. The women do all the work and carry *heavy* loads, while the men walk around with nothing in their hands. The *Yanks* have *won them over*. It's a common sight to see a native all dressed up in a *Yank* uniform.

Well, little girl of mine, I don't have to tell you I miss you very much. You know that I do and I love you more each day.

All my Love, Johnny

On the Southwest Pacific War Front in New Guinea
Dad enjoyed another *outdoor* movie with Charles Boyer and Ingrid Bergman. He tells mom the Aussie expressions are *odd*. Of course, he has enclosed more pictures for her to save for their album.

08/03/44

My Darling,

I just got back from the local movie. It was called **Gaslight** and I thought it was pretty good. However, Charles Boyer was very rough on Ingrid Bergmann. You better not go to see it for I know it would make you cry, you *softy* you.

I'm listening to my radio and it's playing some Aussie expressions. They are funny or should I say *odd*. A gal that is a hot number is called a *live wire*. The fellows in the jungle are called *jungle jokers*. One guy has a children's program that he named **The kid Chickadie**.

The movies I've seen sure make you think wars are won *fast*. I think I'm looking at twenty three months so far. Enclosed are a few pictures I cut out of magazines and they show the places where I was stationed. I'm sending them home to you before they get *wrecked*. Boy Hon, these *love movies* make me feel awful at times but I struggle through them by imagining you and I together. I guess this covers the current situation.

With Love and Lots of Kisses, Your Johnny

On the Southwest Pacific War Front in New Guinea
Dad has the *blues* but hopes mom is okay. He knows a letter from her will bring *out the sunshine* and *snap* him out of his mood. News that the war in Europe and in the South Pacific is *escalating* reaches him. He is hoping this is a good sign. He really misses dancing *cheek to cheek* with mom.

08/05/44

My Dear Mary,

This is one of those days I feel *down in the dumps*. I hope everything is okay with you, sweetheart. I know a letter from you would *bring out the sunshine* and *snap* me out of this mood. However, I had no luck receiving anything today.

The war in Europe and the situation here in the South Pacific has been *escalating* at a high rate of speed. I'm hoping this means we're getting closer to the end. On September 1, 1944, I will have two year's overseas, wars sure take time out of one's life. My radio is my pal. I don't know how I would get by without it. The songs are so *good* these days and I can't wait to try them out on the dance floor with you. I can still remember how we used to dance *cheek to cheek*. It was *pure heaven*!

I guess the *ban* on gas will be lifted and new cars will start to appear. I would like to get one but we'll see how much they will cost. So long my sweet and take care of yourself.

With All my Love, Johnny

On the Southwest Pacific War Front in New Guinea
Dad is looking at mom's picture and says he likes the *shy look* on her face. He gazes at her in a *house dress*. He is not the *least bit* disappointed. He does not want her to work too hard.

08/06/44

My Darling Mary,

It is one of those *exciting* nights in the South Pacific Islands. Yeah, it's so romantic and all that *sort of stuff*. Ha! Ha! It would definitely be greatly improved and much more exciting if you were here, hon. If you only knew how much you mean to me. If I were holding you in my arms, I could show you my love in person instead of dreaming about it in my little tent.

I have the picture of you in the *house dress* with the broom in front of me. That shy look on your face is so cute. I can see how you will look as a *housewife* and I'm not the least bit disappointed. I sure wish I had you by my side. I really need a *large dose of tender love* more than ever.

Don't work too hard, sweetheart. I know you have your hands full with your mom being sick, but don't over exert yourself. Remember you are saving yourself for me as I am saving myself for you. So long my sweet one.

All my Love, Johnnie

On the Southwest Pacific War Front in New Guinea
Dad doubted mom's love wondering if it was *on paper only*. He has no worries now because she *proved* herself by *sticking by him* and writing. It seems workers in the States are *striking* for *better* wages. He disagrees with their complaints. He says our soldiers work hard but get paid very little.

08/11/44

Dear Sweetheart Mary,

I often wondered if your love for me was *on paper only*. My heart started *jumping* the day I met you so I know it's true on my end. I have no worries about you now because you have *proved your love* for me by *staying with me and writing to me* all this time.

My radio is playing the songs **No love or nothing until my baby comes home.** Ain't it the truth? By the way, I was offered $150.00 for my radio which I built for myself. It's worth a million to me for it has made my time over here more tolerable.

I heard workers are *striking* in the States for *better* wages. They seem to be complaining to their unions a lot.

Why our soldiers work for *next to nothing* compared to the *average* worker in the States. I'd like to *string them all up or drop them* instead of bombs over Japan! I think that is what they deserve.

Love Always, Johnny

On the Southwest Pacific War Front in New Guinea
Dad relays how much fun he and mom have writing to each other despite the *distance* between them. He becomes interested in a movie about China as it was the first place *invaded* by the Japs who needed to use the *natural rubber* plantations.

08/12/44

My Darling Sweetheart,

I got your two *v-letters* today that were dated July 16, 1944. They came much slower than your regular letter. We have our fun writing even if we are so far apart.

I saw a movie about China. It was the first place the Japs *invaded* because they needed to use the *natural rubber* plantations. However, the Japs lost all their *raw materials* such as rubber and oil because the United States *sank* their cargo ships. China certainly fought with the *odds against them* while the Japs committed so many murders of civilians.

The Japs started their eighth year of war. I hope we won't be in a war conflict that long. How do we stand with our *hot war of love,* sweetheart? Now give me a nice big smile so I can dream about those eyes of yours and your pretty face. So long, my sweet thing.

All my Hot Love, Johnny

On the Southwest Pacific War Front in New Guinea
Dad is disappointed because he has not received a picture of mom in a bathing suit. He asks her if she has ever learned to ice skate or drive a car, if not he would like to teach her both things. He is hoping she isn't *so busy* at the plant where she works. He thinks most of the factories will start working on *civilian* items soon.

08/14/44

My Darling,

Hon, I'm quite disappointed because I don't have a picture of you in your bathing suit. All the other boys seem to have received them. Oh well, I can be patient but hurry up, hon. Mary, I believe you told me once you don't know how to ice skate. Did you ever learn to drive a car? I would like to teach you both of these skills if you haven't tried them already. I hope you're not *so busy* at the factory now. I think there is a *slow period of time* of making *war* materials. Am I correct? Are *private* people able to buy tires?

I guess most of the factories will begin working on *civilian* materials soon. Were shoes ever rationed? I believe I heard something about that from my family.

Do you think you will be brave enough about us to *shut off* the light in your parlor? It won't matter either way to me for I can be romantic in light or dark. Tell me, did the picnic grove have their outdoor dances this year?

Sweetheart, I'll close now for it is 10:45 p.m. and I must *hit the hay*.

With All My Love, Johnny

On the Home Front in Manville, New Jersey
Mom has received a *boatload* of letters from dad describing everything about his surroundings where he is stationed. He also describes Army life in general.

08/16/44

Dear Johnnie,

You'll never know how happy you make me feel when I receive your letters and cards. You are too good to me, Johnnie. In one week I received six postcards, one twelve page letter, one four page letter and that *beautiful* compact all for me. I don't know how to thank you so I'll just say plain "thank you" and when I see you again I can make it more personal. You make me proud of you honey. Your letters are as interesting as they are beautiful. I can't help but tell my folks the cute things you write.

I was sorry to hear how tough the Army has gotten. Oh gosh, darn it, why doesn't somebody do something to end this whole *fighting* battle? I can't get over how hard you have to work. I wish this war would end right away. When I walk home from work, I always think of you marching left, right, etc.

I'm reading your twelve page letter now. You tell me everything and honestly I just can't seem to think of anything to answer your letters. How could I ever forget you? How sweet of you to figure out how many hours have passed since you last saw me. You are a sweet monkey!

With Love, Your Sweet Mary

On the Southwest Pacific War Front in New Guinea
Dad is relieved and pleased as he has finally gotten a picture of mom in her bathing suit. She describes a picture of herself waiting for dad with her hair *spread out on her pillow*. Dad gets all *tingly and excited* at the thought of it.

08/17/44

Dearest Darling,

What a relief and a pleasure. I finally got you to send me a picture of you in a bathing suit. Woo! Hoo! I have two bottles of beer in front of me so I'll have one on you. You should go out and have at least one drink for me. This picture will *keep me company* on these cold nights here. The picture you describe of you waiting for me with your hair *spread out on your pillow* gets me *tingly and excited* in more ways than one. Honey, it sure is nice for me to get *wrapped up* in your letters. All I think about is us, you and me. I love you two years, one month and thirteen and ½ days more than I did before.

Lots of Love, Your *old* Man

On the Home Front in Manville, New Jersey
Mom informs dad about the activities at home when it is 10:45 p.m. Times are tough so if a family can save money by making their own meat supply. They are resourceful.

08/20/44

My Dear Johnny,

Guess what my Dad is doing right now? It's exactly 10:45 p.m. and he's chopping up a fresh lamb. He bought it, killed it and now he's making lamb chops from it. Johnny, don't worry about me for there are no others in my mind or heart. It's very hard but so far I have managed to stay away from loving someone *except you* until the war is over.

Dear, I know you're lonely and would be happy if I was with you, but don't be a sissy. Face it and show yourself that nothing is getting the best of you. We can always dream, hope, pray and picture each other. I guess our letters are *censored*, but I don't care.

Your Woman, Mary

On the Southwest Pacific War Front in New Guinea
Dad gets word from home that some of his school mates are *missing in action*. He says "everyone can't be lucky while fighting a war". He hears a rumor about the release of a lot of soldiers after the war ends. He hopes this dream will come true.

08/20/44

My Dear Sweetheart,

My mail from home tells me some of my school mates are *missing in action*. I guess everyone can't be lucky while fighting a war. There is talk about releasing a lot of men after the war. I hope this dream will come true and I'll get to come home. I hope, I hope.

At any rate, it is a nice dream. So long *wife to be*, I'll be hunting you down soon.

Love Always, Johnny

On the Home Front in Manville, New Jersey
Mom and dad are still writing to each other. Mom is describing how she took care of her own mother as well as her brothers and sisters.

09/01/44

My Darling Johnny,

When I was small, I was always the big sister or the mother in our play house. Mostly I kept house for mother. I used to hold one of my baby sisters or brothers and they used to cry and crawl away from me for I was small too. She used to tie the baby and me to the back of a chair.

Movies, what were they? I hadn't seen one until I went to clean houses in Somerville, New Jersey and I was fifteen at the time. That's when I really became a *lady*! All my younger life, I was a *grown up* girl. I never owned a doll and I never had a bicycle of my own so I never learned to ride one. Mother never had to tell me what to do. I quit school at the age of thirteen and took care of our home and three children while mother and dad went to work. At fifteen I left home to clean houses and I never returned home to stay until I was twenty-three even though I always sent Mom and Dad some money to help out.

With All my Love, Mary

On the Southwest Pacific War Front in New Guinea
Dad is elated because he has received some *snapshots* of mom in her two piece bathing suit. He praises her *figure* and reminds her that she is the *reason* he's fighting now more than ever. The *pose* of her waving and the one of her sitting on the lawn with his letters spread around really *touched* him.

09/04/44

My Darling Sweetheart,

Well Hon, I received your *snapshots* and you bet I was happy. The two piece bathing suit looks very nice on you and also what's inside it too! Gosh Hon, you do have a *very nice figure* so don't think anything different. I like the *pose* of you waving very much.

I can really see what I'm fighting for more than ever.

The picture of you sitting on the lawn with all my letters *spread around* was very touching. I just had to show the boys the pictures.

They all thought with a figure like yours, you should be a dancer. Whatever you decide to do in the future is alright with me as long as I am a part of it. I will support you all the way.

Love, Johnny

On the Home Front in Manville, New Jersey
Mom and dad are as close as they can get. They also pray for one another in church.

09/10/44

My Darling,

I loved receiving the silver ring with the two hearts on it made from a Jap zero. Oh honey, you can imagine what all the girls at the plant thought when I showed them my ring. It warmed my heart to think of your heart and my heart together on one ring as we always will be two hearts together.

This is a little poem from the blessed Mother Mary called **Hymn for Soldiers**:

> Mary help our valiant solders, guard them all on land and sea.
> Keep them ever close to Jesus and sweet Mother near to thee.
> Help them in all care and sorrows, bring our boys home safe we pray.
> Mary, help our daring sailors, guard them all on land and sea.
> Keep them ever free from danger, ever close to God and thee.
>
> Mary, help our absent loved ones. Oh we miss their presence here,
> Help our fathers, friends and brothers dear.
> Help them, guide them far and near.

My Love to You, Mary

On the Southwest Pacific War Front in the Philippines
Dad's having fun riding in an Army *duck*. He becomes *busy as a bee* helping to set up camp and unload supplies. He describes mom as a *sweet little girl* with golden hair and a nice, *curvy* body.

09/16/44

My Darling Mary,

This place isn't bad but it does rain quite often. In fact, we got off the boat in a *driving rain* in one of those Army *ducks*. Ducks are vehicles with wheels that can transport people either on land or water. I'm *busy as a bee* now helping set up camp and unload supplies.

Hon, did you ever get the ring I sent you with the two hearts on it? Please let me know. I still can find the time to write to you even if I'm busy for you are very important to me. I can now say I have a *sweet little girl* waiting at home for me. She has golden hair, weighs only ninety eight pounds and has a nice, *curvy* body. She has dimples on her knees and a vaccination as well. The rest of her is a *military secret*.

Remember there is a *sad* soldier waiting to see his honey.

Love and Kisses, Johnnie

On the Southwest Pacific War Front somewhere in the Philippines
Dad is paying *close* attention to the number of men sent home. He shocked his mom when he sent her the *grand* to put in the bank for him. He describes the *babes* in this new location as they look like our American *Negroes*.

09/17/44

Dearest Darling,

Well Hon, we sent a few men home before we moved. Now we have sent more from here. I am paying close attention to this. Yes Darling, we will make all those *little* things you want for our home. I am sure now that we can have one.

My Mom almost fell over when she received the *grand* I sent her to put in the bank for me. I guess she didn't know her sonny was capable of saving so much money.

The *babes* around here wear *a lot* of clothes so we have no more *scenery* above the belt. They look more like our American *Negroes* and they work very hard. I saw one woman carrying at least *one hundred eighty* pounds on her back, while the old man carried a cane and nothing else.

I can't tell you much about this place yet. I was glad to hear of the landing three hundred miles near the Philippines. I'm hoping my letters reach you quicker after you start using this new APO. Take care of yourself.

Your Sweetheart, Johnny

On the Southwest Pacific War Front braving the weather near the Philippines
The mail is a little *mixed up* because dad keeps moving from one location to another. The war seems to be *spreading out* and Finland is now fighting Germany.

09/19/44

My Dear Mary,

I'm still *very* busy but it rains off and on so it *slows us down* a lot. Despite the weather, we are making good *headway*. Everything is a little *mixed up* with the mail situation. The Post Office boys from our old location used to eat with us so they are sending our mail in one bag. This means we get our mail over time.

Even though I have been busy, I can always find the time to write to you. I was on guard duty last night from 3:00 a.m. to 5:30 a.m. so I slept the rest of the morning. I kept looking at the sky and the stars thinking of you so the time went fast for me.

I heard Finland is now fighting Germany. The war is *spreading out*. Any place I visit or move to surprises me for it is fixed in *Yank* style. Boy, the Japs better give it up now. I miss you more than ever.

All my Love to You, Johnny

On the Southwest Pacific War Front located near the Philippines
Mom and dad agree on the *large* size of their wedding. They're thinking of a *possible* location. Dad does not like to hear she is working *so hard* every

day. He says he will have to *concentrate* on getting home as soon as he can to do something about it.

09/21/44

My Dearest Mary,

I understand the picnic grove at Diehl's Manufacturing must be quite a place. I can see you have your heart *set* on having a *big* wedding. I like the idea and maybe we can get the place for it.

It's so muddy here, especially when you drive jeeps and trucks all over the area. Gosh Hon, it makes me feel bad to hear that you have to work *so hard* every day. I'll just have to *concentrate* on getting home as soon as possible to do something about it. I can't say much about this place for no one is sure what the *real score* is here. This does it for now, honey.

All my Love Always, Johnny

On the Southwest Pacific War Front near the Philippines
Dad explains to mom he has heard *almost all* the outfits have sent their September rotation men home. He is thankful for the cooks who live with him as they listen to the radio and give dad *war* news they hear while he is working.

09/23/44

Dear Darling,

A rumor went out *all over* this island to the effect that Germany gave up, but I knew better. I have the radio on all day and the cooks who live with me listen to it when I am working. Almost all the outfits have sent their September rotation men home. We still are two months behind compared to them. Closing now before I fall asleep.

All my Love to You, Johnny

On the Southwest Pacific War Front somewhere near the Philippines
The boys are discussing *girls* as their favorite topic. Dad gets a letter from his mom telling him she bought him a new bed with his money instead of using it for herself. His stuff was moved *without incidence* and he has hung up mom's picture.

09/25/44

My Dearest One,

Right now the boys are discussing our favorite topic which is *girls*. In my tent I now live with one radio man and three cooks. I have to live with them for this is a very *G. I.* place. It is surprising to me considering where I am to find it this way.

I received a letter from my Mom. Gosh, she's so good to me. I keep sending her money so she can save it, because after we get married, I won't be able to help her financially. What does she do? She bought me a new bed. She is always doing something for me, but I wish she would take the *hint* and keep the money for herself.

I just heard a good one. An Aussie said "In the next war, we *Yanks* won't have to go there in person". "All they need is for us to send uniforms because there are so many *Yank* kids in Australia. Well my *little* one, I have said my mouthful for this time so I'll call it quits.

Love and Kisses, Johnny

On the Southwest Pacific War Front near the Philippines
Dad has put up his *permanent* tent. He says all the guys can *arrange* their things to get organized. He tells mom he hung her picture above his head so he can study her *curves*.

09/26/44

My Darling Mary,

It's another *rainy* night so we will have no *outdoor* movie tonight. I finally put up our *permanent* tent and it's not too bad. Now we can *arrange* our things and get organized. All my *stuff* came through although some guys were not as *lucky* and lost a few things. I have your picture hanging up again in my tent. That was *priority #1* for me.

I now have you standing right above my head waving to me with your *curves* behind your bathing suit. My Mom is sending me six rolls of film. As soon as I get myself *in shape*, I'll snap a few *terrible* pictures of myself and the boys.

Now I'm smoking a big El Rapo cigar. No, I'm not celebrating a guy becoming a father, rather it's a *two bit* cigar just for the heck of it. I'm settling down now for the night with a prayer to hurry up and end this war so I can see you again.

My Love Always, Johnny

On the Southwest Pacific War Front in the Philippines
Dad swears someone has *messed up* the process of sending men home. Morale has hit *rock bottom* for many of the boys. He feels this *jungle life* has taken a *toll* on him.

09/27/44

My Dearest Darling,

There is a group that has half as many men eligible to go home, yet they will send seven men home this month while we are sending only one *lucky stiff* home. Surely, someone must have *messed up!* This really makes morale low and in fact, it could hit *rock bottom*. Luckily for me, I just think about you and that makes me forget everything. I get by *much easier* than those guys who haven't a gal waiting for them.

This *jungle life* has taken a *toll* on me. I have the utmost confidence in you to help *snap me* back in shape. I hope to have at least seventy five years with you so there is no hurry. You were made for me to love even though it took twenty seven months to hear you talk.

With Lots of Love, Your Johnny

On the Southwest Pacific War Front in the Philippines
Dad has lost patience with the *wet* weather in his area. The weather is so *wet* for long periods of time, nothing has a chance to *dry out* before the next rain starts.

09/28/44

My Dear Mary,

I wish this place wasn't so *wet*. Gosh it's awful because nothing has a chance to dry out. I had clothes hanging on a line for six days and they're still wet. There are a lot of palm leaves around here I can wear. I can always wear my *birthday suit*.

With Love, Johnnie

On the Southwest Pacific War Front in the Philippines
Dad is living in the *jungle* presently so he thinks he might be here long enough to learn the Jap language. He already knows some *naughty* words. He's sending more pictures home for the album.

09/29/44

My Darling,

Well, I'm *still* in the *jungle* so I guess I'll be over here long enough to learn the Jap language. I already have a good head start with the *naughty* words. I have some exciting news! All the boys were delighted and we never knew it could happen to us. Guess what, it did not rain today!

Enclosed are a few pictures I want you to save for our album. I now have eight rolls of film on their way so I will be able to take pictures of some scenes around here.

So long Sweetheart.

Love Always, Your Johnny

On the Southwest Pacific War Front arriving in the Netherlands, East Indies Dad is now located somewhere in the Netherlands, East Indies and he says it is a lot like New Guinea. He likes his new location. He hasn't the slightest idea what to get mom for her birthday or Christmas. He tells her a *sad* story about one of the boy's girlfriend who suddenly passed away. It was a big shock to everyone as she was very young.

10/03/44

Dearest Mary,

I am somewhere in the Netherlands, East Indies. It seems to be about the same as New Guinea. My old company was in Australia in a large city. I would rather be here even if it's just *dog faces* on natives that we see around here.

I still don't know what you want for your birthday or Christmas. You mentioned that another letter will tell me what I need to know, but I haven't received it yet. One of the boys got word that his gal died. It was a big shock for she was very young. He had twenty six months overseas and might have had a chance to go home soon. All this kind of news makes a person stop and think. Be sure to take good care of yourself this winter. I think that is the most dangerous part of the year.

I'll close now before I get myself in a *blue* mood.

All my Love, Johnny

On the Southwest Pacific War Front in the Netherlands, East Indies Dad is overcome by the *tropical* heat. He says the heat drains all his energy. He is sending mom more pictures for the album.

10/04/44

Dear Mary,

Gosh honey, this place really makes a person *tired*. It's the *tropical heat* that does it. I have enclosed a few more pictures for our album. They get ruined over here so easily because of the humidity so I hope you don't mind saving them for me.

Love, Johnny

On the Southwest Pacific War Front in the Netherlands, East Indies Dad describes this location as *very different* from the *big* city. In other locations, the whole town comes out to greet the *Yanks*. He wants to send mom *a sum of* money to cover her birthday and Christmas presents.

10/07/44

My Darling Mary,

The Southwest Pacific hasn't anything of the *big city* stuff, where the whole town comes out to greet the Yanks. On the other hand, you probably would worry about me if I were in France. The picture you sent me shows women *jumping all over* the men. You might think I have a *babe*, but honestly you're *all the babe* I need.

It's getting closer to your birthday and I still don't know if it would be okay to send you a *sum of* money to cover your birthday and Christmas. As you know, I can't find anything here for you. You know darn well if I had a choice, I would try to pick out something nice for you. I'm sure all the Christmas gifts you picked out for me will come in handy. Besides, you know me better than I do myself.

Take care, Hon. When you look in the mirror, pretend I am standing there beside you.

Love and Many Kisses, Johnny

On the Southwest Pacific War Front in the Netherlands, East Indies
Dad credits mom for *inspiring* him to lead his Army life. He doesn't know how he would have done it without her encouragement.

10/12/44

My Sweetheart,

I had no idea what I could say to a girl who I haven't seen for twenty eight months. All it took was a *little one* like you to inspire me. I don't know how I would have stayed with this Army life alone without someone like you.

I try to send a few pictures in each letter. It's better for you to get something besides my boring letters. Our album must be pretty full of pictures by now. Our kids will get a kick out of them.

Love Always, Johnny

On the Southwest Pacific War Front in the Netherlands, East Indies

Dad has decided to send mom a $50.00 money order to cover her birthday and Christmas present. He hopes she gets his birthday card in time. Even though he is not always pictured in each photo, he wants to save these pictures to remember the boys he served with overseas.

10/14/44

My Darling Mary,

Some time ago, I asked if I could send you a sum of money for your birthday and Christmas presents. Well, I have waited for two weeks so I decided to send you a money order in the amount of $50.00 to cover both occasions. I certainly would have done more if I were home in the States.

I hope you got my birthday card in time. I also sent a few pictures some of the boys gave me. That is the reason I'm not in them. They probably won't mean much to you but to me they will. I want to be able to remember the guys who I spent my overseas time with in the future.

Loads of Love, Johnnie

On the Home Front in Manville, New Jersey
Dad has been sending mom a lot of pictures to save for him. He plans to make an album of the places he visited, the people he saw and the friends he made. He also wants to be able to show their kids what Army life and the war showed him.

10/15/44

My Loved One,

Oh Darling, I am so happy I could almost scream, cry, dance and sing all at the same time! For two weeks now I have been so miserable because I had not received even one letter from you. This week it is only Tuesday and I already got fourteen letters all from you! Johnny, your little girl is simply *overjoyed* with happiness! Honey, all these pictures you are sending me will look nice in an album. You will be able to put them in order and show them to your family and friends. I can't wait until you are able to finally come home to us.

Love Always, Mary

On the Southwest Pacific War Front in the Netherlands, East Indies
Dad can't wait to get started doing *radio work*. Dad says it is a contest between all the radios and only the loudest wins. He feels so sorry for his friend as he has lost all his *spirit*. He wants mom to go ahead and buy a nice *hope chest*.

10/15/44

My Darling,

I am back to being busy again. Sometimes I work days and sometimes nights, but I always make an effort to write to you. I'll be glad when we will be doing *radio work* again. There is a radio in almost every tent around me so you can hear three or four programs at the same time. It's a case of which one can play the loudest.

Remember me telling you about the boy whose girlfriend died? He used to run to mail call. Now he doesn't even move and he lets someone else check to see if he got a letter from home. What a change in him. He has no happiness or inspiration any more. A sweetheart sure makes a big difference in one's life.

With All My Love, Johnny

On the Southwest Pacific War Front in the Netherlands, East Indies
Dad is encouraging mom to buy a nice *hope chest*. He reminds her they are both helping their parents financially, however, they will need some *nice* things for their own house as well. He has enclosed a special letter that was given to all the guys who have crossed the equator. He wants mom to save it for him.

10/16/44

My Darling Sweetheart,

I received your letter of October 1, 1944. Gosh honey, it was one of the *dearest* letters I ever got from you. It's the one with the blue bow and all those cute *cutouts* pasted in it. Please go ahead and buy yourself a *hope chest*. Honey, please do what I say. After all I have made more money in the past two years no matter how much you made.

I have saved all my money except the $25.00 or $30.00 a month I send to my Mom. Besides, you are still helping your folks get straightened out financially before we are married. My folks are all set now.

I have enclosed a paper given to all those who have crossed the equator. Please save it for me. Our little junior will not have *two strikes* on him like we started with in life. He will start off on top thanks to your inspiration and love.

Love and Kisses, Johnny

On the Southwest Pacific War Front in the Netherlands, East Indies
An article in the *Yank* newspaper informs Dad he is now *permitted* to reveal the places where he was stationed. He starts describing each place and reassures mom by saying he was never even near *any* action. He reiterates that she should not worry about the Japs finding him as it is like *looking for a needle for a haystack*.

10/18/44

My Darling Mary,

I read in the *Yank* newspaper that we are now *permitted* to tell about all the places we were stationed in Australia. I spent a few months initially in Brisbane. After that, I travelled 1,000 miles north by train to Townsville.

I stayed there a few days then I went to Charter Towers. It is a small town west of Townsville. I stayed there for the rest of my time until my transfer.

The population was almost 8,000 people and the town had only three streets. Now you know I wasn't even near *any* action until I went to New Guinea. I spent quite a few nights in a trench while the Jap planes flew over our heads. Since I left New Guinea, I have spent only five minutes in a little hole built for two people. It is surprising how many people can fit in them during a raid.

Don't worry Hon, for the Japs it is like *looking for a needle in a haystack*. They have a few planes and none are any bigger than our medium bombers. All *Yank* newspapers are *censored* and any articles are changed before they are printed in it.

I'm still trying to throw out more junk. One of the boys in my tent got a letter from a girl weighing 175 pounds. Boy, are we having fun kidding him. Imagine him trying to sleep in a single bed with that *big of a babe*.

With A Ton of Love, Johnnie

On the Southwest Pacific War Front in the Netherlands, East Indies Dad describes the *dengue virus* spread by mosquitoes and tells mom he had a fever due to a stomach problem luckily not the *dengue fever*. He did have to spend six days in the hospital. The Japs lied about many things, however, Dad and the boys find out the truth about the war status.

10/19/44

My Darling,

Our First Sergeant went home on a twenty one day furlough and he will be back in about four months. Also, a very *small* number of men went home on rotation so I'm still a long way off from my dream of coming home.

Hon, all my life I have never gotten sick and that includes both civilian time and time spent in the Army. I developed a fever due to a stomach problem. There were many cases of *dengue fever* around so I had to spend six days in the hospital. The fever is part of the disease and the *dengue virus* is spread by mosquitoes.

By the way, the Japs lied about the things we now know about. We sure must have given them *hell* in Formosa. Formosa is an island off the coast of China and is present day Taiwan.

I guess this ought to bore you enough so I will close my trap before my bridge falls out.

With All my Love, Johnny

On the Southwest Pacific War Front still in the Netherlands, East Indies Dad hasn't stopped writing to mom but could not mail his letters all at the same time. He explains that the Indian Ocean is lacking mail boxes. He was tested in Radio School but did not have any problem with the test.

10/20/44

Sweetheart of Mine,

I told you in the past that there may come a time when you might not hear from me for a couple of weeks. You say you received fourteen letters at one time. You see, I didn't stop writing but I couldn't mail the letters at that time. After all, the Indian Ocean has no mail boxes. Even though I'm *nine thousand* miles from home, I have you in my heart.

We took a test for Radio School today. It was just like asking a good cook how many vitamins are in a meal. In other words, they're not actual *operative* questions and only used for Radio School entrance. Only an *equipment* designer would have a use for them.

I guess this covers the situation for now. Give my regards to your folks.

With Oceans of Love, Johnny

On the Southwest Pacific War Front in the Netherlands, East Indies Dad hears a Jap report that says American troops landed in the Philippines two days ago. The Filipino people are very generous so it is thought that if they offer you something you must accept it otherwise you will *hurt* their feelings. He explains the airplane pictures and how each mission is *painted* on the *body of* the plane. Dad also found out some of the first boys who were sent home ended up in an Overseas Replacement Center so they will be sent overseas a second time.

10/22/44

My Darling Mary,

According to the Jap reports, American troops landed in the Philippines two days ago. We did not hear this from the Army reports we usually get here. They say it *hurts* the feelings of the Filipino people if they offer you something and you *refuse* to take it from them. Most of the people are Spanish or Malaysian. I do hope I get a chance to visit some of these places one day.

All the plane pictures I sent you are of our airplanes. A bomb is *painted* on them for each mission and a plane is *painted* for each Jap shot down. This also applies to ships so if we sink a ship then a ship is *painted* on the plane.

B-29 plane signifying one Jap airplane shot down

Some of the first boys who went home are now in an Overseas *Replacement* Center so I'm guessing they will be sent overseas a second time. I may be rather busy for some time now so I might not be able to write to you every day. However, don't worry Hon, you will hear from me.

Love and Many Kisses, Johnnie

On the Southwest Pacific War Front in the Netherlands, East Indies Dad is surprised when a *large rain* hits a tent and then runs right through it. He says at his previous location they slept on wooden pallets, however, here they just have *coral*. The boys say my tan is as *dark as a native* so mom might not recognize him when he returns. He has another amusing tale about how one guy was able to acquire whiskey from home in mouthwash bottles.

10/24/44

My Darling,

Once again, we had a *large rain* last night. One tent started to *fill up* because it was a little low and water ran right through it. At my previous location, we made wood pallets to sleep on but here we just have coral. I do miss my personal tent. There I could think in peace.

All the boys tell me my tan is as *dark as* a native so you might not recognize me when I get home. All the boys in my tent are growing mustaches. We are kidding everyone into thinking Filipino women like them so that is the reason. We do need something to pass the time away.

One of the boys called home and they sent him whiskey in *mouthwash* bottles. This is one way of getting it here *unnoticed*. A base rule now says we must wear complete uniforms whenever we are away from the company area. We are also required to wear our stripes. I hope we will leave this place before they tell us we have to wear neckties as well.

Closing with All my Love, Johnny

On the Home Front in Manville, New Jersey
Mom and dad enjoy writing and reading letters so much they even reread the letters.
Mom likes to send him some prayers and poems.

10/29/44

My Darling,

Honey, I think I finally caught up with rereading and answering your letters for now. I better get some sleep so I am going upstairs and sharing my bed with your picture. With your picture next to my heart and this prayer on my lips I fell asleep after saying this prayer:

Heavenly Father up above, please protect the one I love.
Keep him safe keep him sound no matter when or where he's bound.
Help him to know, help him to see that I love him make him love me.

Oh dear God help me to be the kind of girl he wants me to be.
Keep us now keep us forever, happy, loving and trusting together.

Dear one, I hope you are staying well, I'm thinking of you daily.

Lots of Love, Mary

On the Southwest Pacific War Front in the Netherlands, East Indies Dad warns mom not to *fall* for any *baloney* where people ask for a donation to buy cigarettes for the boys overseas. He says they have never seen any evidence of this fund. He tells her about two new Red Cross girls who load up a jeep with lemonade and cookies for the guys. They were surprised as the guys told them "This is the first Red Cross visit they have had in nineteen months".

10/29/44

Sweetheart of Mine,

I often wondered if you believe all that *baloney* they *dish out* when they ask for donations to buy cigarettes for the troops overseas. We have never seen any *evidence* of such a fund here.

I had an experience at my former location. It seems two new Red Cross gals who had just arrived decided to load a jeep with lemonade and cookies. They drove to our area where we were working and gave out these items. Then they asked if the Red Cross was ever here before. We said "this was the first visit in nineteen months". Boy, were they surprised! They said "In the States they told us a lot of things and now we find out there are many things that don't exist overseas".

So Hon, don't fall for any of it. The situation is not like the previous war. During the last war, the Red Cross gals were nurses. Now they only give out books, ice water or a few cookies. The food is only for anyone passing through but not for the permanent men stationed at the base. Don't worry about me because I feel fine and very healthy at 154 pounds. Give yourself a nice big squeeze and try to imagine it's my arms doing it.

Love, Johnny

On the Southwest Pacific War Front in the Netherlands, East Indies
Dad encloses a picture of a Mess Sergeant who is *Slovack* and has become his buddy. He can't get over the fact the natives have almost more G. I. equipment than he owns.

10/30/44

Dearest Mary,

I have enclosed a picture of our Mess Sergeant. He's Slovak and we get along swell. You ought to see the natives around here. They have almost more G. I. equipment than I have myself.

Honey, now we know a lot more about each other so you can imagine how great it will be for us to be together. Our love has stood the *time* test so nothing can break us apart now. Sweetheart, I guess this is all for the time being. Don't let this get you down. Cheer up and remember we still have our *deep* love to keep us going.

Love with Many Kisses, Johnny

On the Southwest Pacific War Front in the Netherlands, East Indies
Dad calls attention to his change in rank and he is proud to be a Technical Fourth Grade, otherwise known as a Sergeant. He is happy to receive a pay increase and says this was *somewhat* of a surprise as he was not aware of any positions being open.

MARY JANE JUZWIN

11/02/44

My Darling Mary,

First of all, I must call your attention to the change of my rank. I am now a Technical Fourth Grade or otherwise known as a Sergeant. I can now get $96.00 per month. It was *somewhat* of a surprise for I had no idea any positions were open. You see we had received at least eight men with the rank of Sergeant from the States. It sure looked *hopeless* for us older men to attain another rank.

However, since we sent some men home, the ranks were *reconstructed* so now we are on an even grade. I sent you more pictures to save for me as they spoil easily in this climate.

Lots of Love and Kisses, Johnny

On the Southwest Pacific War Front in the Netherland, East Indies
Dad begins with a funny poem about a *boy wolf* and a *girl wolf*. He says he is very busy during the day but gets plenty of rest at night. He is sending more pictures which need explanations and he will do this when he returns home.

11/04/44

Hi Honey,

I will start right away with some humor.

The Wolf

> If he parks in his *flivver*, down beside the moonlit river,
> and you feel him all a *quiver*, Baby he's a wolf.
> If he says you're gorgeous looking, and your dark eyes set him cooking,
> but your eyes aren't where he's looking, Baby he's a wolf.

If he says that you're an *eyeful*, but his hands begin to *trifle*,
and his heart pumps like a *rifle*, Baby he's a wolf.
If by chance when you're kissing, you can hear his heart a *missing*,
and you plead but he won't listen, Baby he's a wolf.

She Wolf

If she throws her little *quiver*, in the front seat of your *flivver*,
and says it's pleasant on the river, Brother she's a wolf.

If the *get-up* she's wearing turns your head and keeps you staring
cause the lengths a little d*aring*, Brother she's a wolf.

If she really is *bewitching*, and she kisses with a *twitching*,
and if her rosy lips are *itching*, Brother she's a wolf.

It's cute eh, hon. I am still very busy during the day but don't worry I get lots of rest at night. I have enclosed a few more pictures. I'll explain them when I get home.

All my Love, Johnny

On the Southwest Pacific War Front in the Netherlands, East Indies Dad tells mom about a regular fellow they called *Chief* who was due to go home and how the boys gave him *three* cheers after he got through thanking them for being like *brothers* to him. He also comes out with an *amusing* but interesting story about a native who visited their tent.

11/06/44

My Dearest Sweetheart,

It must be very nice this time of the year at home. I would be so happy just to *snuggle* in your arms and pitch some *Woo*! I sure could stand a lot of that stuff and I do mean stuff.

One of our officers has left our company. It's the one we all called *Chief*. He sure was a *regular* fellow and we gave him three cheers when he got through thanking us for being like *brothers* to him.

We had a native visit us in our tent today. He couldn't speak English very well but his handwriting was very neat. About fifteen boys gathered around him and kept asking him how to say this or that. We sure had some fun with him. You should have seen the native *making* all kinds of *expressions* when the guys with false teeth pulled out their bridges. I don't know what he was thinking but just watching him was entertaining.

Take good care of yourself for me, honey.

Love and Kisses, Johnnie

On the Southwest Pacific War Front in the Netherlands, East Indies
Dad has *fixed up* a radio and sold it for $140.00. He says the guys think *nothing* of paying this much and are delighted to get one. He hears a *disturbing* story and finds it hard to believe how some of the guys who went home on rotation wearing overseas stripes and visiting bars in San Francisco, California are being *beaten or robbed*.

11/07/44

My Darling Girl,

Everything is going fine with me and I hope all is the same with you. I sold a radio today for $140.00. All the guys think *nothing* of paying this amount of money and the guy was delighted to get the radio.

One of the guys whose brother went home on rotation told him that in San Francisco, California you must *watch out* for yourself. The guys who are seen with overseas stripes on are being *robbed* by civilians and in many cases *beaten as well*. Some of these guys have fifty to sixty missions to their credit. They only wish to go home and when they finally get there, they are *robbed* when they go out to a bar.

I have some funny stuff to share with you. These are definitions:

> Stork---------------- A bird who has *none* of the fun in bringing the baby
> Spring Fever--------- The time when the *iron* in your blood turns to *lead* in your pants.
> Private secretary----- A good one never misses a period.
> Pajamas-------------- An item of clothing that newlyweds place beside their bed in case of a fire! Tee! Hee!

I hope you enjoyed my definitions. Perhaps you know some of the same and would like to *let your hair down* and tell me them. After all, we do know each other pretty well by now. I bet you are still giving your hair a *rough* time. Those golden curls could stand a lot of *fussing from* these hands.

All my Love, Johnnie

On the Southwest Pacific War Front somewhere near the Philippines
Dad is very happy to receive his *good conduct* pin. He had to wait quite a while for it as he was caught without *dog tags* on and was told it was an *infraction* on his record. In this location, the guys must be aware of the times when they need to *shut off* the lights.

11/09/44

Dearest Mary,

I finally got my *good conduct* pin. I had to wait until now because at my last location I forgot to wear my *dog tags* one day. I now have four pins. I'll probably accumulate more of them before I come home.

If I don't seem like I'm writing as often, please do not worry about me. In this area, we are required to *shut off* the lights several times during a day. The Japs only make one or two *passes* over us.

Therefore, we cannot have *bright* lights on because they could identify our location. However, it's like *duck hunting* for our pilots and they easily shoot them down.

Take care, my sweet one.

Love and kisses, Johnny

On the Home Front in Manville, New Jersey
Dad sends mom a picture of himself in a grass skirt. Both he and mom are enjoying their senses of humor. This goes a long way to keeping dad's morale positive.

11/12/44

My Darling Johnny,

You have the sweetest ways of starting your letters as *My Darling Girl*. That sends chills as well as thrills all through my system. I'm simply crazy about the pictures of you in the grass skirt! That's my favorite picture and I laughed so hard my sides nearly split. When I showed Mother and Daddy the picture, they laughed hard too.

I have seen and heard Mother and Daddy laughing and sharing jokes with each other many times. I have heard sharing a sense of humor is very important for both husband and wife. Let's hope we can share a sense of humor no matter whether we have hard times or good times in our life together.

Love Always, Your Mary

On the Southwest Pacific War Front near the Philippines
Dad is now sharing his experiences in travelling. He cites the various branches of the service with the fact that he and the boys got through all their travels without the *slightest bit of* trouble. He describes some *cute* little Filipino children walking around wearing all kinds of G. I. hats and clothing.

11/16/44

My Dearest Darling,

I will now share with you a little about my experiences in travelling. I had a very long voyage. Thanks to our various branches of the service, we got through it all without the *slightest bit of* trouble. We landed and unloaded very quickly just to make sure we were away from the water front as soon as possible.

We turned around and saw some *cute* little Filipino children walking around with all kinds of G. I. hats and clothing. Here and there I saw a few men and women. I was too busy to go to the village that first day. I needed some rest as I could still feel the boat *rocking* even when I was no longer on board.

Everything is *pretty messed up* at the present time. We haven't got our camp site yet.

I also have to wait for my new APO address so Hon, you will get a bunch of letters all at one time! I hope you haven't worried too much about me. I'll do my best to write often so just keep your letters coming too.

Lots of Love, Johnnie

On the Southwest Pacific War Front near the Philippines
Dad has seen quite a bit of *action* in the air when one of our pilots shot down a Jap *zero*. Dad assures mom the Japs cannot see them because

the lights are shut off many times a day. He is not happy with the *awful* mosquito population and says he's camped out in some coconut trees. Rumors say that the December quota on rotation may be larger.

11/19/44

Dear Mary,

I have seen a lot of *action* in the air. I saw a Jap *zero* shot down by the same kind of plane I put on the ashtray made for you. This action occurred right over our heads, however, he fell down a mile or so away. If I am not able to write as often, please don't worry your pretty little head. In this area, we are required to shut off the lights many times a day so the Japs cannot see us.

Boy, the mosquito population is *awful* here and there are plenty of them. I'm camped out among some coconut trees so if it ain't *Tojo* it will be a *coconut* falling on us. We are told we will have some civilians helping us tomorrow to clean our area. I'm in a village and the homes here are just *huts made of bamboo polls*. This place is very *G. I.* It's because the headquarters we are a part of has only been here for eleven months. None of those comfortable places any more. The latest rumor says that our December quota on rotation will be larger. I have finally been able to get this letter completed and sent.

With Lots of Love, Johnny

On the Southwest Pacific War Front near the Philippines
Dad hasn't gotten a chance to *explore* the larger villages but he does not have *high expections*. He tells mom the really *modern* islands are still occupied by the Japs. His tent now includes an *indoor* foxhole right next to his bed protected from the rain. Little kids are running all over the place and the boys are looking forward to getting *organized* so they'll be able to buy some chickens. He also says he has eaten *way too much* coconut.

11/20/44

My Dearest Sweetheart,

I'm writing to you during lunch time. It looks like the food will be very good here. One of the fellows got a letter today so I'm hoping I'll get mine soon. I haven't gotten a chance to see some of the larger villages, but it's not as if I have *high* expectations. All the really modern islands are still under Jap control.

Little kids are running all over. Most of them can understand a little English and speak a little as well. As soon as we get *set up and organized*, we'll be able to buy some chickens by returning the favor with cash or goods. They leave this up to us.

I've eaten so much coconut that I hate to look at one *straight* in the face. At our old place, I was paid in Dutch currency. I wasn't able to send any money home because of regulations. It worked like this. One *guilder* was $.53 American money. They had 1's, 5's, 10's, 50's and 100's guilder notes in paper. Some day you will see them all when I get home. I think it is a long way off, unfortunately. Now we get paid in *pesos*. One is worth $.50. The silver works just like the Dutch 100 *centaros* to the peso. One *centaro* is $.01 in Philippine money.

Please don't tell anyone about the air raids. I don't want my Mom to worry. She worries enough about *little* things so she doesn't need to know any *big* things. Remember civilians in England go through twice as much and serve for four years as well. I haven't heard the news on the radio for some time, but I plan to set up my set soon. There is no other way to find out the news.

Well sweetie, this is all for now.

All my Love and Lots of Kisses, Johnny

On the Southwest Pacific War Front near the Philippines

Dad goes on an *exploration* of one city that was *badly* damaged by the war. He saw some Jap *pill boxes* which are small Japanese planes. The boys met some very *polite*, young Filipino boys. They decide to ask the youngsters to help them construct a wooden floor for the tent to keep it off the ground and protected from the rain. Foxholes also need to be made and covered with trees.

11/23/44

Dearest Mary,

Your birthday passed while I was still *on the water* travelling to yet another camp. I do hope you received my birthday card. I thought of you so much all day wishing I could have been there with you to help you celebrate and enjoy.

I went to a larger place today. It looked like a combination of Chinatown, Negroetown and Shantytown due to the war. I saw a few Jap *pill boxes which are* small Japanese planes that were slightly damaged. I'm guessing the Japs who were in this area at one time got a good *hot foot* from a flame thrower. They looked very much *burnt to a crisp.*

We keep seeing young Filipino boys around our area all day. I never saw more polite children. They say "Yes sir" or "No sir" to us and "thank you" all the time. We are going to ask them to help us make a wooden floor for our tent to keep it off the ground a few feet. This would enable us to stay *high and dry* in even rainy days. We also have to make some foxholes and cover them with trees.

If the rumors I heard about the December quota are true, this puts me about 26th on the list to go home. There is *a squadron of* mosquitoes attacking me at the moment so I will close for the present.

Love and Lots of Kisses, Johnnie

On the Southwest Pacific War Front near the Philippines
The mail from the States must once again *catch up* to the Pacific. Dad sees women carrying *large* bundles on their heads which they seem to be *balancing* without using their arms or hands. He finds out that they prefer to eat rice more than anything else. However, the natives didn't grow rice as the Japs would have stolen it for themselves.

11/24/44

My Dear Sweetheart,

My mail hasn't *caught up* to me in this location, however, there were packages at my former place that arrived the same day we left for the Philippines. We are getting our camp in *better* shape now. The Filipinos get $.60 a day working for the U. S. government. They prefer to eat rice rather than anything else.

The women carry *large* bundles on their heads and balance them without holding them. It is quite something to see. Every man carries a *big* knife. The men use their knives to do some work. One of the Filipino foremen got married today and was back on the job anyway. He said "This is war time so I must work".

They did not grow rice when the Japs were here because the Japs would have taken it all. I hear there is a drink that is served here that is similar to *jungle juice* but it is made from coconut milk and doesn't taste as good. None of that for me! I have almost forgotten what it feels like to get lots of mail. I think it might be close by but not unloaded or sorted out yet. Gosh, how I miss hearing from my sweetheart.

I can't wait to see the latest picture of you. That is always one of my best gifts from you. Please repeat anything of *real* importance. Mail travels through *dangerous* waters at night and might get lost once in a while.

Also please don't let the newspapers fool you. The Philippine Islands are under our control and aren't much different than New Guinea. Of course there are no big, tall trees or mines but the swamps are the same.

I'm finding it hard to write interesting letters to you partly due to the fact that I haven't received any mail for a while. However, I can always find something to say to you.

Love Always, Your Johnny

On the Southwest Pacific War Front near the Philippines
Everyone feels better for they have finally received their *first* mail delivery at this location. *Tojo* is attacking the area at night, however, American anti aircraft guns shoot down the Jap planes. Dad tells mom about a famous fighter pilot named Major Richard Bong and he speculates the end of the air battle. Dad speaks with pride as he has *serviced* the same group of fighter planes used by Major Bong.

11/26/44

Dear Mary,

Today we received our *first mail delivery* in the Philippines. I didn't get one letter, I got more than one. I got two *large* letters from you, two *v-letters* and letters from *almost* everyone I wrote to as well. Now we all feel better.

Tojo is trying to see how long he can keep us up at night. I will never get excited about seeing fireworks again. You ought to see *ack ack* otherwise known as anti aircraft guns. What a *sight* to see gunfire at night! One night he *overdid it* so I saw one get shot down by our anti aircraft guns. It sure was a welcome sight.

Don't worry Hon, Major Bong can take care of *Tojo*. Major Richard I. Bong was a member of the Army Air Force in World War II and a Medal of Honor recipient. He was one of the *most decorated* fighter pilots and the U.

S. highest scoring *air ace* in the war. He was credited with shooting down forty Japanese aircraft. All of his *aerial* victories were in the Lockheed P-38 Lightning fighter.

Our company serviced the same fighter group of planes he is in since our outfit has been overseas. Perhaps, at one time I worked on equipment from his plane. I'm not sure of this because the outfit brings sets of equipment we work on for the planes.

I sure am happy you got my birthday card. I sent it very early for I knew the Philippines were going to be invaded. You do get *sentimental*. I can only imagine you sleeping with my mail next to your cheeks. You sure are sweet to me. I got seven packages from my sweetheart for Christmas. How can I ever keep up with you? I have just enough time to say "good night".

Love always, Johnny

On the Southwest Pacific War Front located near the Philippines
Dad points out to mom how both of them have been helping their folks out financially trying to get their home and property paid in full. He states, however, *Junior* will not have to do this for he and mom in the future.

11/27/44

Sweetheart of Mine,

I want to explain to you clearly about our *junior* being behind the *8 ball* or *having two strikes* against him. You and I have been helping our folks out financially since we were around twelve years old. We were trying to get their home and property *paid in full*. Now we are twenty six years old and this situation is just about done. Well, our kids will not have to do this for us.

Here is the reason I say this. You asked me which is safer keeping some *war bonds* or putting money in the bank? Well hon, both of them are backed by the U. S. government so you need not worry about losing your money. Besides, war bonds are for a ten year period so it isn't *too hard* to pay them in full. Here is where I have my money and the specific amounts. I have $2,000.00 in soldier's deposits with 3% interest and they can be taken out whenever the owner wants them. I have $500.00 at home in a bank and I also have a little over $500.00 in war bonds. I put a little change in our company safe so when I go home, I will have enough to drink and celebrate. I haven't spent my money on wild women, drinks or cigarettes.

I know how you feel about all this. When we get married, we will have more than a few bucks our folks had when they got hooked. When one feels love *deep down* in one's heart, those extras are not important. Only our true love matters.

All my Heart, Johnnie

On the Southwest Pacific War Front near the Philippines
Mom tells dad she received the money he sent for her *hope chest* which she will fill with

various household items for their future home. The fellow who lost his gal is now in dad's tent and he is observing the *change* in the man's demeanor. There is a new Colonel so dad now has to wear his uniform in this location.

11/29/44

My Sweet One,

I am glad you received the money I sent for your *hope chest*. You say you have accumulated quite a collection. After we get engaged, we can buy plenty more items to save in your *hope chest*. I think maple is very nice and your taste is like mine so I know your choice will be wonderful.

The fellow who lost his gal by death is in my tent now. He seems okay but changed a lot. I know it was quite a shock to him. We have a new Colonel here so you can guess what we have to do now. That's right, we have to wear our uniforms.

Oceans of Love, Johnny

On the Southwest Pacific War Front near the Philippines
Dad relays that he now has a *bamboo* hut off the ground with a floor as well. The Filipino boys built it and now they are working K. P. for the American soldiers. Dad is impressed with how *clean* these people appear. He read mom's list of gifts she will be sending to him and tells her she has great taste and picked out good choices.

12/01/44

My Dear Sweet Darling,

I now have a *bamboo* hut off the ground with a floor as well. It was built by the Filipinos and it is just the way I wanted it. We also have them working K.P. for us and I must say they sure are *clean* people. We are finally getting things in better shape here. Luckily, the rain stopped for a few days so we could work easier.

I have read your list of gifts you are sending me and honey you have *great* taste and picked out good choices. It can't be much more than six months before I see you in person. Just don't get yourself all excited and in a *flutter*. Maybe I'll sneak up and surprise you. Of course, I better duck my head for I know you would swing at me.

All My Love, Johnny

On the Southwest Pacific War Front near the Philippines
Dad is in another location and says this is a *much* cooler place and *much more* interesting to him. He describes a B-24 heavy bomber and the amount of gas it takes to fly a *fighter* plane. He also shares more *funny* definitions with mom.

Mary Jane Juzwin

12/03/44

My Darling Love,

Well, I am travelling once again. I am feeling *blue* for I haven't received any mail from you for about a week before I had to sail to another place.

This year I was unable to get an assortment of Christmas cards so that's why I only sent one for the whole family. This is a much cooler place than my last one and much more interesting to me.

I know I will never see Australia again. Some of the boys landed in New Guinea initially and never got to see the land *down under*. At least I saw quite a bit of it. My old outfit was *busted up* and guys were sent all over the place.

I thought you might be interested in my explanation of our B-24 heavy bomber. It takes many gallons of gas an hour to run a B-24 heavy bomber. It also takes many gallons an hour just to fly slowly in a fighter plane. The next time you hear someone complaining about the gas shortage, tell him this. When a plane flies in combat, the gas intake increases by *l-caps and borends*. They considered the B-24's to be *flying boxcars* because they were *spacious* with a slab sided fuselage.

Here are a few more funny definitions:

    Mothers Day---Nine months after Fathers Day
    Nursery-------- A place to park last year's fun until it grows up.
    Spouse----------A combination of a domestic servant, a hot water bottle and incubator
    Horse show---- A bunch of horses showing their asses to a bunch of horses asses who are judges.
    Bathing suit----A garment without hooks but with plenty of eyes on it.

I thought you would enjoy these. I am hoping you're enjoying collecting things for your *hope chest*. Little armful of mine, don't worry about me. Just keep those letters coming.

Lovingly, Johnny

On the Southwest Pacific War Front near the Philippines
Mom feels it is better for dad to *share* a tent with a *gang* instead of being alone. They keep each other company and help one another when necessary.

He is telling her about *excellent* Filipino workers. One even knows how much sugar he likes in his coffee. All the guys work in the Radio and Supply Dept.

12/06/44

My Dearest Sweetheart,

You're right when you said it is better for me to be *among* the boys rather than be alone. I have a new bunch of guys and we all work in the Radio and Supply department. This is the gang I work with all day.

Our Filipino workers on K.P. are doing fine. In fact, one of them always remembers how much sugar I use for my coffee. There are two men about twenty three years old and one boy about sixteen years old. They sure come in handy although some of the boys were hoping we would have WACs instead. So long my Darling.

Your Old Man, Johnny

On the Southwest Pacific War Front near the Philippines
Dad is happy to report that he had his teeth *cleaned* by the one and only dentist he has ever met in the Army. He and the dentist are pretty good friends and dad has *hung out* with him in his tent quite a few times. Both

he and mom think the picture of him in the *grass skirt* is their *favorite* snapshot.

12/07/44

My One and Only,

A moon around here means it is a good night for a visit from *Tojo*. At home it sure means something completely different. Of course, I don't need a moon to get me started.

I had my teeth *cleaned* today by the dentist. He is the *first and only* dentist I have met as long as I have been in the Army. We know each other pretty well so he has invited me to his tent quite a few times to *hang out*.

You say the *grass skirt* picture of me is your *favorite*. It's my *favorite one* of me too. Don't forget to practice the *hula* dance so you can do it for me in the *grass skirt* when I come home. I am *tingling* at the thought of it.

Lovingly, Johnny

On the Southwest Pacific War Front near the Philippines
Dad finds out that his First Sergeant who had been on his way home on furlough remained in New Guinea while he waited two months for transportation.

12/12/44

My Darling,

Here is the latest news for you. Our First Sergeant who was on his way home on furlough was *still* in New Guinea for two months waiting for transportation. Some other guys got home in three weeks. This is just one of those things in the Army.

Boy, are the Japs spreading all kinds of *bullshit* on the radio. It is one big laugh. They say everything we have is *destroyed* yet we can hear our planes flying overhead all day long. I can only believe the information our superiors tell us.

My Love to You, Johnnie

On the Southwest Pacific War Front near the Philippines
Dad is telling mom about some guys he calls *guerrillas*. He saw a First lieutenant who had long black wavy hair and he thought this person was a lady. Much to their surprise, the boys find out the *lady* was actually a man. Apparently, these guys dress in *ladies* clothing and *sneak back* into the village to *spy* on the Japs and find out gun positions.

12/14/44

Sweetheart of Mine,

I went to a large town today in a truck and saw quite a few people. We saw these *guerrillas*. One First Lieutenant had long black wavy hair and we all thought he was a *lady*. On the way back we saw two people hitchhiking so we picked them up. Much to our surprise, the *lady* was a man. In fact, the lieutenant let his hair *down* and he had a fine head of black wavy hair just like a *lady*. They let their hair grow so that they can put on *ladies* clothing and sneak back into the village and spy on the Japs. This way they could find out gun positions.

The people they hate the most are the Filipino *collaborators* because they would expose them to the Japs. You ought to see the people waving to the Lieutenant. He is the *local* hero around here. He has been a First Lieutenant for three and one half years so he is rich as well as good looking. He was a prisoner in Batan which is a city in the Philippines and he escaped. He was a lucky one. The Japs marched the American and Filipino soldiers for hours and if they did not keep up, they were *clubbed or shot to death*. This was called the **March of Death.**

All my Love, Johnny

On the Southwest Pacific War Front near the Philippines
Dad is still *busy as a bee* working on radio sets for planes. He calls himself the only *old man* left as he has *new* guys from the States to train.

He anticipates teaching the *new* guys a lot. They're not as knowledgeable or experienced as he so they will benefit.

12/18/44

My Dearest Sweet One,

I have gotten you a *Jap* jacket and a large *clip of Jap* wooden bullets. These bullets are used in close range fighting. I am still *busy as a bee* during the day. I am the only *old man* left who works on the radio sets for planes. I have a bunch of new guys with me straight from the States. It seems they just teach them how to work on one or two radio sets. I try to work on as many different radio sets as I can. I find it more interesting so I like this work a lot.

By the way, I have my own little portable radio all fixed up. It's a broadcast set but there is a special service station close by that I am using. This set works on batteries or electric. So now Hon, we have a nice portable radio set to use at the beach or while we go on hikes. I especially like music and plenty of you. Woo Hoo!

Loving you Always, Johnny

On the Southwest Pacific War Front near the Philippines
Dad is feeling *down in the dumps for* he has received Christmas cards but no letters. He is concerned about the *lack of* rotation quota for December.

12/31/44

My Darling,

The New Year will be here soon. I don't feel *a bit* excited. I am rather *down in the dumps*. I have gotten Christmas cards but my *regular* mail hasn't arrived.

There isn't a quota for us in December. Other outfits with the same number of men have quotas. I guess they don't want to *break up* our team. Our company has one of the *best* reputations and everyone is *highly* satisfied with our work. They say we're the *best* radio signal company they've ever worked with so it is a big compliment.

I guess you need a *Sugar Daddy*. In five months, the quota might be raised. Men with less than twenty months overseas go home on rotation. I miss you and especially your mail which means everything to me. I can *deep* inside me what your letters do to me. I must not bother you any further for you will be busy looking for that *Sugar Daddy*.

Lots of Love, Your Johnny

CHAPTER FOUR

1945 –
THE WAR WINDS DOWN AND FINALLY ENDS

On the Southwest Pacific War Front reading war news in the Philippines Dad says no civilian in the world has *any* knowledge of the Army or the war. He asks mom if she got her *hope chest* so she can buy a lot of household items for their future home. He's waiting for her Christmas package to arrive. She makes *big points with* her future mother and father-in-law by sending gifts.

01/08/45

My Sweetheart,

I read the article you sent me from your local paper. The only thing wrong is the article is written by a civilian. There isn't a civilian in the world who *knows* what the score is in the Army. The article itself was good though. I always say only the *weak minded* ones fall on the wrong side of life.

You keep worrying about me Hon, and you have no reason to fear. I'm telling you that I have strong willpower. It is a good thing to have in the Army wherever you are placed. Remember I'll be a good boy. A lot of boys lose their girl and start drinking and oh well you know the rest. I have everything in the world I could ever want now. I would never do anything to spoil it. I will try my hardest not to make you unhappy. I feel sure you share the same concept.

By the way hon, did you get your *hope chest* yet? Did the amount of money I sent to you cover the cost? If not, I'll peel off a few *greenbacks* and send them along to you. I have $500.00 in our company safe and can get my hands on it quickly so if you ever need it, just let me know. Please do this, emergency or otherwise.

I wish I knew what you want or need. I would take care of it. I know there is a lot of things I want to do if only I had you by my side. Just keep smiling and I will try to imagine what your pretty face looks like.

Loving you truly, Your Johnnie

On the Southwest Pacific War Front in the Philippines
Dad hasn't received any of mom's Christmas packages, however, he says everyone should remember this war is moving fast and ships are needed for men and materials.

01/11/45

Dear Mary,

I haven't received *any* of your Christmas packages yet. However, I remember I did get them around this time last year so there is a lot of hope they will come soon. We have to remember this war is *moving fast*. Ships are needed for men and materials so if mail service is *slow* there is a very good reason.

I still have some of my Christmas beer left from last year. I try to make it last. I think my handwriting is getting poor. It looks more like *chicken scratch*. I have my mind on you and you are a darling to remember my folks at Christmas time. It was very nice of you to send them those gifts. I guess I really have a very thoughtful and sweet girl. I'll never figure out how I rate by finding you, but I'm not complaining.

Love, Johnny

On the Southwest Pacific War Front in the Philippines
Dad calls mom his *darling sweater girl* as he has a picture of her wearing a sweater with all her *curves*. He's been able to get a Jap rifle, sword and bayonet from an infantry man who has returned from the war front.

01/12/45

My *Darling Sweater Girl,*

I just can't take my eyes off those latest pictures. My, what a pretty sweater you are wearing. We can hang some pictures over our fireplace or on the wall in our living room. All the boys keep asking me to see them. They say "Johnny let me see your *sweater girl* so I can keep my morale up to standard".

I got myself a Jap rifle, sword and bayonet from an infantry man who recently returned from action. To be on the safe side, I'll bring these things home in person. I have built myself a short wave and long wave receiver from an Aussie battery set so I have music at my fingertips again. This is in addition to my little portable radio set I'm saving for us.

We'll be able to take it with us to go on a picnic or on the beach. I can just picture you and I at the beach. We will be laying out in the sun listening to the radio. You will be all dressed up with your *curves* and I will be so proud of you. I'll never forget those *warm and tender* cheeks. Oh how I trouble myself just talking about them.

Love, Johnny

On the Southwest Pacific War Front in the Philippines
Dad continues to *accumulate points* toward his furlough. He met a fellow from his old company who was transferred into a bomb squadron and they catch up with the war news together. He remains positive the Japs are *slowly* losing the battle.

01/14/45

Dearest Mary,

I'm half way to my furlough and after three days of waiting, I'm still getting *nowhere* in a hurry. I'm waiting for transportation by air. Oh well, I'll get there in a *fortnight* as the Aussies say.

I met a fellow who transferred out of my old company into a bomb squadron. He is on his way home for he was able to get fifty missions in and came out *without a scratch*. He only flew for seven months so you can see he was really very busy. He took part in all those things you heard in the newspaper a few months ago. Every time a zero is shot down at the front, it's *stripped of almost everything* in ten minutes after crashing. All the boys want to get a sample of it.

Love, Johnnie

On the Home Front in Manville, New Jersey
Dad has been sending mom copies of **Yank** and **Guinea Gold** newspapers. It is a new year and they are still writing and waiting for each other. They really want the war to end so that they can be together.

01/14/45

My Darling Johnnie,

Even though I sent you a nice booklet last week, I thought I would write this letter. Now, Mr. Poslusny, how do you expect me to answer these twenty-five letters I received all at one time! You are so wonderful to me so I will do my best to start answering them. I've been receiving your **Yank** and **Guinea Gold** newspapers all this time and I am saving them for you. You know, dear you are my biggest worry. If only I knew you are well, safe and happy, I would feel more relieved.

The idea you had about writing my New Year letters each with a few hours in between, was so cute, Johnny. One was written December 31, 1944 and the other one was written at 1:45 a.m. I received them both at the same time. You always ask me why I insist on keeping the living room light on when we sit on the sofa. We shall see if I am able to shut it off when you come home.

We had a lovely Christmas and New Year, honey. I went to midnight mass with my sister, Margie, my brother, Leon and one of my friends. It was a lovely service, but I missed you terribly. A friend of ours dropped by to say hello to us. He brought his little *victrola* and some swell records.

This fellow is young but he isn't able to work because he has asthma. He got sick at Pearl Harbor where he was an electrician for the government. Now he is a football coach for the kids around here. They are all crazy about him. I told him all about our *love affair* and he can't believe the fact that two people live so far apart but they are so in love.

Your Sweetheart, Mary

On the Home Front in Manville, New Jersey
Mom tells dad how she spent her New Year's Eve. She also treated herself to a movie. She took her sister, Jeannie and mother as well.

01/15/45

My Dearest,

Let me tell you a little bit about New Years Eve. Jeannie's boyfriend Frankie had to play his accordion at some club that night so she and I felt very much alone. When the church bells rang at 12:00 pm, I pressed your picture to my heart and said a prayer for you.

Oh honey, I like all those pictures you send me. They will help us make a nice album after we are married. I would like to see more pictures of you as I could never get tired of looking at pictures of you. The other night Jeannie, mother and I went out to the movies. We saw **The Story of Dr. Wessel** with Gary Cooper and Lorraine Day. I was thinking about the time we walked to the theater in Manville one evening. I'll never forget how you dried my tears with your large white handkerchief. You were so *gentle* and kind to me.

Your loving sweetheart, Mary

On the Southwest Pacific War Front in the Philippines
The American boys consider the Australian Ninth Division the *best fighting outfit* in the world. Dad receives a Christmas card from mom. She and dad agree about the way they express "my wish is your wish for the coming New Year".

01/16/45

My Dearest One,

Our boys consider the Australian Ninth Division the *best fighting outfit* in the world. They truly are *great jungle fighters*. This Ninth Division was at Tobruk, Libya so they're seasoned troops. All the Aussies marvel at our vast equipment. It's *so superior* to anything else they've ever seen. It takes a short time for our *Yanks* to get Jap trucks, planes and equipment to any *newly recaptured* island. The Japs just don't have a chance.

I've been keeping my eyes on a line of guys in front of the American Red Cross. Now I see the line is short so I guess I'll go over and get myself a shot of coffee and a few sandwiches to fill my empty stomach. Don't ever think for a moment that because I'm going on my leave, I should forget everything and you too. You know I couldn't do that.

Sweetheart, I received your Christmas card today and I want to thank you for it. The way you said, "My wish is your wish for the coming New

Year" was sweet music to my ears. The little saying inside expresses what we both feel about each other.

You congratulated me for doing more work in the Army. Now you have that all wrong. Rank does not determine how much work a soldier completes. What it means is that recognition for work one did is given. Of course, if no position was open, I'd still be a private even if I was doing General's work. Back in the States it's different because you might have to drill men.

That was very nice of the gang at your factory to give you a birthday cake. I can just picture that cake with the twenty six candles on it. It was very sweet of you to place my picture next to it even though it might have spoiled the celebration. What I wouldn't give to have been in that picture's place. That would have been a swell time to announce our engagement, eh Hon? Now no tears, Sweetheart.

Love, Johnny

On the Home Front in Manville, New Jersey
Mom congratulates dad on earning the rank of Staff Sergeant. She finds out dad really knows how to save money. He wants to save it for their marriage and *dream home.*

01/18/45

My loving Sweetheart,

Congratulations Staff Sergeant and lots of luck to you honey. However, you didn't surprise me because I know you are *smart as a whip*. I do hope you will be home before Christmas so I can decide on a gift for you. My whole family cannot wait to welcome you home for good.

John in his staff sergeant uniform

We all continue to think of you and pray for your safe return to the States.

Your Honey, Mary

On the Southwest Pacific War Front in the Philippines
Dad has filled his stomach with ice cream and enjoyed three glasses of beer after a tennis match. The infantry men told him two years fighting in Africa is as *hard* as six months in New Guinea. He feels lucky to be working for the Army Air Corp.

Mary Jane Juzwin

01/20/45

Hello Hon,

How are you? I'm just filled up with ice cream. I shouldn't eat any more, I'm afraid my teeth will *rattle* almost as loud as that little car of mine.

This place is the kind where you can *let your hair down* and the military police won't bother you at all. I enjoyed three glasses of beer after my tennis match. This was my first taste of beer in a long while, so you see I do behave myself.

I was told by infantry men that fighting for two years in Africa is as *hard* as six months in New Guinea. They finished their two years of fighting in Africa and now they are presently fighting at the front lines in New Guinea. As you can see, it's no party here. That is true in the infantry but not so much in the other parts of the Army Air Corp. I can safely say my work is the most pleasant in the Army. I am very lucky and also blessed to have you as my gal. I love you very much.

U. S. O. Commando, Johnny

On the Southwest Pacific War Front in the Philippines
Dad describes his activities shown by the pictures he is sending mom to save for the album. He apologizes for the lighting in the pictures seem to be dark.

01/22/45

Dear Mary,

I have enclosed a few pictures. They might have been *damaged* by travelling through the mail so I will describe them to you. The picture with the two ears is the way you will see me when I get home. The sign is on our supply room. There is the one with me holding a Jap sniper's gun. That's my apartment in the background. The dark picture is in Radio Repair. The last one is how I'm working with my mess equipment. How about coming over to help me dry my knife, fork and spoon? Another one was taken in front of our projection room.

I don't care too much for these pictures for I know they're not the best. Oh well, you asked for them so here they are. Disappointed? Now don't tell me I look thin because I'm not thin. I weigh 158 pounds so there.

Darling, I feel *so alone* without you. Each night, just after I get ready for bed, I take a picture of yours and look at it for a while. Then I'm happy when I *hit the hay* for I know I have someone who is waiting at home for me. You mean the world to me and nothing can ever stop me from loving you so much.

Lots of Love, Johnnie

On the Southwest Pacific War Front still in the Philippines
Dad is curious and asks mom to confirm the rumor that women in the States are starting to *smoke pipes*. He helped out at the Post Office and saw a lot of mail bags. He says he earned enough money to buy six rolls of film by fixing a guy's radio.

01/24/45

Dear Sweater Gal,

How's my *sweater gal* these days? That picture of you in the sweater sure made me feel warm and cozy. I heard the women in the States are starting to *smoke pipes*. Would you know by any chance if they are using a *corn cob*?

I just got back from the Post Office. I helped them with the packages and tin holders. If you ever want to send me something, the best way is to send it first class and in a paper box or tin holder. I never saw so many bags of mail lying under canvas tape. In case you wondered, I didn't get any mail. Darn it!

Take care of yourself and remember this guy thinks you are *some dish*. You're plenty of everything. That's figuratively speaking with the *accent* on the figure if you know what I mean.

Love, Your Johnny

On the Southwest Pacific War Front in the Philippines
Dad notices some of the boys *making some time* with the local gals. He is so handy that he can make money by tuning up radios for the guys. Luckily, he has acquired quite a few rolls of film.

01/26/45

Hi Hon,

I just wanted to tell you some of the boys seem to be *making some time* with the local gals around here. I can't see what the attraction is for they look too much like a Negro to me. None of that for me!

I got six rolls of film from a fellow for tuning up his radio. I now have quite a few rolls, ten at least. Of course, if you behave yourself, I'll send some along to you. You now have a copy of all the pictures I could lay my hands on. It's not a bad collection we own, huh kid? Our kids sure will get *a kick* out of them when they grow up. I know *don't count the chickens before time.* You know how it is my sweet one.

There is a small rotation quota for this month, however, no one with the same number of months as I have accumulated has gone home. Time sometimes seems to be *flying by* fast for me. However, when I start thinking of you, it feels like a lifetime. You have me thinking this way. Now what are you going to do about it? I'll do plenty.

Your lover boy, Johnny

On the Southwest Pacific War Front remaining in the Philippines

Dad is feeling pretty good due to the fact that he received three letters from mom. He assures mom of his love and is looking forward to marriage and their future together.

02/03/45

Dearest Mary,

I'm feeling pretty good right now because I received three letters from you. It seems you and I dream the same way. Hon, I say a prayer every night for us. I know you *cherish* pictures of me like I do yours. I wish I could take my picture's place under your pillow.

I know how it is when a pretty girl like you gets many invitations from fellows. Even then I can imagine you refuse in a polite way. Honey, that's how I know you love me. You are my only love that holds my heart. Also, you are the only girl I ever want to have as my wife. I know we'll make more definite plans later.

My Love to You, Johnny

On the Southwest Pacific War Front in the Philippines
Dad is looking forward to seeing mom once again and moving on toward their wedding day. This time he developed some pictures himself and is sending them to her.

02/06/45

My Dear Honey,

One of the biggest moments of our lives will be when I come back to you after all this time spent overseas. It will feel like *our greatest moment* as well as our wedding day. I can almost imagine how it will feel to have you wrap yourself in my arms. Your tears will be running down your face and I will be *fluffing* your hair with my hands. I can't wait for those *sweet* kisses I love and haven't had for so long.

I have enclosed more pictures that I developed myself. Some of them did not come out so well. The paper used may have been old and the prints could have had some moisture on them. I want you to have them. I still miss you a lot and love you with all my heart.

Love, Lonesome Johnny

On the Southwest Pacific War Front in the Philippines
Dad feels like the luckiest guy because he knows mom will be there for him when he returns. He's hopeful all this positive *war news* means a closer end of the war.

02/08/45

Dearest Mary,

I am answering your letter with the *cute* feather in it. You say you are worried about me smoking my pipe. Well kid, it's not as bad as you think. I am happy and about one of the luckiest guys for many reasons.

You are my biggest reason I'm happy so I have no reason to smoke too much. Please don't worry about me so much. I don't want to find any wrinkles on your face unless it's from that cute little grin of yours.

Hasn't the *war news* been good lately? All this positive information means a lot to us. The sooner this war is over, the sooner we can be together again. All we can do is hope and pray for this situation to be resolved.

Love, Your Johnny

On the Home Front in Manville, New Jersey
Dad asks mom to accept some money to save for him, however, mom does not want to be held *responsible* for it. He also wanted to know if women on the home front are smoking pipes. Mom says women are even starting to smoke cigars!

02/10/45

Hello My Love,

Listen Mr. Poslusny, don't you dare offer me $50.00 to hold onto for you. You and I are in love sure but I don't want the *responsibility* of holding onto all that money! You hold onto it or put it in a bank for safekeeping.

Gosh honey, one of your letters sure was interesting. The letter was about how those Filipino men had to go out and fight in the jungle as *guerillas*. They didn't have to see the Japs because they could smell them first. That's quite amazing. I hate to think of you having to go and fight in the jungle. You better be careful and come home in one piece.

You are right about women starting to smoke pipes. Some have even started to smoke cigars. Men have to roll their own cigarettes as you have no idea how hard it is to get them. No store has any. There was a *black market* seller in Manville but now he's in jail.

My Love to You, Mary

On the Southwest Pacific War Front in the Philippines
Dad teases mom pretending to be afraid of her ways. Mom's New Year's Eve party in the States was *very quiet* compared to the Army celebration. The guys had an *air raid alert* for an hour followed by guns going off loudly. They also got *tipsy*.

02/10/45

My Dear Sweetheart,

You say the stationary isn't long enough to write what you will do to me when I return. My, are you really going to be that rough on poor little me? I'm afraid! Oh yeah!

I have a few things up my sleeve besides my arm. What is this *snow job* you are giving me? *We shall see what we shall see.* I'll really melt when I see you, just wait and see.

I see you spent your New Years *very quietly.* Well here it certainly was different. We had an *air raid alert* for almost an hour and so many guns were going off that it ended up being quite loud. If you saw all the *tipsy* boys everywhere and you had people calling on the phone every five minutes, you would be mixed up as well.

It was very sweet of you to hold my picture close to your heart and say a prayer for us. Boy, wouldn't that have been a great time for me to walk into your room! You give me *heck* for not sending you more pictures of myself. Well it has been very hard to find film, but now I have enough. I do hope my new pictures come out better. Maybe, I should get my face lifted or something, mostly something. On the other hand, if I go to see you at night, it wouldn't be so noticeable.

Your Honey, Johnny

On the Southwest Pacific War Front in the Philippines
Mom tells dad the insurance company won't permit anyone to wear dresses. For the first time in months, dad is hopeful his incoming mail is going to a correct APO address.

02/13/45

Dearest Mary,

You say the insurance company doesn't *permit you* to wear dresses anymore. What a shame! You sure put that situation in *cute* words. No one will get a *treat* seeing you in a dress with those lovely legs. I guess you can only wear slacks. I have heard there is a shortage of nylon stockings. Now you know us men don't pay any attention to that. Ain't I the biggest liar?

Now for the first time in months, our mail is finally going to the correct APO address. I do hope you are getting my *Yank* newspapers. I think the magazine of January 12, 1945 is very interesting, don't you?

Now I have a poem for you:

> Someone once said a speech ought to be like a woman's skirt.
> It should be long enough to cover the subject yet short enough to sustain interest.
> A speaker says: "I am a man of few words. I've been married a long time".
>
> I was addressing a girl's school the other day and I said: "I'm happy to see so many shining faces before me". All the girls yanked out their powder puffs and touched up their faces.

Love Always, Johnny

On the Southwest Pacific War Front in the Philippines
Dad is indulging himself with ice cream and malted milkshakes. He is still dancing whenever he has time. He also had an opportunity to show off his *floral designer skills* by making corsages for a local lady who owns a florist and is *a good egg*.

02/15/45

Dear Mary,

I'm filling myself up with ice cream and malted milkshakes. I'm also dancing my *fool* head off. I can practice on these babes here so when I do get home, I won't be *trampling* my best gal's toes. See how lucky you are!

I spent half of my day at a local florist next door to our American Red Cross. The lady who runs it is *a good egg* and nice to me. I made about twenty five corsages for her. She had rather a *big* demand for corsages. There is going to be a Yank and Aussie wedding so that's why she was so busy. She couldn't believe ones I made for her only weighed six ounces each. She said "All the others that people made weighed a ton". It was fun helping her. The days drag on so by spending it this way it felt different.

When I'm trying to write to other people, it is so hard to think of the words I want to say. However, with you the words just come our naturally. Could it be love? You bet my sweet one. Of course with me telling you everything in my letters, it will leave me speechless when I get home. All I'll be good for is kissing and holding hands and that sort of stuff. Some stuff, eh kid? I hope my next move is in the direction of your heart.

I guess this covers most of the old news, so I'll give you some good news. I am going to shut my *trap* and mail this letter. Keep those lips nice and tender for me, Hon.

Love, Johnny

On the Southwest Pacific War Front in the Philippines
Dad seems very happy and shares some funny poems with mom in his letter.

02/17/45

Hello My Dearest Mary,

Just a few words to let you know I'm still alive and thinking of you. I am missing you an awful lot. The little dog walked by the tree. The tree said "Have one on me". The dog blinked like Mickey Mouse and said "No thanks, I just had one on the house"!

Here's a little poem for you:

> I had sworn to be a bachelor. She had sworn to be a bride,
> I guess you know the answer, she had nature on her side.
> Some girls talking: "Men are all alike" said the first cutie.
> The second cutie said "Yeah, men are all I like too"!

"I had a date with a mind reader last night". "Really" said Bill. "Did you have any fun"? "No" he said. "She sat around all night and blushed".

"We manicurists are luckier than most girls". "Why is that"?
It's because we have so many men at our fingertips".
"No, it's because we always know where their hands are".

You must think your Johnny has a screw loose. Can you help this old boy out? I'm *going to the dogs*. What have I ever done to them except chase them out of my bed?

Love, Your Johnnie

On the Southwest Pacific War Front reminiscing in the Philippines Dad remembers how he and mom celebrated their *first* Valentines Day with roses and kisses. He is really missing her face, hair, eyes and hands.

02/18/45

Dear Mary,

Talk about timing, you sure did a good job. I received your Valentines card today. I found it under my pillow for the fellows put it there and almost forgot to tell me. It was a sweet one, darling. I love that *lady like smell*. Boy, how you do spoil me.

You remembered the roses I gave you on our *first* Valentines Day. What a memory you have! You know me Hon, if it's for my Mary, I'll do anything. You think of me an awful lot, don't you Hon? That goes double for me.

All the fellows wonder how I am happy all the time. That's when I pull your picture off my tent and show them the reason. It seems I'm *lucky in love*, everything is good. Now you can see why I'm always happy. I am because I know I have you for *my very own*.

With love, Johnnie

On the Southwest Pacific War Front in the Philippines
Dad is remembering dancing *cheek to cheek* with mom and he tells her he is more determined to have her for his *very own*.

02/19/45

My little Darling,

You don't have to explain anything to me about that Sunday we had our date. That was my biggest test. I found out from that experience how much you meant to me. I tried to get my mind off of you. Nothing could make me forget us dancing *cheek to cheek*. I finally drove home with tears in my eyes. I was never more determined in my life to have you *for my very own*. Little did you know how I felt when I was looking at you. I took in your face, your beautiful hair, those eyes and your hands. I even noticed that figure with the *curves* in all the right places. I can picture you in that white *fluffy* blouse.

You even took a chance of spoiling it with the pin from the corsage I made for you. I don't remember if I told you what I did on my last furlough. I helped an Aussie florist and made forty corsages for her in a few hours.

I wish you wouldn't worry so much about me being *a bad boy*. Didn't I behave when I was with you? Why shouldn't I be the same now? You know you are always in my heart no matter where I go. Keep on wondering Hon, but don't ever worry for I'll never do anything to hurt you. I would like to cover those sweet warm lips of yours with mine and hold you tight. All in good time, I hope.

Love, Johnny

On the Southwest Pacific War Front getting mail still in the Philippines

Dad is wondering what he ever did to deserve such loving treatment from mom. He is reminiscing about the first time he brought her to meet his folks.

02/20/45

Dearest Mary,

I received your letter of January 21, 1945 today. Man oh man, why are you *so sweet* to me? What did I ever do to you to deserve such treatment? I'd love to see you in your work slacks. I bet you look cute. It's not the clothes but what is poured into the outfit that makes the difference. Nature sure treated you in the right places. P. S. Blush, woman, blush! Be sure to save a few blushes for me.

I remember the first suit I bought for myself. It was the one I wore the day I took you to see my folks. I was so nervous I stuttered. You were *scared stiff* that day even though I told you not to be afraid. You were so cute. How could anyone object to having their son go out with a girl like you?

I never told my folks much about our attention to each other even up to this day. You know mothers can always figure things out. Speaking of figures, take good care of yours.

Here are some jokes for you:

> Did you hear about the drunk who stood on a corner singing "I am a pole". In a few minutes, an Airedale walked up to him. He looked him over and said
> "Ok buddy, you asked for it".

> Many a rural romance started off with a bushel
> of corn and ended up with a crib!

Love always, Johnny

On the Southwest Pacific War Front still in the Philippines
Dad loves teasing mom in a way that is loving and amusing. He remembers he did not say "Mary, I love you" on their first date. However, he realized it was written all over his face.

02/23/45

Dearest Mary,

I'm starting to set you straight as to who my *little* darling is and how much I love her. She is not too tall, has beautiful hair and is caring and thoughtful. I wouldn't go into guessing her size, but her figure is perfect. She is wearing a grin and as an added feature, she just rolls those eyes. I'm trying my best to say what I mean. She rolls her stockings up her lovely legs. Can you guess who I am describing? Okay, I better give you a few more clues. She is always fussing with her hair and never do I have to say "Woman stay away from me". I'd be a damn fool wouldn't I? She takes so long to say good night. It's no wonder she is *my cup of tea*. When I say something sweet to her she says, "Oh Johnnie" and hugs me tight. When I kiss her, she says "Why do you moan"? I'll always remember you for that sound. It's so clear to me even after two years, that I love that hungry look on your face. I hope you can take this kid, for I'm really rubbing it in!

She would always take me for a little walk. We walked so close together, one would think we were holding each other so no one could fall. At the end of the walk, I'd give her a hug and kiss. I'm telling you it was *pure heaven* to hold such a girl in my arms. I never came out and said "Mary, I love you". I knew it was written all over my face even in the dark! I would drive away thinking about this special girl who makes my eyes water. You didn't know at the time, but I was afraid I'd lose you. I hadn't staked a claim to your affection. Each time I saw you, I got progressively braver. Soon I could see that she did care for me. Off I went to the Army you see, and the greatest gift went with me.

Love, Your Johnny

On the Southwest Pacific War Front in the Philippines
Dad feels blessed to have a *beautiful* person at home waiting for him. He finds it easier to tell mom anything when he writes to her.

02/24/45

Dear Mary,

I am so blessed to have a beautiful person would be home waiting for me. I have tried so hard to make her proud of me. I hope I have succeeded. Mary, now you see what kind of shape I see myself. I'm happy as a lark. If I sound like I talk in riddles hon, it's because I find it easier to speak this way in my letters. You know darn well that this old boy loves you a lot. When I get a chance to show you in person lady, watch out! You will lose your last name and become a Mrs. You'll be so sweet to me forever and a day.

Some jokes for you:

> Long ago the private asked his friend "I want to know how long girls should be courted"? The PFC said "the same as short ones"!
> In modern times in the good old days when a fellow told a girl a naughty story,
> she blushed. At the present day, she memorizes it!

Lots of Love, Johnny

On the Southwest Pacific War Front in the Philippines
Dad knows how grateful guys are when he fixes their radio equipment and he makes a *deal* with his friend to find him some developer. The boys hear good news from San Francisco telling everyone all restrictions on furloughs to home are lifted.

Mary Jane Juzwin

02/25/45

Dear Honey,

We really will have a swell picture album after this war for I'll still be sending more pictures to you. I'm short of developer but if the fellow who promised to get me some comes through, I'll have plenty to use for more shots. I fixed his radio for him and he was so grateful, he told me he would try to get what I needed.

Our cook, Joe, is on his way home on rotation now. On the radio from San Francisco, California, we heard Chief of Staff Marshall say that all restrictions on furloughs to home were lifted. Anyone can go on furlough whether he holds a key position or any other position. We had one man who tried and was turned down. I guess all that talk was for the morale of the people at home and not for us. It's just like the statement that after Army Air Core men come home, they are not inducted into the infantry in the States.

I hope you got the things I sent to you. I would like to tell you that I got your packages but I cannot. I saw a U. S. O. show with plenty of gals with that stuff boys love to see and girls love to have. You know what I mean for baby, you got it! No kidding aside!

Love, Johnnie

On the Southwest Pacific War Front in the Philippines
It is an exciting time for Dad because he gets mom's holiday packages filled with goodies and new pictures of his sweetheart. He wears her medal to church.

02/26/45

Dearest Mary,

I really don't have to say a word about the gifts you sent. You can tell by this paper I'm using that I finally got your packages. The main one came through *in perfect shape* and with pictures. The fruitcake was okay but a little *flat and squished*. The candy was *a little sticky* but we enjoyed it. The package that had noodle soup and sardines was great!

Gosh darling, you sure have good taste. Those pictures you sent were very nice. You look wonderful with those hungry lips and beautiful hair. I see you are wearing all the things I sent to you. I still think a ring on that certain finger would look well, don't you?

I wore the medal you sent me to church and will always have it with me. It also had such a sweet little prayer. You sure are spoiling this boy! Soon you will be able to practice that *grass skirt* dance you promised me for I am sending you one. I wish I could see your face when you read some of my letters. I see you are making sure I keep writing to you by sending me all those stamps and envelopes. They will come in handy. I'm sure all the good news on the radio and in newspapers makes you as happy as it does for me.

I have a joke for you: Love is a game that is never postponed on account of darkness.

Love, Johnny

On the Southwest Pacific War Front in the Philippines
Dad explains how he spends his money as well as saves his money for their future. He's very happy to serve in the Army Air Corp.

03/09/45

Dear Mary,

I see you are giving me the *works* about saving money. Hon, you don't ever have to worry about that. After all, haven't I shown you results of it? I try to spend my money on you alone. Anything I have is yours as much as it is mine. I still send my Mom $25.00 a month and the rest is saved. I wanted to tell you everything a long time ago, but first I had to make sure where I stood in your heart. I had to tell you about my financial standing.

At that time I was telling you that we will do this together. You still think I have it rough, but really the Army Air Corp. is the best.

Since I am a Radio Repairman and quite handy it's a snap. By the way, I have accumulated thirty months overseas. Long time no see and baby long time no kiss either. Boo! Hoo!

Your Lover Boy, Johnnie

On the Southwest Pacific War Front feeling lonely in the Philippines Dad is speculating if the war had not begun, he and mom could have married and begun their family with a *little junior*. He tells her he sent the *grass skirt* to her today.

03/11/45

Hello Hon,

Yes, I can just see your sigh of relief when I catch up with you at the age of twenty seven. I'm thinking if this war hadn't started, we could have been married for two and one half years by now. Also, *little Junior* could be about nine months old.

It all looks and sounds good on paper, doesn't it? Oh well, we will make up for all this loneliness by being that much more in need of each other. I feel so lost without you and miss you so much. Don't worry I'll pull through for you. I sent the *grass skirt* today so be sure to practice that dance. Would you really do this for me? I know the answer already. *We shall see what we shall see*, am I right?

Love ya lots, Johnny

On the Southwest Pacific War Front in the Philippines
He tries to spell his last name phonetically as Pas-loose-knee. He keeps talking about a church wedding. Mom wants a big one.

03/16/45

My Darling,

You want to know more about this *marriage business*. You sound like I'm an *old timer* at marriages. I understand the gals you work with are having a hard time pronouncing my last name. It's easy, say Pas-loose-knee and you have it. You sound like you have many friends. I guess we'll have to reserve Yankee Stadium.

I certainly would never get married by *proxy*. There should be only one wedding in church and not any of those $20.00 jobs for us. After all, a wedding is something that happens once in a lifetime so ours will be as beautiful as I can make it. I have thought so much of marriage and talked with married men. I have a good idea what it's all about and what it means. You're asking me when it can be arranged. It can't be soon enough for me, but we'll see when I get back. I know the look on your face will *melt me away*.

You say I look like Earl Flynn, the movie star, my what an imagination you have. Here we have everything we can get. If we don't have it, we can't get it! We have no idea what item will become scarce. I know this for

I've worked with over one thousand units. It was tough to acquire all the essentials to work with in order to complete the job.

Love, Johnny

On the Southwest Pacific War Front in the Philippines
Dad tells mom about a USO show and how much he enjoyed the acting and the songs.

03/18/45

Dearest Mary,

I must tell you about the *swell* USO show I saw. It had one hundred people in it. It was called **This is the Army**. The cast was made up of all men but it was wonderful. Irving Berlin sang a few of his songs. He sang **White Christmas** and **Oh I hate to get up in the morning**. There are only a few places that have a large enough stage to take care of this USO production so many people travelled a lot of miles to see it.

Darling, you know that sending me a picture of yourself is the best present you could give me unless you came in person, so just keep them coming. Now about these women soldiers, I don't want any part of it. One of the fellows asked me if I wanted to go on a double date with him. I didn't go and don't expect to for I'm saving myself all for you.

Your faith in me is priority number one and I have the same faith in you. I'll never do anything that could destroy our love. I'm yours completely now and always.

Love, Johnny

On the Southwest Pacific War Front in the Philippines

He tells mom to keep the letters coming. He is sending her a pair of **Filipino** slippers. He is able to see a Sears and Roebuck catalogue filled with household items.

03/25/45

Dearest Mary,

In a few days, I'm sending you a pair of *Filipino* slippers made from hemp. I hope I got the right size. I sure am looking forward to the end of the war soon. Did you get our *hope chest* yet? Were you able to get the type you wanted? I wish I was in the States so I could help you fill it to the top! One of the guys received a Sears and Roebuck catalog so I spent some time looking at things we'll need for our home. I saw a set of twin beds. Don't get excited as they would be for our twins not us. Baby, I want you by my side.

You ought to see the Filipino gals take showers out in the open. Now don't jump to conclusions, they wear their dresses and just pour water over their heads.

I went to town recently but I haven't been able to get there too often. Yes Hon, there are more pictures. I've sent all kinds and I guess they were okay for you never objected to any of them yet.

All my Love to You, Johnny

On the Southwest Pacific War Front serving in the Philippines
Dad takes advantage of the time he spends in the Command Headquarters Office by writing to mom and listening for any current *war news*. The news is it could be only a matter of days before Germany falls. He's dreaming about marriage and how they will find their *dream home*.

03/28/45

Dear Mary,

It is my turn in CQ *Command Headquarters Office* so this gives me a very good chance to catch up on my letter writing. It is generally not too busy in here. I'm also paying close attention to war news. It looks like only a matter of days before Germany falls. That should affect this theater of war a lot with all the added help we will get.

This place sure is *dead*, no excitement at all. Summer is just around the corner for you. It would be so nice to come home sometime in the middle of it. I'm hoping I can get a new car without waiting too long. My old one is no good and has seen better days. I guess there might not be many choices. We'll pick one out and it will have to do for us.

I keep dreaming of our home and everything we'll do together. It can't be soon enough for me. Waiting and hoping is rough, but as long as I have you I can face anything. Without you it would have been rough. I love you with all my heart now and always.

Love, Your Johnny

On the Southwest Pacific War Front in the Philippines
Dad teases mom about keeping the light on in her parlor for him to see when he returns.

04/08/45

Hi Baby doll,

How's my *sweater girl* these days? I can still picture you in that sweater with all your *curves* in the right places, hon. Do you think you can arrange to have that light on in the parlor for me? I promise to behave, ahem. You know kid I never met a girl that meant so much to me. I can only dream how it will be to have you make a fuss over me and kiss me for no reason. You do so much to me even if I didn't show it at the time we were last together. I wasn't sure I had a right to love you.

Now that I have won your heart, I'll do everything I can to show you I'll take good care of you. I have so many tricks in mind to play on you and you probably have plenty in store for me.

Love, Johnny

On the Southwest Pacific War Front in the Philippines
Dad receives a very sweet letter from mom. He tells her to go out and have a little fun.

04/12/45

Dearest Mary,

I received your letter of March 25, 1945 today and what a letter! You keep giving up movies and dances so you can write to me. That's very sweet of you but I would like you to have a little fun. I will be overjoyed when you give up your last name in exchange for mine. I'll have to take a few more pictures of myself and send you my best copies.

Love, Johnny

On the Southwest Pacific War Front in the Philippines
Dad describes the reaction all the boys had when hearing about the passing of President Franklin Delano Roosevelt. He's hoping to be stationed near home when he returns to the States. He assures mom he no longer wishes to remain a bachelor.

Mary Jane Juzwin

04/14/45

Dear Mary,

The toast you and the girls had on my birthday was very sweet. Darling, you are a brave girl and I love you. These are trying times and you've gone through them like a lady. You have no idea what you mean to me. I can imagine how you'll look doing that hula!

I heard the bad news on the radio about Roosevelt who died on April 12, 1945. When we first heard this on the radio, we were eating breakfast, everyone just stopped and you couldn't hear a pin drop. We all felt bad and I'm sure it was the same with the civilians.

I know you are a sensible girl so I'm going to tell you something. I heard on the radio that a couple of million men in the States are slated for overseas service just as soon as men overseas are relieved. If I am hearing this information correctly, that means I will stay in the States when I get back. That would be great! Don't get excited for even if I'm one of the luckiest guys in the Army, I can't hope too much for anything. It would be great if I got to stay at Fort Monmouth which is only four miles from home, but there are no guarantees. I'm sure everything will turn out for the best.

All my heart's love to my one and only, Johnny

On the Home Front in Manville, New Jersey
Mom and dad discuss the President's passing and how their friends reacted to the news.

04/15/45

My Darling Sweetheart,

I miss you so. Today was a beautiful day and I sat on the front porch thinking of you and wondering what you would be doing at that moment.

Gosh honey, isn't it awful about our President Roosevelt passing away? You should see people here mourning for him. Manville is a *democratic* city. They especially liked him. I hope his death won't cause you to stay in that *hell hole* longer or continue this war.

Missing you, Mary

On the Southwest Pacific War Front in the Philippines
Dad says mom asks some serious questions. He reminisced about the day they met and how he said "Some day I am going to marry you". He says their future is secure.

04/15/45

Dear Mary,

Mary, you do come out with serious questions. For instance, you asked me "Would you really want this girl to be your wife"? Why you monkey, I only told you a few thousand times and in many ways. It's been a long time since I gave up being a bachelor. Don't you remember what I said to you when we met and after our first dance? I said "Some day I am going to marry you". I know you thought I was crazy at the time, especially since you were not thinking about marriage at all.

There you go again telling me how nice I look in my pictures. You really must be in love to say that about me. I'll never forget the last big kiss I got before I said *good night*. I drove home a very happy boy, sleepy sure, but it was worth it. The only thing that worried me then was how can I give my Mary all she deserves when I'm almost broke?

Time has solved everything for us. We have our love and our future is secure. We can settle down right away and start our *baseball team*. What an inspiration you are to me. Dry those tears from your eyes and read the last line on this letter. You will learn a great secret. I love you with all my heart and soul. I want you to share my life with me.

Love, Johnny

On the Southwest Pacific War Front keeping tabs on rotation in the Philippines
The war news keeps getting better each day so the boys' morale is high. Dad's group gets a new *big shot* who they hope will work on the rotation policy.

04/20/45

Dearest Mary,

The news around here keeps getting better each day. There is a new *big shot* in charge of the rotation policy so we're sweating him out. It can't be any worse, that's for sure. We've been getting quite a few replacements from the States. In fact, my replacement has arrived. I'm just thirty two days closer to seeing you now so it can't be too long. I can almost safely say I don't think I'll have to go overseas again.

Love, Johnny

On the Southwest Pacific War Front in the Philippines
He tells mom the longer he is overseas, the better chance he has to stay in the States.

04/24/45

Dear Mary,

I received your letter of April 15, 1945 today. I was impressed with the speed in which this letter took through the mail. What a sweet letter! I still have a big grin on my face.

Yes the President's passing away was a big shock to us. I think we were affected more than the civilians at home, but it wouldn't have anything to do with my stay over here longer. After all Hon, you have to remember the longer I stay here, the less chance I will have of being sent overseas again.

It's tough to stay away from a girl like you, but darling, all the breaks have come my way. It will be so much better to stay here four more months than to come home and have to go overseas again. Well my darling, I'll keep answering your letters a bit each day. I still want to read your letters a few dozen times as it does my heart good.

Love, Your Johnnie

On the Southwest Pacific War Front in the Philippines
Travelling around the world and observing people has shown dad he has the best girl.

04/25/45

Dear Mary,

You keep telling me that when I get home I might not love you like I do now. That's impossible for if I didn't, I would fall in love with you all over again. Do you realize it just took two dances and you had me? Don't you dare talk like that!

Travelling a lot and seeing so much has made me a better man for you. After all, I know how the rest of the world lives. I know what it means to do without things you long to own. I know what it means to be lonely, homesick, lovesick, happy and sad. I saw what makes the world go round. I met all kinds of girls some good and some bad. I had a lot of opportunities to do anything and I do mean anything. Don't think I did darling, for I have saved myself for you and our future. That means never doing anything that is not proper or frivolous.

Love, Johnnie

On the Southwest Pacific War Front in the Philippines
Dad enjoys teasing mom giving her a taste of her own *medicine*. He explains the drinking water situation and the purity process to her.

04/26/45

Dearest Mary,

You don't know what you're in for when you say "Just come home and fool around with me". You always say "We shall see what we shall see". I wonder how you like some of your own *medicine*? Ain't I a meanie? Woman, you made me this way!

Our water well is for showers only. We get our drinking water from a trailer truck. It is a big central water well and it is tasted every two hours for purity. If you only knew what I have done in my *spare time*, you would realize how little time I had to do anything except make money to prepare for our future. You wait and see, you will love me for it.

I know how *free girls* are and I want you to know you'll marry a clean, pure man. I don't mess around. I have willpower to handle any situation. Take good care of *sweet you*.

All my heart and soul, Johnny

On the Southwest Pacific War Front in the Philippines
He tells mom he doesn't care about her age. It's not important when it comes to love.

04/27/45

My Sweet Armful,

You say you went to church and said a prayer for us. I have done the same thing. You keep telling me you're four months older than me. I don't care about our ages. I fell in love with you as a person and knowing your age makes no difference to me. Whatever you have done before I met you would never change my love for you, so don't worry. I will try to answer your questions in a way that would make my remarks as cute as yours.

Love, Johnny

On the Southwest Pacific War Front in the Philippines
Dad is looking forward to hearing definite news of the end of the war. He asks mom if her Mother liked the special Mother's Day card he made for her.

04/30/45

Dearest Honey,

The news in Germany sure is good and it's only days before it's all over. When the war is finally over, it will take about three months before it affects our chances of getting home. You are so brave about all this. I'm glad you never get excited about this until we know what is definite. Waiting so long for me after only a few dates is amazing to me.

Darling, you will never know what all this meant to me when I am alone and so far away.

Let me know how your mother likes the Mother's Day card I made especially for her. I couldn't find any in the stores so I made my own. Our life together will begin perhaps our or five years later, but we'll make up for it. I wish I met you long ago as that's when we should have married. Stay as sweet as you are and before you know it a kiss will appear on those lips and you'll find yourself in my arms forever. Hoping and waiting has brought us close to each other. We realize we need one another to complete our lives.

Lovingly, Johnny

On the Southwest Pacific War Front realizing three years service in the Philippines
Dad realized he has been in the Army for three years. He is proud to have fulfilled his obligation to his country. Rumors are floating around saying the war is almost over.

05/01/45

Dearest Mary,

Do you realize that June 20, 1945 will be three years in the Army for me? That is a long time to be away from you, isn't it? However, I can always say I have fulfilled my service obligation. It's more than those strikers can say. They let us down we won't forget it.

There are plenty of rumors about the war floating around, but nothing is official. There will probably be fifteen girls for one man at home after the war. I know I have my one and only so that doesn't interest me in the least bit. Well little girl with the beauty marks all over, I'll close for now.

All my love to you, Johnny

On the Southwest Pacific War Front in the Philippines
Dad says "the roughest part of the war was being away from mom for such a long time".

05/03/45

Dear Sweet Mary,

Now that the war is almost over, those so called *4f big shots* will join the Army and get stationed near their homes. I can picture them telling people how rough the war was on them. The roughest part was being away from you so long. I never want to go that again. Our twelve children will keep me out of the next war, heaven forbid. Just wait and see.

Love, Johnny

On the Southwest Pacific War Front in the Philippines
Dad likes the pictures mom sent him but says the tropical weather is *no good* for them. He tells her the war in Europe is ninety eight percent over.

05/05/45

Dear Mary,

I received your *v-letter* dated April 12, 1945. In it you told me about the pictures you sent me. I also got the picture of you as a bridesmaid. It has a small brown spot near your knee. Most all of the small ones you sent are now either a little yellow or spotted. This tropical weather is no good for them. Luckily, your large pictures are just fine.

I saw a very good picture last night called **Bring on the Girls**. There were plenty of curves and all that sort of stuff. It only made me miss you more. However, each day brings us closer to our day. The war in Europe is ninety eight percent over, so things should start coming this way. These Japs are all *suicide* types and will die over anything so it wouldn't be a push over. Our Air Force will take care of everything.

Love ya Always, Johnny

On the Southwest Pacific War Front in the Philippines
Hearing that the war is *officially over at least on paper* is good news, however, there could still be many soldiers who will die even after the order to stop fighting is given. Dad is becoming hopeful he will be home in the States for mom's next birthday.

05/09/45

Dear Mary,

With the war in Europe *officially over at least on paper*, there could still be many soldiers who will die there even after the order to stop fighting is given. I guess a lot of people are celebrating. Even though it's good news for all, they should stop and think. What have I done to help out before they start? Over here the news was received rather calm by most of the *old timers*.

We're all wondering how soon we will get help and when will we be getting our chance to go home. I do hope it's soon. I am pretty certain I'll be home by the time your next birthday arrives. Darling, I want you to know I didn't celebrate even though some of the boys did. I've heard too much about this *Filipino* drink from fellows who had to take care of the guys affected by it. If I ever drink, it will be you and I together and on very special occasions. I'll be coming around one of these days.

Yours Always, Johnny

On the Southwest Pacific War Front in the Philippines
Dad remains optimistic about when he'll be able to go home on rotation. He says guys with kids get a break, even those who had kids so they could stay away from the Army.

05/13/45

Dearest Mary,

I have no doubt you have heard the news about the point system of discharge from the Army. It's one of those things you can't always count on, so please don't get excited. I will have my eighty five points in three months time and it could be at least four to six months before I go home on rotation. We will just have to wait and hope for the best.

Fellows with kids get the break, even those who had kids only with the intention of trying to stay out of the Army. Just think if we had gotten married and had some kids, I would now have points to spare.

Mail is awful now with very little being distributed. As soon as I have more information, I'll let you know. Start dreaming, it's not going to be long before our dreams come true.

Your dreamboat, Johnnie

On the Southwest Pacific War Front in the Philippines
Dad teases mom by saying he's counting his fourteen kids with his first three wives to gain points. He then says he expects to get thirty four points for his overseas service. He has earned three bronze company stars as well.

05/19/45

Dearest Mary,

I don't know if you are wondering how many points I have accumulated. Well, not counting my fourteen kids by my first three wives, exactly eighty one points today. I get thirty four points for being overseas. The sixteen days of my furlough aren't counted in credit for being overseas but are for time in the Army. The twentieth of June I'll start getting five percent more base pay.

5 points = Paprian campaign 5 points = New Guinea 5 points = Philippines

I have earned three bronze company stars which are worn on my Southwest Pacific ribbon. I also have a fourth star and another ribbon which is the liberation of the Philippines. Don't let fourteen kids worry you, you'll like them all!

Love, Your Johnnie

On the Southwest Pacific War Front in the Philippines

All the guys keep hearing about the points one must accumulate in order to qualify for rotation and have a chance to go home. He thinks their time overseas is viewed the same as time spent living in a city in the States.

05/23/45

Dear Mary,

I keep hearing all day and half the night is points and more points. Twelve points for a kid seems like a lot to a single guy and he feels it's just as much a married man's war as it is a single person's war. I received eighty points for overseas time and of course the States included the rest of the time in the service. My First Sergeant got back after almost seven months. We were so glad to see him.

Hon, I can lay in my bed and stare at your pictures for hours. I shut my eyes and try to imagine it's really you in person. However, nothing can make me feel like I did when I had you in my arms. Well, little sweater girl of mine, take care of yourself and remember you fulfill all my dreams.

Love, Johnnie

On the Southwest Pacific War Front in the Philippines
Dad is happy to get some beer to enjoy. He keeps hearing about big raids in Tokyo. He thinks everyone will have to wait for the end of the war before they will be able to go home. He says he has served in the *forgotten* war and his jungle time is considered the same as living in a city in the States.

05/25/45

Dear Mary,

Well, we finally got a beer issue again, six bottles per person. This will definitely take care of my thirst. All those big raids on Tokyo are music to our ears. By the looks of things, the end of the war will be the only way to get home.

It will be the same old excuse, *no shipping space on board*. However, the ships are going back with their holds full of water so that the propellers will be under enough water. I have seen this with my own eyes and I have heard from merchant seamen many times.

They would rather fill their holds with water to keep it afloat instead of filling the ship with soldiers who are ready to go home. The more I think of it the madder I get. We're still the *forgotten war* and jungle time is considered just like living in a city. Prior to the war, the blacks did the work in the jungle and the boss sat under a shade tree with two natives fanning him. An inspector was here today to listen to any complaints. This is a regular routine, however, a chaplain could have done more good.

Please don't worry if mail slows down for a week or so. Packages are not permitted to be sent home at the present time.

Love, Johnny

On the Home Front in Manville, New Jersey
Dad tells mom how her letters and pictures have cheered him up and kept him company.

05/27/45

Hello my Sweetheart,

Boy, we sure have been busy writing letters back and forth ever since we met. Your letters have kept me going and I hope I've cheered you up by answering your letters and sending you poems and stories. Oh honey, I sure enjoyed receiving the picture of you in your bathing suit. Whoo Hoo! You *sexy* little devil!

Lovingly yours, Mary

On the Southwest Pacific War Front still in the Philippines

Dad feels low as he doesn't see evidence of anyone working hard to get boys overseas home. No one has been interviewed in order to determine points needed to acomplish this task.

05/28/45

Dearest Honey,

How are you Hon? I'm still on the *blue side* just from general principles. Only your letters keep me going. The European war hasn't done anything for us. The permanent party stays in the Southwest Pacific. It seems nobody is going out of the way to get us home.

However, Air Transport Command who are our allies does send men home in eighteen months. The 13th Air Force who are also our allies send them home in twenty nine months or less. We service both units but we're different. We have to wait and let the months collect and read about furloughs, strikes and discharges.

No one has found a single soldier in the Southwest Pacific who has been interviewed in the so-called *survey* to determine points. I want to get back home for I feel I have done my share in a theater of war where things were done with very little supplies. When I got here, I saw maybe five airplanes at one time. I thought it was something at the time, but now I see one hundred planes or more as a common occurrence.

I'm not worried about you because I know I can depend on you. However, I can't help thinking about how long you've waited giving up your time for me. That's why I want to come home so I can show you I'm okay. I want to hold you in my arms, dry your tears and mess with your hair. I can't wait to have you next to my heart on a dance floor.

Love Always, Johnny

On the Southwest Pacific War Front in the Philippines

Dad is noticing both the American Negroes and some white boys are entertaining the babes living in the area. Okinawa, Japan is the island where fighting is still going on. He is shocked to hear about public baths where men and women bathe out in the open.

05/30/45

Dear Mary,

My kid brother, Walter is supposed to be on his way to the Pacific. He will be disappointed with the place. There isn't an appealing area around here. The average person here has a poor education.

Those big raids on Tokyo are very good news. Our only hope of getting home without red tape is the end of the war. The American Negroes sure are *going to town* with these babes here. Of course, there is the usual amount of white boys who have to entertain a babe of any kind. They are also operating. That's not for me.

This place is getting to be a *peace time camp* with inspections. I guess the States are full of men from England with eighteen to twenty four months overseas time. Their time was probably spent mostly in cities over there and on furlough now in the States.

I understand in Okinawa, the island where all the fighting is going on now, there are public baths where everyone goes. The men and the women go together to bathe out in the open. What a place! I keep hearing all kinds of proposals by senators. It seems they want to make it a single young man's war instead of everyone's war as it is and always has been. It's not our fault we're young and single. Oh well, at least I'm still alive.

Tomorrow I will get mail for today. There was a lot of mail delivered today but none for me. When there's a little mail, I seem to get a lot. Lately it always works out that way.

Love Always to You, Johnny

On the Home Front in Manville, New Jersey
Mom finds out she has been helping the *war effort* by making ammunition and parts for B-29 airplanes used for fighting the Japs. She is amazed and proud!

06/03/45

Hello my Darling,

I want to tell you what occured at work last week. Mr. Ward is a *Stock Chaser* and came into my department asking if I have the arms inspected as they were a rush job. I told him I was working on them and he said, "That's wonderful" and patted me on my back.

It was then that he said "You're doing a great job on them and I'm glad you're working so hard on them because they are used for B-29 airplanes". I swallowed so hard as I quickly turned toward him my eyes wide open in amazement and said "Honestly". Johnny, knowing you had something to do with the B-29's as you know how to fix them, I got a *hot* and *cold* chill through my body and then a thrill at the thought of us being a half a world apart and still working side by side!

I told Mr. Ward that my boyfriend works on the B-29's and he said, "See how wonderful it is to help him out". Oh Johnny, I couldn't get over that. I copied some information on that little long silver arm. It has parts on it that are called the *shaft, spine, bearing seals, core and commutator.* *H*oney, this little *armature* is right inside the motor. There are many more *armatures* and *rotors* that I work on but I don't know what they are used for in the war. Honey, no matter where I am or what I'm doing, you are always beside me.

With All my Love, Mary

On the Southwest Pacific War Front in the Philippines

The guys hear news about points. They're trying to remain optimistic the rotation may be in their favor. Dad says Jap radio propaganda has changed its tone.

06/04/45

Dear Mary,

Now we are hearing more news about the points. I will have eighty six points on July 12 if they start counting. It would be better if the eighty five is lowered to eighty. After fourteen months of waiting for rotation, we start a new plan, *our plan*.

The Jap radio propaganda has changed its tone lately. There is no more of that *We are waiting for the right moment to strike a fatal blow* stuff. I keep looking for my brother Walter but I haven't seen him. I've been wondering if you have anything in mind for your *hope chest*. Let me know for I would like to get that item for you.

Love, Johnnie

On the Southwest Pacific War Front in the Philippines
Dad praises mom for she is working on parts used by the Army Air Corp.

06/17/45

Dear Mary,

I received your letter of June 3, 1945 in which I told you how I felt about certain things. Please don't think I'm experiencing any discomfort. What makes me mad is the way the Pacific theater is treated and how things keep changing.

You would think we were a bunch of subjects for experiments. I'm glad you got the story about those *empty* ships. I am thrilled and proud you're working on something that is being used by the Air Force. Thanks again for all that information about your work.

Hon, please don't worry. Your promise to wait for me no matter how long it takes makes me so happy. I hope I'm deserving of it. So long, my sweet one.

Love and a whole lot of Kisses, Johnnie

On the Southwest Pacific War Front in the Philippines
Dad and his boys reach another location and are waiting for their turn to unload the boat. The landscape is not *tropical* but the climate is sunny and dry. He jokes about having bad luck so it might start to pour as soon as they start unloading.

06/20/45

My Dearest Darling,

Guess what Hon? Today I received your large picture and three studio ones. I was never so happy and gosh, you look so beautiful. We finally reached another place. We're just waiting for our turn to unload. There is no more *tropical* landscape and it's sunny and dry. With our luck, it will pour as soon as we start unloading. The climate here is cooler. There is a local radio station on this island so we'll be able to hear the news again.

If replacement troops were arriving like equipment, I'd be home a long time ago. The news on the radio says it looks like eighty five points is another rotation. I will probably wear those pictures out just looking at them and sleeping with them under my pillow.

I've quite a few letters to mail to you just as soon as I get the new APO number for this place. Well my little sweater girl, I have run short of words for the time being.

Love, Johnny

On the Southwest Pacific War Front travelling in the Pacific Ocean
Dad and the boys are taking another boat trip to somewhere in the Philippines.

06/23/45

Dearest Mary,

I am still on the boat taking it easy. Someone fell overboard from one of the other boats so we stopped and searched for him for two hours but couldn't find him. They say he was a *mental case*. The weather hasn't been windy so there haven't been too many cases of sea sickness.

This boat was one of the first boats to hit the beach at Normandy in France. It was damaged and sent to New York for repairs. I have met quite a few sailors who have travelled all over Europe. They consider Australia the best place by far for the people and the climate.

All my Love, Johnny

On the Home Front in Manville, New Jersey
Mom cannot get over the fact that she and dad have *romanced* by writing letters.

06/30/45

Hello Honey,

You should see me now. I'm sitting on the lawn on a rug with my little stationery suitcase near me. I keep your letters in the suitcase so they don't get lost. Hon, you make me so happy in your letters. You know Johnny it's your letters that made me fall in love with you and if it wasn't for all the attention I'm getting from you, I'd never have told you I'm yours. Yes, you *hunk of a dark meat* man you sure are going to get my love treatment when you get home.

My Love Always, Mary

On the Southwest Pacific War Front in the Philippines
The boys peruse the civilians working around their camp. They are Japanese and they learn the custom of how the dead are buried and what ceremony takes place.

07/08/45

I thought this place was going to be cool, but right now it sure is hot. We have seen no rain yet and it seems to be one hundred degrees in the shade. We are surrounded by mountains, valleys and long needle pine trees as well.

The civilians here are Japanese and there are about twenty of them working around our Army camp. The rest of the people are located in camps and must be restricted. There are burial vaults along the hillside containing bones of the dead. A body is placed in these for three years.

Then the body is taken out and all the bones are washed in some kind of wine by the youngest girl in the family. They say it is an honor to be selected for this job. Most vaults have been opened and you see big jars with fancy trimmings. There was one we could identify as a lady by her long hair.

Our tents are set up now. I can safely say we have one of the coldest showers in the Pacific. The water is piped from the mountains and comes right next to our area. We have no electric lights yet so I'm using a flashlight to write this letter. This climate, even when hot, is not *jungle climate*. There should be less *jungle skin rashes* for us.

Love, Johnny

On the Southwest Pacific War Front in the Philippines
Once again, dad is busy making another wooden floor for a new tent. He saw an outdoor movie and met another friend from his hometown.

07/10/45

Dearest Mary,

What a day I had! I was busy as can be and finally got our tent higher off the ground and things arranged better. I feel much better now that everything is in pretty good shape and organized. I managed to see another outdoor movie called **Without Love**. Spencer Tracy and Katherine Hepburn played the couple and I enjoyed it very much.

That same evening I met a friend from my hometown. He lives next door to me back home. We talked about old times and had a great time. He was sent overseas fourteen months ago and he brought me up to date. Guess what he said? After not seeing me for over thirty seven months, he tells me I haven't *changed a bit*.

My radio is playing and it sure feels good to hear it on again. Sometimes if the weather is hot, we get so tired so we go to bed early.

Here is the latest news on getting furloughs to go home. You have to sign a paper saying you will come back and spend one year over here. They think of anything to discourage us from thinking about asking for a furlough. Perhaps the end of the war is in sight so that must be the reason. At any rate, we sure are getting a *raw deal*. Oh well, it doesn't affect me anymore. I know I have the sweetest girl in the world waiting for me at home so I am as *happy as a clam!*

Love, Johnny

On the Southwest Pacific War Front in the Philippines
The guys treat themselves to an evening sail and did not return until 2:30 a.m. They found high prices in the stores, however, once they told the Filipinos about their service time spent overseas, they automatically cut the prices in half.

Mary Jane Juzwin

07/13/45

Dear Honey,

I had a wonderful time last night. We were on the beach waiting for our boat so we went swimming. There was a large boat on the beach so we took it for a sail. It was a Filipino fishing boat so each side of the boat has an out rig to keep it from turning over. We sailed all over the place and I guess it was 2:30 a.m. when we got back. After that we had to travel by truck and we arrived at almost the same spot we landed on the first day.

Prices were high but when we told the Filipinos we had been here for nine months, they automatically cut the prices in half. It's the same old story, Americans *have money* so ask high prices and they will pay them. This has been the case at any place I visited. I'll be glad to get off this island. Another Air Force is taking over the island.

The Japs aren't around anymore so we rule the sea in the Pacific. When I'm on my way home, I'll hit San Francisco to get plenty of *malted milk* and brush up on my dancing skills. I still haven't decided where and how I should meet you for the first time when I get home. No matter what happens, I know it will be a moment I will never forget.

We left an area built with framework for tents, wooden floors, drainage ditches, bridges, a day room and a mess hall. We had a water supply well and showers and still the *big shots* weren't satisfied. They wouldn't accept the area because there were a few tin cans out in the weeds about one hundred yards away from our immediate area. I'm glad we left before we had to put up their tents, tuck them in and serve them breakfast in bed.

Love, Johnny

On the Southwest Pacific War Front learning customs in the Philippines Dad is amused talking to the Filipino laundry gal. She says "Filipino custom, no touch". He also points out some of the sights he observed in the shacks where the people live.

07/15/45

Dear Mary,

There is a funny phrase here *Filipino custom, no touch*. This is what the gals say. When our laundry gal would come around, we would tease her. If we came too close to her, she would use this saying. Some of the fellows took a few babes out but were discouraged when they had to take the whole family along.

It's common to see an old shack with pigs living under the house. There is usually ten people including kids on the first floor and chickens on the roof and porch. There's nothing modern about this place. One girl is checking another girl's hair for fleas.

Love, Johnny

On the Southwest Pacific War Front in the Philippines
Dad is teasing mom about what she should wear as a blouse with her *grass skirt*. He enjoys telling her how much she has affected his life.

07/16/45

My Darling,

I see you are still having trouble thinking about what to wear with the *grass skirt*. How about settling for a big smile! Woo! Hoo! I'll let you surprise me so use anything you wish, sweetheart. I'll settle for a smile with a twinkle in your eyes any time.

You have no idea how you have affected my life. I've been so happy knowing you are my very own. We have so much in common and that means a lot in a happy marriage. Well, little woman of mine, you can see what the future will be when we're together. You better leave town before it's too late! You can leave me your address.

All my Love, Johnnie

On the Southwest Pacific War Front in the Philippines
Dad wants to know what *sweet smelling stuff* mom has been putting in her letters. He believes *absence makes the heart fonder.*

07/17/45

Dear Mary,

I received your letter of June 30, 1945. Woman, what is that *sweet smelling stuff* you put in your letters? It smells very feminine. I know what the rest of the *sweet stuff* is because it's you in the letter.

Yes honey, *absence makes the heart grow fonder.* This saying is for us. You say the mosquitoes near your house are beginning to enjoy themselves. It might be the two piece outfit you are wearing. I know if I were a mosquito, I'd be more interested in what's inside that outfit.

Loads of Love, Your Johnny

On the Southwest Pacific War Front noticing regulations in the Philippines
Dad is frustrated with the Army's practice of changing rules and regulations so often. He is sending his Japanese gun home so his older brother, Stanley can grease it for him.

07/17/45

Dearest Mary,

You might be wondering why I haven't dated my letters or numbered them. Well, it's military regulations and might not last too long. The Army keeps changing rules and regulations all the time. Now I see it will be okay for me to send my Jap gun home.

I'm taking my chances sending it while I can. I want my older brother Stanley to grease it up because right now it's shellacked. I will make a lamp stand out of it for our home.

I was going to send it to you, but it is heavy. I know Stanley will take good care of it.

The mail is finally reaching us. The valleys around here are full of deep caves. I don't want to explore them because there could be a booby trap inside. I'm hoping this will be my last move and the next should be coming home.

An Armful of Love, Johnnie

On the Southwest Pacific War Front in the Philippines
Mom and dad are discussing wedding ceremonies. She is busy filling up her *hope chest*. If there is a shortage later, dad wants to help her fill it up with necessities.

07/19/45

Dear Sweet Mary,

Well you asked for my opinion about wedding ceremonies so here goes. My ideal wedding is a bride and groom in a church saying their vows. To me that's the only real wedding. The rest of the arrangements I would leave up to the bride. I would, however, like a *Polish* wedding with all the trimmings. I hope we both agree on the subject. However it gets done, I know it will be the happiest occasion of our lives.

You mentioned a while ago that you are busy filling the *hope chest* with things we will need. You also said there could be a *real shortage* later so please darling, let me help you fill it with the necessities. I want you to have everything your heart wants. I have all the faith in the world in you, so please tell me how much money I should send to you.

Love, Johnny

On the Southwest Pacific War Front still in the Philippines
Dad receives a letter from his folks describing the neighbor's raising of turkeys. The other neighbors don't approve but dad can't do much about this situation. He discusses their *future* home and how his handyman skills will make it nice.

07/21/45

Dearest Mary,

It sure is hot and dry here. Yesterday it was so windy half of the tents blew over. We were lucky ours stayed up in some mysterious manner.

My Mom and Pop tell me there is a *city slicker* using the home next door to raise turkeys. There are one thousand of them and the neighbors are angry. There is nothing I can do about this situation from overseas.

I hope we get a nice place to live. I don't know where you want to live, but even if we get a small place, I can add a room or two and I can put a lot of extras in myself to make it real cozy and nice.

Love, Johnny

On the Southwest Pacific War Front in Okinawa, Japan
Dad says everything is *dead* in this location. They got a new Mess Sergeant so he's hoping for some changes in the meals that are prepared.

07/25/45

Dear Mary,

It's very *dead* around here. Before we left the Philippines, our outfit got a new Mess Sergeant. It sure makes a difference to have someone who has interest in his work. We also have a new First Sergeant and he is a very nice guy.

Here's a little dope about the Army. The staff is buck leaders of men. One day before the First Sergeant was promoted, he wasn't a leader of men because he was only a T-4. The moment his rank changed to First Sergeant, he became a leader. You're a leader if you hold the rank. If you were drafted or joined any outfit with ratings, you still could not be a leader. In the Army, you don't have the rank even if you were the best leader in the world. A private is as good in a majority of cases as a Sergeant. He can probably do a better job of leading than those holding the rank. If six men are working on a detail, the highest is in charge unless the outfit is not G.I. A private with thirty years experience might run a detail and have the ranks helping. I could go on about the Army, but other things are more interesting. That is how different the Army operates.

We had a few raids since we landed but none near us. They were shot down. It's no use teaching Japs how to land a plane, they make one trip up and down for a crash. I keep hearing about men coming home from Europe. I guess you know how I feel about this. Sooner or later I'll get back safely, that's the major thing because it will be for good.

Love always, Johnny

On the Southwest Pacific War Front in Okinawa, Japan
Mom receives a letter from dad describing some of the work he has been doing. He is very hopeful the Japs will stop fighting so it will lead to the end of World War II.

07/26/45

Dear Mary,

Well, we finally got some mail with APO 331 on it. Of course the APO now is 337. I am hoping our mail should reach us. While I've been in the Army, I haven't done anything rough or hard yet. The hardest thing is being away from you, my sweet one.

You say I scared you at times when you caught me looking at you. You made me that way so it serves you right. When I'm with you, I'm one hundred percent heart and soul so shouldn't I have my eyes on you? You'll be my wife as soon as I divorce Uncle Sam.

My work is the most pleasant detail. I fix airborne and ground radio equipment. This includes receivers, transmitters and the accessories. This work doesn't need strength but calls for common sense. The way Japanese radio broadcasts are talking, they don't want to fight anymore. I hope this will be the end soon. I must close it's *lights out* in my tent.

Love to You Always, Johnny

On the Southwest Pacific War Front in Okinawa, Japan
Dad is looking forward to the end of the war. He is so happy he sends mom a poem.

07/28/45

Dearest Mary,

Here is a poem for you:

> If we were sitting in the parlor just us two, and my big arms were encircling you, and you were sure nobody knew, would you?
>
> If the world was good and bright, and we stayed up half the night and I kept looking at you while all the time we knew our hearts were true, would you?
>
> If you closed your eyes to dream and promise not to scream when you opened your eyes and saw my gleam, and you knew all the time it wasn't for ice cream, would you?
>
> In this world there were but two, and we saw here at last is our chance

for some real romance, and you found yourself in a trance, would you?

If the cuckoo in the clock said "woo woo" every time I said I love you, and the moon outside seemed to say, wouldn't I love to be you, would you?

My Love Always, Your Johnny

On the Southwest Pacific War Front now located somewhere near Ryukyu, Japan
Dad still feels the war was strictly for the Europeans because they got all the breaks and received newer supplies as well as help from their allies.

08/04/45

Dear Mary,

I am somewhere in Ryukyu, Japan which is the southwest island. The point system looks like a *stall* tactic until the war is over. This war is strictly for the Europeans. They got the breaks and had the allies helping them. We were alone except for limited help from Australia. We're still alone except for help from the British Navy and the Dutch.

A couple of the boys in our company visited Manila on business. It's a wide open town in the Philippines. I might take a trip there if I get a chance. I have enclosed some bills that are U. S. currency used on this island. We get paid with it. Ten yen is $1.00, ten sen is $.01. One yen is $.10, five yen is $.50. It is as clear as mud. I got 1,418 yen or $41,800.00 but we have to use it on their territory.

Love, Johnny

On the Southwest Pacific War Front somewhere near Ryukyu, Japan
Dad explains a little history about the atomic bomb. He is lucky to have a friend from his hometown nearby to come and *hang out* with him.

08/06/45

My Darling,

You must have heard news about the new bomb for the United States. The first time the atomic bomb killed 200,000 people. The second time it was used in Nagasaki, Japan and killed more people. All I keep hearing on the radio is information about the new bomb. Once again, I expect to be working on a wooden floor for our tent in the next few days.

My friend from my hometown comes over to see me quite often. He and I were *little angels* in reverse at school. One of my old teachers saw me ten years later and said "My, that Johnnie turned out to be a pretty nice guy after all". There were thousands of stars out last night but it reminded me how much more I miss you by my side.

Love, Johnny

On the Southwest Pacific War Front still in Ryukyu, Japan
Dad thinks the war will end soon. He's excited as he tells mom she'll be a June, 1946 bride. He is busy keeping the planes flying. They require maintenance even though the war seems to be slowing down.

08/09/45

Dear Mary,

I am pretty sure of the war's end soon now. You have no idea what this means to us over here. It should be over in about a month and then all I have to do is wait. There will be a plan that we will hear about when and where they start sending men home.

I hope they do it by points or overseas time. You will be a June, 1946 bride for sure, maybe sooner. My mother will be happy to hear great news. I'm so glad she is well and will still be there when I get back. A lot of the boys weren't lucky and lost their parents.

Love, Your Johnny

On the Home Front in Manville, New Jersey
Mom and dad find out the WAR IS OVER and they are delighted! It doesn't mean dad will be coming home right away, only that he is no longer in any danger. Mom describes how the whole family celebrated this news.

08/14/45

My Darling Johnny,

Hurray! THE WAR IS OVER! Please darling, don't stay there too long now. Come home soon! Hurry, I'm still your girl and I'm still waiting for you to come to me Johnny.

At five minutes after seven we heard the news! Jeannie and I and the girl next door got into our little cotton dresses and went to church right away. My, you should see all the people crying in there. All three of us lit a candle and prayed until the tears rolled down our cheeks. My Darling, I can't wait until you come home so we can say a prayer in each others arms and look into each others eyes too!

When we got home, Mother and Dad and our whole family were all dressed up ready to go out and celebrate this happy occasion. Frank, the neighbor from upstairs was shooting from his shot gun so what do you think? Yep, I even took a shot, one for the *dirty Japs*. The whole gang went out down the highway and we blew the horn and sang happy songs.

We went to a pretty nice place called **Pal's Inn** in Manville, New Jersey and we had a nice time for about two hours. Then the cops came and we had to leave as they had to close the place. Jeannie and I took a tablecloth each to remember the place and time. Now here I am hon, all curled up on the sofa in our living room writing this letter to you. Jeannie and the children are asleep already. The people across the way from us are sure celebrating. Most everyone has been celebrating for two days. I still can't believe it. Even now it seems unbelievable! So much time has passed since we got into this war.

The time I'll really be happy is when I'm in your arms. That will be heaven. My dreams, hopes and prayers will come true then and especially when I can hear you whisper to me *Mary I love you*. Please my love, be careful now and remember I'm here waiting for you.

With All my Love, Mary

On the Southwest Pacific War Front in Ryukyu, Japan
Dad thinks mom might not have a job pretty soon as the war is nearly over.

08/17/45

Dear Lover,

I have been very busy so I finally got some things caught up around here. Even if the war is over, our company keeps busy because planes keep on flying. Anyway, you know with the future coming it will mean more airplane travel than ever.

You might be out of a job now because the war is nearly over. I think once the prisoners of war are dealt with, it should be my turn to come home. I should be in the first million to go. There are supposed to be one and one half million in this theater.

Love, Johnny

On the Home Front in Manville, New Jersey

Mom informs dad she has been laid off from her job. She did not expect this to happen this quickly. However, she is exploring the unemployment office choices.

08/18/45

My Darling Johnnie,

I've got a surprise for you. I am one of the 1,500 people who have been laid off from the Diehl's Manufacturing Company. I didn't expect this to happen suddenly but it has. Today I went to the unemployment office to collect some money I earned while working for three years and four months. You should have seen the crowd of people and all from the same place. I don't mind it as much because the war is over. Nothing can be better than that. I do, however, hate the idea of being out of a job. I don't know exactly how much I will be able to get but I think it's close to $20.00 a week for twenty-six weeks.

Your Loving Mary

On the Southwest Pacific War Front in Ryukyu, Japan
Dad assures mom that the information she might have heard about air raids taking place over Okinawa, Japan are not near his current location. He finds the campaign star policy to be unfair. However, the good news is the Japs are ready to surrender to General MacArthur. He also heard Jap pilots talking to the radio tower in Junam Island.

08/18/45

Dear Mary,

Let your hair down and relax. The wait can't be too long now. I see you got two handkerchiefs for your top and you wore a smile with the *grass skirt*. I'm just looking at those lovely legs. Woo! Hoo! Yes, that is some outfit and I love what's in it very much.

We only had a few raids since I landed here. The information you heard about planes raiding Okinawa, Japan does not mean it is in our area. None came close to us at any time and the Okinawa Islands are large.

When we were in the Philippines, we had about two months of raids and all of them were close. We were very busy for our company took care of the Philippine campaign by ourselves. We did this for almost four months, and then when things got slow along came a lot of other companies to help out. I can safely say we took part in every campaign over here. The single star we earned was the Southern Campaign star.

Some fellows would bring radio sets in for me to fix. They would only drive it from the plane to my location yet they got a campaign star because the plane took part in a similar campaign. I did all the work. I'll get by on the eighty one points I have accumulated.

Isn't there *taming stuff* you can use to *tame me down* so you'll be able to handle me?

Love, Johnny

On the Southwest Pacific War Front in Ryukyu, Japan
Dad is not sympathetic toward infantry men who are slated to be Occupation troops in Japan. There are outfits of infantry men who spent five times as long fighting here.

08/19/45

My Dearest Mary,

I just heard that some infantry unit who fought in Europe is protesting because they fought one hundred and forty five days in Europe and are slated to be Occupation troops in Japan. Why there are outfits of infantry men here who spent five times as long fighting here. So, yes they should not complain.

Today I saw a plane fly overhead that took the Japs to Manila to surrender to General MacArthur. I also heard the Jap pilots talking to the radio tower at the airstrip where they landed in Junam Island. It was not too far away by plane from us.

You told me what type of home you have in mind and by all means we will have a fireplace. I always wanted one. I feel happy now I can do everything I want to do for you.

Love, Johnny

On the Southwest Pacific War Front still in Ryukyu, Japan
Dad is quite upset when he tells mom about the sad story of a guy who has a child who is *gravely ill* but is not permitted to take emergency leave. On the positive side, it seems the WAR IS OVER and perhaps things will be happening more quickly.

08/21/45

Dearest Mary,

I must tell you about this. One of the fellows in my tent has two children and his four year old is *gravely ill*. The child has a short time to live. This guy has been overseas for two years. The doctor and his wife are trying to get him an emergency leave. So far he has seen only *red tape* but there is still hope. I do hope he gets home in time. It's been three weeks now and he hasn't heard a word.

Well little darling, don't worry about writing to me as the mail is bound to be slow both ways. You just practice your *hula dance* so I can get a good eyeful when I get home.

Love, Johnny

On the Home Front in Manville, New Jersey

Mom feels lost and sad now that she is unemployed. She roams around the house feeling more lonesome than ever. However, Dad tries to cheer her up with *love letters*.

08/22/45

Hello *Snookums,*

Last night I just couldn't sleep. I kept picturing our little home but somehow I couldn't fit furniture in it. You know, darling, you are so sweet to listen to all my wishes and hopes. You try so hard to make all my dreams come true. Johnny, please don't fail me now, I've got my heart set on you.

I feel more lonesome now that I'm unemployed and I keep roaming around the house. I can picture you walking into our home without saying a word and staring at me. I guess you would say "Hello sweetheart". I'm almost afraid of that.

I hope you'll let me know approximately when you might come home. I miss you and need you so very much. You really made me laugh when you said "You better enjoy single life young lady for your days are numbered now". That was such a cute sentence. Gosh, I hope you are safe and it won't be long until I get you in my arms. You're my everything, darling.

Speaking of my engagement ring, I would love to help you pick it out at the jewelry store. I had tears in my eyes when you wrote *you'll be a June, 1946 bride for sure.* Now, about the light in the living room, honey, I didn't want to turn it off back then but I have changed my mind. When you come home, would you please turn it off for me?

My love Always, Mary

On the Southwest Pacific War Front in Ryukyu, Japan
Dad is excited because the WAR IS OVER! It's a mystery as to when he will able to come home to the States.

08/24/45

My Dearest One,

Gosh Hon, things are happening quickly now that THE WAR IS OVER! My real happiness won't come until I get home. The war still continues on a small scale because a lot of Japs just don't want to give up. The estimate of when I will be able to come home remains a mystery. There are one and one half million troops with eighty five points or more. The five million to be released should reach me eventually.

Don't get excited yet as the end of the war caught everyone by surprise so no arrangements were made in advance. The speed of homecoming will take time. Everyone thinks I should be home by the end of the year. I'm hoping it will be before your birthday.

We started on our wooden floor and tent setup even with the news on the radio telling us the end is near. It only took three days. Almost all the other tents did not go up for at least one to two weeks. Two of us really worked the majority of the time for the others are not so handy with a saw and hammer.

People have started celebrating but there is still some fighting as well as air raids continuing overseas. Don't worry, we will *celebrate in style* when I get home.

Love, Johnny

On the Southwest Pacific War Front still located in Ryukyu, Japan
Mom gets a letter from dad describing information about the equipment dad worked on during the war in Radio Repair and other departments. He is hoping as soon as the occupation of Japan by American forces begins there will not be any trouble.

08/25/45

Dear Mary,

First of all, I want to tell you not to worry about Christmas this year and don't bother to get anything for me. By October all eighty five point men will start on their way home. That puts me on the top of the list. Yes, things sure look good now. Even if there are boys going home long before their *fair time*, they were able to get around the point system set forth by Washington. If all the eighty five point men leave for home in our outfit by October, it will leave only the Section Chief and me in Radio Repair.

As soon as the occupation of Japan begins and no further trouble is encountered, the point system should be lowered. Even though the war is over, we are busier than before. It seems it takes a couple of months for other signal companies like ours to setup. We were able to setup in seven days and were ready to operate. During two weeks of driving rain in the Philippines, it took nine days and we didn't even get a letter of commendation. We were taking care of over three quarters of the island by ourselves.

Lots of Love, Johnny

On the Southwest Pacific War Front located somewhere in Japan
Dad is still located somewhere in Japan. He is finally able to tell mom about all the equipment he fixed. He helped run a telephone switchboard and message center, fixed electric motors for other outfits and encrypted messages which were then transferred into codes to keep them secret from the Japs.

08/26/45

Dear Mary,

You can see by the picture I sent you what a small group we had. Our work was to repair all radio equipment found on a plane. We also ran a telephone switchboard and message center. Telephone lineman had to set up and keep repaired the phone lines around here. We had to maintain teletype machine communication with headquarters. We ran our own *motor pool* where we fixed all our trucks.

We fixed electric motors for other outfits and the radio equipment we work on is used by a lot of planes from a *small cub plane* up to a *B-29 bomber*. Many planes have up to twelve different radio units in them. I worked on almost all of the units. All together there are over fifty different types of radios. In my old outfit, I worked in the message center for six months. I encrypted messages and transferred them into codes in order to keep them secret from the Japs.

That was the time I was busted after being assigned the task of running eighty shifts by myself. I just did not like the way the First Sergeant ran the operation so I told him what I thought about it. By the way, it turned out to be the best break I ever got.

Hardly any of the fellows in my old company have campaign stars and are still located in Brisbane, Australia.

I have a very good chance of becoming Staff Sergeant in the next thirty days as long as no restrictions are made on men who have high points like me.

Love, Johnny

On the Southwest Pacific War Front still in Japan
Dad is very excited about a new point system which he hears is granting all men who have eighty five points or more a definite ride to the States. He is not taking on any extra work, however, he is grateful for all the knowledge he has gained in this man's Army.

08/27/45

Dearest Mary,

Last night the most exciting thing happened. A message on the radio told us that all eighty five point men can pack their bags to be ready to leave in the morning! Yes, this means every single eighty five point man will be put on the top of the list. As soon as the occupation of Japan starts and there is no more trouble, I should be on my way home by Christmas at the latest! Isn't this news wonderful, my darling?

I have ended my extra work so I'm taking it easy waiting for my turn. If I had not taken on extra work, I wouldn't be where I am today. Everybody envies me now instead of saying "Why do you work so much"? I always tell them the time passed quicker and I learned more skills. The war lasted forty five months and I spent thirty six months of it overseas in New Guinea and Australia.

It makes me so mad when guys brag and say "I've been overseas for fifty two months". I ask them where they were and they say their time was spent in Hawaii for three years and nine months. They try to tell you how rough it was, but Hawaii was American territory and after Pearl Harbor occurred they never had an air raid again.

Well little sweetheart of mine, I'll be seeing you soon. I am overjoyed just thinking about it!

Love always, Johnnie

On the Southwest Pacific War Front celebrating a church service located in Japan
Dad finds out how mom celebrated the end of the war and tells her how the guys had a special church service to thank God just like she had at home. He is estimating the time when he might arrive in the States.

Then he receives word that the planes and ships are now tied up with the occupation of Japan.

08/30/45

Dear Mary,

I received your letter of August 14, 1945 and I see you got the news of the end of the war at the same time I did. We are in agreement about it and when I get home we will have a *real celebration*. We had a special church service as well. I kept thinking all the time about us and how wonderful it was to have been taken care of by God. You don't have to worry now, my sweet because unless they change something all men with eighty to eighty four points will begin to come home. If the points are counted again, I'll have ninety two points. No matter how it's done, I'll be one of the first on the list to go. I'll write the moment I receive my notice. I am estimating it should be during the next four to six weeks. Maybe I will be there for your birthday in November. I really have nothing to do right now. Every night I get one quart of ice cream courtesy of my *connections*. This news about the end of the war feels like a *dream* to me all of a sudden.

Honey, I have so much to tell you. If it is okay with you, don't bother to write very long letters to me just short one page ones if you wish. I just might not receive any of your mail if my orders come soon. Take care of yourself and when my telegram reaches you it will be the best clue to say I have landed in the States.

My Love to you, Johnny

On the Southwest Pacific War Front elevated to Staff Sergeant somewhere in Japan
Dad is proud to say he has been promoted to T-3 or what is known as Staff Sergeant. His record for completing work orders is amazing and he is very pleased with all the work he accomplished. The food is awful. He thinks they need to use up the *bully beef.*

Mary Jane Juzwin

09/01/45

Dearest Mary,

I'm just letting you know all the planes and ships are tied up at the present time with the occupation of Japan. This place is not dangerous and never was since I landed here. In the Philippines it was a different story. However, the few raids we did have were so far away from our camp that it took a few days before we found out any information.

Hon, I've finally been elevated to T-3 or Staff Sergeant. I probably would have become Technical Sergeant if I stuck around longer. I now make about $118.00 a month. Of course it will be for a short time. I had been *number three man* in Radio Repair for a long time, but I finally got my break when the opening was created.

I turned over three thousand work orders which kept a lot of planes flying in good shape. I had some fun the other day with Signal Supply. I told them I would fix five radios in the shortest possible time. I finished them in one and one half hours. In an average day during a week, I fix about three sets a day if I don't run into any complications.

I had a lot of fun saying *next* and asking for parts. It takes some knowledge about the weakness each set contains plus a good amount of experience. You ought to see some of the junk that was sold to the government.

Love and Many Kisses, Johnny

On the Southwest Pacific War Front somewhere in Japan
Dad is not sure how or when he might be able to come home. He hates eating *bully beef* but is thankful that the P. X. store has plenty of tasty canned goods.

09/03/45

My Dearest Darling,

I don't know how or when I will be coming home and time seems to be going so slow. The food is awful and I know it won't improve for a long time. I guess all the *bully beef* has to be used up over here. Luckily, we have a lot of canned goods and crackers in our P.X. store so I won't starve.

As usual, the married men get the breaks in this war. All of a sudden, it is a single man's war. Don't mind me Hon, I'm not as unhappy as I sound. I know I didn't get malaria for I feel healthy. I stopped taking the prevention pills about six months ago, but I have been fine just a little bit bored. I am getting more sleep and resting up now so I'll have more energy to keep up with you.

With Love Always, Johnny

On the Southwest Pacific War Front still in Japan
Finally, the Army has lifted *censorship* of letters now that the war has ended. Dad tells mom he will soon be sailing to Keijo, Korea. He thinks they will be stopping in Manila and possibly the Philippine Islands on the way home to the States.

09/05/45

Dearest Mary,

Well hon, all *censorship* has been lifted so now I suppose you expect to hear me complain a lot. I really don't have many complaints. I must tell you I will sail to Korea in the next few days. I will be stationed near a city called Kinjo. It has a population of 700,000 people. It's really a waste of time because I will only have to come back to Okinawa, Japan when my order for home comes through.

I probably will stop in Manila and the Philippine Islands on the way home. Okinawa was a snap. We landed three months after the first wave of air raids. We just had a handful of raids that were not close. We landed at Leyte in the Philippines nineteen days later. It was two and a half months that there were air raids both day and night.

There was plenty of anti aircraft fire shots at the Japs and we saw a lot of planes shot down. The Jap paratroopers landed in Leyte about ten miles away and *raised hell* for a while but were soon silenced.

So here is how it went. After I landed in Brisbane, Australia, I went to western Australia, then to Buna, New Guinea. Following that I went to Nemours which is an island in the Dutch East Indies. It is the small island off northern New Guinea. Finally I went on to Leyte in the Philippines and then to Okinawa, Japan. I always hoped you would try to guess where I was but I could not tell you because of military restrictions.

All my Love, Johnny

On the Home Front in Manville, New Jersey
Mom *lays down the law* about how she feels when dealing with men. Dad takes her letter *in stride* and tells her not too worry as he feels like a boy instead of a man.

09/06/45

My Loving Sweetheart,

Staff Sergeant John Poslusny, Congratulations honey! I can't stop writing to you as you told me in your last letter. I wouldn't feel right. I'm still your loving sweetheart and I miss you more each day. Please take care of yourself. I must tell you how excited I felt when I opened your letter and found many kisses on the bottom, all for me. You are so sweet and make me so happy. Please Johnny, don't ever change. As long as you stay as sweet as you are, you will always have me and my heart.

Actually, I hate men and can easily learn to hate you if you turn out to be as *mean, vulgar* and *inhuman* as some men are. Many men don't understand their women. They only know when they want something, yet don't understand a girl's wishes. I hate men that think a woman should do as he says, or commands because he thinks he's the boss. I hate men who don't love or cherish their woman especially if she belongs only to him.

Some men think a woman is some sort of *gadget* they can *use* or *discard* whenever they feel like it. Also, a man who chose his sweetheart for his very own and asks her to marry him along with his own desires. This kind of man promises her everything under the sun, and then leaves her night after night *hanging out* with his gang just *tramping around* town. He really has nothing to do or no place to go, but he still escapes from his wife and sneaks out alone. I hate and *despise* men of that sort.

Yes, I've seen and met them and they scare me. They seem so wonderful when they are single and change completely after they married. I just thought I would let you know how I feel when it comes to a man and a woman's relationship. Please Johnny, don't ever change as I love you just the way you are, a loving sweet man.

Your Sweet Mary

On the Southwest Pacific War Front moving to Korea
Dad noticed Korea is not like Japan. It was a war-free country of its own before the Japs took it over. He and his crew observe Okinawa and clear up any evidence of war before they move on to Buckner Bay where they're waiting for the convoy to move to Korea.

09/06/45

Dearest Mary,

Gosh darling, I was so happy to get another letter before I left for Korea. Korea isn't really like Japan. It was taken over just like so many other places. It was a war free country of its own before the Japs took over.

Our company is small, only about one hundred men so you get to know everyone very quickly. Boy, Okinawa sure is a busy place. The highways are full of all kinds of trucks and jeeps. Why it seems almost as busy as the highways in New Jersey. I'm very glad the war is over in many ways. A lot of the material that was sent over here is useless. It was made for Europe and we just couldn't use the same material over here at all.

We took care of Okinawa, Japan except for one strip of land by Naha. This place has a lot of airplanes. I missed out on a campaign star for this island by one day. Three months of really hard work and I got no points for it. That's the Army for you.

We now travel by *L. S. T.* otherwise known as a *landing ship tank*. This is a large boat that can sail right up onto a beach. The whole front of it opens up and you ride off in a jeep, tank or truck. Infantry troops land this way on new beach heads.

Hon, I'm very anxious for the day when we can see each other and be able to look at houses together. Of course, a lot of changes will be made. After all, it has to be the way we want it so we can really call it our *dream home*. I'm so glad you are comfortable with me and hope you will always act naturally. You are sweet just being human. That's one of the 1,000,000,000 reasons I love you so much.

Your sweetheart, Johnny

On the Southwest Pacific War Front still moving to Korea
Dad gathers all the letters he can hold to take with him to his new location.

09/07/45

Hello Honey,

How is my little armful of love today? I sent all your letters back to you. They are without envelopes because I didn't have enough room to carry them around so long. A few of them got mixed up when we moved and the rats ate a few, but I still have ninety five percent of them.

Please keep them safe for they are my prized possessions and so dear to me. I sent three packages home. Two are for you and one to my folks. The letters are in one package, all my pictures except a few I kept are in package number two. The third package contained my gun. I finally sent it home now for it should be safe. You will see that some of your pictures have spots on them from the tropical weather.

I kept the picture of you standing in Dukes Park, New Jersey wearing that sweater. Read the book the 59th Service Group put out on V. J. day. The book explains the victory in Japan and the end of World War II. There is a 1024 section in it.

Love, Johnny

On the Southwest Pacific War Front in Buckner Bay near Okinawa, Japan Dad's outfit waits for a convoy to take them to Korea. He says General MacArthur will give a speech for people in the States where he'll say "Your boys are on their way home".

09/09/45

Dearest Mary,

I'm out in Buckner Bay, Okinawa waiting for the convoy to start going to Korea. I was stationed on the Youton Strip which is an airstrip between the two of them. The other was Gardenia fifteen miles north of Naha. Naha is the capital city of Okinawa, Japan.

After General MacArthur gives his big speech, I will be on my way to Korea. This is what he said "Your boys are on their way home so take good care of them". It's how heroes are made in the eyes of those who don't know the whole story. Every speech given by a *big shot* is broadcasted so notes can be taken by the bunch back home.

I have two bags packed. One is all the things I have to take home with me and the other bag I must turn in before I leave. My friend whose daughter did die never got a yes or a no for his emergency leave.

Many officers were *good-for-nothing* bums as civilians and don't have the slightest idea what hard work is on any day. The most they did was censor a few letters. They tried to be bosses over jobs they never saw or did in their lives and had nerve to act like experts.

Love, Johnny

On the Southwest Pacific War Front on the way to Korea
Dad is on a boat in the China Sea waiting to sail to Korea. He hates travelling by boat and the sea is rocking. The men are *burning mad* at *big shots* for delaying their return.

09/11/45

Dearest Mary,

Hon, I'm out in the China Sea on my way to Korea. It is a small convoy compared to the old days. I sure hope I get a chance to fly home because I hate travelling by boat in the sea. This trip will take at least four days. The food isn't bad at all. The only duty I have is Sergeant of the guard. I have sixteen men on guard at different hours. Our Radio Department had twenty six men in it and I was third in charge for a long time.

Boy is this tub rocking now! I'm hoping to be home in time for your birthday so I can buy you something nice. Hon, you are my whole life and soul. All this time over here was a snap for I knew I had my sweet Mary back home waiting for me. When things looked bad, along came a sweet letter from you. These always made me happy and I'd be good for another couple of weeks.

I'm telling you the boys sure are *burning mad* at the *big shots* over here. All we get is a lot of talk and no action. There has not been one occasion when a general here spoke up and said anything to us. Yes, they say a lot of *phony words* to the people back home. People in the states think these men are heroes so they get away with it. This place may be home to General MacArthur, but it is not home to us. There has not been a single *crackpot* in Washington, D.C. that has ever proposed any steps to help us.

I guess I sound pretty low hon, don't let it get you down. This is a normal feeling among us all over here. I just wanted you to know the score so you can shoot down people who are complaining and have no reason.

All my Love, Johnnie

On the Home Front in Manville, New Jersey
Mom describes her feelings being the oldest at home and still single. She is not happy about this however she displays her strong love and devotion to her family.

09/12/45

Dearest Johnny,

Honey, I'm glad the war is over. I have been busy with the troubles at home. I am the oldest one at home and still single. I feel it's my duty to take interest and responsibility of everyone and everything. I feel like an *old married* woman with a large family and a home to care for but I have no husband. Honestly sometimes I feel I just can't take it anymore. I become overwhelmed and can't do anything. I realize there is no one else to do the work and worry about everyone so I just go ahead and take care of it. It's a wonder I feel and look half as well as I do now.

My Love Always, Mary

On the Southwest Pacific War Front in the China Sea moving to Korea
Dad and the boys have reached the harbor on the coast of Korea. The harbor is full of American boats and the climate is delightfully cool.

09/15/45

My Sweet One,

We finally reached the harbor on the coast of Korea. We have to drive inland about thirty miles before we get to the capitol city of Kinjo. The climate here is cool and wonderful. The harbor is full of American boats. There shouldn't be much trouble getting a ride home from here. There is a large boat on the top deck of our *L. S. T.* which is our *landing ship tank*. They slide it into the water by tipping our boat a little on its side. The chains will be removed and it will slide on grease skids into the water.

I am seeing my share of big buildings and factories. I also saw a few Navy hospital ships. This place has its mountains and valleys. To the west is China, the east is the mainland of Japan. Still north is Russia.

I met a guy from Red Bank, New Jersey and we had a good time talking. There are many small boats in the harbor with Koreans in them. They look like Filipinos. Tomorrow morning we should start unloading and it will probably be three days of hard work.

Love always, Johnny

On the Southwest Pacific War front in the harbor of Korea
Dad and the boys are on the boat docked in the harbor waiting to unload and set foot on land in Korea. He's happy he didn't get *seasick*. He wants mom to get an engagement ring so all he has to do is *pop the question*.

09/16/45

Dear Sweet Mary,

I'm still in the harbor waiting to unload. We might get to shore this afternoon. This place gets chilly at night. I hate sitting here waiting off shore. On land, at least you can stretch your feet. I must be used to these trips for I didn't get *seasick*. We had a young priest on board so we had Catholic mass every day except when the sea was too rough.

I see the strikes are happening in the States. It looks like they don't care how long it takes for the country to get back to normal again. Keep your eyes open when you go shopping for all the things you want. Remember to pick out your engagement ring. Mary, it's up to you to pick it out so I have the easy part for myself. I'll just pick you up and swing you around like a top! While your head is spinning, we'll become engaged.

Love, Your Johnny

On the Home Front in Manville, New Jersey
Mom and dad are proud of themselves for sticking by each other and they feel confident in their love. Mom says if we are truly meant for each other, it will happen.

09/17/45

Hello Honey,

I'm so glad to hear that everyone is envious of you because you worked so hard and saved all your money. I can't wait until you come home so all our plans can work out together. When I think of you being in such a dangerous place, I am so proud of you. I think we can prove to everyone how hard work, saving, true love and devotion has worked for us even though we have waited so long to get together. I don't care how much money you have saved. I want to love you with all my heart and soul just because you are John Poslusny not for what you have or what you have done. If we are truly meant for each other, we will never keep secrets from one another.

My sister just walked in with two letters from you, dated September 5 and 9, 1945. The letter from September 9, 1945 had no A.P.O. address because you were in Buckner Bay waiting for the convoy to take you to Korea. You left me in the summer, but I guess you will return in the winter and I can't wait to finally see you in person. Hon, I'm all yours.

I'm so sorry about your friend who lost his daughter and couldn't get home to his wife. I hated this war and everything about it. I've seen more *dirty tricks* and *cheating* these past three years than ever before. I'm so glad you decided to give me an idea of when you might be coming home.

What is this you say I should *rest up* now? Do you expect to run me *ragged* when you come home? Maybe I'd like *running ragged* with you in fact it sounds like fun. I'll settle for that as long as you don't make me wait too long to see you. Honey, you say you've got plenty of good news and interesting things to tell me. I want to hear everything no matter how long it takes. Our *love affair* will change into a wedding and honeymoon.

Your Darling Mary

On the South West Pacific War Front in the Pacific Ocean
Dad is looking forward to coming home to the States. He says the Japs are now behaving like angels. The Koreans are doing all the work for the Americans. He says there are so many kids around the place his guess is all they do is eat, sleep and raise kids.

09/18/45

Dear Mary,

Guess what, we finally received our order to get ready to leave for home! In the next week or two I should be moving slowly toward the States.

It's been a long wait darling, and you showed me what you really meant to me even while we were apart. Don't get too excited yet. Remember I have 8,000 miles to travel. A boat averages about two hundred miles a day unless it is a very fast one. I think I'll definitely be there for your birthday. I'm cutting this short for I have a lot to do before we land on shore.

At present there is no word about moving toward home. The Japs are behaving like angels. The Koreans do all the work for us. There are so many kids here, more than any place I have ever seen. I guess all they do here is eat, sleep and raise kids. The funny thing is the kids all stare at you as if you were Frank Sinatra.

Oceans of Love, Johnnie

On the Southwest Pacific War Front moving around in Korea
Dad and the guys have moved into a big building and it is filled with all kinds of bugs, rock roaches and bed bugs. He describes the rooms lined with sand on a wooden floor and outside each room is a *trap door* in the floor. He is having trouble understanding the fashions worn by the people.

09/22/45

Dear Mary,

We moved into a big building that has five hundred rooms, store rooms, lots of closets and it includes a big stage. There is also a large room three times bigger than the Polish American Home in New Jersey. This building is filled with all kinds of bugs, rock roaches and bed bugs. Apparently they sprayed inside the building, but the bugs still appear. It seems bugs aren't objectionable to people over here. I am not kidding when I say most of them live like pigs. The floors in the rooms are lined with sand on a wooden floor and then covered with paper. Outside each room is a little *trap door* in the wooden floor. The Japs have a custom in which they take their shoes off and walk inside barefoot. The women here wear some crazy combinations of clothes. I can't tell whether a babe is wearing *bloomers* or some sort of dress.

I'm telling you ten American soldiers can disarm one thousand Japs and the Jap officers will line up their men. The Japs stand at attention while American soldiers go through their bags taking away any form of weapon. That's how easy it is now.

Things are screwed up here. No one knows why we're here or what we're supposed to do. Officers are taking over big, beautiful Japanese officers' homes. We get two hundred bottles of beer to share while officers get four thousand bottles. Then they take a jeep and go sightseeing. We outnumber the officers yet we're the ones expected to work on planes and landing strips. It is *officer's paradise* here and enlisted men don't count. You will always count with me and I want you to know you can always count on me.

More Love to Come, Johnny

On the Southwest Pacific War Front in Korea
Dad joked with a guy about the food served. He says this Navy guy was complaining so Dad told him he should've seen what the Army gave them for dinner in the past.

09/20/45

My Dearest,

It's getting dark but I decided to write another letter to my sweet one. We had meatloaf and fresh bread with pie for dessert. One Navy guy was complaining about the food. I told him if he ate what we used to eat most of the time, they would bury half the Navy! According to our standards, this was great food.

One would think it was another country the way the Navy guys complained. The Sea Beas were non-military personnel who functioned as engineers also complained. Why it's just like home if not better to most of our guys. The Army serves *junk*. The better the cooks, the better the *junk* tastes to us. The hospitals serve the same food we eat.

We had a *desk lawyer* who is an officer try to tell a forty year old private how to build a building. The private had twenty five years of experience in carpentry work. The officer didn't know how to drive a nail straight. He was an officer so he tried to make people believe he knew everything. The truth is he knew nothing. This is why wars take so long and why ninety five percent of the men hate the Army and how it is run. If I had ninety nine years experience in one type of work and was a private, I would have some Sergeant with no experience try to boss me around. That's the Army for you.

Days usually go by so fast, however, since the point system was dropped to eighty points it just crawls day to day. Oh well it's not such a long wait now, it only seems like it. I'm in the Yellow Sea now and it's not quite as rough as before.

Love with All my Heart, Johnny

On the Southwest Pacific War Front in Kinjo, Korea
Dad is not impressed with the city of Kinjo, Korea. He tells mom it is basically a *slum* and he thinks all places in the Orient are in the same condition.

09/23/45

My Dearest Mary,

I visited the city of Kinjo, Korea. What a mess! There are lots of people and everyone is buying or selling something. The place is basically a *slum*. In fact the whole Orient is that way. The buildings are very big but in front of them are little old *broken down* stores. It is hard to buy anything because most of these people do not speak any English. Maybe a handful of the nine hundred thousand people speak or understand English.

There are Japs and Koreans and they look alike to me. As soon as a Jap appears, a bunch of Korean kids run to you and say *Jap*. I guess they expected us to shoot them on sight.

When you stop to buy something, before you realize it, there are about one hundred people watching you bargain. If the price remains too high, we just walk away and people watching shout a cheer. We sure are lucky in a way for our small company was the first in the 59th Service Group to get here. The rest of the groups are in Okinawa. There are over one thousand men in a Service Group and we had the pick of the souvenirs. I have two Jap guns, two dress swords and one large battle saber. This is the kind that usually sells for $200.00. I also got a *hari kari knife* and flags.

I have had plenty of sake, that's Jap wine with a little kick. I know this to be true for I got a little woozy from it. The best part is it costs $300.00 for a two quart bottle and you get no hangovers from it. Well darling, I am sorry to say this but there is still no word as to when I will able to head home.

Missing you and Loving you, Johnny

On the Southwest Pacific War Front waiting for orders in Korea
The guys in dad's group are running out of patience while they wait for the *big shots* to issue orders to pack their bags and get ready to return to the States. The Jap soldiers salute the American guys and the Jap kids like to hang on to them. There seems to be a lot of looting and stealing from the stores by civilians in Korea.

09/26/45

Dearest Honey,

Yes, I'm still waiting for orders. Other outfits got their orders already. You ought to see the women walking around here. It is quite a sight because they strap their chest down. Apparently, you are considered good looking if you have a flat chest.

The married women wear their hair in a bun behind their heads. When they are nursing babies, they wear a shirt that's open and their milk bottles stick right out.

It seems the women are supposed to raise lots of children and do ninety five percent of the work. If I am standing around when the Jap women walk by, they take a bow all together. The Jap soldiers salute us and the kids like to hang all over us. The place I'm living in was a large factory. Actually, it was a cotton mill and cotton material factory. It's bigger than a factory in Manville, New Jersey or even New Brunswick, New Jersey. Korea is intact because it was never bombed.

There is plenty of looting and stealing things from the stores by civilians. Most of the boys get drunk and pay nothing for the Koreans treat them like kings. There are also night clubs where a guy can get a girl to stay with him and pour his drinks. They're always dressed neatly and hired because of their good looks.

Of course, some of the *honky tonk joints* are full of wild babes and they don't care what the boys do to them. That's not for me. I'm yours and I'll never do anything to hurt our love for each other.

The thing about oriental countries is that you could catch several diseases so one should be very careful. The occupation of countries sure is a mess. It will take a long time for the factories to be reopened and people are off the streets. All the large factories and buildings were run by Japs, so it's hard to say who owns them now.

All my Love, Johnny

On the Southwest Pacific War Front officers are getting drunk or sightseeing in Korea
Dad cannot understand why the officers are *carousing around* Korea yet not working hard to get the men home. The guys have to go to a private factory to get beer while the officers drive off with truckloads of beer for

themselves. Dad's best guess about when he might return to the States is probably by Christmas.

09/27/45

Dearest Mary,

The officers are just getting drunk and sightseeing instead of trying to get our orders. They have 700,000 Koreans and 1,000 Japs doing work but they still want us to make them comfortable. They have lots of Jap or Korean house boys, maids and cooks.

The *big shot Jap* owns the five mile square factory here. He is still living in a castle while we have to live in a building full of bed bugs. I have so much powder on my bed that it looks as white as snow.

We really told off one of our Lieutenants today. Tomorrow we meet the company officers and get things straight. We want to know why they can get a jeep anytime they want and visit the city every day.

Meanwhile, we get no jeep and only one pass every seven days after thirty seven months overseas. We go to a private factory to buy beer. The officers try to stop us from buying beer while they ride away with truckloads for themselves.

It seems no one cares how long we stay over here. My best guess is I'll definitely be home by Christmas. I sent home silk materials to you so you can make anything you want out of them. I also have two Japanese kimonos that I will give you in person.

We have not received a single letter for a month now. We are the *lost company* alright and it's everyone for himself. Here is one guy who doesn't stand short. I did my share of work a long time ago. Well darling, I sure hope someone does something to get us home.

Your loving man, Johnny

On the Southwest Pacific War Front in Korea
Dad says he understands arrangements are finally underway to help the guys get home. Since the war has ended, mom has been laid off from her job. On the better side of things, dad is happy they have their own personal supply of ice cream.

10/01/45

My Dearest One,

After flying all the officers up to Korea for sightseeing, we are getting a few headquarter men here. All the eighty point men in the 59th Service Group left for the States from Okinawa four days ago. I understand arrangements are being made to get us home. I'm sure I'll get a definite answer sometime this week.

We have our own personal supply of ice cream and so far the officers haven't chiseled in but give them time. There are a few Negro troops in town. One of the guys saw a barmaid try to rub off the black on the Negro's skin. We have the whole room, which is 14 square feet, lined with beer bottles. We have to buy our own because officers take too long to get it for us.

Gosh Hon, it must be rough on you to hear all the stories about the plans to discharge soldiers and yet those of us who are overseas are waiting here. It's too bad you are now out of a job. I know you have a lot of work to do at home but I'm sure you're thinking about all this. Well darling, our dreams are getting closer day by day now.

Lots of Love, Johnny

On the Southwest Pacific War Front in Korea
Dad is counting points toward going home and paying attention to any news of departing.

10/03/45

My Dearest Honey,

I am still in Korea with eighty nine points. In Okinawa, outfits in the 59th Service Group are sending men home with sixty points which is twenty nine points less than us here. I never saw such injustice like this.

Don't worry about me Hon, I'm very disappointed but I don't get *sloppy drunk*. I do come close once in a while. The Army Air Core here in Korea is only guarding the beer for officers and cleaning the place. I wrote to the Inspector General about the situation, but it might not do any good at all. Everything on the radio is *baloney*. The land Army is fighting the Air Corp. We think this is the reason we aren't getting out of here sooner. I don't know how we will be processed.

There are going to be a lot of bitter men after the war. The lesson would be because the Army is so unfair to us yet they try to tell the people back home how well they treat us.

Love, Your Johnnie

On the Southwest Pacific War Front waiting to go home still in Korea Dad can't wait to see mom so he says his job now is to answer her letters. He gets a serious letter from her telling him how men in general and husbands treat their sweethearts and wives. He explains to Mom that he's just a soldier boy who is devoted to his *one and only*. Dad is shocked to hear he was praised by one of the superior officers.

10/09/45

Dear Mary,

My job now is to answer your letters. You sure have your hands full of troubles being the oldest girl in the family. One of these days, I'll be your main trouble. The only trouble I could possibly give you is more love and devotion. I'm sure you wouldn't mind that kind of trouble.

So you hate men, eh kid. It's a good thing I'm a boy. You sure wind up and tell me how mean some men get after marriage. Well Hon, I know just how you feel. I always feel I love you than you could dream possible, so you don't have to worry about me changing. I never hung out with gangs even if I did know and get along with them.

My idea of life is all the little things put together. I like to feel I need no one's shoulders to help me out, except you, of course. Even while I have been in the Army, I never depended on anyone else to do or get me anything.

Here's what our commanding officer said to a bunch of boys who submitted their names for Officers Training. You boys will have to remember some things. In order to be an officer, you have to do more than your regular job well. You have to be able to go out and do things on your own and not depend on others to help you. Take John Poslusny, he may not be officer material, but that's one guy who goes out and does things for himself without depending on others. He has the ambition and initiative to be successful. How about that! The boys told me this after they came back and I was really surprised. At least one officer recognized my hard work.

Don't worry I'm saving my heart and soul for you only. My appetite sure is doing well. The climate here is so much better and I feel wonderful. I hope I look the same.

Love Always, Johnny

On the Southwest Pacific War Front in Korea
Dad is trying to help mom locate Korea. He is hoping his records will be given a final check so he can finally expect to be going home.

Mary Jane Juzwin

10/14/45

Dear Mary,

I am as happy as a lark because I got my first letters in over a month. I got four *v-letters* and one large letter. I see you don't know where Korea is located. Well, it's actually Chasten, but before the Japs took it over twenty five years ago it was called Korea. We are about one hundred miles north of Okinawa. On the west is China, and on our east is Tokyo, Japan. About sixty miles north is Siberia, Russia. I hope this will tell you more about where I am at the present time.

Tomorrow our records will be checked. This is usually the last thing done before you go on a boat headed for the States. The latest rumor says this will happen about October 20. I am lucky to get away from Okinawa because three very dangerous hurricanes hit the island. It wrecked ninety five percent of the buildings, killed a lot of guys and destroyed over five hundred airplanes. Whew that was close! We left two days before it hit.

I'm glad in a way that I saw Korea. I know how the Orient lives. It sure is a mess! The women are treated roughly. They do most of the work and strap everything down. This is common throughout the Orient. I saw a Korean stage show with Korean players in an American run theater.

The little kids aged two and up all say *hello* to us and when we answer they feel so proud. They all know how to ask for chocolate and gum. Sometimes dozens of kids grab you and it's hard to get away from them. Most places are off limits until inspected. Our $1.00 bill is worth 15 yen here. The Koreans consider a $1.00 bill like a quarter and boy do they throw them around like water.

All my Love, Johnny

On the South West Pacific War Front still in Korea

Dad has been through processing and is given an approximate time to return to the States. He states he is due to leave Korea on or about October 20, 1945. Unfortunately, he will miss another one of mom's birthdays, but is elated about landing in San Francisco.

10/15/45

Dearest Mary,

Well, I went through the processing line today. I still have eighty nine points and everything is all set for the boat ride to the States. Our service records state that we're due to leave on or about October 20, 1945. Of course, this is uncertain as the Army gives out the information. This time I'm sure it's the *real thing*.

After I get on the boat, it will be fifteen days or so before I reach San Francisco, California. I will send you a telegram just as soon as I arrive.

I am on *detached* service to the 1024 Signal Company now. My old gang is leaving.

The fellow in my room whose daughter died finally got his emergency leave three months late. He left for Okinawa this morning and I think he will probably be stuck there for a while. I might make it home before him now. They tried to take points away from some of the thirty eight month overseas men, but it didn't pan out. We got our American beer issued today along with Coca Cola.

Well little darling, things are starting to look better day by day. You better eat those *wheaties* for you will need extra energy to keep up with me.

Joyously in Love, Johnny

On the Southwest Pacific Front hearing a rumor for departure but still in Korea

Dad is issued a sleeping bag and describes it to mom. He also says there are flags on buildings all over town and signs welcoming the American soldiers' home.

10/16/45

Dearest Mary,

As usual after being processed to go home, the new rumor says we will be shipped out around October 27, 1945. I don't believe it but we shall see what occurs. We were issued sleeping bags. You open a big zipper, jump inside and zip it up to your neck. It is nice and warm and only your head sticks out.

I have been just taking it easy and sightseeing. You can see by the postcards I sent, it is a large and strange city. It looks like everyone is selling his furniture and clothes. There is always a cart full of stuff passing you on the street.

When the train pulls into the station, they hurry and pack themselves in like sardines. Some people even get on the roof outside. Around the city are big archways with flags painted very nicely saying *Welcome Home* all over the place. Some buildings and taverns have *Welcome U. S. Army* painted on them. The markets are so full of people you can hardly move. I guess all parents teach their kids to say *hello* and ask for chocolate and gum. Mothers also strap their kids on their backs.

The rest of the 59th Service Group arrived today. They left Okinawa six hours before the storm. We finally have warm water. This is wonderful because it is cold at night.

According to the newspaper, 17,600 troops are leaving Korea for home in October. If it is true, I am among the two hundred on the list to leave. Every day the town is decorated with all kinds of *Welcome U. S. Army* signs. It looks like each group wants to outdo the other group.

All my Love, Johnny

On the Southwest Pacific War Front thinking about his *rattle trap* car still in Korea
Dad wants to scrap his old car and buy a new one, however, he realizes they might be too expensive to buy at the present time. The town celebrates *Korean Liberation Day* and more signs stating *Welcome U. S. Army* are appearing daily.

10/20/45

My Sweetheart,

Today was *Korean Liberation Day*. They had a large parade. Different political parties had fights with each other and a few bricks were thrown. I was watching the parade, when all of a sudden bricks and torn papers were flying down from a third story window.

Our military police were mounted on horses and the city looked like a guarded fortress. There were so many military police around. I only saw one Korean man get hurt by a brick on his head. I sort of stayed clear to one side for this is no joke. Darling, I'm getting so sick of this place now. We have to wait until October 28, 1945 to get on a boat unless the Army changes the date. I have enclosed some picture cards of Kinjo, Saul on Chung Song. It is all the same place.

Tonight I got home and fried ten eggs and believe it or not, I still felt hungry. Don't let it worry you as I'm not always that hungry except for you. Here is a story for you. A weak minded American soldier walked into a Korean home. He was impersonating a military policeman. He tried to give the woman in the house *the works*. He was drunk or maybe mentally ill. How anyone could get excited about any Korean babe is beyond me.

Korean women are very cold and are brought up to obey their husbands. When a single Korean man dates a girl, he tells her where and when to meet him. I was told this by an educated Korean interpreter for our Service Group. If it is a lunch date, she must walk alone to the restaurant to sit with him. I have not seen one bit of affection between Korean couples. The Japs are different in many ways.

I asked my brother Stanley to get my *old rattle trap* checked over and fixed. I was told by some car dealers that new cars will be hard to get for some time. I guess I'll have to stick with my old car for a while. One has to realize that civilians and soldiers are the same now that the war is over, so they each have the same chance to buy new cars. Well, Hon, this is all for now.

With Love Always, Johnny

On the Southwest Pacific War Front finally getting orders to leave Korea Dad finds out he is actually leaving today. He is overjoyed! He tells mom he will have a few stops before he can reach the east coast of the United States.

10/28/45

Dearest Mary,

I am LEAVING KOREA FOR HOME TODAY! Remember I will have to stop a few places before I get to San Francisco. Please don't get too anxious as it will take a little time. I sure feel as happy as can be darling, and I can't wait to see you. I love you with all my heart. I am asking you to take it easy until I get there. I will send you a telegram as soon as I get to San Francisco, California. Hallelujah!

More Love Coming, Johnnie

On the Home Front in the United States AT LAST!
Dad arrives in Seattle, Washington after a sixteen day trip on a Marine Flasher 575 foot Troop ship. Back in the United States AT LAST! He is overjoyed!

11/12/45

My Darling Mary,

I LANDED IN SEATTLE, WASHINGTON TODAY after a sixteen day trip on a Marine Flasher 575 foot troop ship. I feel very happy! I think I will also have to check in with some Army personnel in Tacoma, Washington as well.

Promise me you will not make any plans to travel to see me at Fort Dix in New Jersey for I will be very busy. I will have to stand in line to get my final discharge. If you wait at home, I'll let you know one day in advance when I can come to see you. I will send you a telegram telling you the day and time you can expect me. After a five day trip, I know I'll look like a wreck so one day at home will give me a chance to catch up. Our dreams are getter better all the time.

Your dreamboat, Johnny

On the Home Front waiting for transportation from west coast to the east coast of U. S.
Dad has been checked and issued orders for his return to Fort Dix, New Jersey. It will still take about twenty days before he might be able to visit mom.

11/13/45

Dearest Mary,

I am still on the west coast waiting for transportation. I have been checked and issued orders for Fort Dix, New Jersey. In about seven days or less I should be leaving here. Then it will be a five day trip to Fort Dix combined with a four day or less stay once I get there. After all this, I will finally get to go home and see my folks.

You can see by the details above, it will be about twenty days yet before I can visit you. Please relax baby and take it easy. I really hate this waiting period especially because we don't do a stitch of work so the time passes too slowly.

The K.P. duty is done by German prisoners of war so all we do is check this and that. The food is *top of the line*. I ate two quarts of ice cream the first day as well as a steak dinner with all the trimmings. The first telegram you already received was a standard one which we were able to get while on the boat.

I am as happy as can be sweetheart and I can't wait to come home to you. The Army sure is slow in getting us on our way. Each place claims they didn't have any word we were coming and then they give some other excuses. Oh well Mary, it's only a matter of days now instead of years.

All my Love to You, Johnny

On the Home Front in Tacoma, Washington
Dad is still waiting for any word about his transfer to Fort Dix, New Jersey where he will be issued his discharge papers.

11/19/45

Dear Sweetheart,

It's my seventh day here in Tacoma, Washington and by the looks of things every place is slow and far behind. If I have to wait when I get to Fort Dix, I'll try to get a furlough with pay. The Army works on your discharge papers even if you are not there in person.

I can't wait to haunt you up close and personal. We can go shopping together, driving around and oh yes parking too as well as a lot of other things.

We have so much catching up to do. These last seven days have been the roughest for me for I know you are near yet so far as well. I feel sad because your birthday came and I couldn't get there to celebrate it with you. However, this is one Christmas we will spend together. We will celebrate *in style*, young lady.

We will have to use my old car for now until new ones can be purchased. I hear even used cars cost a fortune. We will get a new car with cash. I am guessing we can't be too fussy about what color or model it will be as long as it is a new one.

Darling, we are supposed to leave sometime today so I will close for now.

An Armful of Love, Johnnie

On the Home Front in Fort Dix, New Jersey
Dad finally arrives in Fort Dix, New Jersey where he will be *officially discharged* from the Army. Of course he is so anxious to see mom, he does not wait for discharge papers. Instead he jumps a fence, hitchhikes to his house and collects his *rattle trap* of a car. This will help him to get to Manville, New Jersey sooner. His anticipation is bubbling over!

11/25/45

Dear Mary,

I ARRIVED IN FORT DIX, NEW JERSEY YESTERDAY and ten minutes after I found my bed and barracks number. I knew it would take time before I would be issued my final discharge papers so I jumped over the fence and headed home in my worse clothes. I was able to get by the main gate with a fake pass.

I took a bus to Bordentown, New Jersey just to get away from the camp. The reason I did this is because I wanted to get my car. We aren't able to get a pass to leave camp because our stay is too short. I reached Bordentown and in twenty minutes I was able to get a ride to Red Bank, New Jersey. I took a bus to the other end of town and was able to then get a ride right to my backyard from a lady who lives in my hometown.

I got home in less than two hours but I sure looked a mess! I needed a shower and a shave and I left my good clothes at Fort Dix. I didn't have any idea how long it would take to be issued discharge papers and be able to leave the Army and return to civilian life. I looked like a hobo after six days of train riding, but at least I had my car with me. I got back to Fort Dix. No one stopped me so I drove straight through the front gate.

On Monday, I will start my discharge schedule so by Tuesday I should be free to leave. The time on my paperwork says 11:45 a.m. but the time may not be definite. It should be around 6:00 p.m. when I reach my folks home. Hon, please get ready starting at 6:45 p.m. and as late as 8:00 p.m. for I definitely will be coming to see you! Don't tell me I didn't warn you. Gosh Hon, I feel wonderful and excited!

My brother Walter got my car fixed and I now have four brand new tires on it. Of course, it will need other repairs but I can fix the rest myself.

I CAN'T BELIEVE I'M HOME AT LAST! Keep an eye out for a Polish dance. I think there is one in South River, New Jersey on Wednesday night. I'll check on it to be sure. Oh yes, I'll be seeing you in the daytime too. All I need is a little gas money and I'm ready to go. Well Mary, I can't sit around here anticipating my departure. I want you to go easy on me and remember I have a lot of *jungle time* in my system.

So much Love, Johnny

On the Home Front in Fort Dix, New Jersey
Dad has a nasty cold but it won't stop him from seeing his Mary. He is thrilled and blessed to be HOME AT LAST!

12/08/45

My Darling,

I received your letter Tuesday afternoon and was I surprised. I just got back from the garage where my car is all apart. The radiator fell out and the entire motor is out including the part with the gear shift handle. I had to hitchhike to Perth Amboy to buy parts. It only cost $60.00 so I was very happy and now my oil will not leak out. I didn't have to wait more than ten minutes to get a ride there and back.

I am sneezing and yes, I've got a bad, nasty cold. It's going to be rough to wait until Thursday, but I have no choice. I went to bed early on Monday and got plenty of rest for you, of course! You say your friends at the plant liked the engagement ring you picked out. I am so glad for I wanted an extra special ring for an extra special girl who waited such a long time for me. I can't wait to have so many more wonderful days together.

I'm in bed all alone listening to my radio. I feel handicapped because I have no odometer but I'll get one soon. I will have to get some *repairman cards* and stationary printed so I will be able to fix radios and receive parts at a forty percent discount.

You are so sweet darling, and I miss you so much. If you need further information about my love for you, just park your ear next to my lips and I'll let my heart tell you.

All my Love, Johnny

On the Home Front in Manville, New Jersey
Mom surprises dad with another love letter. She tells him she wore her engagement ring to church and got a lot of compliments about it.

Mary Jane Juzwin

12/10/45

Johnny, My Sweetheart,

Are you surprised to hear from me? Don't be as I miss you dear so very much, so I had to sit down and write to tell you. Honey, just in case you have forgotten, I want to tell you "I love you with all my heart and soul".

Please Johnny, I want you to take care of yourself for me. The weather is getting nasty and I don't want you to neglect yourself in any way. Remember, you sneezed exactly three times while I was with you. One sneeze was at home and twice you sneezed at the little place we went to spend time together that evening.

Did you really have a wonderful time as you said you had? A few of the girls mentioned that they saw us there. I was so proud of you. I'm so much *in love* that I feel like I'm *floating in air*.

Stay just the way you are and keep all the words you say. Also, please don't ever change your attitude, for if you do, you will change my love for you.

Darling, I wore my ring to church today. Sweetheart, I can't begin to tell you all the compliments I received. Remember dear, when I told you the girls will look at my ring and think of the wonderful fellow who helped to choose it. You see, Johnny, you are a wonderful fellow, my wonderful fellow!

I hope you didn't have any trouble with our car. I'm sure you are attending to it so the car will run much better. It seems to have improved since you came home. Johnny, no matter what is broken or hurt, just one touch from you and all is well again.

I love you so very, very much. Take care of your health and don't rush around. I will wait for you as I have always done for a long, long time.

Your Lover, Mary

On the Home Front in Manville, New Jersey
Mom and dad are engaged and supremely happy. Now they are thinking about their *dream home*. Mom sends dad a picture of a home she is thinking will be perfect for them.

01/01/46

My Loving Sweetheart,

This is our *dream home* Darling. Some day soon we shall have one similar to it and then I really will be proud of you and all the blessings we will have together. I love you Johnny and I can't wait to show you off to the rest of my family in your dress jacket complete with stripes, all your ribbons and special hat.

You have been so nice to me ever since the day I met you. Don't ever change your ways if you want to keep me happy. We had some visitors from my family recently and I showed them all the beautiful items you brought home for us. They think you are wonderful and so do I in case you forgot.

You know hon, I saw you this morning but that is seven hours ago! Gosh, I hope the next few days go by quickly. My cold is worse and I can only talk above a whisper but I will make sure I take care of myself and heal. I know I have some wonderful things in store for us. Well, darling, good night. I can't wait to see you in a few days nice and healthy.

Your Loving Sweetheart, Mary

John and Mary June 8, 1946

Mary and John in front of their dream house in Somerville NJ

John at the air Force Museum

ACKNOWLEDGEMENTS

First of all I would like to thank my husband, Steve, for encouraging me to write this story. He also added his literary creativity which I had no idea he possessed and helped to prepare the pictures contained in this book. I also want to thank him for helping me keep my home in order as well as share the babysitting responsibility for our grandson during the four years I worked on this book.

I would then like to thank my brother, John R. Poslusny, for his help in organizing and counting the six hundred and twenty letters that were written and for providing some of the historic references.

Next, I would like to thank my sister-in-law, Diane, for her enthusiasm and help with the picture portion of this endeavor and also helping us to count the letters.

I am grateful and blessed to have my children, Steven and Lauren and my nieces, Jocelyn and Kristen as well as my nephew Nathan for their encouragement. I am confident that this special love story will remain one of their prized possessions.

Finally, I must thank my Aunt Doris Kraemer, who is my mother's only living sister. She was very helpful in remembering and filling in some of the details regarding my mom, Mary, my grandmother Rose and my grandfather John.

DESCRIPTION OF LOCATIONS FOR 1024 SIGNAL COMPANY

Ballarat Vic. – This city, Victoria, Australia was the location of the Royal Australian Army Air Force No. 1 Inland Aircraft Fuel Depot which was completed in 1942 and defended Australia against a Japanese attack. It held the supply and storage of fuel for the Allied Military base.

Northern Territory – This was considered Darwin, Australia and it was the target of Japanese air raids in February, 1942 with many bombs dropped on this city. More than 100 air raids took place across this region during World War II. The Japanese did not plan to invade Australia, and if they tried, they would have been limited to the northwest coast of Australia. It would have little or no impact during World War II.

Mareeba Qld. – This town was the major U. S. Army Air Force Base from 1942 to 1945. It was in the northeastern section of Australia, namely, in the town of Queensland. Mareeba housed both heavy bomber and fighter squadrons in 1942 and 1943.

Port Moresby – There were fifteen airstrips located in the southeastern corner of New Guinea known as Papua. The Battle of Port Moresby was an aerial battle with the Royal Australian Air Force including the United States Force on one side against the Imperial Japanese Army and Navy on the other side. It took place between February 3, 1942 and August 17, 1943. In the beginning, the defenders consisted of only Australian Army anti-aircraft batteries and machine guns. However, in late March, the Kittyhawk fighters appeared and they were part of the No. 75 Squadron in the Royal Australian Air Force.

Dobodura – The database Airfield complex was located west of Dobodura and fifteen miles south of Buna. The United States Army Air Force developed approximately fifteen runways and airfields in this area. Dobodura No. 4 was initially used by C-47 Dakota transport aircraft during late November, 1942 until January, 1943 in support of the Battle of the Beachheads including Buna, Gona and Sananada.

Noemfoor Island – The island was part of Dutch New Guinea and was where the Battle of Noemfoor took place between July 2, 1944 and August 31, 1944. The United States and Australian forces attacked the Japanese who were using this area for airfield bases. Noemfoor was also known as one of the Scouten Islands in Papua province, western New Guinea, northeastern Indonesia. Allied troops initially landed around Kamiri Airfield on the northwest edge of the island. Although the Japanese had built large defensive adjustments in this area, there was little resistence by them. As they were engaged in battle, they were so stunned from the bombardment that all the fight in them disappeared.

Leyte P. I. – The Battle of Leyte Gulf occurred from October 23 through October 26, 1944. It was an air and sea battle that crippled the Japanese combined fleet and reinforced the Allies' control of the Pacific. It was the largest Naval battle ever fought and destroyed the Imperial Japanese Navy. Leyte Gulf was also the scene of the first organized use of the Kamikaze *suicide* aircraft by the Japanese. In total there were approximately 40,000,000 to 50,000,000 deaths during World War II.

BIBLIOGRAPHY FOR LOCATIONS OF THE 1024 SIGNAL COMPANY

1. Australia. Royal Australian Air Force, Historical section, (1995) Logistics units, AGPS Press
2. Dunnigan, James F. and Nofi, Albert A., The Pacific War Encyclopedia, Copyright 1998, Article: Australia, Commomwealth of, Imprint of Facts on File Inc., New York, NY
3. Maurer, Maurer, ed. (1982) (1969) Combat Squadrons of the Air Force, World War II, Washington, D. C. Office of Air Force History
4. Basilisk Passage, Indicator Loops. Com/Port Moresby, Royal Australian Navy Harbour Defences,
5. Pacific Wrecks Inc., 1995 – 2018
6. Parillo, M. "The Imperial Japanese Navy in World War II" in S. Sadkovich (ed.) Re-evaluting Major Naval Combatants of World War II, New York: Greenwood Press, 1990
7. Encyclopedia Britannica, Article: Battle of Leyte Gulf, 15th ed., (2005) Volume 7, Page 318

BIBLIOGRAPHY

Major Richard I. Bong, P-38 Association, Veterans Historical Center, 305 Harbor View Parkway, Superior, WI 54880.

Zoot Suit Riots, The Editors of Encyclopaedia Britannica, Coroian, George.

March of Death, United States Holocaust Memorial Museum. Archived from the original on 2009, 09-08-25.